Lecture Notes in Computer Science 15732

Founding Editors

Gerhard Goos
Juris Hartmanis

Series Editors

Elisa Bertino, *Purdue University, West Lafayette, IN, USA*
Wen Gao, *Peking University, Beijing, China*
Bernhard Steffen, *TU Dortmund University, Dortmund, Germany*
Moti Yung, *Columbia University, New York, NY, USA*

The series Lecture Notes in Computer Science (LNCS), including its subseries Lecture Notes in Artificial Intelligence (LNAI) and Lecture Notes in Bioinformatics (LNBI), has established itself as a medium for the publication of new developments in computer science and information technology research, teaching, and education.

LNCS enjoys close cooperation with the computer science R & D community, the series counts many renowned academics among its volume editors and paper authors, and collaborates with prestigious societies. Its mission is to serve this international community by providing an invaluable service, mainly focused on the publication of conference and workshop proceedings and postproceedings. LNCS commenced publication in 1973.

Carla Ferreira · Claudio Antares Mezzina
Editors

Formal Techniques for Distributed Objects, Components, and Systems

45th IFIP WG 6.1 International Conference, FORTE 2025
Held as Part of the 20th International Federated Conference
on Distributed Computing Techniques, DisCoTec 2025
Lille, France, June 16–20, 2025
Proceedings

Editors
Carla Ferreira ⓘ
Universidade NOVA de Lisboa
Costa da Caparica, Portugal

Claudio Antares Mezzina ⓘ
University of Urbino
Urbino, Pesaro-Urbino, Italy

ISSN 0302-9743   ISSN 1611-3349 (electronic)
Lecture Notes in Computer Science
ISBN 978-3-031-95496-2   ISBN 978-3-031-95497-9 (eBook)
https://doi.org/10.1007/978-3-031-95497-9

© IFIP International Federation for Information Processing 2025

This work is subject to copyright. All rights are solely and exclusively licensed by the Publisher, whether the whole or part of the material is concerned, specifically the rights of translation, reprinting, reuse of illustrations, recitation, broadcasting, reproduction on microfilms or in any other physical way, and transmission or information storage and retrieval, electronic adaptation, computer software, or by similar or dissimilar methodology now known or hereafter developed.
The use of general descriptive names, registered names, trademarks, service marks, etc. in this publication does not imply, even in the absence of a specific statement, that such names are exempt from the relevant protective laws and regulations and therefore free for general use.
The publisher, the authors and the editors are safe to assume that the advice and information in this book are believed to be true and accurate at the date of publication. Neither the publisher nor the authors or the editors give a warranty, expressed or implied, with respect to the material contained herein or for any errors or omissions that may have been made. The publisher remains neutral with regard to jurisdictional claims in published maps and institutional affiliations.

This Springer imprint is published by the registered company Springer Nature Switzerland AG
The registered company address is: Gewerbestrasse 11, 6330 Cham, Switzerland

If disposing of this product, please recycle the paper.

Preface

This book constitutes the refereed proceedings of the 45th IFIP WG 6.1 International Conference on Formal Techniques for Distributed Objects, Components, and Systems, FORTE 2025, held in Lille, France, as part of the 20th International Federated Conference on Distributed Computing Techniques, DisCoTec 2025, during June 16–20, 2025.

FORTE is a well-established forum for fundamental research on theory, models, tools, and applications for distributed systems. It solicits submissions focused on foundational aspects of distributed software systems, presenting approaches or tools to formally model, soundly implement, and rigorously validate these demanding but ever more necessary systems and applications. As our dependency on such software systems grows, also our responsibility as researchers grows to provide both trustworthy and usable solutions.

This year, 25 submissions were received. Each was reviewed by at least three Program Committee members or additional reviewers. Following a rigorous single-blind review process in which each submission received three reviews, the Program Committee accepted 8 regular papers and 5 short papers. We would like to sincerely thank the Program Committee members and all additional reviewers for their professional work and strong commitment to the success of FORTE 2025. We are also grateful to the authors for thoughtfully addressing the reviewers' comments and suggestions during the preparation of their final papers.

As program chairs of FORTE 2025, we actively contributed to the selection of the keynote speaker and tutorial talk for FORTE.

We are most grateful to Burcu Kulahcioglu Ozkan for accepting our invitation to be the FORTE-related keynote speaker.

We also thank Emilio Tuosto for accepting our invitation to deliver the FORTE-related tutorial. This volume contains the invited paper accompanying his tutorial entitled *"A choreographic view of Smart Contracts"*.

April 2025

Carla Ferreira
Claudio Antares Mezzina

Organization

Program Committee

Ana Almeida Matos	Universidade de Lisboa, Portugal
Davide Basile	ISTI CNR, Italy
Matteo Cimini	University of Massachusetts Lowell, USA
João Costa Seco	NOVA University Lisbon, Portugal
Carla Ferreira	NOVA University of Lisbon, Portugal
Wan Fokkink	Vrije Universiteit Amsterdam, The Netherlands
Adrian Francalanza	University of Malta, Malta
Simon Gay	University of Glasgow, UK
Elisa Gonzalez Boix	Vrije Universiteit Brussel, Belgium
Ping Hou	University of Oxford, UK
Emilio Incerto	IMT Lucca, Italy
Tobias Kappé	Leiden University, The Netherlands
Vasileios Koutavas	Trinity College Dublin, Ireland
Jean Krivine	CNRS, France
Cosimo Laneve	University of Bologna, Italy
Daniele Masti	Gran Sasso Science Institute, Italy
Hernán Melgratti	Universidad de Buenos Aires, Argentina
Claudio Antares Mezzina	University of Urbino, Italy
Luca Padovani	University of Bologna, Italy
Jovanka Pantovic	University of Novi Sad, Serbia
Anna Philippou	University of Cyprus, Cyprus
G. Michele Pinna	Università di Cagliari, Italy
Violet Ka I Pun	Western Norway University of Applied Sciences, Norway
Jorge A. Pérez	University of Groningen, The Netherlands
Dominika Regéciová	Brno University of Technology, Czech Republic
Alceste Scalas	Technical University of Denmark, Denmark
Alan Schmitt	Inria, France
Gerard Tabone	University of Malta, Malta
Simon Thompson	University of Kent, UK
Bernardo Toninho	Universidade Nova de Lisboa, Portugal
Emilio Tuosto	Gran Sasso Science Institute, Italy
Bas van den Heuvel	Karlsruhe University of Applied Sciences, Germany

German Vidal   Universitat Politècnica de València, Spain
Shoji Yuen   Nagoya University, Japan

Additional Reviewers

Galea, Marietta
Husson, Adrien
King, Daragh

Contents

Tutorial Paper

A Choreographic View of Smart Contracts 3
   Emilio Tuosto

Regular Papers

Temporal and Spatial Fault Detection for Connected Cyber-Physical
Systems 17
   Hugo Araujo, Mohammad Reza Mousavi, and Shiva Nejati

Sequential Composition of BDD Transition Systems for Model-Based
Testing 37
   Tannaz Zameni, Petra van den Bos, Johan Foederer, and Arend Rensink

Scaling Information Flow Control By-Construction to Component-Based
Software Architectures 55
   *Rasmus C. Rønneberg, Tabea Bordis, Christopher Gerking,
   Asmae Heydari Tabar, and Ina Schaefer*

Noninterference Analysis of Stochastically Timed Reversible Systems 75
   Andrea Esposito, Alessandro Aldini, and Marco Bernardo

Attribute-Based Communication over Pub/Sub: Transactional
Coordination for Smart Systems 96
   Marco Comini, Luca Gemolotto, and Marino Miculan

Probabilistic Safety Verification of Distributed Systems: A Statistical
Approach for Monitoring 114
   Bineet Ghosh and Étienne André

Towards Efficient Verification of Parallel Applications with Mc SimGrid 134
   Mathieu Laurent, Thierry Jéron, and Martin Quinson

Revisited Convergence of a Self-stabilizing BFS Spanning Tree Algorithm 154
   Karine Altisen and Marius Bozga

Short/Tool Papers

Choreographies for Program Understanding 173
   Gabriele Genovese, Ivan Lanese, Cinzia Di Giusto, Emilio Tuosto,
   and Germán Vidal

An Approach to Formalize Information-Theoretic Security of Multiparty
Computation Protocols 182
   Cheng-Hui Weng, Reynald Affeldt, Jacques Garrigue,
   and Takafumi Saikawa

SNexpression: A New Component for SN Matrix-Based Structural
Analysis 193
   Lorenzo Capra, Massimiliano De Pierro, and Giuliana Franceschinis

Assessing Code Understanding in LLMs 202
   C. Laneve, A. Spanò, D. Ressi, S. Rossi, and M. Bugliesi

LolaPrompts: Assisting the General Public in Performing Real-Driving
Emission Tests 211
   Melane Navaratnarajah, Ma'ayan Armony, Sebastian Biewer,
   Holger Hermanns, and Mohammad Reza Mousavi

Author Index 221

Tutorial Paper

A Choreographic View of Smart Contracts

Emilio Tuosto[✉]

Gran Sasso Science Institute, L'Aquila, Italy
emilio.tuosto@gssi.it

Abstract. This tutorial concerns the use of a novel model of coordination of distributed systems. The model combines ideas from choreographic approaches and smart contracts. More precisely, application protocols regulating the coordination of a distributed application are rendered as *global views* that specify the expected behaviour of the system. Unlike in standard choreographic models though, participants are not necessarily obtained by projection from global views and can behave in completely unexpected ways. The adopted countermeasure to erroneous or malicious behaviour of participants is the one adopted in smart contracts: disabled interactions are just ignored.

1 Introduction

The design and implementation of distributed computations requires great attention to information and control flows. In fact, distributed computation require suitable mechanisms and protocols to properly share information about the state of the computation among the unit of computations.[1] Paramount questions for "correctness" in this context are:

1. what information should participants use to coordinate among themselves?
2. how is this information supposed to be shared among participants?
3. when should the information sharing happen?

How to address these questions depends on which properties one wants to enforce (e.g., classical properties such deadlock freedom, security such as confidentiality, etc.), on which assumptions are made on participants (e.g., if they are cooperative, competitive, malicious, etc.), and on which interaction mechanisms are adopted (e.g., message passing, remote procedure call, etc.).

Increasing attention has been recently paid to *choreographic approaches* [10] both in academia and industry [3,4,6,16] since choreographies stand out for a

---
[1] We will call such units 'participants'; alternative terminology refers to such units as 'agents', 'processes', 'components'.

Research partly supported by the PRIN PNRR project DeLICE (F53D23009130001), by the MUR dipartimento di eccellenza 2023–2027.

neat separation of concerns which (*i*) abstracts away local computations from participants' interactions and (*ii*) advocates a two-pronged description of computations consisting of a *global view* and a *local view* of systems.

This tutorial hinges on a recent approach leveraging global views of choreographies to specify the coordination of participants through mechanisms inspired by execution models of *smart contracts* [17]. Our approach hinges on an attempt to formalise the informal model advocated in the Azure initiative of Microsoft [14] where models for the coordination of smart contract (SC for short) are given as finite-state machines (FMSs). Albeit commendable, this idea is only informally sketched; we illustrate this proposal using the simple marketplace (SMP) scenario.

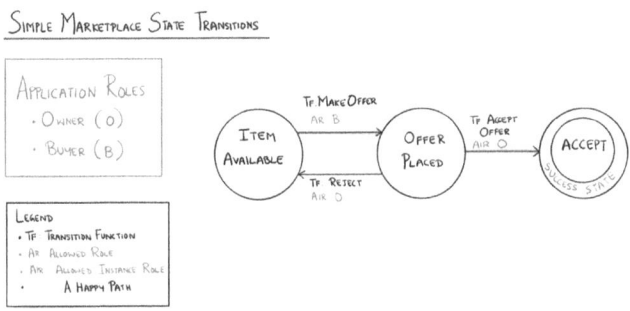

Fig. 1. The simple marketplace

Figure 1 borrows the sketch of the SMP specification as given in [15]. The key elements of the sketch are *roles* (OWNER and BUYER) played by participants of the protocol. The initial state ITEM AVAILABLE enables the transition MAKEOFFER for participants acting as buyers since, according to the Azure notation, the green decoration on transitions specifies the roles allowed to invoke the operation transition function (in the Azure jargon). On successful completion of this invocation, the protocol moves to the next state OFFER PLACED; in this state the owner can choose either to ACCEPT or REJECT the offer. In the former case, the protocol reaches the success state ACCEPT, otherwise the protocol moves back to ITEM AVAILABLE. The expected behaviour (the HAPPY PATH in Azure jargon) is the one highlighted in Fig. 1; in our example, the happy path can be interpreted as "an offer is eventually accepted".

As noted in [1], this idea is reminiscent of monitors [7,8] which encapsulate a state accessible through an API whose operations are guarded by conditions set to maintain an invariant on the state (in the SMP scenario the operations are MAKEOFFER, ACCEPTOFFER, and REJECT). Crucial aspects, however, tell apart monitors from this model. Firstly, our participants are distributed and do not share memory; secondly, callers of disabled operation do not suspend.

As said, the Azure approach is appealing but not formal. The sketch of the SMP scenario, for instance, blurs away some important details. For instance, the informal description hints that there is a single owner but, instead of being explicitly stated, this is implied by the use of ALLOWED ROLE and ALLOWED ROLE INSTANCE. Likewise, the description is unclear if an owner participant can also act as buyers. (Other ambiguities are described in [1].)

The model we use in this tutorial is based on a new class of symbolic finite-state machines formalising the Azure approach. Our model, at the same time, exposes the APIs of each participant of the protocol as well as the expected behaviour of the system. As global specifications such as global types [9], our model is instrumental to define a notion of *well-formedness*. Interestingly data-dependency, crucial in many contexts, can be explicitly represented. This is a quintessential aspect to handle properties that, like well-formedness, depend on the payloads of components' interactions such as those typical in smart contracts.

The natural application domain of our module are smart contracts; this tutorial shows this by covering the modelling and analysis of some smart contracts with a companion tool supporting our approach.

Structure of the Paper. Section 2 adapts the model presented in [1] to this tutorial (with minor adaptations to make the presentation lighter). Section 3 briefly discuss the intricacies of non-determinism in our model. Section 4 informally discusses our well-formedness conditions. Finally, Sect. 5 outlines our tool and the DSL it uses for the analysis.

2 Smart Contract Inspired Coordination

In our model, protocols' *participants* p, p', ... cooperate through a *coordinator* c according to their *role roles* R, R', ... Each coordinator c has:

- A finite set of *state variables* u, v, ...; each state variable has an associated data type, e.g., Int, Bool, ...; we also admit usual structured data types like arrays.
- A set of *function names* f, g, ... representing the operations available in c. Function parameters x, y, ... can be either data or participants variables.

An *assignment* u := e updates the state variable u to a *pure* expression e which may contain function parameters or the lexeme old u; the latter denotes the value of the state variable u before the assignment.[2] We let $B, B', \ldots$ range over finite sets of assignments where each variable can be assigned at most once. For simplicity, the syntax of expressions is kept implicit; the reader can assume that the syntax of expressions is standard (but for the use of the old _ qualifier).

A *coordinator* c *on state variables* $u_1, \ldots, u_n$ is a finite-state machine "instantiated" by a participant p whose transitions are essentially of two kinds.[3] A transition like

---

[2] We adapt the mechanism based on the old keyword from the Eiffel language [13] which, as explained in [12] is necessary to render assignments into logical formulae since e.g., $x = x + 1 \iff$ False.

[3] See [1, Def. 1]; here we just simplified the notation and adapted it to our needs.

$$\xrightarrow{\nu\;p\colon R \triangleright \mathsf{start}(c,\cdots,T_i\;x_i,\cdots)\;\{\cdots u_j := e_j \cdots\}} \bigcirc$$

allows participant p to create a fresh instance of coordinator c instantiating state variables u_j with expressions e_j on state variables and the parameters x_i. Transitions of the kind

$$\bigcirc \xrightarrow{\{\gamma\}\;\pi \triangleright f(\cdots, T_i\;x_i, \cdots)\;B} \bigcirc$$

are enabled when their *guard* γ, that is a boolean expression, holds true; in this case a *qualified participant* π defined by the following grammar:

$$\pi ::= \nu\;p\colon R \;\mid\; \mathsf{any}\;p\colon R \;\mid\; p$$

can call f with parameters x_i which reassigns state variables as defined by the set of assignments B. Intuitively, a qualified participant ν p: R specifies that variable p represents a fresh participant with role R while any p: R qualifies p as an existing participant with role R.

This model can be used to specify the conditions that enable the operations of a coordinator, how participants are expected to invoke the operations according to their role, and how successful invocation modify the state variables of the coordinator.

Exercise 1. *Give a contract for the SMP protocol in Sect. 1 resolving the ambiguities discussed there.*

3 A Note on Non-determinism

Sometimes determinism is required; for instance, smart contracts are usually required to behave deterministically [5]). Introducing a notion of deterministic coordinator requires some care as the labels of our automata use guards and symbolic expressions.

Exercise 2. *Consider the coordinator below*

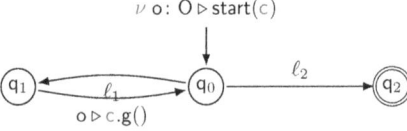

and say if it is deterministic in each of the following cases:
- $\ell_1 = \ell_2 = \mathsf{o} \triangleright \mathsf{c.g}()$
- $\ell_1 = \nu\;\mathsf{p}\colon \mathsf{R} \triangleright \mathsf{c.g}()$ *and* $\ell_2 = \mathsf{any}\;\mathsf{p}\colon \mathsf{R} \triangleright \mathsf{c.g}()$
- $\ell_1 = \{x \leq 10\}\;\mathsf{o} \triangleright \mathsf{c.g}(\mathsf{Int}\;x)$ *and* $\ell_2 = \{x > 10\}\;\mathsf{o} \triangleright \mathsf{c.g}(\mathsf{Int}\;x)$

We now introduce a binary relation instrumental to the definition of determinism. Let $\# \subseteq \mathcal{P} \times \mathcal{P}$ be the least symmetric relation such that

- $(\nu\;\mathsf{p}\colon \mathsf{R})\,\#\,\mathsf{p}'$,

- $(\nu\,\mathsf{p}\colon\mathsf{R})\,\#\,(\mathsf{any}\,\mathsf{p}'\colon\mathsf{O})$, and
- $\mathsf{R} \neq \mathsf{O} \implies (\mathsf{any}\,\mathsf{p}\colon\mathsf{R})\,\#\,(\mathsf{any}\,\mathsf{p}'\colon\mathsf{O})$.

Intuitively, if $\pi_1 \# \pi_2$, then the participants in π_1 and π_2 *differ*. Indeed, the first two items just say that a new participant is necessarily different from an existing one. The third item says that two participants with different roles are necessarily different (since we require that every participant can have at most one role).

We now define *strong determinism* which basically ensures that different transitions calling the same function from a same participant have mutually exclusive guards. A coordinator is *(strongly) deterministic* if for all of its transitions $\mathsf{t}_1 \neq \mathsf{t}_2$ from the same source state and calling the same function we have:
$$(\mathsf{g}_1 \wedge \mathsf{g}_2) \implies (\pi_1 \# \pi_2)$$
where, for $i \in \{1, 2\}$, g_i is the guard of t_i and π_i is the qualified participant of t_i.

Exercise 3. *Consider the coordinator*

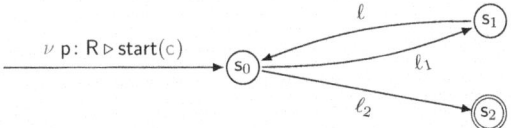

1. *Find two labels $\ell_1 = \ell_2$ such that the coordinator is deterministic.*
2. *Find two labels $\ell_1 \neq \ell_2$ that make the coordinator non-deterministic.*

4 Do All coordinators Make Sense?

In our model care is necessary to avoid specifying nonsensical coordinators. We consider a few cases that are evidently problematic.

Qualified participants of the form $\nu\,\mathsf{p}\colon\mathsf{R}$ and $\mathsf{any}\,\mathsf{p}\colon\mathsf{R}$, and parameter declarations of the form $\mathsf{p}\colon\mathsf{R}$ act as binders. Therefore, we should rule out coordinators like (1) below

$$\xrightarrow{\nu\,\mathsf{o}\colon\mathsf{O}\,\triangleright\,\mathsf{start}(\mathsf{c})} \bigcirc \xrightarrow{\mathsf{p}\,\triangleright\,@()} \bigcirc \qquad (1)$$

since p is a free occurrence which cannot denote any of the participants of the protocol. This can be simply attained by imposing the following property.

Name freeness: for each path of a coordinator, all free occurrences of participant variables should be after a quantifier.

Another problem arises when the role of a qualified participant is empty; consider

$$\xrightarrow{\nu\,\mathsf{o}\colon\mathsf{O}\,\triangleright\,\mathsf{start}(\mathsf{c})} \bigcirc \xrightarrow{\mathsf{any}\,\mathsf{p}\colon\mathsf{R}\,\triangleright\,@()} \bigcirc \qquad (2)$$

Arguably, the coordinator (2) is ill-formed since R is necessarily empty in s_0 and therefore the execution gets stuck in the initial state since no action is possible.

Role emptyness: all the roles in a path of a coordinator must appear in a transition with a freshly qualified participant.

We adopt a simple syntactical check that avoids the problem of empty roles. In fact, a sound and complete procedure for empty-roles detection subsumes reachability which, depending on the chosen expressivity of constraints and expressions, may be undecidable.

Progress can also be prevented in cases like the following

$$\xrightarrow{\nu\, \mathsf{o}:\, \mathsf{O} \triangleright \mathsf{start}(\mathsf{c})\ \{u:=0\}} \bigcirc \xrightarrow{\{u>0\}\ \nu\, \mathsf{p}:\, \mathsf{R} \triangleright @()} \circledcirc \qquad (3)$$

where the assignment in the start-transition of the coordinator (3) falsifies the guard of the transition from the initial state.

Consistency: the disjunction of the guards of the outgoing transitions of each state should not be a contradiction.

Similarly to empty roles, no-progress is undecidable in general. Our algorithmic verification checks that every transition t, regardless of the "history" of the current execution, leads to a state which is either accepting or it has at least a transition enabled. This is intuitively accomplished by checking that the guard of t, after being updated according to the assignments of t, implies the disjunction of the guards of the outgoing transitions from the target state of t.

Finally, we restrict to *well-formed* coordinators, that is coordinators that are deterministic closed, empty-role free, and consistent.

Exercise 4. *Is the coordinator*

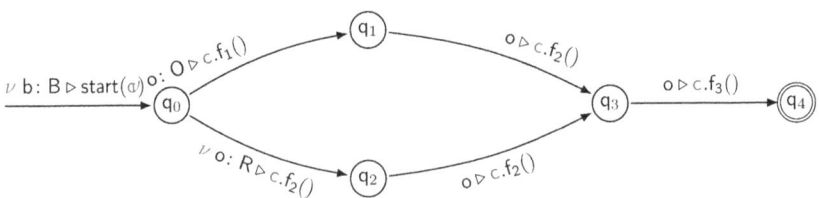

well-formed? Justify your answer.

Our notion of well-formedness is not complete as shown by reflecting on the solution of the following exercise.

Exercise 5. *Explain why the following coordinator*

$$\xrightarrow{\nu\, \mathsf{o}:\, \mathsf{O} \triangleright \mathsf{start}(\mathsf{c})\ \{\mathsf{c}.x:=1\}} (q_0) \xrightarrow{\mathsf{o} \triangleright \mathsf{c}.f_1()} (q_1) \xrightarrow{\{\mathsf{c}.x>0\}\ \mathsf{o} \triangleright \mathsf{c}.f_2()} (\!(q_2)\!)$$

is not well-formed.

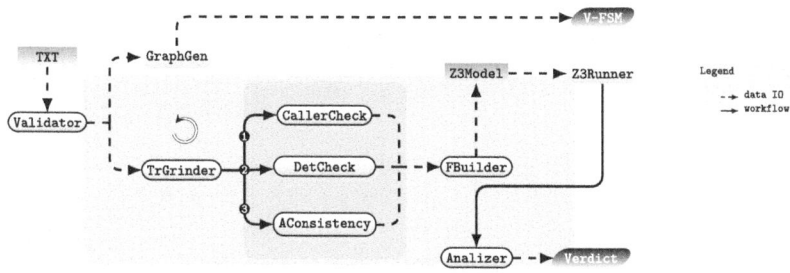

Fig. 2. Architecture of TRAC

5 Checking Well-Formedness

Figure 2 borrows from [1] the architecture of our *tool* for *resource-aware* coordination (TRAC). The architecture of TRAC consists of two principal modules: one for parsing and visualisation (yellow box) and a module for the core functionalities (orange box). The latter module implements well-formedness check (green box).

The Validator transforms a textual representation of the coordinator in the V-FSM format suitable for visualisation through GraphGen or in an internal format suitable for our analysis.

The component TrGrinder relays each transition of the coordinator in input to the components in the green box that perform the verification of well-formedness according to Sect. 2; more precisely:

- CallerCheck (arrow ❶) checks for closedness and role emptyness;
- DetCheck (arrow ❷) builds a Z3 formula equivalent to strong determinism;
- AConsistency (arrow ❸) generates a Z3 formula equivalent to consistency.

These three outputs form the conjuncts of another Z3 formula built by the component FBuilder which finally yields a Z3Model passed to the Z3Runner component. The verification process ends with the Analizer component that diagnoses the output of Z3 and produces a Verdict which reports (if any) the violations of well-formedness of the coordinatorin input.

We now give some details on TRACinstrumental for this tutorial; further details can be found in [2] while the installation instructions are at [11].

To invoke TRACone has to prepare a .trac text-file to pass to the Validator. The content of the file is a sugared lists of transitions of a coordinator preceded by initial assignments of its state variables and a guard. The general form of a coordinator is given on the left below according to the DSL whose syntax is given by the grammar on the right below (where non-terminal symbols are in angled brackets):

```
1   dafsm c(⟨pars⟩) by p : R {
      ⋮
4     ⟨dcl⟩ := e ;
      ⋮
5     if γ
    }
7   ⟨str⟩ ⟨lbl⟩ ⟨str⟩ ;
      ⋮
```

⟨pars⟩ ::= ε | ⟨dcl⟩(,⟨dcl⟩)*

⟨dcl⟩ ::= ⟨str⟩ ⟨str⟩

⟨lbl⟩ ::= {γ} ⟨qlf⟩ > ⟨str⟩(⟨pars⟩) {⟨asg⟩}
⟨qlf⟩ ::= new p : R | any p : R | p
⟨asg⟩ ::= ⟨str⟩:=⟨expr⟩
⟨asgs⟩ ::= ε | ⟨asg⟩(;⟨asg⟩)*

Essentially, our format declares a coordinator c.u (cf. line 1) that can be instantiated by passing some actual values for the formal parameters defined in ⟨pars⟩. A parameter declaration is a (possibly empty) list of declarations ⟨dcl⟩ that is pairs assigning a type T to an identifier x, written T x. State variables (if any), declared and initially assigned an expression (line 3) are followed by a guard (line 5); the free variables occurring in the expression or the guard must be either state variables of formal parameters. Finally, the list of transitions is specified (line 7) as triplets consisting of source state, label, and target state where states are simple strings and labels have essentially the syntax described in Sect. 2.

Exercise 6. *Edit a .trac file for the SMP protocol.*
You can inspect the coordinator you provide using GraphGen.

6 Concluding Remarks

This tutorial surveyed a coordination model inspired by smart contracts and showed how to use TRAC to analyse DAFSMs in this settings.

A version of this paper with solutions to the exercises is available at https://emwww.github.io/home/tr/forte2025.pdf.

Currently we are extending both the model and the tool in several directions. Specifically, we are extending the model to support dynamic change of roles and inter-coordinators invocations. This extension is the ground for automatic generation of Solidity code from our coordinators as well as of automatic test generation.

Another interesting direction is to use our models as a basis for statistical model checking.

Acknowledgements. The coordination model presented in this tutorial has been developed in collaboration with Elvis Gerardin Konjoh Selabi (Università di Camerino and GSSI), Antonio Ravara (NOVA), and Maurizio Murgia (GSSI). I am responsible however for any imprecision and inaccuracy in this paper.

I thank Elvis for his technical assistance.

References

1. Afonso, J., Selabi, E.K., Murgia, M., Ravara, A., Tuosto, E.: TRAC: a tool for data-aware coordination - (with an application to smart contracts). In: Castellani, I., Tiezzi, F. (eds.) Coordination Models and Languages - 26th IFIP WG

6.1 International Conference, COORDINATION 2024, Held as Part of the 19th International Federated Conference on Distributed Computing Techniques, DisCoTec 2024, Groningen, The Netherlands, 17–21 June 2024, Proceedings, vol. 14676. LNCS, pp. 239–257. Springer, Heidelberg (2024)
2. Afonso, J., Selabi, E.K., Murgia, M., Tuosto, E., Ravara, A.: Artefact submission for paper #8 of COORDINATION 2024 (2024)
3. Autili, M., Inverardi, P., Tivoli, M.: Automated synthesis of service choreographies. IEEE Softw. **32**(1), 50–57 (2015)
4. Bonér, J.: Reactive Microsystems - The Evolution Of Microservices At Scale. O'Reilly (2018)
5. Buterin, V.: Ethereum: a next generation smart contract and decentralized application platform (2014). https://ethereum.org/whitepaper
6. Frittelli, L., Maldonado, F., Melgratti, H., Tuosto, E.: A choreography-driven approach to APIs: the OpenDXL case study. In: Bliudze, S., Bocchi, L. (eds.) COORDINATION 2020. LNCS, vol. 12134, pp. 107–124. Springer, Cham (2020). https://doi.org/10.1007/978-3-030-50029-0_7
7. Hansen, P.B.: Operating System Principles. Prentice-Hall, Upper Saddle river (1973)
8. Hansen, P.B.: Monitors and concurrent pascal: a personal history. In: The Second ACM SIGPLAN Conference on History of Programming Languages, HOPL-II, pp. 1–35. Association for Computing Machinery, New York (1993)
9. Honda, K., Yoshida, N., Carbone, M.: Multiparty asynchronous session types. JACM **63**(1), 9:1–9:67 (2016)
10. Kavantzas, N., Burdett, D., Ritzinger, G., Fletcher, T., Lafon, Y.: Web services choreography description language version 1.0. http://www.w3.org/TR/2004/WD-ws-cdl-10-20041217. Working Draft 17 December 2004
11. Selabi, E.G.K.: TRAC: a tool for data-aware coordination (2024). https://github.com/loctet/TRAC
12. Meyer, B.: Introduction to the Theory of Programming Languages. Prentice-Hall, Upper Saddle River (1990)
13. Meyer, B.: Eiffel: The Language. Prentice-Hall, Upper Saddle River (1991)
14. Microsoft. The blockchain workbench (2019). https://github.com/Azure-Samples/blockchain/tree/master/blockchain-workbench
15. Microsoft. Simple marketplace sample application for azure blockchain workbench (2019). https://github.com/Azure-Samples/blockchain/tree/master/blockchain-workbench/application-and-smart-contract-samples/simple-marketplace
16. Object Management Group. Business Process Model and Notation. http://www.bpmn.org
17. Tolmach, P., Li, Y., Lin, S.W., Liu, Y., Li, Z.: A survey of smart contract formal specification and verification. ACM Comput. Surv. **54**(7) (2021)

Regular Papers

Temporal and Spatial Fault Detection for Connected Cyber-Physical Systems

Hugo Araujo[1(✉)], Mohammad Reza Mousavi[1], and Shiva Nejati[2]

[1] King's College London, London, UK
{hugo.araujo,mohammad.mousavi}@kcl.ac.uk
[2] University of Ottawa, Ottawa, Canada
snejati@uottawa.ca

Abstract. Testing connected cyber-physical systems (CPS) is a complex task. Connected CPS feature complex stochastic dynamic behaviour in interaction with the physical and human environment as well as communication over networks. Devising an oracle for testing connected CPS is a challenge; the oracle should be able to quantitatively reason about the stochastic nature of the interactions between the CPS and its environment. The quantitative reasoning should be sensitive to significant deviations in the dynamics and neglect minor deviations, e.g., due to measurement errors. To address this challenge, we provide the mathematical framework for conformance testing of connected CPS. We define a quantitative measure of closeness for two distributions of trajectories (i.e., output distributions from two distinct stochastic systems that are provided with the same input stimuli) that allows for capturing significant temporal and spatial deviations and neglecting subtle ones. This measure forms the basis for our notion of stochastic conformance, which determines when two stochastic systems conform to each other. We implement our proposed notion of stochastic conformance and compare our notion against a state-of-the-art baseline by applying both approaches to a case study involving a platoon of connected vehicles. Our notion detects a variety of different types of faults whilst allowing subtle deviations resulting from naturally occurring perturbations inherent to CPS.

Keywords: Cyber-physical systems · Conformance testing · Stochastic

1 Introduction

Connected Cyber-Physical Systems (CPS) represent an integration of computation, networking, and physical processes, where embedded computers and networks monitor and control physical processes [9]. As these systems are highly prevalent in critical domains such as healthcare, automotive, and aerospace, ensuring their correctness and reliability is paramount [24]. However, verifying CPS is challenging and many techniques have been developed to ensure their correctness [6,38]. One such approach is *conformance testing*, which verifies whether a system complies with its specification by comparing their outputs through a well-defined mathematical relation (i.e., a conformance notion) [27]. Conformance testing is highly relevant to CPS, as comparing the system against its specification supports automated test oracles. Nonetheless, applying conformance testing to CPS presents several challenges.

One of the key challenges in conformance testing for CPS is to define a quantitative measure that detects significant deviations, yet disregards subtle perturbations in the system behaviour caused by naturally occurring physical phenomena and measurement errors. For instance, sensor noise, mechanical backlash, and communication delays can affect the behaviour of such systems in a negligible way. If not accounted for, this can lead to false negatives, i.e., failing a test case, even when the system is within the expected boundaries [2]. Thus, conformance testing techniques should provide adjustable temporal and spatial bounds (to be defined by domain experts) to allow for detecting significant deviations between a system's output and its specification while neglecting the minor ones. The second key challenge arises from the stochastic nature of connected CPS and their environments, necessitating conformance testing that accounts for the probabilistic distributions of outcomes. The need for such a notion has been identified in the literature: it has been demonstrated that test results for CPS are often stochastic, leading to variability in outputs when the same test is re-executed multiple times [18].

In the literature, existing conformance notions can accommodate for (i) temporal error margins and (ii) spatial error margins [1], or (iii) stochasticity [32], exclusively. However, to our knowledge, there is no conformance testing approach that covers these three aspects simultaneously. The aim of this work is to propose a conformance notion that responds to the identified need and addresses all three aspects. To this end, we define a quantitative measure that compares output distributions and checks whether their distance is within user-defined margins. This lets us uncover deviating stochastic behaviour that indicates a failure whilst allowing for subtle, naturally occurring temporal and spatial deviations. We implement our conformance testing notion and compare it against the state-of-the-art it using a case study of a connected platoon. Our results show that our conformance notion can detect a higher number of inserted faults and common faulty signal patterns (identified by a taxonomy on signal-based properties of CPS [14]), given the same test suite, compared to the alternative.

In summary, the main contributions of this work are as follows. We first introduce a novel conformance notion that allows for (i) reasoning about the stochastic nature of connected CPS (by considering distributions of outputs) and for (ii) quantitative temporal and spatial error margins in the outputs (which are needed to fail major deviations while reducing the number of false negatives). Then, we implement our conformance notion into a publicly-available tool. Lastly, we present the results of an empirical evaluation that compares our notion against a baseline [32]; we make the assets and data resulting from the study publicly available at https://zenodo.org/records/14906880.

We assess the performance of our conformance testing approach using the true positive (a *correct* fail verdict) and false positive (an *incorrect* fail verdict) metrics. We devise the following research questions based on these two metrics.

- **RQ1.** Is our conformance testing approach effective in detecting substantial discrepancies between the outputs of two CPS and, hence, yielding true positive verdicts?
- **RQ2.** Is our conformance testing approach adaptable to allow negligible discrepancies between the outputs of two CPS and, hence, avoiding false positive verdicts?

The notion of false positives and negatives is related to the parameters of the conformance notion. That is, any deviating behaviour within the allowed margins should not result in a fail verdict. The opposite must also be true: any deviating behaviour beyond the allowed margins should result in a fail verdict.

2 Related Work

Classical methods for automatic verification of CPS, such as reachability analysis [8] and, more generally, model checking [16] have been extensively studied and applied [3,10,15,22,33]; such methods typically rely on exhaustively exploring the state-space of the system (or its model). However, these methods are prone to the state-space explosion problem and cannot be used for large-scale systems. Classical conformance testing approaches [1,19,36] address this problem by non-exhaustively falsifying a specification through comparing the specification against the system under test. This is typically done using distance metrics such as Euclidean [1] and Skorokhod [19] to compute the degree of dissimilarity between the observed and expected output. However, they fail to account for stochastic behaviour, limiting their applicability to real-world CPS. To address the limitations of traditional verification approaches, stochastic approaches have been proposed. They range from exhaustive model-checking approaches [28] to non-exhaustive formal verification [17,25] and conformance testing [29,32] approaches. In the remainder of this section, we review the most significant contributions in this area and compare them to ours.

Clarke et al. [17] developed a strategy for statistical model checking of CPS by combining the Monte Carlo method with temporal logic model checking. They sample simulations of the system model and check their conformance with respect to a temporal formula by applying a statistical estimation technique to compute the probability that the formula is satisfied. Unlike our work, they focus on verifying compliance with respect to properties whereas our methodology works by verifying that the distance between (expected and observed) output distributions is smaller than a pre-defined value. More closely related to our work, Qin et al. [32] propose a notion of conformance for stochastic system that checks whether the probability of the distance between outputs is less than the failure probability. Unlike their work, we consider not only spatial but also temporal distance between outputs. This allows us to cater for delays that naturally occur in CPS. Furthermore, our notion of distance considers point-by-point and not the overall distance between the entire output signal; hence, we propose a more thorough formalism that can catch short bursts of discrepancy that violate conformance. Similarly, Leemans et al. [29] use the Wasserstein distance to quantify the distance between two stochastic Petri systems. Their notion of distance is based on the "earth movers' distance" and measures the effort to transform the distributions of traces in one model into the distribution of traces in another. Their approach substantially differs from ours, as it has only been considered for discrete systems (using traces based on event logs). The effect of using different distance measures (such as total variation distance [35] or Wasserstein [23]) on the effectiveness of conformance testing can be further investigated.

3 Preliminaries

In this section, we provide the preliminary concepts used to define conformance. We start with a running example of a CPS (Sect. 3.1), and, in Sect. 3.2, we provide the mathematical background to describe stochastic systems. Lastly, in Sect. 3.3, we recall a basic notion of conformance [2] (for non-stochastic systems) that we extend to deal with the stochastic nature of CPS.

3.1 Running Example

Consider a system where a convoy of cars autonomously follow a leading human-driven car. The leading car sends its acceleration, velocity, and location via wireless communication channels to the followers. It is critical that the follower cars are up-to-date with the information received from the connected cars; therefore, following the literature, we employ the concept of data age as a safety metric for the platoon [13]. Due to network congestion, the transmission of a packet has a probability distribution. In the remainder, we use this running example to explain the basic concepts and further elaborate on it as our case study.

3.2 Probability Theory

To formally model stochastic systems, we start by defining probability spaces.

Definition 1 (Probability Space). *A probability space is a triple, denoted by $(\Omega, \mathcal{F}, P)$, comprising the sample space Ω, a set $\mathcal{F}$ of events that is a σ-algebra of Ω, and a function $P : \mathcal{F} \to [0, 1]$ that provides the probability measure for the set of events. A σ-algebra of a set X is defined as a non-empty collection of subsets of X closed under complement, countable unions, and countable intersections.*

A probability space is a triple that comprises the sample space Ω (i.e., the set of all possible outcomes), a collection of events within the sample space $\mathcal{F}$ that may or may not comprise every outcome in Ω (i.e., the σ-algebra of Ω), and a probability measure P that assigns a probability to each event in $\mathcal{F}$.

Example 1 (Probability Space). A probability space for our running example comprises the set of all possible outcomes for data-age ($\Omega = \mathbb{R}_{>0}$), a possible collection of events is the sets of intervals of size 1 between natural numbers less than 5 ($\mathcal{F} = \{[1,2], [2,3], [3,4], [4,5]\}$), and the probability of the event where the data-age X falls within $[1,2]$ is $P(1 \leq X \leq 2) = \frac{2}{3}$.

The concepts of probability space and random variables are closely related; in this work, a random variable is a function that assigns a numerical value to each elementary outcome. We formally define it below.

Definition 2 (Random Variable). *Consider the probability space $(\Omega, \mathcal{F}, P)$ where Ω is the sample space, $\mathcal{F}$ is a σ-algebra of Ω, and $P : \mathcal{F} \to [0,1]$ is a probability measure. A random variable X is a function $X : \Omega \to \mathbb{R}$ from the sample space Ω into the set of numerical values $\mathbb{R}$.*

In probability theory, the probability of a continuous random variable X taking a specific value is always equal to zero; instead, its probability is measured over a range of values (i.e., $P[a \leq X \leq b]$). For such variables, in order to calculate probabilities, we use a probability density function (pdf), denoted by $f(t)$. Essentially, the area beneath the two points (a, b) in the plot of such a function constitutes the probability density within the range $P[a \leq X \leq b]$. We recall the formal definition of probability density functions below.

Definition 3 (Probability Density Function). *Consider the probability space $(\Omega, \mathcal{F}, P)$, and a random variable $X : \Omega \to \mathbb{R}$. A probability density function of X, denoted by $f(t)$, is a function that obeys the following properties:*

- *$P(X \in [a, b]) = \int_b^a f(t)dt$;*
- *$f(t) \geq 0$ for all possible values of t;*
- *$\int_{-\infty}^{+\infty} f(t)dt = 1$;*

We denote by $Dens(V)$ the set of the density functions over the set of random variables V. The first property specifies that the probability of an event X to be within the range $[a, b]$ is equal to the integral of $f(t)$ (the pdf of X) from a to b; this corresponds to the area beneath the plotted line formed by $f(t)$ within $[a, b]$. The second and third properties specify that a pdf is never negative and that the total area beneath the plot is always equals to 1, respectively. The last property essentially states that the probability of an event to be between $[-\infty, +\infty]$ is 1.

Example 2 (Probability density function). Consider our running example; the pdf for the data-age (D) is the normal distributions function, defined by:

$$f_D(t) = \frac{1}{\sigma\sqrt{2\pi}} e^{-\frac{1}{2}(\frac{t-u}{\sigma})^2},$$

where σ and u are the location and scale parameters and, for this example, are set to 0.25 and 1, respectively. The plot of this function is shown in Fig. 1, where we highlight in grey the area that corresponds to $P(0.8 \leq D \leq 1.2) = 0.64$.

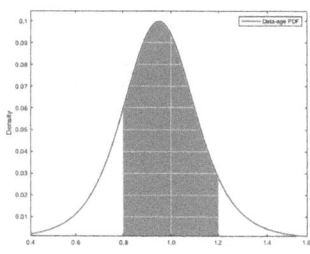

Fig. 1. Running example PDF.

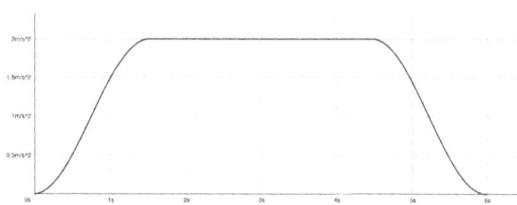

Fig. 2. Example of an acceleration trajectory.

In order to determine conformance between two systems, one first needs a way to quantify the degree of similarity between them. For stochastic systems, we can make use of statistical distance metrics such as the total variation distance [35], the Wasserstein metric [23], and the Hellinger distance [12]. Throughout the remainder of this paper, we employ the last definition (defined below) as our distance metric as it is akin to the Euclidean distance for stochastic system and, hence, more intuitive to understand. In the experiment section (Section 6), however, we also compare the results of using the other two metrics and we show that, in fact, Hellinger distance does perform better than the alternatives.

Definition 4 (Hellinger distance). *Given two probability density functions $f(x)$ and $g(x)$, the Hellinger distance $d(f,g)$ is given by the formula:*

$$d(f,g) = \frac{1}{2} \int (\sqrt{f(t)} - \sqrt{g(t)})^2 dt$$

Essentially, the Hellinger distance can be seen as the ℓ_2 norm between two distributions (more specifically, between the square root of the distributions).

3.3 Conformance

In what follows, we recall a basic theory to define stochastic systems and use the notions of pdf (Definition 3) and a measure of distance (Definition 4) to develop our stochastic conformance notion. We start with the notion of valuation, which provides the values for set of variables and serves as the basis for our definitions.

Definition 5 (Valuation). *Given a set of variables $V = \{X_1, \ldots, X_n\}$, we denote by $Val(V) = V \to \mathbb{R}$ the set of all total functions from V to the real domain $\mathbb{R}$.*

In cyber-physical systems, variables have continuous valuation over time. This can be represented using trajectories, which are collections of variable valuations within a time interval.

Definition 6 (Trajectory). *Given a set of variables V, the set of trajectories over V, denoted by $Trajs(V) = \{x_1, \ldots, x_m\}$, is the set of all mappings $T \to Val(V)$, where T is the time domain, assumed to be a convex subset of $\mathbb{R}_{\geq 0}$.*

Example 3 (Acceleration trajectory). Consider our running example and that, in this example, the acceleration can be depicted by a trajectory that increases for the first 1.5 s, stays constant for 3 s and then decreases for another 1.5 s. This trajectory is depicted in Fig. 2.

The trajectory of a variable maps the moments in time to values. Given two trajectories, their similarity can be evaluated using a parametric notion that caters for spatial and temporal discrepancies. This allows for conformance verdicts in scenarios where slight deviations are acceptable.

Definition 7 ((τ,ϵ)-closeness [1]). *Consider the maximum temporal and spatial distances $\tau, \epsilon \in \mathbb{R} \mid \tau, \epsilon > 0$, and the time domain T; then, two trajectories y_1 and y_2 are said to be (τ,ϵ)-close, denoted by $y_1 \approx_{(\tau,\epsilon)} y_2$, if*

1. *for all $t \in \text{dom}(y_1)$ with $t \leq T$, there exists $s \in \text{dom}(y_2)$ such that $|t - s| \leq \tau$ and $\|y_1(t) - y_2(s)\| \leq \epsilon$, and*
2. *for all $t \in \text{dom}(y_2)$ with $t \leq T$, there exists $s \in \text{dom}(y_1)$ such that $|t - s| \leq \tau$ and $\|y_2(t) - y_1(s)\| \leq \epsilon$.*

The notion of (τ,ϵ)-closeness [2] is defined based on the continuous behaviour associated with a continuous physical system, and, hence, this notion does not require the output signals to behave in exact synchronisation. In practice, due to physical phenomena such as measurement errors, transport delays, or mechanical backlash, two implementations of the same system will often slightly deviate from each other [2]. The closeness notion that we adopt in this work to determine how close two trajectories are, in terms of valuation, is based on maximum error margins τ (to account for temporal deviations) and ϵ (to account for spatial deviations). Given the notion of trajectory, we define a deterministic cyber-physical system as an input-output relation based on trajectories; the system is deterministic if each input trajectory yields only one possible output trajectory.

Definition 8 (Deterministic Cyber-Physical System). *A continuous cyber-physical system S is described by the input output relation $S : Trajs(I) \rightarrow Trajs(O)$ where I is the set of input variables and O is the set of output variables. The system S is deterministic if, and only if, $\forall x \in Trajs(I), \forall y_1, y_2 \in Trajs(O)$, we have that $S(x) = y_1 \land S(x) = y_2 \implies y_1 = y_2$.*

Lastly, we define a parametric notion of conformance between CPS. Essentially, for every input stimuli that is fed to both systems, the corresponding output trajectories must not deviate beyond the τ and ϵ bounds.

Definition 9 ((τ,ϵ)-conformance [1]). *Given two deterministic cyber-physical systems S_1 and S_2, a maximum temporal distance $\tau \in \mathbb{R}_{>0}$, and a maximum spatial distance $\epsilon \in \mathbb{R}_{>0}$, we say that S_1 (τ,ϵ)-conforms to S_2, denoted by $S_1 \approx_{\tau,\epsilon} S_2$, if, and only if, for any input trajectory $x \in \text{dom}(S_1) \cup \text{dom}(S_2)$, we have that $S_1(x) \approx_{\tau,\epsilon} S_2(x)$.*

4 Stochastic Conformance

In this section, we first present the mathematical formalism to compare two stochastic systems given parametric error margins. Then, we provide some intuition about the differences between our notion and the state-of-the-art [32].

4.1 Stochastic Conformance

In stochastic systems, instead of specific values, trajectories map a moment in time to a possible distribution of outcomes. In this work, given the continuous nature of our systems, the distribution is represented by density functions.

Definition 10 (Stochastic trajectory). *Given the probability space $(\Omega, \mathcal{F}, P)$ and a set of random variables V, an stochastic trajectory $x : T \to Dens(V)$ is the set of all mappings of the time domain into a set of density functions over V.*

We denote by $STrajs(V)$ the set of all possible stochastic trajectories over the set of random variables V. Next, we define an stochastic cyber-physical system as a system that, given an input trajectory, outputs a stochastic trajectory.

Definition 11 (Stochastic CPS).

Example 4 (Leader-Follower example). Consider that we use the acceleration trajectory a depicted in Example 3 as the input trajectory for our running example. The output for such a system is a stochastic trajectory that represents the data-age (D) and comprises a density function $f_X^t(x)$ (i.e., a distribution of values for D) for each $t \in \text{dom}(a)$.

We note that, even in a stochastic system, some variables may have a deterministic value (a value with probability 1). In this work, we use a Dirac distribution in order to model such variables. Essentially, a Dirac distribution is a function that is mapped to positive infinity for a specific value and is zero at any other point. The integral of any interval containing that one point is equals to one as its density function.

To define stochastic closeness, we lift the definition of (τ, ϵ)-closeness (see Sect. 3.3) to work with stochastic trajectories. Essentially, two stochastic trajectories y_1 and y_2 are close if, for every distribution $y_1(t)$ there exists a point in time $s \in [t - \tau, t + \tau]$ that results in a distribution $y_2(s)$ and the Hellinger distance between $y_1(t)$ and $y_2(s)$ is lower than a predetermined ϵ.

Definition 12 (Stochastic Closeness). *Given two stochastic trajectories y_1 and y_2, a maximum temporal distance τ, the Hellinger distance function $d()$, and a maximum distribution distance ϵ, we say that y_1 is stochastically close to y_2, denoted by $y_1 \approx_{\tau,\epsilon}^s y_2$, iff:*

- *for all $t \in \text{dom}(y_1)$, there exists $s \in \text{dom}(y_2)$ such that $|t - s| \leq \tau$ and $d(y_1(t), y_2(s)) \leq \epsilon$*

- for all $t \in dom(y_2)$, there exists $s \in dom(y_1)$ such that $|t - s| \leq \tau$ and $d(y_2(t), y_1(s)) \leq \epsilon$

Analogously, we lift the definition of (τ, ϵ)-conformance [1] to work with stochastic systems. Two stochastic systems conform to each other when, for all possible inputs, the resulting stochastic trajectories are stochastically close.

Definition 13 (Stochastic Conformance). *Given two stochastic systems S_1 and S_2, a maximum temporal distance τ, and a maximum distribution distance ϵ, we say that S_1 (τ,ϵ)-stochastically conforms to S_2, denoted by $S_1 \approx_{\tau,\epsilon}^{s} S_2$, if, and only if, for any input trajectory $x \in dom(S_1) \cup dom(S_2)$, we have that $S_1(x) \approx_{\tau,\epsilon}^{s} S_2(x)$.*

4.2 Comparison with the State of the Art

Qin et al. [32] defined a conformance notion for stochastic continuous systems that computes the distribution between trajectory distances. Their models of cyber-physical systems comprise stochastic input and output trajectories. Given a system of probability space $(\Omega, \mathcal{F}, P)$, inputs and outputs are defined as a function $Y : T \times \Omega \to \mathbb{R}^m$, where the sample space is part of the domain but the outcome are specific values. Hence, given an outcome $\omega \in \Omega$, one can produce a specific trajectory $y = Y(\bullet, \omega)$ (called a realisation of Y). The possible values for the outcome ω leads to a distribution of realisations of Y.

Now, consider two stochastic outputs Y_1 and Y_2 and two realisations y_1 and y_2. The authors define a distance metric between two trajectories as $d_p(y_1, y_2) := (\int_T ||y_1(t) - y_2(t)||^p dt)^{\frac{1}{p}}$. A distribution on the possible trajectories for Y_1 and Y_2 leads to a distribution on their distance, denoted by $d(Y_1, Y_2)$. Thus, given a maximum distance ϵ and a failure rate δ, they define a conformance notions as $P(d(Y_1, Y_2) \leq \epsilon) \geq 1 - \delta$.

There are a few key differences between our and their strategies. Overall, our work aims to compute the distance between probabilities distribution; Qin's work, instead, computes the probability of the distance between distributions of trajectories. Additionally, in Qin's work, the degree of closeness between two trajectories is given by the integral of their distance and produces an overall value. The (τ,ϵ)-closeness relation, instead, checks if conformance holds for every point in the trajectories. We motivate our work by identifying two main distinctions.

Firstly, our conformance notion caters for temporal deviations. As an example, consider two identical trajectories in the shape of a signal that has high frequency and high amplitude. If we apply a tiny delay to one of them, this may result in a significant difference between their overall distance, whereas point-wise the distance may be negligible. Hence, allowing for temporal deviations may result in conformance to hold, and, from the literature [1,19], it seems necessary to accommodate such delays.

Secondly, our conformance notion captures short bursts of high deviation. Consider two trajectories that are identical except during a short time interval where they abruptly deviate from each other significantly. In our approach, this abrupt deviation will be considered and this may result in a non-conforming verdict. In Qin's work however, due to the fact that the two trajectories are mostly identical, this may not result in non conformance.

The literature [14] consider such bursts and spikes as significant fault categories that need to be detected by a notion of conformance. To confirm our intuition, we have devised a controlled experiment (see Sect. 6) where we evaluate our implementation of both conformance notions.

5 Mechanisation

Our approach is mechanised as illustrated in Algorithm 1. Given an input trajectory x that is fed into two systems S_S and S_I (e.g., the system specification and its implementation), the algorithms estimates the distributions for the outputs of $S_S(x)$ and $S_I(x)$.

The algorithm works as follows. As per Definition 12, the closeness notion between two trajectories checks that every point in the first trajectory is close enough to a neighbouring point in the second trajectory; additionally, the reverse

---

Algorithm 1: Pseudo-code for conformance check algorithm.

input : Trajectory x, Time error margin τ, Value error margin ϵ, , Specification S_S, Implementation S_I;
output: Boolean $conforms$;

1 **Function** Main() :
2   **if** StochasticCloseness(x,τ,ϵ,S_S,S_I) **then**
3   **return** StochasticCloseness(x,τ,ϵ,S_I,S_S);
4   **end**
5   **return** False;
6 **end**
7 **Function** StochasticCloseness(x,τ,ϵ,S_1,S_2) :
8   **for** $t \leftarrow 0$ **to** T **do**
9   Boolean $conforms$ = False;
10   Distribution D_1 = Sample(x,t,S_1);
11   **for** $s \leftarrow$ Min$(0, t - \tau)$ **to** Max$(T, t + \tau)$ **do**
12   Distribution D_2 = Sample(x,s,S_2);
13   Real $distance$ = HellingerDistance(D_1,D_2);
14   **if** $distance \leq \epsilon$ **then**
15   **return** $conforms$ = True;
16   **end**
17   **end**
18   **if** !conforms **then**
19   **return** False;
20   **end**
21   **end**
22   **return** True;
23 **end**
24 **Function** Sample(x,t,S) :
25   Set [Real] $outputs$ = {};
26   **for** $i \leftarrow 0$ **to** 50 **do**
27      $outputs$.Add(Execute(S,x,t));
28   **end**
29   Distribution D = EstimateDistribution($outputs$);
30   **return** D;
31 **end**

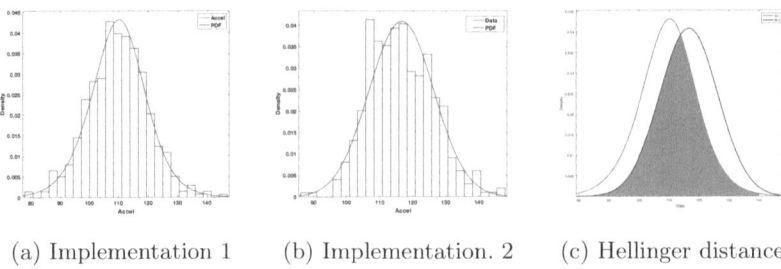

(a) Implementation 1   (b) Implementation. 2   (c) Hellinger distance.

Fig. 3. Output distribution.

must also hold. Hence, our algorithm performs the closeness check both ways (lines 02 and 03). The closeness check iterates through every $t \in T$ (line 08). For every t, we sample the possible outcomes for S_1 (line 10). Essentially, the sampling process executes S_1 using x as input several times (lines 25 - 27) and estimates its distribution (line 28). Then, we compute the distributions for the other system $S_2(x)$ within the $[t - \tau, t + \tau]$ time interval (lines 11 and 12) and check if there is at least one point within the interval where the Hellinger distance between $S_1(x)$ and $S_2(x)$ is smaller than ϵ (lines 13 and 14). If no such point exists, then the conformance does not hold (line 19).

As an example, Fig. 3 shows the comparison between two output distributions. Consider two implementations of the running example. Given the same input to both systems, Fig. 3a shows the output distribution for a time t in the first implementation and, analogously, Fig. 3b shows the distribution for the same time t in the second implementation. Our algorithm checks whether the distance (Fig. 3c) between both distributions (and also, distributions in the neighbourhood) is greater than ϵ, and, if so, the systems are deemed non-conformant with respect to each other.

6 Empirical Evaluation

In this section, we present the application of the strategy proposed in Sect. 5 to a case study in which we detect inserted faults in a model of a convoy of autonomous vehicles.

6.1 Research Objectives

Our evaluation assesses the effectiveness of our proposed stochastic conformance notion for testing CPS by comparing it to the state-of-the-art [32]. Using a Simulink [20] model of a connected vehicle platoon, we manually introduce faults and analyse test outputs from both correct and faulty models. Our baseline is the approach by Qin et al. [32] (see Sect. 4.2 for its description). To the best of our knowledge, this approach is the only stochastic conformance testing approach relevant to trajectories. We aim to answer two key questions:

- **RQ1.** Is our conformance testing approach effective in detecting substantial discrepancies between the outputs of two CPS and, hence, yielding true positive verdicts?
- **RQ2.** Is our conformance testing approach adaptable to allow for negligible discrepancies between the outputs of two CPS and, hence, avoiding false positive verdicts?

The above research questions aim to assess if our conformance notion can efficiently identify common types of programming faults (via insertion of mutants) and common types of failures observed in cyber-physical systems (via insertion of anti-patterns), benchmarking against existing alternatives.

6.2 Case Study: Connected Platoon

Vehicular platooning is an autonomous driving technology that uses wireless communication to maintain a close but safe distance between vehicles in a convoy. We use an open-source model from a previous study [5] where a human-driven lead vehicle sets the pace and autonomous followers adjust their speed accordingly. Communication follows the ETSI EN 302 637-2 standard [21], which, among others, describes the rules for the frequency of packet transmission. These packets comprise Cooperative Awareness Messages (CAM), which contain information about the vehicle, such as acceleration and position. We employ the Intelligent Driver Model [34] as the controller for the vehicles.

The platoon model consists of five vehicles moving along a straight road, with followers adapting to the lead vehicle's acceleration via communication. The main input of our system is the behaviour of the driver in the lead vehicle (i.e., its acceleration), and the output is the acceleration of the follower vehicles.

6.3 Experiment Design

In this section, we explain the experiment design. Particularly, we describe the methodology, and our metrics and hypotheses.

Methodology. An overview of our methodology is as follows. We first generate faulty variants for a correct model of the platooning system. Then, we automatically generate and execute test cases in our models. Lastly, we employ the conformance notions (ours and a state-of-the-art from the literature [31]) on the outputs obtained in the previous step to reach the test verdicts.

We work with two types of fault insertion: (i) code mutation and (ii) signal-based patterns. In the first approach, we manually insert mutations to the correct model in order to create faulty variants. The mutation operators used in this experiment were inserted via a mutation tool for Simulink (FIM [11]). We used the *Delay Operator* (simulates the addition of delays), *Noise Operator* (adds noise to the signals), *Package Drop* (modifies the value of a variable), and also the *Logical* and *Arithmetic Operator Replacements* (swaps an operator with another of the same type). In total, we inserted 100 faults to the model. As the second method for fault insertion, we insert three types of anti-patterns (i.e., common and significant fault types identified by a taxonomy on signal-based properties of CPSs [14]) to a correct system output, depicted in Fig. 4. We incorporate the *spike, oscillatory behaviour*, and *overshoot* types of anti-pattern. We have inserted 100 faults for each type by manually modifying the output of the system to match a type of anti-pattern; we consider that the faulty output needs to be identified by the conformance notions.

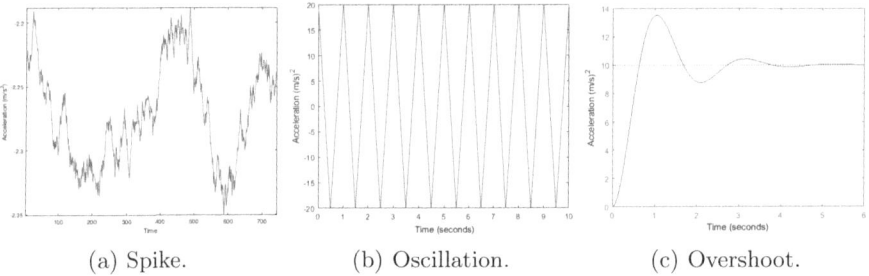

(a) Spike.   (b) Oscillation.   (c) Overshoot.

Fig. 4. Examples of signal-based patterns.

To generate inputs for the simulations, we use one random-based generation approach and two multi-objective search-based algorithms (standard simulated annealing [26] and genetic algorithm [30]). The former generates valid but completely random test cases and this can be used as a baseline measurement. The two other options are search-based heuristics which have been shown to generate tests that are more likely to exhibit failures [4,7,37]. Both search heuristics adopted in this case study employ 'fitness functions' to optimise the search, and we consider a notion of closeness, coverage, and diversity as the objectives; they have been demonstrated to lead the SUT towards conformance violations [4].

The verdict of a test is given by a conformance notion. For this study, to be considered an actual failure, the deviations need to be above error margins. The values chosen here are based on a maximum spatial deviation of $0.5 m/s^2$ for the acceleration trajectories and a maximum temporal deviation of $1s$, which are used in a study conducted by domain experts [5]. With respect to our conformance notion, we chose to replicate the specific values of maximum allowed deviation and, hence, we have chosen $\tau = 1s$ and $\epsilon = 0.5$. Qin's conformance notion, however, requires two parameters: the overall difference between error margins for the entire trajectory (λ) and a failure rate (δ), which are set to 2.5 and 0.25, respectively. If distance between two trajectories is set to constant 0.5 for 10 seconds, this results in lambda value (i.e., the integral of the distance between the two trajectories) of 5. Hence, we chose 2.5 as it is half of this value.

Metrics and Hypotheses. In this experiment, we make use of the number of true positives (TP) and false positives (FP) verdicts. These metrics essentially quantify the fault detection rate of each conformance notion. Detecting more faults is generally the goal of any testing approach. We have defined one hypothesis for each of our research questions. With respect to RQ1, which focusses on fault detection capabilities of the conformance notion, we have devised the hypotheses $H_{A0} : TP_{our} \leq TP_{alt}$ and $H_{A1} : TP_{our} > TP_{alt}$. Essentially, a test suite will be generated and the same test suite will be fed to both the correct and faulty models. The conformance notion that detects a higher number of mutants correctly is deemed more effective in the True Positive rate. The null hypothesis (H_{A0}) states that the number of True Positives detected by our conformance notion (TP_{our}) is lower or equal to the one obtained by the alternative notion (TP_{alt}). This experiment aims to refute such a hypothesis. Thus, an alternative hypothesis (H_{A1}) is also defined, which has a complementary role to the null one, and can be accepted in case their counterpart is rejected. Analogously, we have defined the hypotheses $H_{B0} : FP_{our} \geq FP_{alt}$ and $H_{B1} : FP_{our} < FP_{alt}$ to compare the number of false positives resulting from ours (FP_{our}) and the alternative (FP_{alt}) conformance notion.

6.4 Results

We split the main results into two tables. Table 1 shows the false and true positive rates (as well as other metrics) for the mutation operators and Table 3 focuses on the detection of anti-patterns. We show the results of applying our three variants of our conformance notion: Hellinger distance, Wasserstein metric, and Total Variation Distance (TVD) and the baseline to the three types of input generation: Random, Simulated Annealing (SA), and Genetic Algorithms (GA).

The numbers shown in Table 1 represent the number of false positives (FP), true positives (TP), false negatives (FN), and true negatives (TN). A false positive occurs when a test fails when it should not have. On the other hand, true positives represent tests that have failed correctly. Analogously, true and false negatives are tests that have correctly and incorrectly passed, respectively. The numbers represent how many verdicts are in each category. Moreover, we also display the values for Accuracy, Precision, Recall and F1 metrics.

The results indicate a small but significant difference for the true positive rates for the detection of mutations in favour of our approach. The difference increases with the complexity of the input generation approach. In terms of distance metric, Hellinger and Total Variation distances seemed to yield similar and better results compared to Wasserstein metric. By analysing the results more closely (see Table 2 for results per operator), we note how our conformance notion tends to detect the *Noise* more predominantly than the alternative. This is because the *Noise* operator is more likely to lead to a short burst of deviation between the results from the correct and faulty implementations. The operators *Package Drop* and *Logical Operator Replacement* showed little difference between the notions, however.

As for the false positives (shown in Table 1), most of them occurred with the *Delay* operator. The reasoning is that by allowing for temporal error margins, our conformance notions tends to disregard negligible deviations resulting from small *Delay* mutations (below the error margin). Such mutants are not killed

Table 1. Detection of mutation operators.

(a) Random Input

	FP	TP	FN	TN	Acc.	Prec.	Rec.	F1
Ours - Hellinger	0	71	19	10	0.81	1.00	0.79	0.88
Ours - Wasserstein	0	70	20	10	0.80	1.00	0.78	0.88
Ours - TVD	0	71	19	10	0.81	1.00	0.79	0.88
State-of-the-art	5	70	20	5	0.75	0.93	0.78	0.85

(b) Simulated Annealing

	FP	TP	FN	TN	Acc.	Prec.	Rec.	F1
Ours - Hellinger	0	81	9	10	0.91	1.00	0.90	0.95
Ours - Wasserstein	0	79	11	10	0.88	1.00	0.87	0.93
Ours - TVD	0	82	8	10	0.92	1.00	0.91	0.95
State-of-the-art	6	77	23	4	0.74	0.93	0.77	0.84

(c) Genetic Algorithms

	FP	TP	FN	TN	Acc.	Prec.	Rec.	F1
Ours - Hellinger	0	85	5	10	0.95	1.00	0.94	0.97
Ours - Wasserstein	0	82	8	10	0.91	1.00	0.90	0.95
Ours - TVD	0	84	6	10	0.94	1.00	0.93	0.97
State-of-the-art	4	79	11	6	0.84	0.94	0.88	0.91

Table 2. TP per mutant operator.

	Noise	PD	LOR	AOR	Delay
Ours - RA	16	08	17	16	14
Alt - RA	15	08	17	16	14
Ours - SA	16	13	20	17	15
Alt - SA	14	12	20	16	15
Ours - GA	19	15	20	17	14
Alt - GA	15	14	20	16	14

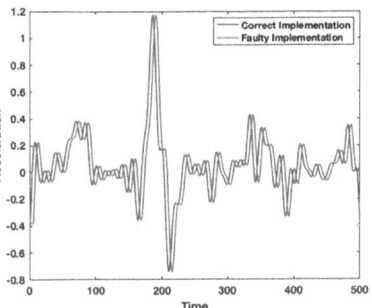

Fig. 5. Trajectory with a delay.

and, hence, we avoid false positives. As an example, Fig. 5 shows the output of the correct and of an implementation with a small *Delay* operator. Even though both outputs are very similar, this slight delay in time has led to a drastic distance using Qin's notion due to a high degree of accumulated variation. Our conformance notion, however, permits such divergences depending on the value of τ, which gives flexibility to the verification process.

Analogously, our methods (especially Hellinger and TVD) consistently produce fewer false negatives than the state-of-the-art, across all types of input generation. Hence, they are less likely to incorrectly pass faulty systems. The difference is more pronounced as input generation gets more sophisticated (from Random to SA to GA). For instance, with Simulated Annealing, the FN count dropped from 23 (baseline) to as low as 8 (ours), showing a significant improvement. Wasserstein performs slightly worse than Hellinger and TVD in terms of false negatives, though still better than the baseline. Improved FN rates lead to higher recall, which is reflected in the metrics: when using simulated annealing, recall improves from 0.77 (baseline) to > 0.90 (ours - Hellinger and TVD).

Lastly, Table 3 shows the results for the detection rates of anti-patterns. Similarly to noise mutation operator, the spike anti-pattern tends to result in short bursts of discrepancy, which leads to our conformance notion detecting more of them compared to the alternative. The oscillation anti-pattern has been efficiently detected by both approaches and, as for overshoots, there is a small but significant difference in favour of our strategy.

Table 3. Detection of anti-patterns.

(a) Spike

	FP	TP	FN	TN	Acc.	Prec.	Rec.	F1
Ours - Hellinger	0	82	8	10	0.89	1.00	0.89	0.94
Ours - Wasserstein	0	71	19	10	0.78	1.00	0.78	0.88
Ours - TVD	0	82	8	10	0.89	1.00	0.89	0.94
State-of-the-art	0	65	25	10	0.72	1.00	0.72	0.84

(b) Oscillation

	FP	TP	FN	TN	Acc.	Prec.	Rec.	F1
Ours - Hellinger	0	88	2	10	0.95	1.00	0.95	0.97
Ours - Wasserstein	0	86	4	10	0.93	1.00	0.93	0.96
Ours - TVD	0	87	2	10	0.94	1.00	0.94	0.97
State-of-the-art	0	88	2	10	0.95	1.00	0.95	0.97

(c) Overshoot

	FP	TP	FN	TN	Acc.	Prec.	Rec.	F1
Ours - Hellinger	0	60	29	10	0.67	1.00	0.67	0.80
Ours - Wasserstein	0	60	29	10	0.67	1.00	0.67	0.80
Ours - TVD	0	59	31	10	0.66	1.00	0.66	0.80
State-of-the-art	0	56	34	10	0.63	1.00	0.63	0.77

6.5 Threats to Validity

As threats to the validity of our experiment, we note that the choice of mutant operators is made by domain experts, but a thorough and formal study of their relation to real faults needs to be conducted. To mitigate this issue, we have also introduced anti-patterns (spike, overshoot, and oscillation) common in CPS to mimic failures. Furthermore, the error margin values in the oracle impact the results: small values would detect all mutants and large ones would detected none. As a mitigation measure, the values we have chosen throughout the work (e.g., τ, ϵ, and δ, as well as the mutation operators) are based on prior experiments and domain knowledge. Moreover, we fit the distributions of the outputs in the experiment to a normal distribution. This is an assumption based on data gathered from the experiments; we have chosen a distribution fit that most closely matches with the observed ones. Lastly, this experiment only considers one (albeit, complex) example of connected CPS. This makes it hard to generalise the outcome of this experiment for a general class of cyber-physical systems. This is mitigated by the large number of mutants that were inserted into this system.

7 Conclusions

We have developed a novel stochastic conformance notion to test connected Cyber-Physical Systems (CPS) that takes error margins into account. Our approach is well-suited to test CPS, where the interaction between computational, physical, and environmental components may lead to a probabilistic distribution of outcomes. Our notion is adaptable so that negligible perturbations (e.g., subtle measurement errors) are not mistakenly flagged as failures. Our approach verifies CPS by checking whether the distance between two output distributions (the observed and the expected one) falls within safety bounds. Our notion is able to detect deviations in stochastic behaviour that manifest under faulty conditions, while accommodating for natural temporal and spatial variations. In the mechanisation of our approach, we implemented our conformance as a tool and evaluated its effectiveness through a case study involving a connected platoon of autonomous vehicles. We show that our approach can detect faulty behaviour, such as oscillation and spikes (common types of anti-patterns in CPS) more reliably than alternatives found in the literature.

Acknowledgements. Hugo Araujo and Mohammad Reza Mousavi have been partially supported by the UKRI Trustworthy Autonomous Systems Node in Verifiability, Grant Award Reference EP/V026801/2, EPSRC project on Verified Simulation for Large Quantum Systems (VSL-Q), grant reference EP/Y005244/1, and the EPSRC project on Robust and Reliable Quantum Computing (RoaRQ), Investigation 009 Model-based monitoring and calibration of quantum computations (ModeMCQ), grant reference EP/W032635/1, as well as the ITEA/InnovateUK projects GENIUS and GreenCode.

References

1. Abbas, H., Hoxha, B., Fainekos, G.E., Deshmukh, J.V., Kapinski, J., Ueda, K.: WiP abstract: conformance testing as falsification for cyber-physical systems. In: Proceedings of the ACM/IEEE 5th International Conference on Cyber-Physical Systems (ICCPS 2014), p. 211. IEEE CS (2014), http://arxiv.org/abs/1401.5200
2. Abbas, H., Mittelmann, H., Fainekos, G.: Formal property verification in a conformance testing framework. In: Formal methods and models for codesign (memocode), 2014 twelfth ACM/IEEE International Conference on, pp. 155–164. IEEE (2014)
3. Althoff, M.: Reachability analysis and its application to the safety assessment of autonomous cars. Ph.D. thesis, Technische Universität München (2010)
4. Araujo, H., Carvalho, G., Mousavi, M., Sampaio, A.: Multi-objective search for effective testing of cyber-physical systems. In: Proceedings of the 17th International Conference on Software Engineering and Formal Methods, Springer (2019)
5. Araujo, H., Hoenselaar, T., Mousavi, M.R., Vinel, A.: Connected automated driving: a model-based approach to the analysis of basic awareness services. In: 2020 IEEE 31st Annual International Symposium on Personal, Indoor and Mobile Radio Communications, pp. 1–7. IEEE (2020)
6. Araujo, H., Mousavi, M.R., Varshosaz, M.: Testing, validation, and verification of robotic and autonomous systems: a systematic review. ACM Trans. Softw. Eng. Methodol. **32**(2), 1–61 (2023)
7. Arrieta, A., Wang, S., Markiegi, U., Sagardui, G., Etxeberria, L.: Search-based test case generation for cyber-physical systems. In: 2017 IEEE Congress on Evolutionary Computation (CEC), pp. 688–697 (2017). https://doi.org/10.1109/CEC.2017.7969377
8. Asarin, E., Dang, T., Frehse, G., Girard, A., Le Guernic, C., Maler, O.: Recent progress in continuous and hybrid reachability analysis. In: 2006 IEEE Conference on Computer Aided Control System Design, 2006 IEEE International Conference on Control Applications, 2006 IEEE International Symposium on Intelligent Control, pp. 1582–1587 (2006). https://doi.org/10.1109/CACSD-CCA-ISIC.2006.4776877

9. Baheti, R., Gill, H.: Cyber-physical systems. Impact Control Technol. **12**(1), 161–166 (2011)
10. Bak, S., Chaki, S.: Verifying cyber-physical systems by combining software model checking with hybrid systems reachability. In: Proceedings of the 13th International Conference on Embedded Software, pp. 1–10 (2016)
11. Bartocci, E., Mariani, L., Ničković, D., Yadav, D.: Fim: fault injection and mutation for simulink. In: Proceedings of the 30th ACM Joint European Software Engineering Conference and Symposium on the Foundations of Software Engineering, ESEC/FSE 2022, pp. 1716–1720. Association for Computing Machinery, New York, NY, USA (2022). https://doi.org/10.1145/3540250.3558932
12. Beran, R.: Minimum hellinger distance estimates for parametric models. Ann. Stat. 445–463 (1977)
13. Böhm, A., Kunert, K.: Data age based retransmission scheme for reliable control data exchange in platooning applications. In: 2015 IEEE International Conference on Communication Workshop (ICCW), pp. 2412–2418. IEEE (2015)
14. Boufaied, C., Jukss, M., Bianculli, D., Briand, L.C., Parache, Y.I.: Signal-based properties of cyber-physical systems: taxonomy and logic-based characterization. J. Syst. Softw. **174**, 110881 (2021)
15. Chen, X., Sankaranarayanan, S.: Reachability analysis for cyber-physical systems: are we there yet? In: NASA Formal Methods Symposium, pp. 109–130. Springer (2022)
16. Clarke, E.M.: Model checking. In: Ramesh, S., Sivakumar, G. (eds.) FSTTCS 1997. LNCS, vol. 1346, pp. 54–56. Springer, Heidelberg (1997). https://doi.org/10.1007/BFb0058022
17. Clarke, E.M., Zuliani, P.: Statistical model checking for cyber-physical systems. In: International Symposium on Automated Technology for Verification and Analysis, pp. 1–12. Springer (2011)
18. Corso, A., Moss, R., Koren, M., Lee, R., Kochenderfer, M.: A survey of algorithms for black-box safety validation of cyber-physical systems. J. Artif. Intell. Res. **72**, 377–428 (2021)
19. Deshmukh, J.V., Majumdar, R., Prabhu, V.S.: Quantifying conformance using the skorokhod metric. In: Kroening, D., Păsăreanu, C.S. (eds.) CAV 2015. LNCS, vol. 9207, pp. 234–250. Springer, Cham (2015). https://doi.org/10.1007/978-3-319-21668-3_14
20. Documentation, S.: Simulation and model-based design (2020). https://www.mathworks.com/products/simulink.html
21. ETSI EN 302 637- 2; Intelligent Transport Systems (ITS); vehicular communications; basic set of applications; part 2: Specification of cooperative awareness basic service (2013)

22. Gerking, C., Schäfer, W., Dziwok, S., Heinzemann, C.: Domain-specific model checking for cyber-physical systems. In: MoDeVVa@ Models, pp. 18–27 (2015)
23. Givens, C.R., Shortt, R.M.: A class of wasserstein metrics for probability distributions. Mich. Math. J. **31**(2), 231–240 (1984)
24. Hamzah, M., et al.: Distributed control of cyber physical system on various domains: a critical review. Systems **11**(4), 208 (2023)
25. Hashemi, N., Lindemann, L., Deshmukh, J.V.: Statistical reachability analysis of stochastic cyber-physical systems under distribution shift. arXiv preprint arXiv:2407.11609 (2024)
26. Kirkpatrick, S., Gelatt, C.D., Vecchi, M.P.: Optimization by simulated annealing. Science **220**(4598), 671–680 (1983)
27. Krichen, M., Tripakis, S.: Conformance testing for real-time systems. Formal Methods Syst. Des. **34**(3), 238–304 (2009)
28. Kwiatkowska, M., Norman, G., Parker, D.: PRISM 4.0: verification of probabilistic real-time systems. In: Gopalakrishnan, G., Qadeer, S. (eds.) CAV 2011. LNCS, vol. 6806, pp. 585–591. Springer, Heidelberg (2011). https://doi.org/10.1007/978-3-642-22110-1_47
29. Leemans, S.J., Syring, A.F., van der Aalst, W.M.: Earth movers' stochastic conformance checking. In: Business Process Management Forum: BPM Forum 2019, Vienna, Austria, 1–6 September 2019, Proceedings 17, pp. 127–143. Springer (2019)
30. Mitchell, M.: An Introduction to Genetic Algorithms. MIT Press (1998)
31. Qin, X., Aréchiga, N., Deshmukh, J., Best, A.: Robust testing for cyber-physical systems using reinforcement learning. In: Proceedings of the 21st ACM-IEEE International Conference on Formal Methods and Models for System Design, pp. 36–46 (2023)
32. Qin, X., Hashemi, N., Lindemann, L., Deshmukh, J.V.: Conformance testing for stochastic cyber-physical systems. In: Conference on Formal Methods in Computer-Aided Design, FMCAD, p. 294 (2023)
33. Sirjani, M., Lee, E.A., Khamespanah, E.: Model checking software in cyberphysical systems. In: 2020 IEEE 44th Annual Computers, Software, and Applications Conference (COMPSAC), pp. 1017–1026. IEEE (2020)
34. Treiber, M., Hennecke, A., Helbing, D.: Congested traffic states in empirical observations and microscopic simulations. Phys. Rev. E **62**(2), 1805 (2000)
35. Verdú, S.: Total variation distance and the distribution of relative information. In: 2014 Information Theory and Applications Workshop (ITA), pp. 1–3. IEEE (2014)
36. Woehrle, M., Lampka, K., Thiele, L.: Conformance testing for cyber-physical systems. ACM Trans. Embedded Comput. Syst. (TECS) **11**(4), 1–23 (2013)

37. Zhang, M., Ali, S., Yue, T.: Uncertainty-wise test case generation and minimization for cyber-physical systems. J. Syst. Softw. **153**, 1–21 (2019)
38. Zheng, X., Julien, C., Kim, M., Khurshid, S.: Perceptions on the state of the art in verification and validation in cyber-physical systems. IEEE Syst. J. **11**(4), 2614–2627 (2015)

Sequential Composition of BDD Transition Systems for Model-Based Testing

Tannaz Zameni[1](✉) , Petra van den Bos[1] , Johan Foederer[2] , and Arend Rensink[1]

[1] University of Twente, Enschede, The Netherlands
{t.zameni,p.vandenbos,arend.rensink}@utwente.nl
[2] TOPIC Embedded Systems, Best, The Netherlands
johan.foederer@topic.nl

Abstract. This paper presents a compositional approach to model-based test derivation in Behavior-Driven Development (BDD). In BDD, system behavior is specified through *scenarios* written in natural language. For each scenario, a test case can be derived. However, such test cases do not cover the integration of multiple behaviors, while that is where potential faults may very well occur. To counter this, we introduce a formal composition operator for *sequential composition*, which integrates the individual BDDs while preserving their test coverage. We also report on a prototype tool that integrates model-based features into an existing testing framework that supports BDD-based test derivation. We show the feasibility and advantages of our approach by applying the prototype to a real-world case study.

Keywords: BDD Transition Systems · Symbolic Transition Systems · Composition · Behavior-Driven Development · Model-Based Testing

1 Introduction

Testing is the most widely applied validation method in software development. However, the effort, time, and cost spent on testing cannot keep up with the large and complex systems being developed nowadays. Model-based testing (MBT) has been proposed as an approach to automate part of this process; see, e.g., [16]. In MBT, tests are not only executed automatically but also generated automatically from a *model* that specifies the expected behaviors of the system. Automatic test generation algorithms generate diverse test cases to find many more (potential) bugs than could be found by writing test cases manually. However, one of the factors hindering the widespread adoption of MBT is that a model has to be provided before MBT can be applied. The need to create and maintain such models, typically in unfamiliar languages and formalisms for software developers, in many circumstances negates the potential benefits.

Artifact available at https://doi.org/10.5281/zenodo.14892704.

Behavior-driven development (BDD) is a popular agile software development approach. As part of this approach, behaviors are specified in natural language scenarios. These scenarios are formulated as a result of the understanding reached between the involved stakeholders; typically a product owner, developer, and tester of an agile team. They are often written in a structured format, using the Given-When-Then style of the Gherkin notation [4,12]. Such a BDD scenario expresses a behavior in three steps: *Given* a precondition for the required system state, *When* an action is performed on or by the system, *Then* specified actions and resulting state are expected. There exist BDD tools, like Cucumber [5] and SpecFlow [15], that allow users to manually implement how each step in a scenario is performed in the system, after which they automatically compose the implemented steps into test cases. Though the required manual effort and the unspecified semantics of these tools mean that they do not meet the standards of MBT, their adoption in practice shows that BDD scenarios are an interesting candidate to fill the modeling gap.

In [18], we outlined an approach to translate BDD scenarios to models suitable for formal test generation, called BDD Transition Systems (BDDTSs). Being derived from a single scenario, each BDDTS comprises a single sequence of actions and checks. Although the generated test cases adhere to the formal semantics of BDDTS, they remain singular and do not integrate behaviors, just like the tests generated from BDD tools. To really harvest the power of MBT, in [19] we sketched the idea to compose individual BDDTSs into more complex models. In this paper, we formally define *sequential composition* on (an improved version of) BDDTSs, i.e., invoking them one after the other. This is valid if the *Then*-step of one scenario (called the "predecessor" below) implies the *Given*-step of another scenario.

The main strength of this composition lies in its *integration* capability: from the composed model, we can derive test cases that cover the integration of scenarios, i.e., whether they work together as expected. This has three advantages. Firstly, in standard BDD-based testing, achieving the desired state for a *Given* step may require complex *setup* and *teardown* phases, adding overhead and imposing a fixed test execution order. Sequential composition reduces spurious setups and teardowns, and enables the generation of varied, integrated test sequences. Secondly, testers might make assumptions in implementing tests, that are only true when tests are run in a certain order. The varied combinations of tests derived from a composed model help reveal incomplete test implementations, thereby improving test quality. Last but not least, different features of the system (embodied in different BDD scenarios) may interact in unexpected ways that are difficult to predict and detect. Scenario composition helps to identify issues missed by the standard BDD approach.

Results of the Paper. This paper formally defines and practically applies sequential composition, as well as the corresponding test cases, and demonstrates their application through a practical case study. The key contributions are:

1. **Formal definition of sequential composition.** We formalize the idea suggested in [19], where the sequential composition was proposed but lacked a formal definition.
2. **Proof of soundness and completeness.** We show that sequential composition preserves the *potential* test coverage; that is, the test suite derived from the individual scenarios *potentially* tests for the same faults as that derived from their composition – namely, if the tests would be applied exhaustively, meaning that each test is repeated for all possible setups that bring the system to a state satisfying its *Given* clause.
3. **Formal definition of test case derivation.** In [18] we discussed three potential methods to convert BDDTSs to test cases. Here, we adopt and formalize one, based on retrieving variable values in the System under Test (SuT) and in output guards, as well as satisfying the initial input guard (while others are validated through composition).
4. **Practical application and results.** We show the practical feasibility of our approach by developing an extension of Robot Framework [13] with MBT and applying it to a real-world case study: a distributed system that controls the lamps on airfields. The tool and case study are available in the artifact [17].

The paper outline is as follows. We introduce our case study in Sect. 2. We then recall BDD transition systems (Sect. 3), and formally define how to convert them to test cases (Sect. 4). After, we formally define the sequential composition operator and its soundness and completeness properties in Sect. 5. Then we show the results of the case study using our tool in Sect. 6. Finally, we discuss related work (Sect. 7), conclusions, and future work (Sect. 8).

2 Introduction to the Case Study

The case study concerns the software system of the company TKH Airport Solutions. The software controls airfield lamps, a so-called Airfield Ground Lighting system (AGL). Lamps are grouped into AGL functions, which each correspond to something meaningful to the Air Traffic Controller, like a certain runway or taxiway. Lamps are locally powered and managed by basestations. Typically, multiple basestations are used to operate a single AGL function.

The main purpose of the feature specified by our scenarios is to demonstrate that if maintenance is required for a specific basestation, it can be carried out in isolation: only the AGL function it serves is affected, and other parts of the airfield stay operational. There are three roles involved in the BDD scenarios:

- *Air Traffic Controller* (ATC), responsible for operating AGL functions. They do not need to be aware of basestations.
- *Maintenance Manager* (MM), responsible for basestation maintenance and their impact on AGL functions. They can release a basestation from operation when an AGL function is cleared by the ATC and no longer in use.

– *Maintenance Engineer* (ME), responsible for installing and maintaining basestations and their connected lamps. They access a basestation airside, where the airplanes operate, once it has been released by the MM.

ATC and MM use the same interface to interact with the system, while ME uses a different interface. So unlike the BDD scenarios, we make no difference between ATC and MM in the derived models and test implementations.

Below we provide a selection of the BDD scenarios we used in the case study. The Background scenario ensures we have the correct system configuration, the others describe three relevant behaviours. For readability, we slightly simplified the phrasing of the original scenarios for this paper.

Scenarios 0 Background
 - **Given** Given airfield of airportA is operated by CEDD-AGL system
 - **And** basestation07 serves the runway
 - **And** basestation13 serves the taxiway
 - **And** basestation14 serves the taxiway

Scenarios 1 The runway stays open during maintenance on the taxiway
 - **Given** Given the runway is under the operation of the Air Traffic Controller
 - **And** the taxiway is under the operation of the Air Traffic Controller
 - **When** the Maintenance Manager confirms that only the taxiway is affected by basestation13
 - **And** the Maintenance Manager releases basestation13 from operation
 - **And** the Maintenance Engineer puts basestation13 into maintenance
 - **Then** the Maintenance Engineer has basestation13 in maintenance
 - **And** the runway is (still) under the operation of the Air Traffic Controller

Scenarios 2 A single basestation is handed over for maintenance
 - **Given** Basestation13 is under the control of the Air Traffic Controller
 - **When** the Maintenance Manager releases basestation13 from operation
 - **And** the Maintenance Enigneer puts basestation13 into maintenance
 - **Then** the Maintenance Engineer has basestation13 in maintenance

Scenarios 3 A basestation is handed back without configuration change
 - **Given** the Maintenance Engineer has basestation13 in maintenance
 - **When** the Maintenance Engineer releases basestation13 from maintenance
 - **And** the Maintenance Manager puts basestation13 into operation
 - **Then** the mode of basestation13 is operational
 - **And** the taxiway is under the operation of the Air Traffic Controller

3 BDD Transition Systems

Before introducing BDD Transition Systems, we need some auxiliary notation. We write $f : X \to Y$ or $f \in Y^X$ for a total function f from domain X to codomain Y, and $f : X \hookrightarrow Y$ if f is partial. In the latter case, $f \downarrow x$ denotes that f is defined for x, and $f \uparrow x$ that it is undefined. $f\upharpoonright_Z$ denotes the restriction of f to the subdomain $Z \subseteq X$, $f \uplus g$ the union of (compatible) functions.

In this paper, we often use *transition relations*, which are always defined as $\to \subseteq Q \times A \times Q$ for a set Q of states (sometimes called locations) and a set A of labels. For this, we adopt some common notations. In particular, $q_0 \xrightarrow{a_0 \cdots a_{n-1}} q_n$ denotes $(q_i, a_i, q_{i+1}) \in \to$ for $0 \le i < n$, and $q \xrightarrow{\sigma}$ for $\sigma \in A^*$ means that there is some q' such that $q \xrightarrow{\sigma} q'$. A state q is called a *sink*, denoted $Sink(q)$, if $\nexists a : q \xrightarrow{a}$, and the *traces* of q are given by $traces(q) = \{\sigma \in A^* \mid q \xrightarrow{\sigma}\}$.

In several cases, the set Q will be partitioned into $Q = Q^\circ \cup Q^\bullet$ of *open* and *closed* elements to further distinguish between actions that lead to failing tests (from closed locations) and the ones that lead to inconclusive or pass (from open locations). We call such sets $\stackrel{\circ}{\bullet}$-natured. For a $\stackrel{\circ}{\bullet}$-natured set X we will use $\mathsf{N} : X \to \{\circ, \bullet\}$ to retrieve the nature (hence $x \in X^{\mathsf{N}(x)}$ for all x).

The core models of this paper are *BDD Transition Systems* (BDDTSs). These are *symbolic* in the sense that the labels, as well as some other components, are built using syntactic *terms*, e.g. $\mathsf{x} + 1$ or $\mathsf{a} \wedge \mathsf{b}$, the value of which will be computed later. We use $\mathcal{T}_s(V)$ to denote the set of s-typed terms over some set of variables V; omitting s gives us *all* terms. We also use $\mathcal{I}(G, IV)$ to denote *interactions*, which are pairs $(g, \bar{iv})$ of *gates* $g \in G$ and sequences of *interaction variables* $\bar{iv} \in IV^*$. Every gate g has a fixed set of interaction variables. Terms and interactions are typed in the standard way; we omit the details here.

Definition 1. *A BDD Transition System (BDDTS) is a tuple $\mathcal{B}$ consisting of $\langle L, V, G, \to, il, IG, OG \rangle$, where*

- L is a $\stackrel{\circ}{\bullet}$-natured set of locations;
- V is a set of variables, partitioned into MV *(model variables)*, CV *(context variables)* and IV *(interaction variables)*.
- G is a set of gates, partitioned into G_i *(input gates)* and G_o *(output gates)*;
- $\to \subseteq L \times \mathcal{I}(G, IV) \times \mathcal{T}_{\mathsf{Bool}}(V) \times \mathcal{T}(V)^{MV} \times L$ *is a switch relation;*
- $il \in L^\circ$ *is the initial (open) location;*
- $IG \in \mathcal{T}_{\mathsf{Bool}}(MV \cup CV)$ *is the input guard;*
- $OG : L \hookrightarrow \mathcal{T}_{\mathsf{Bool}}(MV \cup CV)$ *is a partial map from locations to output guards.*

We use $L_\mathcal{B}$, $V_\mathcal{B}$ etc. to denote the components of a BDDTS $\mathcal{B}$; for $\mathcal{B}_i$, we further abbreviate $L_{\mathcal{B}_i}$, $V_{\mathcal{B}_i}$ etc. to L_i, V_i. The components of a switch $t \in \to$ are denoted sl_t (the *source location*), $\alpha_t = (g_t, \bar{iv}_t)$ (the *interaction*), ϕ_t (the *switch guard*, a boolean term), a_t (the *assignment*, a function from MV to terms) and tl_t (the *target location*); for a switch denoted t_i, we write sl_i, α_i etc.

A BDDTS is *instantiated* by assigning values to all *location variables* $LV = CV \cup MV$. After instantiation, the context variables (CV) never change, in contrast to the model variables (MV). The intuition behind a switch t is that it encodes the possibility to move from the source location sl_t to the target location tl_t while interacting with the environment via α_t, but only if the switch guard ϕ_t holds. Upon reaching tl_t, all model variables receive a new value, as dictated by a_t. Upon reaching a *goal location* l, being a location on which OG is defined, the output guard $OG(l)$ is supposed to hold.

$\mathcal{B}$ is called *well-formed* if it satisfies the following additional conditions:

- *Switching is deterministic*: for distinct $t_1, t_2 \in \to$, if $sl_1 = sl_2$ and $\alpha_1 = \alpha_2$ then $\phi_1 \wedge \phi_2 \equiv \mathbf{false}$.
- *Closed locations only have output switches*: $t \in \to$ with $sl_t \in L^\bullet$ implies $g_t \in G_o$.
- *Sink locations are always open*: $Sink(q)$ implies $q \in L^\circ$.

We require all BDDTSs to be well-formed, and henceforth tacitly assume this.

The $\stackrel{\circ}{\bullet}$-nature of a location determines how to treat, during testing, an output action of the SUT that deviates from the outgoing switches specified for that

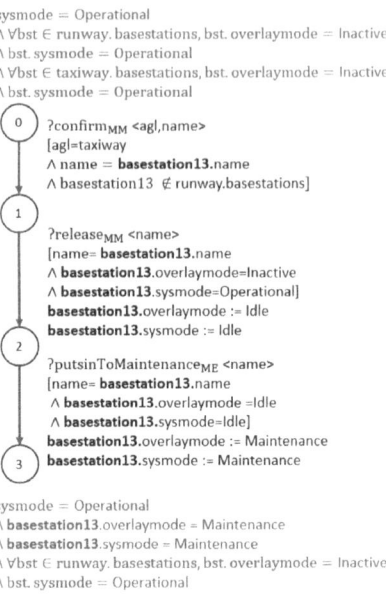

Fig. 1. BDDTS $\mathcal{B}_1$ corresponding to scenario 1: AGL function handover

location. For an open location, such a deviation is taken to mean that the SuT was inadvertently not in the expected state; the test is then marked as *inconclusive*. In a closed location, on the other hand, a deviation is regarded as a fault of the system; the test is marked as *failed*.

Example 1. Figure 1 shows the BDDTS for **Scenario 1**. We extract model elements from the textual scenario through stakeholder discussions and the method in [18]. The BDDTS elements are explained below:

- $L = L° = \{0, 1, 2, 3\}$ and $il = 0$.
- $V = MV \cup CV \cup IV$ with $MV = \{$basestation13$\}$, $CV = \{$sysmode, runway, taxiway$\}$ and $IV = \{$agl, name$\}$
- $G = G_i = \{?\text{confirm}_{MM}, ?\text{release}_{MM}, ?\text{putsinToMaintenance}_{ME}\}$
- The switches are derived from the *When* step. For instance, the first switch $t = (0, ?\text{confirm}_{MM}\text{ agl name}, agl = \text{taxiway}, name = \text{basestation13.name}, id, 1)$
- IG, derived from the *Given* step, is shown in blue on location 0.
- OG, derived from the *Then* step, is only defined for location 3 (in blue).

The BDDTSs for **Scenario 2** and **Scenario 3** are shown in Fig. 2a and b.

4 From BDDTSs to Test Cases

We now come to the first contribution: the formal conversion of BDDTSs to test cases. This follows the steps in Fig. 3, and corresponds to one of the (informally discussed) proposals in [18].

42   T. Zameni et al.

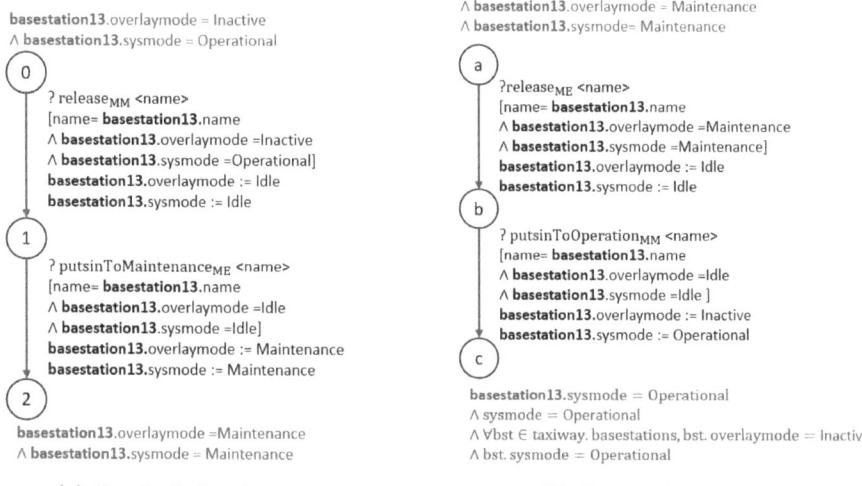

(a) $\mathcal{B}_2$: single handover   (b) $\mathcal{B}_3$: single handback

Fig. 2. BDDTSs corresponding to scenarios of Sect. 2

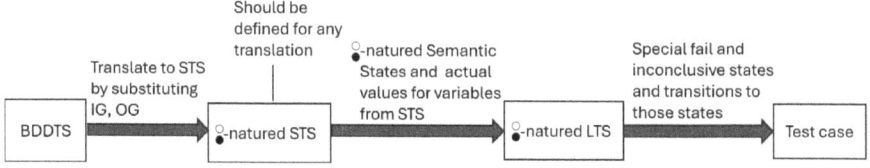

Fig. 3. BDDTS to Test Cases Translation Steps

We first define a translation from BDDTSs to *Symbolic Transition Systems* in which the input and output guards are implemented: the former by instantiating location variables appropriately, whereas the latter are replaced by sequences of *check* and *retrieve* switches.

Definition 2. *A* Symbolic Transition System *(STS) is given by a tuple* $\mathcal{S} = \langle L, V, G, \rightarrow, il, ini \rangle$, *where the first five components are identical to those of a BDDTS with the proviso that* $CV = \emptyset$, *and* $ini \in \mathcal{T}(\emptyset)^{LV}$ *is the initial assignment of the location variables.*

The input guard of a BDDTS can be represented in an STS with an $ini \in \mathcal{T}(\emptyset)^{LV}$ that satisfies the input guard, denoted as $[\![IG]\!]_{ini} \equiv \mathbf{true}$. For the output guards, the translation to STS is more involved. We assume that for all $v \in LV$, there exist special input gates $\mathsf{check}_v \in \mathcal{G}$ and output gates $\mathsf{retrieve}_v \in \mathcal{G}$ with interaction variable iv_v. (For convenience, since there is no risk of confusion, we actually denote iv instead of iv_v.) A $?\mathsf{check}_v$-labelled switch asks the SuT to produce the current value of v; the SuT is expected to respond immediately by $!\mathsf{retrieve}_v\, iv$ with iv instantiated to that value. If v is a model variable, the switch guard immediately compares iv to v; if v is a context variable, the value of iv is assigned to v instead.[1] To define this formally, let $v_1 \cdots v_n$ be the vector of variables occurring in $OG(gl)$, in their order of occurrence. As is shown in Fig. 4, we introduce new locations $\hat{L}_{gl} = \{chl_{gl,i} \mid 1 \leq i \leq n\} \cup \{rtl_{gl,i} \mid 1 \leq i \leq n\}$ (disjoint from L) for check and retrieve locations, with $\circ\!\!\!\bullet$-nature defined by

$$\mathsf{N} : l \mapsto \begin{cases} \mathsf{N}(gl) & \text{if } l = rtl_{gl,n} \\ \circ & \text{if } l = rtl_{gl,i} \text{ for } 1 \leq i < n \\ \bullet & \text{if } l = chl_{gl,i} \text{ for } 1 \leq i \leq n \end{cases}$$

In the following switches between the new locations $\hat{L}_{gl}$, let $rtl_{gl,0} = gl$. Besides check and retrieve switches CH_{gl} and RT_{gl}, we need *connecting* switches CN_{gl} from $rtl_{gl,n}$ for every outgoing switch of gl (if any). Note that the output guard of goal location gl is turned into a switch guard of the last retrieve switch. (We write $t[x/y]$ with $t \in \mathcal{T}(X)$ and $x, y \in X$ for the replacement of all y by x in t.)

$CH_{gl} = \{(rtl_{gl,i-1}, ?\mathsf{check}_{v_i}, \mathbf{true}, id, chl_{gl,i}) \mid 1 \leq i \leq n\}$
$RT_{gl} = \{(chl_{gl,i}, !\mathsf{retrieve}_{v_i} iv, \phi_i, a_i, rtl_{gl,i}) \mid 1 \leq i \leq n\}$

where $\phi_i = \begin{cases} iv{=}v_i \wedge OG & \text{if } i = n \wedge v_i \in MV \\ OG[iv/v_i] & \text{if } i = n \wedge v_i \in CV \\ iv{=}v_i & \text{if } i < n \wedge v_i \in MV \\ \mathbf{true} & \text{otherwise} \end{cases}$ $\quad a_i = \begin{cases} v_i := iv & \text{if } v_i \in CV \\ id & \text{otherwise} \end{cases}$

$CN_{gl} = \{(rtl_{gl,n}, \alpha, \phi, a, tl) \mid gl \xrightarrow{\alpha,\phi,a} tl\}$

With these ingredients, we can define the derived STS of a given BDDTS.

Definition 3. *Let* $\mathcal{B} = \langle L, V, G, \to, il, IG, OG \rangle$ *be a BDDTS, and* $ini \in \mathcal{T}(\emptyset)^{LV}$ *an assignment such that* $[\![IG]\!]_{ini} \equiv \mathbf{true}$. *Then the* check-retrieve symbolic system *for* $\mathcal{B}$ *and* ini *is defined as* $CRSS(\mathcal{B}, ini) = \langle L_c, V_c, G, \to_c, il, ini \rangle$ *where* $L_c = \{l \in L \mid OG \uparrow l\} \cup \bigcup \{\hat{L}_{gl} \mid OG \downarrow gl\}$, $LV_c = MV \cup CV$, *and*

$$\to_c = \{t \in \to \mid OG \uparrow sl_t\} \cup \bigcup \{CH_{gl} \cup RT_{gl} \cup CN_{gl} \mid OG \downarrow gl\} \ .$$

For instance, Fig. 4 shows the CRSS obtained from the BDDTS in Fig. 2a (modelling **Scenario 2**). The bold green transitions in green starting from location 2 are check and retrieve switches for variable basestation13; there is no outgoing transition from $rtl_{2,1}$ because the goal location in Fig. 2a was a sink.

The next step is to translate a CRSS into an $\circ\!\!\!\bullet$-natured LTS, sometimes called the *interpretation* of the STS [3]. From LTSs we are able to derive test cases.

Definition 4. *A labelled transition system is a tuple* $\mathcal{L} = \langle Q, A, \to, q_0 \rangle$ *in which* Q *is a set of states with initial state* q_0, A *is a set of labels partitioned into input labels* A_i *and output labels* A_o, *and* $\to \subseteq Q \times A \times Q$ *is a transition relation.*

---

[1] Note that we do not assign values to context variables: in STSs, all location variables are model variables.

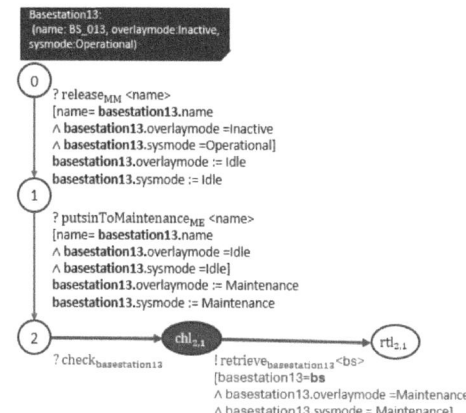

Fig. 4. CRSS of $\mathcal{B}_2$

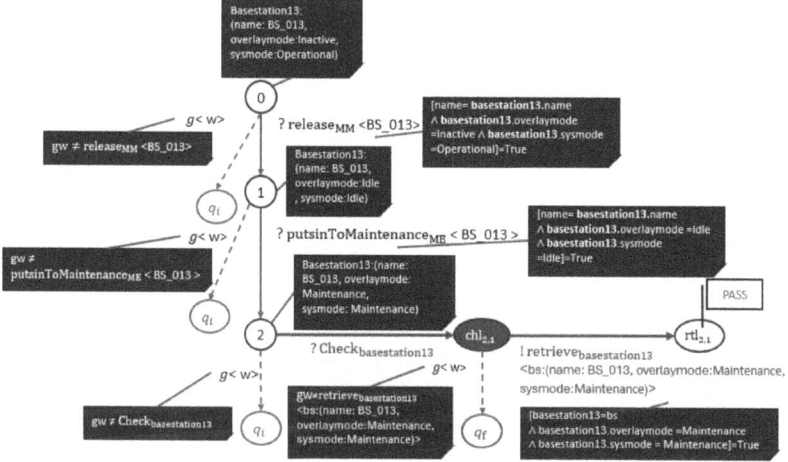

Fig. 5. Test Case for BDDTS $\mathcal{B}_2$

The interpretation of an STS involves a mapping to a semantic domain $\mathcal{U}$ of *values*, defined as usual; in particular, given a valuation $\vartheta : X \to \mathcal{U}$, every term $t \in \mathcal{T}(X)$ gives rise to a value $[\![t]\!]_\vartheta \in \mathcal{U}$, and every assignment $a \in T(X)^Y$ to a valuation $[\![a]\!]_\vartheta \in \mathcal{U}^Y$ such that $[\![a]\!]_\vartheta : v \mapsto [\![a(v)]\!]_\vartheta$ for all $v \in Y$. For ground terms, we may omit the valuation ϑ.

The states of an interpretation are called *semantic states*; the labels are *gate values*. Consider the STS $S = \langle L, V, G, \to, il, ini \rangle$.

- *Semantic states* are elements of $L \times \mathcal{U}^{LV}$. The nature of semantic states is taken from their locations: $\mathsf{N} : (l, \vartheta) \mapsto \mathsf{N}(l)$.
- *Gate values* are sequences $u = g\,\bar{w}$ where $g \in G$ and $\bar{w} \in \mathcal{U}^*$. Every such gate value u gives rise to a valuation $\vartheta_u \in \mathcal{U}^{IV}$.

- LTS transitions exist for every STS switch and every gate value that satisfies the switch guard. For a switch $t \in \rightarrow$ and gate value $u = g\,\bar{w} \in \mathcal{GU}$, we say that t is enabled for u in q, denoted $enab(q, u, t)$, if $[\![\phi_t]\!]_{\vartheta_u \uplus \vartheta_q} = \mathbf{true}$.
- The successor state of a u-labelled transition from q based on switch t is derived from t's target location and assignment: $succ(q, u, t) = (tl_t, [\![a_t]\!]_{\vartheta_u \uplus \vartheta_q})$.

Definition 5. *Let* $\mathcal{S} = \langle L, V, G, \rightarrow, il, ini \rangle$ *be an STS. The* interpretation *of* $\mathcal{S}$ *is defined as the LTS* $[\![\mathcal{S}]\!] = \langle L \times \mathcal{U}^{LV}, G \times \mathcal{U}^*, \rightarrow', (il, [\![ini]\!]) \rangle$ *with*

$$\rightarrow' = \{(q, u, succ(q, u, t)) \mid q \in L \times \mathcal{U}^{LV}, u \in \mathcal{GU}, t \in \rightarrow, enab(q, u, t)\} \ .$$

Finally, we turn ⧬-natured LTSs into *test cases*, which are themselves LTSs in which particular (sink) states are identified as *fail* and *inconclusive*. This is the step in which the ⧬-nature comes into play.

Definition 6. *A* test case *is tuple* $\langle Q, A, \rightarrow, q_0, q_\mathbf{f}, q_\mathbf{i} \rangle$ *where* $\langle Q, A, \rightarrow, q_0 \rangle$ *is an LTS and* $q_\mathbf{f}, q_\mathbf{i} \in Q$ *are special* fail *and* inconclusive *sink states, distinct from* q_0.

A test case TC is used as follows: an SuT (in a given state) is said to *fail TC* when its observable behaviour σ is such that $q_0 \xrightarrow{\sigma} q_\mathbf{f}$; and TC is *inconclusive* if $q_0 \xrightarrow{\sigma} q_\mathbf{i}$. If, finally, $q_0 \xrightarrow{\sigma} q$ for some sink state $q \notin \{q_\mathbf{f}, q_\mathbf{i}\}$, the SuT *passes TC*.

To obtain a test case from a ⧬-natured LTS $\langle Q, A, \rightarrow, q_0 \rangle$, we add fresh states $q_\mathbf{f}, q_\mathbf{i}$ and, moreover, new transitions for every existing non-sink state $q \in Q$ and every output label for which q does not have an outgoing transition. The target state for such a new transition is $q_\mathbf{f}$ if $\mathsf{N}(q) = \bullet$ and $q_\mathbf{i}$ if $\mathsf{N}(q) = \circ$, reflecting the intuition that an unexpected output action from a closed state is an error, whereas from an open state, it is outside the scope of this test. A sink state that is neither $q_\mathbf{f}$ nor $q_\mathbf{i}$ indicates a pass. Formally:

Definition 7. *Let* $T = \langle Q, A, \rightarrow, q_0 \rangle$ *be an* ⧬*-natured LTS and* $q_\mathbf{f}, q_\mathbf{i} \notin Q$. *The test case for* T *is defined by* $TC(T) = \langle Q \cup \{q_\mathbf{f}, q_\mathbf{i}\}, A, \rightarrow', q_0, q_\mathbf{f}, q_\mathbf{i} \rangle$ *such that*

$$\rightarrow' = \rightarrow \cup \{(q, a, q_\mathbf{f}) \mid q \in Q^\bullet, \neg Sink(q), a \in A_o, q \not\xrightarrow{a}\}$$
$$\cup \{(q, a, q_\mathbf{i}) \mid q \in Q^\circ, \neg Sink(q), a \in A, q \not\xrightarrow{a}\} \ .$$

Definition 8. *The test case for a BDDTS* $\mathcal{B}$ *with initialisation* $ini \in \mathcal{T}(\emptyset)^{LV}$ *such that* $[\![IG]\!]_{ini} \equiv \mathbf{true}$ *is defined as:*

$$TC(\mathcal{B}, ini) = TC([\![CRSS(\mathcal{B}, ini)]\!]) \ .$$

For instance, the test case for $\mathcal{B}_2$ is shown in Fig. 5.

5 Sequential Composition

We now come to the second main contribution of this paper: the definition of sequential composition for BDDTSs. Two BDDTSs $\mathcal{B}_1, \mathcal{B}_2$ can be sequentially composed wherever the output guard of an open goal location gl of $\mathcal{B}_1$ implies the input guard of $\mathcal{B}_2$. We call such a location gl *composable*. In fact, every composable goal location gl will be 'connected' to the initial location il_2 of $\mathcal{B}_2$. The connection is constructed by defining for each initial switch $(il_2, \alpha, \phi, a, l_2)$ of $\mathcal{B}_2$ a new switch $(gl, \alpha, \phi, a, l_2)$ starting in gl, with the same label and target location. (In this way, il_2 and thus switches $(il_2, \alpha, \phi, a, l_2)$ may become unreachable, but that does not affect the well-definedness of the sequential composition.)

For sequential composition to be well-defined, we require $\mathcal{B}_1$ and $\mathcal{B}_2$ to be *disjoint*, in the sense that *(i)* their locations are disjoint, i.e., $L_1 \cap L_2 = \emptyset$ (which can be assumed without loss of generality because location identities are irrelevant for the semantics); and *(ii)* $\mathcal{B}_1$'s model variables are disjoint from $\mathcal{B}_2$'s context variables and vice versa, i.e., $MV_1 \cap CV_2 = MV_2 \cap CV_1 = \emptyset$. For shared context and model variables, the sequential composition assumes that they are indeed the same. Note that an assignment to a model variable $v \in MV_1 \cap MV_2$ in the $\mathcal{B}_1$-part of the composition may affect the truth of guards in $\mathcal{B}_2$.

Furthermore, we remove the input guard of $\mathcal{B}_2$, because it is guaranteed by the composition, but keep the output guards of $\mathcal{B}_1$'s composable goal locations, because they remain relevant for testing, i.e. for a check of the *Then* step.

Definition 9. *Let $\mathcal{B}_1, \mathcal{B}_2$ be disjoint BDDTSs. The composable goal locations of $\mathcal{B}_1$ are defined as $L_1^c = \{gl \in L_1^o \mid OG_1 \downarrow gl \wedge OG_1(gl) \Rightarrow IG_2\}$. If $L_1^c \neq \emptyset$, the sequential composition $\mathcal{B}_1 \triangleright \mathcal{B}_2$ is defined as $\langle L_1 \cup L_2, V, G_1 \cup G_2, \rightarrow, il_1, IG_1, OG \rangle$, where:*

- *The $\overset{\circ}{\bullet}$-nature of locations is preserved;*
- *$V = IV \cup MV \cup CV$ where each X in IV, MV, CV is defined as $X_1 \cup X_2$;*
- *$\rightarrow \;=\; \rightarrow_1 \cup \rightarrow_2 \cup \{(l_1, \alpha, \phi, a, l_2) \mid l_1 \in L_1^c, il_2 \xrightarrow{\alpha, \phi, a} l_2\}$;*
- *$OG : l \mapsto \begin{cases} OG_1(l) \wedge OG_2(il_2) & \text{if } l \in L_1^c \text{ and } OG_2 \downarrow il_2 \\ OG_1(l) & \text{if } OG_1 \downarrow l, \text{ and } l \notin L_1^c \text{ or } OG_2 \uparrow il_2 \\ OG_2(l) & \text{if } OG_2 \downarrow l \end{cases}$*

Example 2. We apply the sequential composition on the BDDTS of **Scenario 2** in Fig. 2a and the BDDTS of **Scenario 3** in (Fig. 2b). The result of the sequential composition is shown in Fig. 6. The two BDDTSs can be sequentially composed because the output guard of $\mathcal{B}_2$ at location 2:

$$OG_2(2) = \text{basestation13.overlaymode} = \text{Maintenance}$$
$$\wedge \text{ basestation13.sysmode} = \text{Maintenance}$$

logically implies (here even identical to) the Input Guard of $\mathcal{B}_3$. A new switch (equal to the switch from the initial location of $\mathcal{B}_3$) is added from location 2 of $\mathcal{B}_2$, shown with bold lines in green, and the Input guard of $\mathcal{B}_3$ is removed.

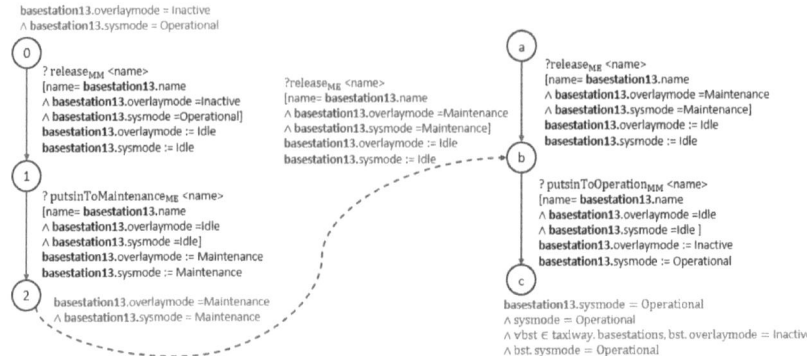

Fig. 6. Sequential Composition $\mathcal{B}_2 \triangleright \mathcal{B}_3$

We note we could slightly adapt the sequential operator to compose two scenarios in a loop if the *Then*-step of each scenario implies the *Given*-step of the other scenario. Looping behavior may well be possible in a software system, while the format of BDD scenarios does not stimulate describing this.

Correctness. We now discuss and show under what circumstances the composed BDDTS $\mathcal{B}_1 \triangleright \mathcal{B}_2$ can replace the original $\mathcal{B}_1$ and $\mathcal{B}_2$ in testing.

Theorem 1 states that if a test derived from the composed system fails on a SuT, the individual systems also generate at least one failing test. In practice, the composed system is capable of finding even more bugs because the model can generate more, various traces due to the different orders the scenarios can be composed, which eventually tests the scenarios with more valuations.

Theorem 2 states the inverse property, namely that any bug found by a test derived from the individual BDDTSs $\mathcal{B}_1$ and $\mathcal{B}_2$ can also be found based on their sequential composition $\mathcal{B}_1 \triangleright \mathcal{B}_2$. This holds when the output guard of the composable locations of $\mathcal{B}_1$ is semantically equivalent to the input guard of $\mathcal{B}_2$— which is not always the case. In fact, when the output guard is strictly stronger than the input guard, this may indicate a missing (unwritten) scenario in the set. To address this, either a new scenario could be added to cover the part of $\mathcal{B}_2$'s input guard that $\mathcal{B}_1$ did not consider, or $\mathcal{B}_2$ should be re-tested in isolation, focusing on the uncovered part in the given.

However, this is generally not an issue in practice. This is because, in most cases, tests are generated and executed with a single arbitrary or special initialization, and if the test passes, it is already a positive sign. By sequentially composing the scenarios, we not only eliminate the need for repeated initialization phase for each scenario but also, if multiple output guards make the input guard of $\mathcal{B}_2$ true, we test more variations with no additional effort.

Preliminaries. The theorems below crucially rely on the fact that the "goal traces"(traces leading to a goal location having an output guard) of a sequentially composed BDDTS $\mathcal{B}_1 \triangleright \mathcal{B}_2$ are fully characterized by those of $\mathcal{B}_1$ and $\mathcal{B}_2$, in the following way. For any BDDTS $\mathcal{B}$ and $L \subseteq L_\mathcal{B}$, let

$$\Sigma_L(\mathcal{B}) = \{(\sigma, OG(gl)) \mid il_i \xrightarrow{\sigma} gl \in L, OG \downarrow gl\}$$

be pairs of traces of $\mathcal{B}$ to goal locations from L, together with the corresponding output guards; and let $\Sigma(\mathcal{B}) = \Sigma_{L_\mathcal{B}}(\mathcal{B})$. It can be shown that $\Sigma(\mathcal{B}_1 \triangleright \mathcal{B}_2) = \Sigma(\mathcal{B}_1) \cup \Sigma_{1 \cdot 2}$, where

$$\Sigma_{1 \cdot 2} = \{(\sigma_1 \sigma_2, \phi_2) \mid (\sigma_1, \phi_1) \in \Sigma_{L_1^c}(\mathcal{B}_1), \phi_1 \Rightarrow IG_2, (\sigma_2, \phi_2) \in \Sigma(\mathcal{B}_2)\}.$$

(recalling that L_1^c is the set of composable locations of $\mathcal{B}_1$, see Definition 9).

Theorem 1 (soundness). *Let $\mathcal{B}_1, \mathcal{B}_2$ be sequentially composable BDDTSs, and let $\mathcal{B} = \mathcal{B}_1 \triangleright \mathcal{B}_2$. If $TC(\mathcal{B}, ini) \xrightarrow{\sigma} q_\mathbf{f}$, then either of the following holds:*

- $TC(\mathcal{B}_1, ini) \xrightarrow{\sigma} q_\mathbf{f}$;
- $\sigma = \sigma_1 \sigma_2$ for some σ_1, σ_2 with $TC(\mathcal{B}_1, ini) \xrightarrow{\sigma_1} (l, \vartheta)$ and $TC(\mathcal{B}_2, ini_2) \xrightarrow{\sigma_2} q_\mathbf{f}$ with $l \in L_1^c$ and $[\![ini_2]\!] = \vartheta\!\restriction_{LV_2}$.

Theorem 2 (completeness). *Let $\mathcal{B}_1, \mathcal{B}_2$ be sequentially composable BDDTSs, and let $\mathcal{B} = \mathcal{B}_1 \triangleright \mathcal{B}_2$ and 0.*

- *If $TC(\mathcal{B}_1, ini_1) \xrightarrow{\sigma} q_\mathbf{f}$ then $TC(\mathcal{B}, ini) \xrightarrow{\sigma} q_\mathbf{f}$;*
- *If $TC(\mathcal{B}_1, ini_1) \xrightarrow{\sigma_1} (l, \vartheta)$ with $l \in L_1^c$ and $TC(\mathcal{B}_2, ini_2) \xrightarrow{\sigma_2} q_\mathbf{f}$ with $\vartheta\!\restriction_{LV_2} = [\![ini_2]\!]$, then $TC(\mathcal{B}, ini) \xrightarrow{\sigma_1 \sigma_2} q_\mathbf{f}$.*

6 Case Study: Results

Our tool: *RobotFrameworkMBT* is an extension to the Robot Framework(RF) [13], inspired by the theory presented, to combine the BDD approach with MBT. Robot Framework is an open-source automation framework for test and robotic process automation. It uses keyword-driven testing to separate test design from execution, defining actions like clicks or keystrokes. RF supports BDD scenarios in the *Given-When-Then* style, implementing each step with Robot keywords.

The theory and tool correspond with each other as follows. The keywords in RF represent the interactions of BDDTS switches. Guards, assignments, and variable initialization are documented as *model info* in RobotFrameworkMBT. Model info, written in Python syntax, includes :IN: and :OUT: expressions containing boolean terms and assignments. The tool can sequentially compose scenarios by analyzing :IN: and :OUT: expressions in the *Given* and *Then* steps. By applying sequential composition multiple times, it obtains tests with loops. In one respect, the tool implementation deviates from the formal constructions presented in this paper, namely concerning the moment at which variables are initialized. Our formal definition of sequential composition is based on BDDTSs, in particular their output and input guards; variable initialization occurs afterwards, in the transformation to STSs (Definition 3). In contrast, for practical reasons, RobotFrameworkMBT first initializes the variables, before checking the guards for composition. Though this is less modular and has to be repeated for every choice of variable initialization, this variation potentially gives rise to more connecting states. The validity of the method is not affected.

Below we show the *model info* for the Given step of **Scenario 1** (with corresponding BDDTS in Fig. 1). We instantiate the ${AGL function} variable with values 'runway' and 'taxiway'.

```
    [Documentation]    *model info*
...   :IN: system.mode==operational |
...        all([bs.overlay_mode == 'inactive' and
             bs.system_mode == 'operational' for bs in ${AGL function}.basestations])
```

We applied RobotMBT on the case study as introduced in Sect. 2, using 21 BDD scenarios, including the four as shown in the paper. We categorize the test results we obtained into three groups:

Testing Various Non-trivial Traces. Figure 7a shows test execution after the tool generated the abstract test cases (which are the sequences of BDD scenarios each representing an actual test case), while Fig. 7b demonstrates a different order based on sequential composition. Without model info, tests follow the stated order. However, **Scenario 1** and **Scenario 2** cannot be executed in the given order, and require a setup when using RF without RobotMBT, to reach the system state as specified in Given. This is the overhead we noted in Sect. 1.

Testing non-trivial traces of a system is important because it allows us to evaluate the system's behavior under complex, real-world scenarios that go beyond simple or expected use cases. The error in Fig. 8 highlights a real scenario where, after the Maintenance Engineer replaces a basestation, it becomes unreachable and is handed back to the Maintenance Manager for operation. The failure occurred because the step implementations did not allow this, though the initial model(the BDDTS as specified by the model info) did. Stakeholders agreed the model should not permit this hand-back.

Finding Issues in Test Implementations. Model-based testing revealed incomplete step implementations that caused false failures when the execution order changed. In Fig. 9, the *Given* step should check basestation.sys_mode $\neq$ Operational but it only checked the more specific constraint basestation.sys_mode

(a) trace 1   (b) trace 2

Fig. 7. RF Test Report for Different Execution Orders

= Maintenance, while there is a third possible sys_mode, namely Idle. Hence this case showed that our approach can expose issues in step implementations.

Uncovering Difficult-to-Find Bugs in the System. Although we found no system bugs for the scenarios of the partial maintenance feature, we challenged ourselves to automatically trigger and detect a previously resolved issue. This issue was missed by automated tests and only discovered later through manual testing. It was particularly hard to detect as it required both repetition and composition of scenarios. As we stated in Sect. 2, the partial maintenance feature aims to keep the system operational during basestation maintenance. The known issue occurred under the following conditions: a) The system is in partial maintenance, meaning that at least one basestation is in maintenance mode. b) The Air Traffic Controller does repetitive mode switching like putting the system into Idle and then making it Operational again. c) And finally when the Air Traffic Controller switches the lamp levels, the lamp levels do not switch correctly.

To replicate the error, we first created BDD scenarios for system mode and lamp level switching, as these were missing. We then modeled the new scenarios and ran them with **Scenario 1**. The error appeared after the third sequential composition the tool tried, revealing the trace that caused it. While we specifically targeted **Scenario 1**, testing earlier with MBT could have uncovered the issue at some point when running the mode-switching feature with partial maintenance feature, as several scenarios in the suite activate partial maintenance. You can see the test report in Fig. 10.

7 Related Work

Composition of BDD Scenarios. Several papers propose the composition of BDD scenarios. In [10], the authors argue that BDD scenarios alone are unsuitable for Cyber-Physical Production Systems due to their complexity. They address this by modeling scenarios with a variant of state machines and composing those with shared events but different pre/post conditions. Unlike their CPPS-specific, manual approach, ours is more general, formally defined, and automated.

Kang et al. provide a translation from BDD scenarios to Timed-Automata (TA) [9]. They formally verify the compatibility of BDD Scenarios and the TA models using UPAAL. With their verification technique, they can also point out

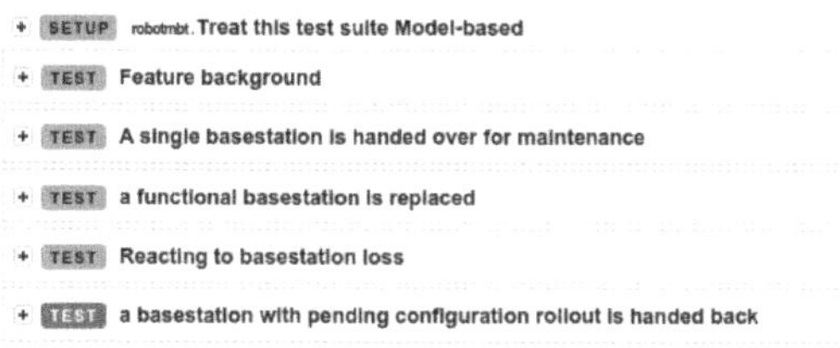

Fig. 8. An example of a non-trivial trace

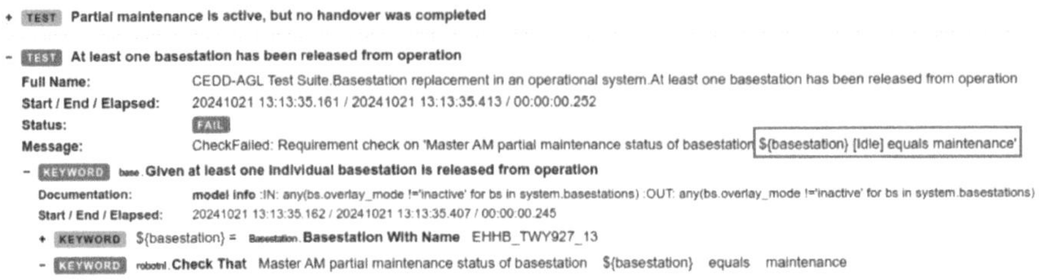

```
+ TEST  Partial maintenance is active, but no handover was completed
- TEST  At least one basestation has been released from operation
   Full Name:            CEDD-AGL Test Suite.Basestation replacement in an operational system.At least one basestation has been released from operation
   Start / End / Elapsed:  20241021 13:13:35.161 / 20241021 13:13:35.413 / 00:00:00.252
   Status:               FAIL
   Message:              CheckFailed: Requirement check on 'Master AM partial maintenance status of basestation ${basestation} [Idle] equals maintenance'
   - KEYWORD  base .Given at least one individual basestation is released from operation
      Documentation:        model info :IN: any(bs.overlay_mode !='inactive' for bs in system.basestations) :OUT: any(bs.overlay_mode !='inactive' for bs in system.basestations)
      Start / End / Elapsed:  20241021 13:13:35.162 / 20241021 13:13:35.407 / 00:00:00.245
      + KEYWORD  ${basestation} = Basestation .Basestation With Name  EHHB_TWY927_13
      - KEYWORD  robotmbt .Check That  Master AM partial maintenance status of basestation  ${basestation}  equals  maintenance
```

Fig. 9. An example of a test implementation issue

the missing behavior in BDD Scenarios. They manually compose some scenarios with shared actions, but no specific composition operator is introduced and one important missing aspect in their work is that output actions are not considered.

Silva introduces a DSL to identify the scenario entities [14]. The DSL contains an abstract Given-When-Then structure. In each step of the abstract scenario, a refined scenario can be written that connects the related scenarios in this abstract way. We currently do not have a formalism for refinement but a prototype implementation of refinement is available in our RobotFrameworkMBT tool. With the tool SkyFire, they generate the BDD scenarios from UML diagrams [11]. The generated scenarios are long, and connect scenarios sequentially, as the UML diagrams specify. They generate tests using Cucumber. Their approach is opposite to ours, we model scenarios while they write scenarios from models.

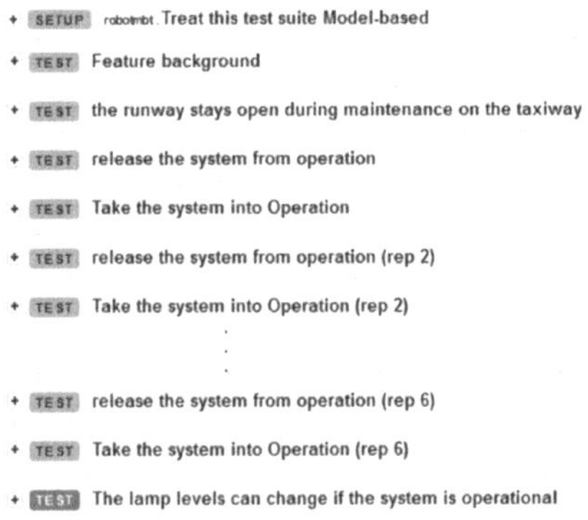

```
+ SETUP  robotmbt .Treat this test suite Model-based
+ TEST  Feature background
+ TEST  the runway stays open during maintenance on the taxiway
+ TEST  release the system from operation
+ TEST  Take the system into Operation
+ TEST  release the system from operation (rep 2)
+ TEST  Take the system into Operation (rep 2)
         ⋮
+ TEST  release the system from operation (rep 6)
+ TEST  Take the system into Operation (rep 6)
+ TEST  The lamp levels can change if the system is operational
```

Fig. 10. An example of a known system bug: Mode Switching Error

Composition Operators for Transition Systems. Several papers have proposed composition operators for Labeled Transition Systems (LTSs). Parallel Composition of LTSs in ioco-theory is defined in [2] and is further improved by formally defining mutual acceptance in [6]. Conjunction, parallel composition, and Quotient are also defined in [1] and the parallel composition is revised in [7]. In [8] a conjunction operator is defined on LTSs with inputs and outputs, such that conjunction expresses the intersection over outputs. Our composition operators for sequentially composing BDD scenarios are defined directly on BDDTS (which is a variant of STS), making them suitable for BDD scenarios.

8 Conclusion and Future Work

This paper presents a compositional approach to Behavior-Driven Development (BDD) where system behavior is specified and tested through scenarios written in natural language. Specifically, we introduced a sequential composition operator for BDD Transition Systems (BDDTS), which are formal models for BDD scenarios. By composing BDDTSs, we can generate more and longer test cases from composed models that account for various integrations of behaviors. These integrations might be challenging to address when writing and testing individual BDD scenarios. The composition also aids in identifying missing scenarios that might be overlooked when only describing small features in single scenarios.

In future work we plan to introduce another composition operator, namely "disjunction", to connect scenarios that share actions or similar pre-conditions. We will evaluate disjunction composition in an industrial case study. We should also investigate how to deal with quiescence [16]. In addition, we could investigate NLP techniques to facilitate the translation between BDD Scenarios and BDDTS or BDD scenarios to some intermediate BDD language [18]. Finally, we would like to experiment with using MBT techniques to generate tests with diverse data values, and how that improves bug detection compared to the standard BDD approach where a BDD scenario has just one test with fixed data values.

Acknowledgement. This publication is part of the project *TiCToC -Testing in Times of Continuous Change-* with project number 17936 of the research program *MasCot-Mastering Complexity-* which is supported by NWO.

References

1. Beneš, N., Daca, P., Henzinger, T.A., Křetínský, J., Ničković, D.: Complete composition operators for IOCO-testing theory. In: Proceedings of the 18th International ACM SIGSOFT Symposium on Component-Based Software Engineering, CBSE '15, pp. 101–110. Association for Computing Machinery, New York (2015). https://doi.org/10.1145/2737166.2737175

2. van der Bijl, M., Rensink, A., Tretmans, J.: Compositional testing with IOCO. In: Petrenko, A., Ulrich, A. (eds.) Formal Approaches to Software Testing, pp. 86–100. Springer, Heidelberg (2004)
3. Van den Bos, P., Tretmans, J.: Coverage-based testing with symbolic transition systems. In: Beyer, D., Keller, C. (eds.) Tests and Proofs, pp. 64–82. Springer, Cham (2019)
4. Chelimsky, D., Astels, D., Helmkamp, B., North, D., Dennis, Z., Hellesoy, A.: The RSpec Book: Behaviour Driven Development with Rspec, Cucumber, and Friends. Pragmatic Bookshelf, 1st edn. (2010). https://dl.acm.org/doi/10.5555/1965448
5. Cucumber. https://cucumber.io/docs/guides/overview/
6. van Cuyck, G., van Arragon, L., Tretmans, J.: Compositionality in model-based testing. In: Bonfanti, S., Gargantini, A., Salvaneschi, P. (eds.) Testing Software and Systems, pp. 202–218. Springer, Cham (2023)
7. Daca, P., Henzinger, T.A., Krenn, W., Nickovic, D.: Compositional specifications for IOCO testing. In: 2014 IEEE Seventh International Conference on Software Testing, Verification and Validation, pp. 373–382 (2014). https://doi.org/10.1109/ICST.2014.50
8. Janssen, R.: Combining partial specifications using alternating interface automata. In: Wehrheim, H., Cabot, J. (eds.) Fundamental Approaches to Software Engineering, pp. 462–481. Springer, Cham (2020)
9. Kang, E.Y., Silva, T.R.: Towards formal verification of behaviour-driven development scenarios using timed automata. In: 2023 30th Asia-Pacific Software Engineering Conference (APSEC), pp. 612–616 (2023). https://doi.org/10.1109/APSEC60848.2023.00081
10. Kannengiesser, U., Krenn, F., Stary, C.: A behaviour-driven development approach for cyber-physical production systems. In: 2020 IEEE Conference on Industrial Cyberphysical Systems (ICPS), vol. 1, pp. 179–184 (2020). https://doi.org/10.1109/ICPS48405.2020.9274755
11. Li, N., Escalona, A., Kamal, T.: Skyfire: model-based testing with cucumber. In: 2016 IEEE International Conference on Software Testing, Verification and Validation (ICST), pp. 393–400 (2016). https://doi.org/10.1109/ICST.2016.41
12. Nagy, G., Rose, S.: The BDD Books - Formulation. Document examples with Given/When/Then. Leanpub (2021). https://leanpub.com/bddbooks-formulation
13. Robot framework. https://robotframework.org/
14. Silva, T.R.: Towards a domain-specific language for behaviour-driven development. In: 2023 IEEE Symposium on Visual Languages and Human-Centric Computing (VL/HCC), pp. 283–286 (2023). https://doi.org/10.1109/VL-HCC57772.2023.00054
15. Specflow. https://docs.specflow.org/en/latest/
16. Tretmans, J.: Model-based testing with labelled transition systems, pp. 1–38. Springer, Heidelberg (2008). https://doi.org/10.1007/978-3-540-78917-8_1
17. Zameni, T.: Executable BDD scenario models for robotframeworkmbt. https://doi.org/10.5281/zenodo.14892704

18. Zameni, T., van den Bos, P., Rensink, A., Tretmans, J.: An intermediate language to integrate behavior-driven development scenarios and model-based testing. In: 2024 IEEE International Conference on Software Analysis, Evolution and Reengineering - Companion (SANER-C), pp. 199–206 (2024). https://doi.org/10.1109/SANER-C62648.2024.00033
19. Zameni, T., van Den Bos, P., Tretmans, J., Foederer, J., Rensink, A.: From BDD scenarios to test case generation. In: 2023 IEEE International Conference on Software Testing, Verification and Validation Workshops (ICSTW), pp. 36–44 (2023). https://doi.org/10.1109/ICSTW58534.2023.00019

Scaling Information Flow Control By-Construction to Component-Based Software Architectures

Rasmus C. Rønneberg[✉], Tabea Bordis, Christopher Gerking, Asmae Heydari Tabar, and Ina Schaefer

Karlsruhe Institute of Technology, Karlsruhe, Germany
{rasmus.ronneberg,tabea.bordis,christopher.gerking,asmae.tabar, ina.schaefer}@kit.edu

Abstract. Building systems that do not violate confidentiality of data through accidental information leakage is an increasingly important challenge. This is especially true for security-critical systems that handle sensitive information. A well-known obstacle for building secure systems is that security properties, such as confidentiality, are only addressed in late development phases. To combat this, information flow control by-construction (IFbC) was proposed. Similarly to correctness-by-construction for functional correctness, it aims at building systems such that they have a secure information flow by-construction. This paper presents an extension of that work in which we scale IFbC to the software architectural level for component-based systems. Our approach allows software architects to create a high-level design of the system using UML component models with explicit provided and required interfaces. We provide information flow specifications for the interfaces of components, which integrates the security concerns of the system in the design phase. We then demonstrate how the individual components can be realized according to information flow control by-construction, such that they adhere to their interface specifications. We provide rules for compatibility of interfaces and implementations that ensure confidential information flow, and prove that all component-based systems that can be constructed by our approach satisfy their security properties. In this way, we allow flexible architectural modeling of component-based systems combined with strong confidentiality guarantees from information flow control by-construction. Finally, we present the tool ArchFlow which assists developers with creating secure component-based systems.

Keywords: By-construction software engineering · Component models · Information flow

1 Introduction

Data confidentiality is an important issue in a digitized society where information is shared and processed at high rates. This is especially true for security-critical systems that handle sensitive information about individuals, e.g., medical data, banking details, and etc. Information leaks in these systems can cause legal consequences for companies and loss of trust in their products, and users might have their information misused [1,2]. A common formalization of security properties *confidentiality* and *integrity* is *information flow* [15], which is concerned with the flow of information between program variables. To ensure confidentiality, secure information should not interfere with public information. This prevents deducing anything from the public information about the secret information. Non-interference is typically enforced by analytical or post-hoc approaches [9,14,20,30], which requires a behavioral specification of the system or source code.

As a result, one of the main issues in developing secure software is that security requirements are often only considered late in the software development life cycle [8]. This makes finding leaks difficult and changing the systems expensive. An important challenge in improving secure software development practice is to provide tools and methods for software architectural design with strong confidentiality guarantees, and thereby placing the security concerns of the system in early development phases. An example of ensuring security properties in the early software development phases, e.g., in the design phase is the extension of modeling languages such as UML for secure development [20]. But such approaches usually do not provide a systematic way to implement the UML components.

Recently, a method to build programs was proposed such that they have a secure information flow control by-construction (IFbC) [26,27]. In this approach, programs are constructed incrementally from an information flow specification. IFbC is inspired by correctness-by-construction (CbC) [22] for functional correctness. In CbC, development starts with a specification in the form of a Hoare triple $\{P\}S\{Q\}$ where P is a precondition, Q is a postcondition and S is an abstract statement to be refined. The abstract statement is refined incrementally and the concrete statement is guaranteed to fulfill the specification. Using IFbC for confidentiality can reduce the need for post-hoc analysis and the costs related to rebuilding the systems. However, IFbC only considers construction on the level of programs and algorithms. Hence, it is not well suited for building large systems, and in its current form it can not be used to incorporate security concerns in the system design phase.

This work aims at scaling IFbC to the software architectural level with the goal of providing constructive methods to address confidentiality concerns in the construction and design phase of larger component-based systems. This will allow software architects to model systems in a UML component diagram and write information flow specifications on the level of UML components. In a later software development phase, a software developer implements the components according to IFbC such that they are guaranteed to comply with the information flow specification of the UML diagram. Alternatively, already implemented IFbC components can be re-used if they meet the specification of the UML component diagram. We achieve this by writing information flow specifications for the interfaces of the UML components. These specifications can be checked against concrete implementations of the components. Specifically, our contributions are as follows:

1. We formally define an information flow specification for component-based systems (Sect. 3) and compatibility between the component specification and concrete implementation (Sect. 4.1) which encourages reuse of secure components.
2. We define sound composition (Sect. 4.3) of components, for both assembly composition and delegation composition (Sect. 4.2), which allows the incorporation of confidentiality in the modeling phase of component-based software architectures.
3. We provide a prototype implementation of the tool ArchFlow (Sect. 5), which supports modeling of secure systems. The tool is open-source and available on GitHub[1]

2 Information Flow Control By-Construction

Information flow control is a prominent approach for ensuring the security properties confidentiality and integrity. One of the main underlying properties of information flow is the notion of non-interference [15]. Intuitively, non-interference states that secret information should not interfere with public information. This intuition can be formalized by considering a program starting in input state $s = (s_l, s_h)$ and ending in output state $s' = (s'_l, s'_h)$ where s_l contains the low (public) parts of the state and s_h contains the high (secret) parts. In this work, we assume that the program is terminating so the program will always end in an output state. We can define a low-equivalence relation $\sim_L$ for two states such that the states are low-equivalent if they agree on low values ($s \sim_L s'$ iff $s_l = s'_l$). A program satisfies non-interference if starting in two low-equivalent states it ends in two low-equivalent states. If two states are low equivalent, an attacker observing the low information can not distinguish the high information in the program and therefore, can not deduce anything about the secret information.

One way to ensure non-interference at the programming language level is through a security type system [30]. Such a type system enables security annotations on variables, and a compiler can statically check that the program satisfies non-interference. For example in program `h:= 1; l:=h;` a high variable is declared and assigned the integer 1. The value of the high variable is then explicitly leaked by the assignment to the low variable. In program `if(h == 1)l:=1; else l:= 0;` there is no explicit leak of the high variable, but it is implicitly leaked when the value of h is 1. Implicit leaks can occur when high values are evaluated as part of a loop or condition guard. Using a security type system, it is possible to detect both the implicit and explicit leaks in the two example programs.

---

[1] https://github.com/KIT-TVA/ArchFlow.

Recently, language-based non-interference was brought into the realm of by-construction engineering with enabling information flow control by-construction in both the guarded command language (GCL) and in object-oriented languages [26,27]. Information flow control by-construction provides a set of refinement rules which incrementally construct a program such that it is guaranteed to satisfy non-interference. We recall some of the main concepts of IFbC from [26].

Definition 1 (Information flow policy). *An information policy P is a lattice $\langle SL, \leq, \top, \bot, lub \rangle$ where SL is a set of security levels, $\leq$: $SL \times SL$ is a partial ordering $\top$ and $\bot$ are the biggest and smallest element in the set, respectively, and lub: $\mathcal{P}(SL) \to SL$ is the least upper bound function, which computes the least upper bound for a given set of security levels.*

The *information flow policy* is a bounded lattice as in the lattice security model by Denning [12]. The information flow policy defines the different security levels and their relation to each other.

Definition 2 (Program information flow specification). *A program information flow specification is a tuple $\langle V^{Pre}, V^{Post}, \eta \rangle$ where V^{Pre}, V^{Post}: Var $\to SL$ are the pre- and post-condition, respectively, mapping program variables Var to security levels. The current security context η: SL keeps track of implicit leaks.*

Figure 1 shows the IFbC refinement rules that we adopt from Runge et al. [26]. The refinements shows which side-conditions must be fulfilled for an abstract statement to be refined into a concrete statement from GCL. Besides the usual commands from GCL [13] the refinements also include *method calls*. All the refinements in Fig. 1 start from an *information flow specification*. An abstract statement is incrementally refined into a concrete statement, and each refinement preserves the specification if correctly applied. The current security context η is updated in conditional statements and loops to prevent implicit information leaks. Security levels used in specifications are from the set SL. The refinements and information flow specifications ensure non-interference with respect to a given information flow policy. To apply the method call refinement rule it is enough to know the specification of the called method, which ensures that methods can be constructed in isolation without the need to know implementation details of other methods.

As an example of application of the assignment refinement consider the program y:= 1; x:=y;. In this example, we have two security levels low l and high h. The information flow policy we wish to enforce is $l < h$. Variables x and y contain low and high information respectively. This can be captured by a specification $V^{Pre}, V^{Post} := \{\text{x: } l, \text{y: } h\}$. Here V^{Pre} and V^{Post} are labeling functions mapping variables to security levels. We omit the security context as there are no conditionals or loops in the example. The first assignment y:=1 does not change the pre and postconditions, but in the second assignment x:=y we need to control the information flow to avoid a leak. This is achieved by updating the postcondition accordingly. Following the refinement in Fig. 1 we can introduce the assignment with the following specification {x: l, y: h} x:=y {x: h, y: h} and, thereby, avoid leaking high information through a low variable by raising the security level of x.

$\{V^{Pre}\} S \{V^{Post}\}[\eta]$	Is refinable to
Skip	$\{V^{Pre}\}Skip\{V^{Post}\}[\eta]$ iff $V^{Post}(x) = V^{Pre}(x) \forall x \in Vars$
Assignment	$\{V^{Pre}\}x := E\{V^{Post}\}[\eta]$ iff $V^{Post}(y) = V^{Pre}(y)$ $\forall y \in Vars \setminus \{x\} \wedge$ $V^{Post}(x) = lub(\{V^{Pre}(v) \mid v \in vars(E)\} \cup \{V^{Pre}(x), \eta\})$
Composition	$\{V^{Pre}\}S1; S2\{V^{Post}\}[\eta]$ iff there exists a labeling function V' such that $\{V^{Pre}\}S1\{V'\}[\eta] \wedge \{V'\}S2\{V^{Post}\}[\eta]$ $\wedge \forall x \in Vars : V^{Pre}(x) \leq V'(x) \leq V^{Post}(x)$
Selection	$\{V^{Pre}\}$ if $G \to S1$ else $S2$ fi $\{V^{Post}\}[\eta]$ iff $\{V^{Pre}\}S1\{V^{Post}\}[\eta'] \wedge \{V^{Pre}\}S2\{V^{Post}\}[\eta']$ with $\eta' = lub(\{V^{Pre}(x) \mid x \in vars(G)\} \cup \{\eta\})$
Repetition	$\{V^{Pre}\}$ do $G \to S1$ od $\{V^{Post}\}[\eta]$ iff $\{V^{Pre}\}S1\{V^{Post}\}[\eta']$ with $\eta' = lub(\{V^{Pre}(x) \mid x \in vars(G)\} \cup \{\eta\})$
Method call	$\{V^{Pre}\}M(a_1...a_n)\{V^{Post}\}[\eta]$ iff for a method $\{V^{Pre}\}M(z_1...z_n)\{V^{Post}\}[\eta]$ and for all parameters we have $V^{Pre}(a_i) \leq V^{Pre}(z_i) \wedge V^{Post}(z_i) \leq V^{Post}(a_i)$ where a_i are the actual parameters and z_i are the formal

Fig. 1. IFbC refinement rules [26]

3 Components and Their Specifications

We extend IFbC to the software architectural level by enabling modeling and reusing of components with UML component models [6,23,29]. In the following, we describe our component model and information flow specifications of components. We also provide formal definitions for the core concepts of our component model.

Component. A components is a basic unit of composition with a clear boundary to other components and the environment. It contains its own internal data and alone or jointly implements functionality. We represent a component with an object. For this reason we extend the language introduced in Fig. 1 with a simple object model. A program is written as an object definition with a set of methods. Objects implement an interface which declares provided methods. This way we group the methods that belong to the same component. Additionally, we introduce object variables which are shared between methods in the same object. Variables can be of primitive types or interface types. In contrast to standard object-oriented languages we don't include inheritance or sub-typing.

We assume a hierarchical component structure in which components can be decomposed into sub-components. The most basic building block of our component model is the *atomic* component, which cannot be decomposed any further. In addition to atomic components, our component model includes *composite* components. Composite components contain sub-components, which in turn can be either a composite or an atomic component. Only atomic components carry an implementation.

Figure 2 shows a UML diagram of the two types of components in our component model. In the figure, components A and C are both atomic components, which are not decomposed any further. Component A contains both a required and provided interface, while component C only contains a provided interface. Component B is a composite component that delegates its provided services to component C. Implicitly the top-level components A and B are contained in a composite component, which makes the composition possible.

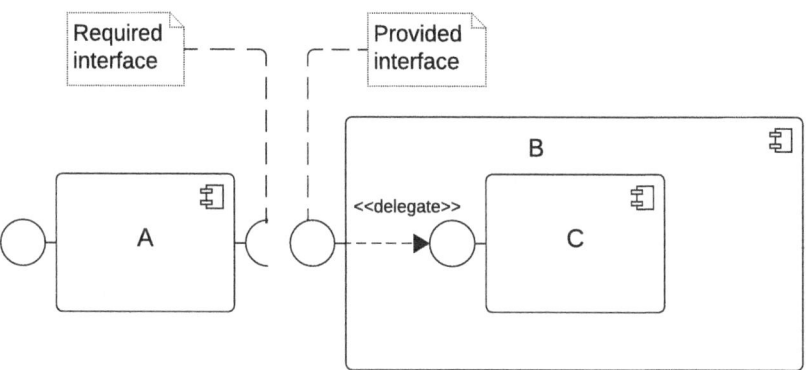

Fig. 2. Example of the two types of components in the component model. An atomic component A and composite component B with a sub-component C.

Interface. Conceptually, a component represents an encapsulated part of the system, which can be exchanged or composed to build more complex functionalities. Components offer functionality to other components and can also have dependencies on functionalities located in other components. Dependencies are collected in *required* interfaces, and offered functionality is collected in *provided* interfaces. Offering functionality corresponds to implementing the methods from the provided interface according to the refinement rules (Sect. 2). Dependencies correspond to storing a reference to another object in a field. On the component level, this is represented by a *binding* between the components (e.g. the delegation binding between component B and C in Fig. 2).

Definition 3 shows the definition for a component interface. It is a set of method signatures, which is either a provided service to other components or required from another component. The method signature consists of a method name, typed input variables and a typed return value.

Definition 3 (Interface). *An interface is either a provided interface I_p or required interface I_r. An interface is a set of method signatures M of the form:* m $in_1, \ldots, in_n \rightarrow$ out *where in_i is a typed input variable,* out *is a typed return variable, and* m *is the method name.*

Interfaces are *compatible* when all method signatures are compatible meaning that the order and types of the input variables are the same and the return type is the same. We are not considering compatible functionality of the methods. For compatible functionality we could consider compatibility of functional specifications as Knüppel et al. [21], however that is not the focus of this paper. We denote compatibility between two method signatures $m_1, m_2 \in M$ by $m_1 \preceq m_2$. In the following, we lift compatibility to interfaces. We introduce a *type* function that returns the type of a variable which is either a primitive type or an interface type.

Definition 4 (Interface compatibility). *Let I and I' be two interfaces with the set of method signatures M and M' respectively. We say that interface I is compatible to interface I' denoted by $I \preceq I'$ iff $\forall m \in M$ where $m =$* m $in_1, \ldots, in_n \rightarrow$ out, *$\exists m' \in M'$ where $m' =$* m' $in'_1, \ldots, in'_n \rightarrow$ out' *such that $\forall i \in \{1...n\}$ $type(in_i) = type(in'_i)$ and $type(out) = type(out')$.*

Interface Specification. Interface specification states the information flow specification on the level of components, which any concrete implementation must ensure. The specifications are written in the same style as in Definition 2, but without the security context η. Importantly, interface specification can only refer to *input* and *output* variables. In contrast, program specification can refer to *input, output*, local variables, and any local fields declared in the object definition. We write $\mathbb{I}$ in front of the pre and postcondition to indicate that the specification is for the interface. When necessary, we distinguish between required and provided interfaces by writing $\mathbb{I}_r$ or $\mathbb{I}_p$ to indicate which interface the specification is for. A global information flow policy sets the security levels in the interface specification.

Definition 5 (Interface specification). *Let m be a method signature:* m $in_1 \ldots in_n \rightarrow$ out. *An interface specification is a tuple $\langle \mathbb{I}V^{Pre}, m, \mathbb{I}V^{Post} \rangle$ where $\mathbb{I}V^{Pre}, \mathbb{I}V^{Post} : Var \rightarrow SL$ are the pre and postcondition which are partial functions mapping variables to security levels. The domain of $\mathbb{I}V^{Pre}$ denoted by $dom(\mathbb{I}V^{Pre})$ is $\cup_{i=1}^{n}\{in_i\}$ and $dom(\mathbb{I}V^{Post})$ is $\cup_{i=1}^{n}\{in_i\} \cup \{out\}$*

Component Model. Here, we formally define the two building blocks of a component model, *atomic* and *composite* components.

An atomic component must include a provided interface, which contains the service that other components can use. Optionally, it can include a required interface if it requires any services from other components. Components can only call methods that are listed in the required interface. Additionally, an atomic component must contain a mapping of the provided interface methods to a concrete implementation.

Definition 6 (Atomic component). *An atomic component C_a is a tuple $\langle I_p, I_r, Impl \rangle$ where I_p is the provided interface, I_r is the optional required interface, $Impl: I_p.m \to m'$ is a mapping from an interface method to a concrete IFbC implementation m'. The mapping Impl must preserve the method signatures.*

Example 1. Consider the `Account` atomic component shown in Fig. 3. The component contains a provided interface, a mapping to a concrete implementation, but no required interface (Definition 6). The component exposes an `Update` method, and the interface (Definition 3) contains the method signature together with a specification (Definition 5). In the example, we assume the following security lattice *public* $\leq$ *private* $\leq$ *secret*. The implementation is written as an object definition and adds a few implementation details, such as local variables to control overdraft and account balance. The implementation contains its own *program information flow specification* (Definition 2). As the example shows, the specification in the interface and the implementation can be different in terms of variables and security levels, however in this case it is not an issue since the security level of the output is raised in the interface. We therefore say that the two specifications are compatible. In Sect. 4.1, we will formally state the conditions for when interface and program specifications are compatible.

Composite components are used for composition through the assembly and delegation binding connectors. Assembly connect required and provided interfaces at the same hierarchical level. Delegation connect provided with provided interfaces and required with required interfaces at different but adjacent hierarchical levels.

Definition 7 (Composite component). *A composite component C is a tuple $\langle I_p, I_r, SubC, Assembly_{i,j}, Delegation(Req/Prov)_i \rangle$ where I_p is a provided interface, I_r is an optional required interface, $SubC = \{C_1, ..., C_n\}$ is a set of subcomponents. $Assembly_{i,j}$ is a partial map from required to provided interfaces $Assembly_{i,j}: C_i.I_r.m' \to C_j.I_p.m$ where $i \neq j$ and $C_i.I_r \preceq C_j.I_p$. $Delegation_{req}$ is a partial map $DelegationReq_i: C_i.I_r.m' \to I_r.m$ where $C_i.I_r \preceq I_r$. Similarly, $DelegationProv_i$ is a partial map $DelegationProv_i: I_p.m' \to C_i.I_p.m$ where $I_p \preceq C_i.I_p$. The methods m and m' refer to the specific methods which are being bound in an assembly or delegation composition.*

Example 2. Consider the composite component `DailyAcount` in Fig. 4. It contains two sub-components `Account` and `DailyLimit`. In the figure we show the

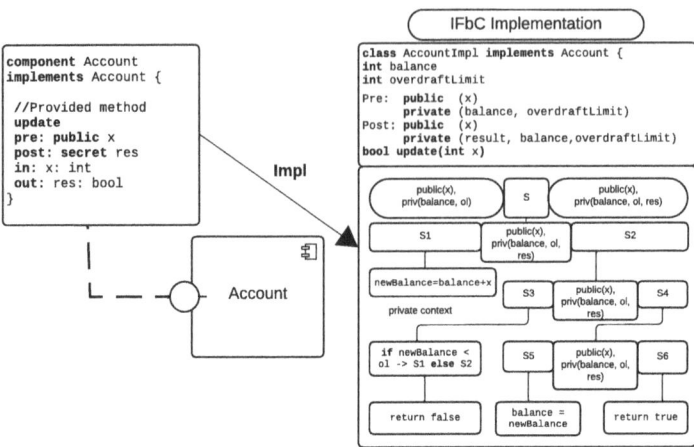

Fig. 3. Atomic Account component and implementation. The method implementation is represented in graphical notation as a refinement tree. Each box represents a statement and each line represent a refinement [26].

component model as an UML component diagram and also described in an architecture description language (ADL) inspired by MontiArch [16]. We declare subcomponents by the keyword **component**. Provided and required methods from the corresponding interfaces (Definition 3) are listed with their names, in and output parameters together with the interface specification (Definition 5). Compositions are declared by the **delegate** or **assembly** keywords. For assemblies we use unique qualified names to specify which required methods are bound to which provided methods. For delegation qualified names are only used for sub-components. In the example, DailyAccount contains the assembly mapping Account.I_r.getLimit → DailyLimit.I_p.getLimit and the delegation I_p.update → Account.I_p.update. As in Example 1 an account provides an update method and checks a daily overdraft limit when money is withdrawn from the account. However, in this example the daily limit is refactored into its own sub-component DailyLimit which provides the limit to the account component. In Sect. 4.2 we address how to ensure that the information flow policy of the system is not broken when component are connected via assembly and delegation.

4 Enforcing Information Flow Policies for Compositions

In the following section, we define the conditions for a secure information flow on composition of atomic and composite components. Specifically, we show the conditions for compatibility of interface specification with program specification, such as in Example 1, and conditions for a secure compositions, such as in Example 2.

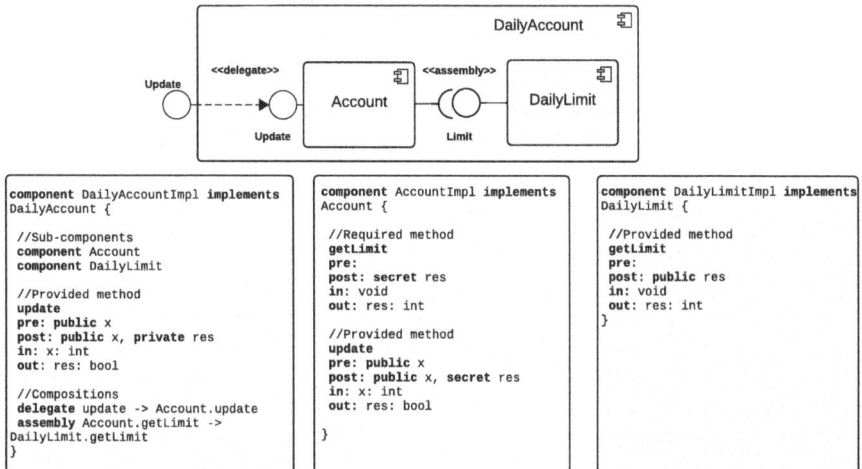

Fig. 4. Composite Daily Account component

4.1 Interface and Implementation Compatibility

We define compatibility between the program specification of a concrete implementation and the interface specification. A component must have a provided interface, but may optionally also contain a required interface. We define the requirements for compatibility between provided interface and the implementation. The main idea of compatibility is to be able to substitute a concrete implementation which is compatible with the interface, and the substitution should not break the overall information flow policy of the system. This allows for a flexible modeling of the system, that abstracts away from implementations of individual components.

Definition 8 (Provided interface compatibility). *Let $C_a = \langle I_p, I_r, Impl \rangle$ be an atomic component. A method m from provided interface I_p and a corresponding concrete IFbC implementation m' where $Impl(I_p.m) = m'$ and $m \preceq m'$ are compatible iff $\forall a \in dom(\mathbb{I}_p V^{Pre})$ and $\forall a' \in dom(\mathbb{I}_p V^{Post})$, $\mathbb{I}_p V^{Pre}(a) \leq V^{Pre}(a) \wedge \mathbb{I}_p V^{Post}(a') \geq V^{Post}(a')$.*

Intuitively, the provided interface specification states a lower bound on the security level of the arguments that the component receives and an upper bound on the security level of the value that the component will return. This way we ensure that any concrete implementation will not accidentally treat data as if it was at a lower security level. We assume that the security levels of the concrete implementation and the interface are directly comparable. This might not always be the case as the information flow policy only defines a partial ordering. In case of non-comparable security levels, the interface is not compatible.

4.2 Interface Specfication Compatibility

We define secure composition of interface specifications. Compatibility must be ensured for both assembly and delegation compositions. For the interface specifications to be compatible first the interfaces must be compatible as in Definition 4. This requirement ensures that the methods in the interfaces will be compatible. We define interface specification compatibility as follows.

Definition 9 (Interface specification compatibility). *Let C be a composite component with sub-components C_i and C_j, provided and required interfaces I_p and I_r, $Assembly_{i,j}(C_i.I_r.m) = C_j.I_p.m'$, $DelegationProv_i(I_p.m) = C_i.I_p.m'$, and $DelegationReq_j(C_j.I_r.m) = I_r.m'$. Let $s = \langle \mathbb{I}V^{Pre}, m, \mathbb{I}V^{Post} \rangle$ be a specification for method m, and let $s' = \langle \mathbb{I}'V^{Pre}, m', \mathbb{I}'V^{Post} \rangle$ be a specification for method m'. The compositions are secure iff $\forall a \in dom(\mathbb{I}V^{Pre})$ and $\forall a' \in dom(\mathbb{I}V^{Post})$, $\mathbb{I}V^{Pre}(a) \leq \mathbb{I}'V^{Pre}(a) \wedge \mathbb{I}V^{Post}(a') \geq \mathbb{I}'V^{Post}(a')$.*

Example 3. Consider again the component model in Fig. 4. The provided interface of `DailyAccount` is connected in a delegation with the provided interface of the `Account` component. The `Account` requires a daily limit from `DailyLimit` component, and they are composed in an assembly. In order to ensure that there are no information leaks the compositions need to satisfy the condition in Definition 9. The delegation of the provided interface trivially satisfies the condition since the interface specifications are the same. The assembly of the required and provided interface also satisfies the condition as the security level of the result is raised in the postcondition of the required interface which is allowed.

4.3 Soundness of Composition

To show soundness, we use the fact that our component model can be unpacked into a set of IFbC methods. We say that the compositions in a component model are sound (Theorem 1), if the unpacked methods satisfy the conditions of IFbC, since these conditions have been proven to satisfy non-interference [26]. Unpacking decomposes a top-level component to the set of methods derived from unpacking all atomic and composite sub-components. An atomic component generates a method with the signature of the provided interface method and a body from the IFbC implementation, and methods with the signature of the called methods from the required interface. Unpacking a composite component requires unpacking all sub-components and composition connectors. Composition connectors generate methods with appropriate signatures which calls the method which is either required or provided. Lemmas (1–4) assert the soundness of unpacking. We refer to appendix A for the proofs. We define an unpacking function as follows:

Definition 10 (Unpacking component model). *Unpacking is a function: Unpack: Component $\rightarrow$ Set(methods). We denote method declarations by $m < b >$ where m is the method signature and b is the method body. We refer to the method body of method m as $m.b$ and method name as $m.name$. The unpacking of each component construct is inductively defined as follows.*

- $\texttt{Unpack}(C_a) = \{I_p\} \cup \{I_r\} \cup \{m < m'.b > \mid m \in I_p, Impl(I_p.m) = m', m \preceq m'\}$
  where $C_a = \langle I_p, I_r, Impl \rangle$ is an atomic component.
- $\texttt{Unpack}(C) = \cup_{c \in SubC}\texttt{Unpack}(c) \cup_{i=1}^{n} \cup_{j=1}^{m} \texttt{UnpackAssembly}(Assembly_{i,j})$
  $\cup_{i=1}^{n} \texttt{UnpackDelProv}(DelegationProv_i)$
  $\cup_{i=1}^{n} \texttt{UnpackDelReq}(DelegationReq_i)$
  where $C = \langle I_p, I_r, SubC, Assembly_{i,j}, Delegation(Req/Prov)_i \rangle$ is a composite component with n delegations and $n \times m$ assembly connections.

With auxiliary functions $\texttt{UnpackAssembly}$, $\texttt{UnpackDelProv}$, $\texttt{UnpackDelReq}$ as follows:
- $\texttt{UnpackAssembly}(Assembly_{i,j}) = \{m < m'.name() > \mid m \in C_i.I_r, Assembly_{i,j}(C_i.I_r.m) = C_j.I_p.m', m \preceq m'\}$
- $\texttt{UnpackDelProv}(DelegationProv_i) = \{m < m'.name() > \mid m \in I_p, DelegationProv_i(I_p.m) = C_i.I_p.m', m \preceq m'\}$
- $\texttt{UnpackDelReq}(DelegationReq_i) = \{m < m'.name() > \mid m \in C_i.I_r, DelegationReq_i(C_i.I_r.m) = I_r.m', m \preceq m'\}$

Lemma 1 (Atomic component). *Let C_a be an atomic component. If the mapping from provided interface to IFbC implementation satisfies the condition Definition 8, then $\texttt{Unpack}(C_a)$ satisfies the IFbC rules.*

Lemma 2 (Assembly). *Let C be a composite component. If Assembly satisfies conditions of compatibility according to Definition 9, then $\texttt{UnpackAssembly}(Assembly_{i,j})$ satisfies the IFbC rules.*

Lemma 3 (Delegation provided interface). *Let C be a composite component. If $DelegatioProv_i$ satisfies the conditions for compatibility in Definition 9, then $\texttt{UnpackDelProv}(DelegationProv_i)$ satisfies the IFbC rules.*

Lemma 4 (Delegation required interface). *Let C be a composite component. If $DelegationReq_i$ satisfies the conditions for compatibility in Definition 9, then $\texttt{UnpackDelReq}(DelegationReq_i)$ satisfies the IFbC rules.*

Theorem 1 (Soundness). *If Component C is constructed according to the definitions presented in Sect. 3 and Sect. 4, then $\texttt{Unpack}(C)$ satisfies the IFbC rules.*

5 Tool Support

We developed the tool *ArchFlow* for developing secure component-based systems and envisioning their development process. Figure 5 shows the entire development process: ① A software architect creates a high-level design of the system with atomic and composite components and specifies their interfaces with interface specifications. ② Atomic components are mapped to a concrete implementations, and the compatibility between interfaces and implementations is checked. A developer can map the components to existing implementations, or construct a new implementation according to IFbC which is compatible with the interface. ③ The compatibility of composition of components is automatically checked in the design phase of the system. ④ Finally, Java code, which is free from information leaks, can be generated.

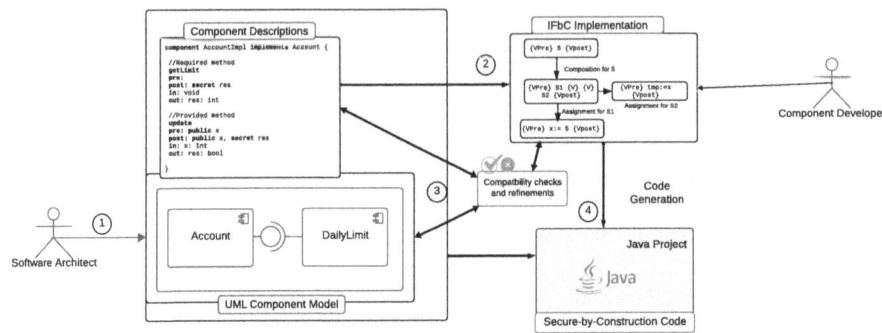

Fig. 5. ArchFlow development process overview

Information Flow Control By-Construction (CorC). Information flow control by-construction is supported by the tool $CorC^2$. CorC is implemented in Java as a plugin extension of Eclipse IDE. In this tool, developers can implement IFbC methods according to the approach described in Sect. 2. The development is supported by a graphical editor in which a program is represented in a refinement tree structure where every node represents a refinement. The refinements are automatically checked, and any information leaks will be detected early. Java code can be generated from the program represented in the graphical editor. CorC allows developing software which is functionally correct-by-construction, and therefore allows secure and functionally correct software development.

ArchFlow. Our open-source tool is realized as a JavaFX GUI application. The tool builds on top of CorC by adding a component view to the IFbC implementations. It includes a model view which can be used to model component-based systems. Component models can be stored and loaded as JSON-files. In the text view, component interfaces can be specified directly. Interfaces specifications can also be stored and loaded for easy reuse. We implemented a parser for the interfaces using the language framework ANTLR [25]. To guide developers any syntax errors detected by the parser when writing the interfaces will be displayed in the text area below. ArchFlow supports checking that composition of components satisfies the requirements described in Sect. 4.

In Fig. 6, we show a part of a model of the travel planner case study [3]. For the full case study we refer to the GitHub repository[3]. A user can book and pay for a trip via a travel planning app. The app uses services from an airline and travel agency to present different flight offers to the user. It is important that the user's credit card details required for the payment is only shared with the

---

[2] The source code for CorC: https://github.com/KIT-TVA/CorC.
[3] The source code for ArchFlow: https://github.com/KIT-TVA/ArchFlow.

airline responsible for processing the payment. To enforce this we use an information flow policy with three security levels: secret (S), private (H), and public (L). The information flow policy used by the system can be defined by the user. Only the user is allowed to see secret information, both a user and the airline can see private information, and everyone is allowed to view public information. A user's credit card information is marked private (H) in the specification of methods which use it, such that only the user and the airline can view it. The figure illustrates the component model view and component specification view of this system. The components are the user, the travel planner with the two sub-components (a travel request and the credit card details), and the composite component service containing the airline and travel agency atomic components. As an example, we show the specification of the app composite component on the right. Component specifications are written in the same style as introduced in Example 2. The specification declares the sub-components and assembly connections. The sub-components in the example are the user, travel planner and service. The assembly declarations show how the sub-components are composed. For instance, the travel planner requires a method `get_flight_offers` which is provided by the backend service. As flight offers are public information, the method specification marks the flight offers public (L). The specification also illustrates that component travel planner requires a method `book` from the backend service. In order to book a flight, the user needs to share credit card details, and the required booking method should therefore mark the credit card details as private (H) in the method specification. In case, the backend service had marked the credit card details as public information (L) in the provided method specification this error would be caught by the tool. In this case, the error would be that private information shared via method arguments would be treated as public information in another component. By clicking check composition button all the declared assemblies and corresponding method specifications are automatically checked in the tool. This is done by finding the specifications containing the required and provided interfaces for the components, and checking that the pre- and postconditions satisfies the conditions for assembly (Definition 9). By using the tool a user can identify confidentiality issues already in the design of the system and functionality implemented using CorC can easily be reused to build secure system.

6 Related Work

Secure Software Architecture Design. Incorporating confidentiality concerns into the architectural design of component-based software is not a new idea. Breu et al. [11] incorporated Role-based Access Control (RBAC) into object-oriented design using the Object Constraint Language (OCL). Their approach is extended further by Alam et al. [5] to also include security policies stated in XACML access control policies. Moebius et al. [24] introduced SecureMDD in which security properties are modeled in UML. From this UML model it is possible to generate executable Java Card code using model to text transformations. Palladio [17]

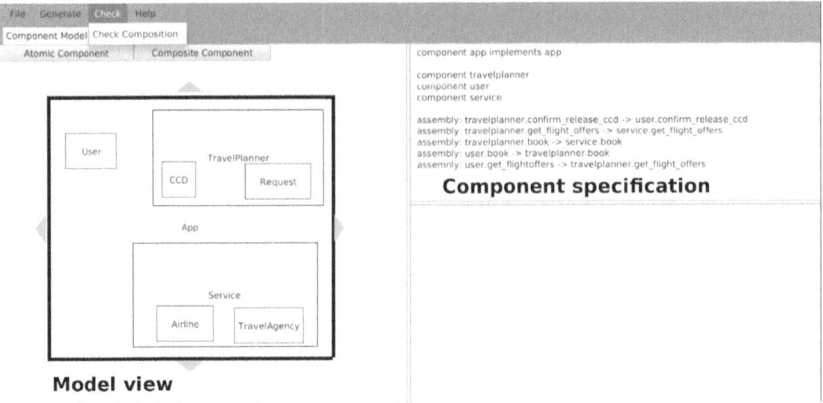

Fig. 6. ArchFlow Tool model view

includes confidentiality concerns in component diagrams by data flow analysis. A crucial difference to our work is that we use information flow policies and noninterference as the main underlying principle for confidentiality. Furthermore, our approach includes both specifications on the architectural level and refinement rules to realize the components contained in the architecture.

Information Flow Analysis and Verification. In the area of program analysis a common approach is to extract the data and control flow dependencies from the program into a program dependence graph (PDG) [4,10,18] which can then be analyzed for potential information leaks. Beckert et al. [9] formalized noninterference in dynamic logic and formally verified it using the KeY program verifier. In these approaches, the analysis and verification of a given information flow policy happens post-hoc meaning only after the program is constructed. In contrast, we propose a constructive method in which the specification is crafted first and the program and system is build such that it is guaranteed to fulfill the specification.

Another approach is MOAT [28], which verifies that there are no leaks even in the presence of an adversary capable of exploiting vulnerabilities at the OS and hardware level. In their approach Sinha et al. use a security type system [30] to secure the application level from information leaks.

Scaling Correctness-by-Construction. With ArchiCorC [21] Knüppel et al. scaled correctness-by-construction to component-based systems. Their approach is similar to this work, specifications are also written on the level of interfaces and they use a similar component model. However, unlike this work, ArchiCorC addresses functional correctness and not confidentiality.

7 Conclusion and Future Work

We have presented an extension of IFbC in which we scale it to component-based software architectures. This was achieved by enabling high-level modeling of systems with UML component models with explicit provided and required interfaces and composition with assembly or delegation connections. We have presented tool support for the approach, which supports developers and software architects in consctructing secure software. We have proven that any component model which can be constructed using our approach will be secure. For the future, we want to extend this work by considering two main lines of work; concurrency and quantification of security. The first line of work considers the construction of secure concurrent component-based systems, which would include asynchronous communication between components. This could be achieved by considering a concurrent object model such as ABS [19], and defining sound refinements for the programming constructs in the ABS language. The second line of future work concerns the relaxation of non-interference, since it is known to be a very strict requirement, which rejects many programs that we intuitively would consider secure. To this end, we wish to be able to construct programs based on a quantitative information flow policy [7], and thereby allow some amount of controlled information leakage.

Acknowledgments. This work was funded by the Topic Engineering Secure Systems of the Helmholtz Association (HGF) and supported by KASTEL Security Research Labs, Karlsruhe.

A Proofs

Lemma 1 (Atomic component). *Let C_a be an atomic component. If the mapping from provided interface to IFbC implementation satisfies the condition Definition 8 then $\text{Unpack}(C_a)$ satisfies the IFbC rules.*

Proof.

1. By assumption $Impl(I_p)$ satisfies the IFbC rules
2. By the condition for provided interface compatibility (cf. Definition 8) we have for the unpacking $m < m'.b >$ the two method signature m and m' satisfies IFbC method call rule.

□

Lemma 2 (Assembly). *Let C be a composite component. If Assembly satisfies conditions of compatibility according to Definition 9 then $\text{UnpackAssembly}(Assembly_{i,j})$ satisfies the IFbC rules.*

Proof. Let A and B be two arbitrary sub-components with $Assembly_{i,j}(A.I_r.m) = B.I_p m'$. Let M_a and M_b be two implementations $Impl(I_p.m') = m_a$ and $Impl(I_r.m) = m_b$ respectively. Let a be an arbitrary but fixed typed variable. We show that given that the components satisfy the interface compatibility conditions Definition 8 then by the condition for assembly composition Definition 9 the implementations m_a and m_b for the unpacked assembly $m_b < m_a.name() >$ satisfies the IFbC method call rule.

$$m_a V^{Pre}(a) \leq \mathbb{I}_r V^{Pre}(a) \wedge m_a V^{Post}(a) \geq \mathbb{I}_r V^{Post}(a) \qquad \text{[By def 8 and 9]}$$
$$\mathbb{I}_r V^{Pre}(a) \leq \mathbb{I}_p V^{Pre}(a) \wedge \mathbb{I}_r V^{Post}(a) \geq \mathbb{I}_p V^{Post}(a) \qquad \text{[By def 9]}$$
$$\mathbb{I}_p V^{Pre}(a) \leq m_b V^{Pre}(a) \wedge \mathbb{I}_p V^{Post}(a) \geq m_b V^{Post}(a) \qquad \text{[By def 8]}$$
$$m_a V^{Pre}(a) \leq m_b V^{Pre}(a) \wedge m_a V^{Post}(a) \geq m_b V^{Post}(a) \qquad \text{[By transitivity]}$$

As it is required by the method call rule. □

Lemma 3 (Delegation provided interface). *Let C be a composite component. If $DelegatioProv_i$ satisfies the conditions for compatibility in Definition 9 then* `UnpackDelProv`*($DelegationProv_i$) satisfies the IFbC rules.*

Proof. Let C be an arbitrary composite component with sub-component C_i and $DelegationProv_i(C.I_p.m) = C_i.I_p.m'$. Let a be an arbitrary but fixed typed variable. We show that for the unpacking $m < m'.name() > C.I_p$ satisfies compatibility with implementation of C_i according to Definition 8 and therefore by Lemma 1 satisfies the IFbC rules.

$$\mathbb{I}_p V^{Pre}(a) \leq \mathbb{I}_p^{C_i} V^{Pre}(a) \wedge \mathbb{I}_p V^{Post}(a) \geq \mathbb{I}_p^{C_i} V^{Post}(a) \qquad \text{[By def 9]}$$
$$\mathbb{I}_p^{C_i} V^{Pre}(a) \leq V^{Pre}(a) \wedge \mathbb{I}_p^{C_i} V^{Post}(a) \geq V^{Post}(a) \qquad \text{[By def 8]}$$
$$\mathbb{I}_p V^{Pre}(a) \leq V^{Pre}(a) \wedge \mathbb{I}_p V^{Post}(a) \geq V^{Post}(a) \qquad \text{[By transitivity]}$$

As it is required for provided interface compatibility (Definition 8). □

Lemma 4 (Delegation required interface). *Let C be a composite component. If $DelegationReq_i$ satisfies the conditions for compatibility in Definition 9 then* `UnpackDelReq`*($DelegationReq_i$) satisfies the IFbC rules.*

Proof. Let C be an arbitrary composite component with sub-component C_i and $DelegationReq_i(C_i.I_r.m) = C.I_r.m'$ Let a be an arbitrary but fixed typed variable. We show that for unpacking $m < m'.name() > C_i.I_r$ satisfies the compatibility of the implementation of $C.I_r$ according to Definition 8 and therefore by Lemma 1 satisfies the IFbC rules.

$$\mathbb{I}_r V^{Pre}(a) \geq \mathbb{I}_r^{C_i} V^{Pre}(a) \wedge \mathbb{I}_r V^{Post}(a') \leq \mathbb{I}_r^{C_i} V^{Post}(a) \qquad \text{[By def 9]}$$
$$\mathbb{I}_r^{C_i} V^{Pre}(a) \geq V^{Pre}(a) \wedge \mathbb{I}_r^{C_i} V^{Post}(a') \leq V^{Post}(a) \qquad \text{[By def 8 and 9]}$$
$$\mathbb{I}_r V^{Pre}(a) \geq V^{Pre}(a) \wedge \mathbb{I}_r V^{Post}(a') \leq V^{Post}(a) \qquad \text{[By transitivity]}$$

As it is required for required interface compatibility (Definition 8). □

Theorem 1 (Soundness). *If Component C is constructed according to the definitions presented in Sect. 3 and Sect. 4 then $\texttt{Unpack}(C)$ satisfies the IFbC rules.*

Proof. Let C be an arbitrary but fixed component and let $Sec(C)$ denote that the set of unpacked methods satisfies the conditions from Sect. 2. We prove by structural induction on the structure of the component model that unpacking will not break the information flow policy.
Base case: Consider the case where C is an atomic component, which can't be unpacked any further. $Sec(\texttt{Unpack}(C))$ follows directly from Lemma 1
Inductive hypothesis: For any sub-component $C_i \in SubC$ of component C $Sec(C_i)$ holds.
Inductive steps: Consider the case where C is a composite component. We show that the condition $Sec(\texttt{Unpack}(C))$ holds for $\texttt{Unpack}(C) = \cup_{c \in SubC} \texttt{Unpack}(c)$ $\cup_{i=1}^{n} \cup_{j=1}^{m}$ $\texttt{UnpackAssembly}(Assembly_{i,j})$ $\cup_{i=1}^{n}$ $\texttt{UnpackDelProv}(DelegationProv_i)$
$\cup_{i=1}^{n} \texttt{UnpackDelReq}(DelegationReq_i)$. By the inductive hypothesis unpacking any sub-component in $SubC$ is secure. We show that unpacking of $Assembly_{i,j}$ and $Delegation(Prov/Req)_i$ is secure.

Case 1 (Assembly). $Sec(\texttt{UnpackAssembly}(Assembly_{i,j}(C_i.I_r.m) = C_j.I_p.m'))$ follows from Lemma 2

Case 2 (Delegation provided). $Sec(\texttt{UnpackDelProv}(DelegationProv_i(C.I_p.m) = C_i.I_p.m'))$ follows from Lemma 3

Case 3 (Delegation required). $Sec(\texttt{UnpackDelReq}(DelegationReq_i(C_i.I_r.m) = C.I_r.m'))$ follows from Lemma 4

□

References

1. Facebook Trust. https://www.nbcnews.com/business/consumer/trust-facebook-has-dropped-51-percent-cambridge-analytica-scandal-n867011. Accessed 09 Sep 2024
2. Linkedin law suit. https://www.zdnet.com/article/linkedin-will-pay-1-25-million-to-settle-suit-over-password-breach/. Accessed 09 Sep 2024
3. Travel planner. https://kiv.isse.de/projects/iflow/TravelPlannerSite/index.html. Accessed 22 Jan 2025
4. Abadi, M., Banerjee, A., Heintze, N., Riecke, J.G.: A core calculus of dependency. In: Proceedings of the 26th ACM SIGPLAN-SIGACT Symposium on Principles of Programming Languages, pp. 147–160. POPL '99, Association for Computing Machinery, New York, NY, USA (1999). https://doi.org/10.1145/292540.292555, https://doi.org/10.1145/292540.292555
5. Alam, M., Breu, R., Breu, M.: Model driven security for web services (MDS4WS). In: 8th International Multitopic Conference, 2004. Proceedings of INMIC 2004, pp. 498–505 (2004). https://doi.org/10.1109/INMIC.2004.1492930
6. Alliance, O.: OSGI Service Platform, Release 3. IOS Press, NLD (2003)

7. Alvim, M., Chatzikokolakis, K., McIver, A., Morgan, C., Palamidessi, C., Smith, G.: The Science of Quantitative Information Flow. Springer (2020)
8. Assal, H., Chiasson, S.: Security in the software development lifecycle, pp. 281–296. SOUPS '18, USENIX Association, USA (2018)
9. Beckert, B., Bruns, D., Klebanov, V., Scheben, C., Schmitt, P.H., Ulbrich, M.: Information flow in object-oriented software. In: Gupta, G., Peña, R. (eds.) Logic-Based Program Synthesis and Transformation, pp. 19–37. Springer International Publishing, Cham (2014)
10. Bergeretti, J.F., Carré, B.A.: Information-flow and data-flow analysis of while-programs **7**(1), 37–61 (1985). https://doi.org/10.1145/2363.2366, https://doi.org/10.1145/2363.2366
11. Breu, R., Popp, G.: Actor-centric modeling of user rights. In: Wermelinger, M., Margaria-Steffen, T. (eds.) Fundamental Approaches to Software Engineering, pp. 165–179. Springer, Berlin Heidelberg, Berlin, Heidelberg (2004)
12. Denning, D.E.: A lattice model of secure information flow. Commun. ACM **19**(5), 236–243 (1976). https://doi.org/10.1145/360051.360056, https://doi.org/10.1145/360051.360056
13. Dijkstra, E.W.: Guarded commands, non determinacy and formal derivation of programs. Commun. ACM **18**(8), 453–457 (1975). https://doi.org/10.1145/360933.360975
14. Gerking, C., Schubert, D.: Component-based refinement and verification of information-flow security policies for cyber-physical microservice architectures. In: 2019 IEEE International Conference on Software Architecture (ICSA), pp. 61–70 (2019). https://doi.org/10.1109/ICSA.2019.00015
15. Goguen, J.A., Meseguer, J.: Security policies and security models. In: 1982 IEEE Symposium on Security and Privacy, pp. 11–11 (1982)
16. Haber, A., Ringert, J.O., Rumpe, B.: Montiarc - architectural modeling of interactive distributed and cyber-physical systems. CoRR (2014). http://arxiv.org/abs/1409.6578v1
17. Hahner, S., Bitschi, T., Walter, M., Bureš, T., Hnětynka, P., Heinrich, R.: Model-based confidentiality analysis under uncertainty. In: 2023 IEEE 20th International Conference on Software Architecture Companion (ICSA-C), pp. 256–263 (2023). https://doi.org/10.1109/ICSA-C57050.2023.00062
18. Hammer, C., Snelting, G.: Flow-sensitive, context-sensitive, and object-sensitive information flow control based on program dependence graphs. Int. J. Inf. Secur. **8**(6), 399–422 (2009). https://doi.org/10.1007/s10207-009-0086-1
19. Johnsen, E.B., Hähnle, R., Schäfer, J., Schlatte, R., Steffen, M.: ABS: a core language for abstract behavioral specification, pp. 142–164. Lecture Notes in Computer Science, Springer Berlin Heidelberg (2011). https://doi.org/10.1007/978-3-642-25271-6_8, http://dx.doi.org/10.1007/978-3-642-25271-6_8
20. Jürjens, J.: UMLsec: extending UML for secure systems development. In: Jézéquel, J.-M., Hussmann, H., Cook, S. (eds.) UML 2002. LNCS, vol. 2460, pp. 412–425. Springer, Heidelberg (2002). https://doi.org/10.1007/3-540-45800-X_32
21. Knüppel, A., Runge, T., Schaefer, I.: Scaling correctness-by-construction. In: Margaria, T., Steffen, B. (eds.) Leveraging Applications of Formal Methods, Verification and Validation: Verification Principles, pp. 187–207. Springer International Publishing, Cham (2020)
22. Kourie, D.G., Watson, B.W.: The Correctness-by-Construction Approach to Programming. Springer, Berlin, Heidelberg (2012). https://doi.org/10.1007/978-3-642-27919-5, http://link.springer.com/10.1007/978-3-642-27919-5

23. Lau, K.K., Tran, C.M.: X-man: An MDE tool for component-based system development. In: 2012 38th Euromicro Conference on Software Engineering and Advanced Applications, pp. 158–165 (2012). https://doi.org/10.1109/SEAA.2012.32
24. Moebius, N., Stenzel, K., Grandy, H., Reif, W.: SecureMDD: a model-driven development method for secure smart card applications. In: 2009 International Conference on Availability, Reliability and Security, pp. 841–846 (2009). https://doi.org/10.1109/ARES.2009.22
25. Parr, T.: The Definitive ANTLR 4 Reference. Pragmatic Bookshelf, 2nd edn. (2013)
26. Runge, T., Knüppel, A., Thüm, T., Schaefer, I.: Lattice-based information flow control-by-construction for security-by-design. In: Proceedings of the 8th International Conference on Formal Methods in Software Engineering, pp. 44–54. ACM (2020)
27. Runge, T., Servetto, M., Potanin, A., Schaefer, I.: Immutability and encapsulation for sound OO information flow control. ACM Trans. Prog. Lang. Syst. **45**(1), 3573270 (2022)
28. Sinha, R., Rajamani, S., Seshia, S., Vaswani, K.: Moat: verifying confidentiality of enclave programs. In: Proceedings of the 22nd ACM SIGSAC Conference on Computer and Communications Security, pp. 1169–1184. CCS '15, Association for Computing Machinery, New York, NY, USA (2015). https://doi.org/10.1145/2810103.2813608
29. Szyperski, C.: Component Software: Beyond Object-Oriented Programming, 2nd edn. Addison-Wesley Longman Publishing Co., Inc, USA (2002)
30. Volpano, D., Irvine, C., Smith, G.: A sound type system for secure flow analysis. J. Comput. Secur. **4**(2–3), 167–187 (1996)

Noninterference Analysis of Stochastically Timed Reversible Systems

Andrea Esposito, Alessandro Aldini, and Marco Bernardo[✉]

Dipartimento di Scienze Pure e Applicate, Università di Urbino, Urbino, Italy
marco.bernardo@uniurb.it

Abstract. Noninterference theory aims at ensuring the absence of covert channels among different security levels. As far as the verification of information-flow properties via equivalence checking is concerned, in nondeterministic and probabilistic settings weak bisimilarity has turned out to be adequate only for standard systems, while branching bisimilarity has proven to be appropriate for reversible systems too. In this paper we investigate noninterference for stochastically timed systems represented in the interactive Markov chain model of Hermanns. After recasting a selection of noninterference properties via Markovian variants of weak and branching bisimilarities, we study their preservation and compositionality aspects, build their taxonomy, and compare it with the nondeterministic and probabilistic taxonomies. We show the adequacy of our proposal through some examples about a database management system.

1 Introduction

The notion of noninterference was introduced in [34] to reason about the way in which illegitimate information flows can occur in multi-level security systems due to covert channels from high-level agents to low-level ones. Since the first definition, conceived for deterministic systems, there have been several extensions to more expressive domains, such as nondeterministic systems, systems in which quantitative aspects like time and probability play a central role, and reversible systems; see, e.g., [26, 2, 47, 37, 64, 59, 8, 5, 3, 41, 25, 24]. Likewise, different verification approaches have been proposed; see, e.g., [67, 30, 27, 48, 4].

Noninterference guarantees that low-level agents cannot infer from their observations what high-level ones are doing. Regardless of its specific definition, noninterference is closely tied to the notion of behavioral equivalence [32] because, given a multi-level security system, the idea is to compare the system behavior with high-level actions being prevented and the system behavior with the same actions being hidden. A natural framework in which to study system behavior is given by process algebra [49]. In this setting, weak bisimilarity has been employed in [26] to reason formally about covert channels and illegitimate information flows as well as to study a classification of noninterference properties for irreversible nondeterministic systems.

Noninterference analysis has been recently extended to reversible systems – featuring forward and backward computations – in the nondeterministic setting [25] and in the probabilistic one [24]. Reversibility has started to gain attention in computing since it has been shown that it may achieve lower levels of energy consumption [43, 9]. Its applications range from biochemical reaction modeling [56, 57] and parallel discrete-event simulation [53, 61] to robotics [46], wireless communications [62], fault-tolerant systems [21, 65, 44, 63], program debugging [29, 45], and distributed algorithms [66, 15].

As shown in [25, 24], noninterference properties based on weak bisimilarity are not adequate in a reversible context because they fail to detect information flows emerging when backward computations are triggered. A more appropriate semantics turns out to be branching bisimilarity [33] because it coincides with weak back-and-forth bisimilarity [22]. The latter behavioral equivalence requires systems to be able to mimic each other's behavior stepwise not only when performing actions in the standard forward direction, but also when undoing those actions in the backward direction. Formally, weak back-and-forth bisimilarity is defined over computation paths instead of states thus preserving not only causality but also history, as backward moves are constrained to take place along the same path followed in the forward direction even in the presence of concurrency.

In this paper we extend the approach of [25, 24] to a stochastically timed setting, so as to address noninterference properties in a framework featuring nondeterminism, time, and reversibility. To accomplish this we move to a model combining nondeterminism and stochastic time given by the interactive Markov chain model of [38], in which transitions are divided into action transitions, each labeled with an action, and rate transition, each labeled with a positive real number called rate that expresses an exponentially distributed delay. The reason for choosing this model in which time passing is orthogonal to action execution, instead of a model in which action execution and time passing are integrated [35, 39, 40, 19, 58, 14, 12, 10] (see [13] for encodings between integrated-time and orthogonal-time calculi), is that the former naturally supports the definition of behavioral equivalences abstracting from unobservable actions [38] – which are necessary for noninterference analysis – whereas this is not the case in the latter [11], which was employed in [3, 41] for stochastic variants of some noninterference properties.

Following [38] we build a process calculus featuring action prefix separated from rate prefix. As for behavioral equivalences, we adopt the weak Markovian bisimilarity of [38] and introduce a novel Markovian branching bisimilarity. By using these two equivalences we recast the noninterference properties of [26, 28] for irreversible systems and the noninterference properties of [25] for reversible systems, respectively, to study their preservation and compositionality aspects as well as to provide a taxonomy similar to those in [26, 25, 24]. Reversibility comes into play by extending one of the results of [22] to the interactive Markov chain model; we show that a Markovian variant of weak back-and-forth bisimilarity coincides with our Markovian branching bisimilarity.

This paper is organized as follows. In Sect. 2 we recall the interactive Markov chain model of [38] along with various definitions of strong and weak bisimilarities for it and a process calculus interpreted on it. In Sect. 3 we recast in our stochastically timed framework a selection of noninterference properties taken from [26, 28, 25]. In Sect. 4 we study their preservation and compositionality characteristics as well as their taxonomy, which in Sect. 5 we relate to the nondeterministic taxonomy of [25] and the probabilistic one of [24]. In Sect. 6 we establish a connection with reversibility by introducing a weak Markovian back-and-forth bisimilarity and proving that it coincides with Markovian branching bisimilarity. In Sect. 7 we present examples of obfuscation and permission mechanisms in database management systems to show the adequacy of our approach to information flows in reversible systems featuring nondeterminism and stochastic time. Finally, in Sect. 8 we provide some concluding remarks.

2 Background Definitions and Results

In this section we recall the interactive Markov chain model of [38] (Sect. 2.1) along with its strong and weak Markovian bisimilarities and define a novel Markovian branching bisimilarity (Sect. 2.2). Then we introduce a Markovian process language inspired by [38] (Sect. 2.3) through which we will express bisimulation-based information-flow security properties accounting for nondeterminism and stochastic time.

2.1 Markovian Labeled Transition Systems

To represent the behavior of a process featuring nondeterminism and stochastic time, we use a Markovian labeled transition system. This is a variant of a labeled transition system [42] where, according to the interactive Markov chain model of [38], transitions are labeled with actions or positive real numbers called rates expressing exponentially distributed delays. We assume that the action set $\mathcal{A}_\tau$ contains a set $\mathcal{A}$ of observable actions and a single action $\tau \notin \mathcal{A}$ representing unobservable actions.

Definition 1. *A* Markovian labeled transition system (MLTS) *is a triple* $(\mathcal{S}, \mathcal{A}_\tau, \longrightarrow)$ *where* $\mathcal{S}$ *is an at most countable set of states,* $\mathcal{A}_\tau = \mathcal{A} \cup \{\tau\}$ *is a countable set of actions, and* $\longrightarrow \,=\, \longrightarrow_a \cup \longrightarrow_r$ *is the transition relation, with* $\longrightarrow_a \,\subseteq\, \mathcal{S} \times \mathcal{A}_\tau \times \mathcal{S}$ *being the action transition relation whilst* $\longrightarrow_r \,\subseteq\, \mathcal{S} \times \mathbb{R}_{>0} \times \mathcal{S}$ *being the rate transition relation.* ∎

An action transition (s, a, s') is written $s \xrightarrow{a}_a s'$ while a rate transition (s, λ, s') is written $s \xrightarrow{\lambda}_r s'$, where s is the source state and s' is the target state. We say that s' is reachable from s, written $s' \in reach(s)$, iff $s' = s$ or there exists a sequence of finitely many transitions such that the target state of each of them coincides with the source state of the subsequent one, with the source of the first one being s and the target of the last one being s'.

The label of a rate transition is the inverse of the average duration of the corresponding exponentially distributed delay, which enjoys the *memoryless property*: the residual duration after the execution starts is still exponentially distributed with the same rate. If the outgoing rate transitions of state s are $s \xrightarrow{\lambda_i}_r s_i$ for $1 \leq i \leq n$, then the *race policy* applies. This means that the average sojourn time in s is given by the minimum of the n exponentially distributed delays –

which is exponentially distributed with rate $\sum_{1 \leq i \leq n} \lambda_i$ – and the execution probability of transition j is given by $\lambda_j / \sum_{1 \leq i \leq n} \lambda_i$. As for the interplay between action transitions and rate transitions, like in [38] we assume *maximal progress*, i.e., τ-transitions take precedence over rate transitions.

2.2 Bisimulation Equivalences

Bisimilarity [52,49] identifies processes that are able to mimic each other's behavior stepwise, i.e., having the same branching structure. In the interactive Markov chain model, this extends to stochastic behavior [38]. Let $rate(s, C) = \sum_{s \xrightarrow{\lambda}_r s', s' \in C} \lambda$ be the cumulative rate with which state s reaches a state in C. Due to maximal progress, cumulative rates are compared only in states with no outgoing τ-transitions, denoted $\xrightarrow{\tau}\!\!\!\!\!/_a$.

Definition 2. *Let $(\mathcal{S}, \mathcal{A}_\tau, \longrightarrow)$ be an MLTS. We say that $s_1, s_2 \in \mathcal{S}$ are strongly Markovian bisimilar, written $s_1 \sim_m s_2$, iff $(s_1, s_2) \in \mathcal{B}$ for some strong Markovian bisimulation $\mathcal{B}$. An equivalence relation $\mathcal{B}$ over $\mathcal{S}$ is a strong Markovian bisimulation iff, whenever $(s_1, s_2) \in \mathcal{B}$, then:*

- *For each $s_1 \xrightarrow{a}_a s_1'$ there exists $s_2 \xrightarrow{a}_a s_2'$ such that $(s_1', s_2') \in \mathcal{B}$.*
- *If $s_1 \xrightarrow{\tau}\!\!\!\!\!/_a$ then $rate(s_1, C) = rate(s_2, C)$ for all equivalence classes C in the quotient set $\mathcal{S}/\mathcal{B}$.* ∎

Weak bisimilarity [49] is additionally capable of abstracting from unobservable actions. Let $s \xRightarrow{\tau^*}_a s'$ mean that $s' \in reach(s)$ and, when $s' \neq s$, there exists a finite sequence of transitions from s to s' each of which is labeled with τ. Moreover let $\xRightarrow{\hat{a}}_a$ stand for $\xRightarrow{\tau^*}_a$ if $a = \tau$ or $\xRightarrow{\tau^*}_a \xrightarrow{a}_a \xRightarrow{\tau^*}_a$ if $a \neq \tau$. The Markovian adaptation below is taken from [38].

Definition 3. *Let $(\mathcal{S}, \mathcal{A}_\tau, \longrightarrow)$ be an MLTS. We say that $s_1, s_2 \in \mathcal{S}$ are weakly Markovian bisimilar, written $s_1 \approx_{mw} s_2$, iff $(s_1, s_2) \in \mathcal{B}$ for some weak Markovian bisimulation $\mathcal{B}$. An equivalence relation $\mathcal{B}$ over $\mathcal{S}$ is a weak Markovian bisimulation iff, whenever $(s_1, s_2) \in \mathcal{B}$, then:*

- *For each $s_1 \xrightarrow{a}_a s_1'$ there exists $s_2 \xRightarrow{\hat{a}}_a s_2'$ such that $(s_1', s_2') \in \mathcal{B}$.*
- *If $s_1 \xrightarrow{\tau}\!\!\!\!\!/_a$ then there exists $s_2 \xRightarrow{\tau^*}_a \bar{s}_2$ such that $\bar{s}_2 \xrightarrow{\tau}\!\!\!\!\!/_a$, $(s_1, \bar{s}_2) \in \mathcal{B}$, and $rate(s_1, C) = rate(\bar{s}_2, C)$ for all equivalence classes $C \in \mathcal{S}/\mathcal{B}$.* ∎

Branching bisimilarity [33] is finer than weak bisimilarity as it preserves the branching structure of processes even when abstracting from τ-actions – see condition $(s_1, \bar{s}_2) \in \mathcal{B}$ in the action transitions matching of the definition below. We adapt it to the Markovian setting as follows.

Definition 4. *Let $(\mathcal{S}, \mathcal{A}_\tau, \longrightarrow)$ be an MLTS. We say that $s_1, s_2 \in \mathcal{S}$ are Markovian branching bisimilar, written $s_1 \approx_{mb} s_2$, iff $(s_1, s_2) \in \mathcal{B}$ for some Markovian branching bisimulation $\mathcal{B}$. An equivalence relation $\mathcal{B}$ over $\mathcal{S}$ is a Markovian branching bisimulation iff, whenever $(s_1, s_2) \in \mathcal{B}$, then:*

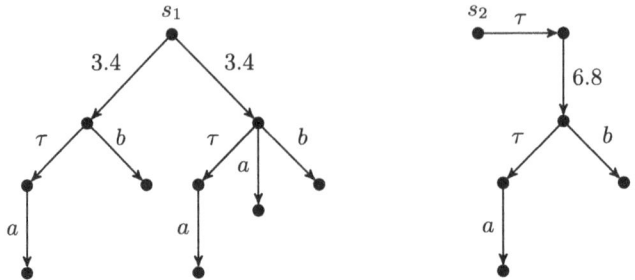

Fig. 1. States s_1 and s_2 are related by $\approx_{\mathrm{mw}}$ but distinguished by $\approx_{\mathrm{mb}}$

- For each $s_1 \xrightarrow{a}_a s'_1$:
  - either $a = \tau$ and $(s'_1, s_2) \in \mathcal{B}$;
  - or there exists $s_2 \xRightarrow{\tau^*}_a \bar{s}_2 \xrightarrow{a}_a s'_2$ such that $(s_1, \bar{s}_2) \in \mathcal{B}$ and $(s'_1, s'_2) \in \mathcal{B}$.
- If $s_1 \not\xrightarrow{\tau}_a$ then there exists $s_2 \xRightarrow{\tau^*}_a \bar{s}_2$ such that $\bar{s}_2 \not\xrightarrow{\tau}_a$, $(s_1, \bar{s}_2) \in \mathcal{B}$, and $rate(s_1, C) = rate(\bar{s}_2, C)$ for all equivalence classes $C \in \mathcal{S}/\mathcal{B}$. ∎

In [38] it is argued that the weak bisimilarity of Definition 3 is already very close to branching bisimilarity, because maximal progress forces a check given by condition $(s_1, \bar{s}_2) \in \mathcal{B}$ on the branching structure of the considered processes. We show that our novel Definition 4, which sticks to the original one of [33], is more discriminating. Consider Fig. 1, where every MLTS is depicted as a directed graph in which vertices represent states and action- or rate-labeled edges represent transitions. The initial states s_1 and s_2 of the two MLTSs are weakly Markovian bisimilar but not Markovian branching bisimilar. On the one hand, each of the two states reachable from s_1 with rate 3.4 and the state reachable from s_2 with rate 6.8 after a τ-transition are all weakly Markovian bisimilar and hence the cumulative rate to reach them is the same from both initial states. On the other hand, the two states reachable from s_1 are not Markovian branching bisimilar, because if the one on the right performs a then the one on the left cannot respond by performing τ followed by a because the state reached after τ no longer enables b. Thus, with respect to Markovian branching bisimilarity, s_1 reaches with rate 3.4 two different equivalence classes, while s_2 reaches with rate 6.8 only one of them.

2.3 A Markovian Process Calculus with High and Low Actions

We now introduce a Markovian process calculus to formalize the security properties of interest. To address two security levels, we partition the set $\mathcal{A}$ of observable actions into $\mathcal{A}_\mathcal{H} \cup \mathcal{A}_\mathcal{L}$, with $\mathcal{A}_\mathcal{H} \cap \mathcal{A}_\mathcal{L} = \emptyset$, where $\mathcal{A}_\mathcal{H}$ is the set of high-level actions, ranged over by h, and $\mathcal{A}_\mathcal{L}$ is the set of low-level actions, ranged over by l. Note that $\tau \notin \mathcal{A}_\mathcal{H} \cup \mathcal{A}_\mathcal{L}$.

Table 1. Operational semantic rules for action transitions

Prefix		$a.P \xrightarrow{a}_a P$
Choice	$\dfrac{P_1 \xrightarrow{a}_a P_1'}{P_1 + P_2 \xrightarrow{a}_a P_1'}$	$\dfrac{P_2 \xrightarrow{a}_a P_2'}{P_1 + P_2 \xrightarrow{a}_a P_2'}$
Parallel	$\dfrac{P_1 \xrightarrow{a}_a P_1' \quad a \notin L}{P_1 \parallel_L P_2 \xrightarrow{a}_a P_1' \parallel_L P_2}$	$\dfrac{P_2 \xrightarrow{a}_a P_2' \quad a \notin L}{P_1 \parallel_L P_2 \xrightarrow{a}_a P_1 \parallel_L P_2'}$
Synch	$\dfrac{P_1 \xrightarrow{a}_a P_1' \quad P_2 \xrightarrow{a}_a P_2' \quad a \in L}{P_1 \parallel_L P_2 \xrightarrow{a}_a P_1' \parallel_L P_2'}$	
Restriction	$\dfrac{P \xrightarrow{a}_a P' \quad a \notin L}{P \setminus L \xrightarrow{a}_a P' \setminus L}$	
Hiding	$\dfrac{P \xrightarrow{a}_a P' \quad a \in L}{P / L \xrightarrow{\tau}_a P' / L}$	$\dfrac{P \xrightarrow{a}_a P' \quad a \notin L}{P / L \xrightarrow{a}_a P' / L}$

The set $\mathbb{P}$ of process terms is obtained by considering typical operators from CCS [49] and CSP [18] together with rate prefix from [38]. In addition to prefix, choice, and parallel composition – which is taken from CSP so as not to hide synchronizations among high-level actions by turning them into τ as would happen with the CCS parallel composition – we include restriction and hiding as they are necessary to formalize noninterference properties. The syntax for $\mathbb{P}$ is:

$$P ::= \underline{0} \mid a.P \mid (\lambda).P \mid P + P \mid P \parallel_L P \mid P \setminus L \mid P / L$$

where:

- $\underline{0}$ is the terminated process.
- $a.\_$, for $a \in \mathcal{A}_\tau$, is the action prefix operator describing a process that can initially perform action a.
- $(\lambda).\_$, for $\lambda \in \mathbb{R}_{>0}$, is the rate prefix operator describing a process that can initially let an exponentially distributed delay pass with average duration $1/\lambda$.
- $\_ + \_$ is the alternative composition operator expressing a choice between two processes, which is nondeterministic in case of actions, probabilistic in case of rates according to the race policy, or subject to maximal progress otherwise.
- $\_ \parallel_L \_$, for $L \subseteq \mathcal{A}$, is the parallel composition operator allowing two processes to proceed independently on any action not in L as well as on rates thanks to the memoryless property of exponential distributions [38] and forcing them to synchronize on every action in L.
- $\_ \setminus L$, for $L \subseteq \mathcal{A}$, is the restriction operator, which prevents the execution of all actions belonging to L.
- $\_ / L$, for $L \subseteq \mathcal{A}$, is the hiding operator, which turns all the executed actions belonging to L into the unobservable action τ.

Table 2. Operational semantic rules for rate transitions

$RatePrefix$	$(\lambda).P \xrightarrow{\lambda}_{r} P$
$RateChoice$	$\dfrac{P_1 \xrightarrow{\lambda}_{r} P_1'}{P_1 + P_2 \xrightarrow{\lambda}_{r} P_1'} \qquad \dfrac{P_2 \xrightarrow{\lambda}_{r} P_2'}{P_1 + P_2 \xrightarrow{\lambda}_{r} P_2'}$
$RateParallel$	$\dfrac{P_1 \xrightarrow{\lambda}_{r} P_1'}{P_1 \parallel_L P_2 \xrightarrow{\lambda}_{r} P_1' \parallel_L P_2} \qquad \dfrac{P_2 \xrightarrow{\lambda}_{r} P_2'}{P_1 \parallel_L P_2 \xrightarrow{\lambda}_{r} P_1 \parallel_L P_2'}$
$RateRestriction$	$\dfrac{P \xrightarrow{\lambda}_{r} P'}{P \setminus L \xrightarrow{\lambda}_{r} P' \setminus L}$
$RateHiding$	$\dfrac{P \xrightarrow{\lambda}_{r} P'}{P / L \xrightarrow{\lambda}_{r} P' / L}$

The operational semantic rules for the process language are shown in Tables 1 and 2 for action and rate transitions respectively. Together they produce the MLTS $(\mathbb{P}, \mathcal{A}_\tau, \longrightarrow)$ where $\longrightarrow \;=\; \longrightarrow_a \cup \longrightarrow_r$, to which the bisimulation equivalences defined in Sect. 2.2 are applicable. While $\longrightarrow_a \;\subseteq\; \mathbb{P} \times \mathcal{A}_\tau \times \mathbb{P}$ is a relation, $\longrightarrow_r \;\subseteq\; \mathbb{P} \times \mathbb{R}_{>0} \times \mathbb{P}$ is deemed to be a multirelation [38]; e.g., from $(\lambda_1).P + (\lambda_2).P$ there must be two rate transitions to P even when $\lambda_1 = \lambda_2$ otherwise the average sojourn time in the source process would be altered.

3 Markovian Information-Flow Security Properties

In this section we recast the definitions of noninteference properties of [26, 28, 25] – *Nondeterministic Non-Interference* (NNI) and *Non-Deducibility on Composition* (NDC) – by taking as behavioral equivalence the weak or branching bisimilarity of Sect. 2.2. The intuition behind noninterference in a two-level security system is that, if a group of agents at the high level performs some actions, the effect of those actions should not be seen by any agent at the low level. To formalize this, the restriction and hiding operators play a central role.

Definition 5. *Let $P \in \mathbb{P}$ and $\approx \;\in\; \{\approx_{\mathrm{mw}}, \approx_{\mathrm{mb}}\}$:*

– $P \in \mathrm{BSNNI}_\approx \iff P \setminus \mathcal{A}_\mathcal{H} \approx P / \mathcal{A}_\mathcal{H}$.
– $P \in \mathrm{BNDC}_\approx \iff$ *for all $Q \in \mathbb{P}$ such that each of its prefixes belongs to $\mathcal{A}_\mathcal{H}$ and for all $L \subseteq \mathcal{A}_\mathcal{H}$, $P \setminus \mathcal{A}_\mathcal{H} \approx ((P \parallel_L Q) / L) \setminus \mathcal{A}_\mathcal{H}$.*
– $P \in \mathrm{SBSNNI}_\approx \iff$ *for all $P' \in \mathit{reach}(P)$, $P' \in \mathrm{BSNNI}_\approx$.*
– $P \in \mathrm{P\_BNDC}_\approx \iff$ *for all $P' \in \mathit{reach}(P)$, $P' \in \mathrm{BNDC}_\approx$.*
– $P \in \mathrm{SBNDC}_\approx \iff$ *for all $P', P'' \in \mathit{reach}(P)$ such that $P' \xrightarrow{h}_a P''$, $P' \setminus \mathcal{A}_\mathcal{H} \approx P'' \setminus \mathcal{A}_\mathcal{H}$.* ∎

Bisimulation-based Strong Nondeterministic Non-Interference (BSNNI) has been one of the first and most intuitive proposals. Basically, it is satisfied by any process P that behaves the same when its high-level actions are prevented (as modeled by $P \setminus \mathcal{A}_\mathcal{H}$) or when they are considered as hidden, unobservable actions (as modeled by $P / \mathcal{A}_\mathcal{H}$). The equivalence between these two low-level views of P states that a low-level agent cannot deduce the high-level behavior of the system. For instance, in our Markovian setting, a low-level agent that observes the execution of l in $P = l.(2 \cdot \lambda).\underline{0} + l.((\lambda).h.l_1.\underline{0} + (\lambda).h.l_2.\underline{0}) + l.((\lambda).l_1.\underline{0} + (\lambda).l_2.\underline{0})$ cannot infer anything about the execution of h. Indeed, after the execution of l, what the low-level agent observes is either a terminal state, reached with rate $2 \cdot \lambda$, or the execution of either l_1 or l_2, both with rate λ. Formally, $P \setminus \{h\} \approx P / \{h\}$ because $l.(2 \cdot \lambda).\underline{0} + l.((\lambda).\underline{0} + (\lambda).\underline{0}) + l.((\lambda).l_1.\underline{0} + (\lambda).l_2.\underline{0}) \approx l.(2 \cdot \lambda).\underline{0} + l.((\lambda).\tau.l_1.\underline{0} + (\lambda).\tau.l_2.\underline{0}) + l.((\lambda).l_1.\underline{0} + (\lambda).l_2.\underline{0})$, hence P is BSNNI$_\approx$.

BSNNI$_\approx$ is not powerful enough to capture covert channels that derive from the behavior of a high-level agent interacting with the system. For instance, $l.(2 \cdot \lambda).\underline{0} + l.((\lambda).h_1.l_1.\underline{0} + (\lambda).h_2.l_2.\underline{0}) + l.((\lambda).l_1.\underline{0} + (\lambda).l_2.\underline{0})$ is BSNNI$_\approx$ for the same reason discussed above. However, a high-level agent could decide to enable only h_1, thus yielding the low-level view of the system $l.(2 \cdot \lambda).\underline{0} + l.((\lambda).\tau.l_1.\underline{0} + (\lambda).\underline{0}) + l.((\lambda).l_1.\underline{0} + (\lambda).l_2.\underline{0})$, which is clearly distinguishable from $l.(2 \cdot \lambda).\underline{0} + l.((\lambda).\underline{0} + (\lambda).\underline{0}) + l.((\lambda).l_1.\underline{0} + (\lambda).l_2.\underline{0})$, as in the former there is a case in which the low-level agent can observe l_1 but not l_2 after the execution of l. To avoid such a limitation, the most obvious solution consists of checking explicitly the interaction on any action set $L \subseteq \mathcal{A}_\mathcal{H}$ between the system and every possible high-level agent Q. The resulting property is the *Bisimulation-based Non-Deducibility on Composition* (BNDC), which features a universal quantification over Q containing only high-level actions.

Note that in this Markovian setting the high-level agent Q cannot exhibit any rate prefix by definition, otherwise no process would satisfy the BNDC property. To see why, consider the trivially safe process $l.\underline{0}$ and the high-level agent $(\lambda).h.\underline{0}$. The processes $(l.\underline{0}) \setminus \mathcal{A}_\mathcal{H}$ and $((l.\underline{0} \|_L (\lambda).h.\underline{0}) / L) \setminus \mathcal{A}_\mathcal{H}$ are not equivalent, regardless of the specific $L \subseteq \mathcal{A}_\mathcal{H}$, because the former can only perform the low-level action l while the latter can also let time pass before or after the execution of l.

To overcome the verification problems related to the quantification over Q, several properties stronger than BNDC have been proposed. They all express some persistency conditions, stating that the security checks have to be extended to all the processes reachable from a secure one. Three of the most representative ones among such properties are the variant of BSNNI that requires every reachable process to satisfy BSNNI itself, called *Strong* BSNNI (SBSNNI), the variant of BNDC that requires every reachable process to satisfy BNDC itself, called *Persistent* BNDC (P_BNDC), and *Strong* BNDC (SBNDC), which requires the low-level view of every reachable process to be the same before and after the execution of any high-level action, meaning that the execution of high-level actions must be completely transparent to low-level agents. In the nondeterministic and probabilistic settings, P_BNDC and SBSNNI have been proven to coincide in the case of both weak bisimilarity and branching bisimilarity [28, 25, 24].

4 Characteristics of Markovian Security Properties

In this section we investigate preservation and compositionality characteristics of the noninterference properties introduced in the previous section (Sect. 4.1) as well as the inclusion relationships between the ones based on $\approx_{\mathrm{mw}}$ and the ones based on $\approx_{\mathrm{mb}}$ (Sect. 4.2).

4.1 Preservation and Compositionality

All the Markovian noninterference properties of Definition 5 turn out to be preserved by the bisimilarity employed in their definition. This means that if a process P_1 is secure under any of such properties, then every other equivalent process P_2 is secure too according to the same property. This is very useful for automated property verification, as it allows us to work with the process with the smallest state space among the equivalent ones.

The preservation result of Theorem 1 immediately follows from Lemma 1 below, which ensures that $\approx_{\mathrm{mw}}$ and $\approx_{\mathrm{mb}}$ are congruences with respect to all the operators occurring in the aforementioned noninterference properties. Congruence with respect to action and rate prefixes is also addressed as it will be exploited in the proof of the compositionality result of Theorem 2. Some of the following congruence properties for $\approx_{\mathrm{mw}}$ are already known from [38].

Lemma 1. *Let* $P_1, P_2 \in \mathbb{P}$ *and* $\approx \in \{\approx_{\mathrm{mw}}, \approx_{\mathrm{mb}}\}$. *If* $P_1 \approx P_2$ *then:*

1. $a . P_1 \approx a . P_2$ *for all* $a \in \mathcal{A}_\tau$.
2. $(\lambda) . P_1 \approx (\lambda) . P_2$ *for all* $\lambda \in \mathbb{R}_{>0}$.
3. $P_1 \|_L P \approx P_2 \|_L P$ *and* $P \|_L P_1 \approx P \|_L P_2$ *for all* $L \subseteq \mathcal{A}$ *and* $P \in \mathbb{P}$.
4. $P_1 \setminus L \approx P_2 \setminus L$ *for all* $L \subseteq \mathcal{A}$.
5. $P_1 / L \approx P_2 / L$ *for all* $L \subseteq \mathcal{A}$. ■

Theorem 1. *Let* $P_1, P_2 \in \mathbb{P}$, $\approx \in \{\approx_{\mathrm{mw}}, \approx_{\mathrm{mb}}\}$, *and* $\mathcal{P} \in \{\mathrm{BSNNI}_{\approx}, \mathrm{BNDC}_{\approx}, \mathrm{SBSNNI}_{\approx}, \mathrm{P\_BNDC}_{\approx}, \mathrm{SBNDC}_{\approx}\}$. *If* $P_1 \approx P_2$ *then* $P_1 \in \mathcal{P} \iff P_2 \in \mathcal{P}$. ■

As far as modular verification is concerned, like in the nondeterministic and probabilistic settings [26,25,24] only the local properties $\mathrm{SBSNNI}_{\approx}$, $\mathrm{P\_BNDC}_{\approx}$, and $\mathrm{SBNDC}_{\approx}$ are compositional, i.e., are preserved by some operators of the calculus in certain circumstances. Moreover, similar to [25,24], compositionality with respect to parallel composition is limited, for $\mathrm{SBSNNI}_{\approx_{\mathrm{mb}}}$ and $\mathrm{P\_BNDC}_{\approx_{\mathrm{mb}}}$, to the case in which synchronizations can take place only among low-level actions, i.e., $L \subseteq \mathcal{A}_\mathcal{L}$. A limitation to low-level actions applies to action prefix and hiding as well, whilst this is not the case for restriction. Another analogy with the nondeterministic and probabilistic settings [26,25,24] is that none of the considered noninterference properties is compositional with respect to alternative composition. As an example, let us examine processes $P_1 = l . \underline{0}$ and $P_2 = h . \underline{0}$. Both processes are $\mathrm{BSNNI}_{\approx}$, as $(l . \underline{0}) \setminus \{h\} \approx (l . \underline{0}) / \{h\}$ and $(h . \underline{0}) \setminus \{h\} \approx (h . \underline{0}) / \{h\}$, but $P_1 + P_2 \notin \mathrm{BSNNI}_{\approx}$, because $(l . \underline{0} + h . \underline{0}) \setminus \{h\} \approx l . \underline{0} \not\approx l . \underline{0} + \tau . \underline{0} \approx (l . \underline{0} + h . \underline{0}) / \{h\}$. It is easy to check that $P_1 + P_2 \notin \mathcal{P}$ also for $\mathcal{P} \in \{\mathrm{BNDC}_{\approx}, \mathrm{SBSNNI}_{\approx}, \mathrm{SBNDC}_{\approx}\}$.

Theorem 2. Let $P, P_1, P_2 \in \mathbb{P}$, $\approx \in \{\approx_{\mathrm{mw}}, \approx_{\mathrm{mb}}\}$, $\mathcal{P} \in \{\mathrm{SBSNNI}_\approx, \mathrm{P\_BNDC}_\approx, \mathrm{SBNDC}_\approx\}$. Then:

1. $P \in \mathcal{P} \Longrightarrow a \,.\, P \in \mathcal{P}$ for all $a \in \mathcal{A}_\mathcal{L} \cup \{\tau\}$.
2. $P \in \mathcal{P} \Longrightarrow (\lambda) \,.\, P \in \mathcal{P}$ for all $\lambda \in \mathbb{R}_{>0}$.
3. $P_1, P_2 \in \mathcal{P} \Longrightarrow P_1 \parallel_L P_2 \in \mathcal{P}$ for $L \subseteq \mathcal{A}_\mathcal{L}$ if $\mathcal{P} \in \{\mathrm{SBSNNI}_{\approx_{\mathrm{mb}}}, \mathrm{P\_BNDC}_{\approx_{\mathrm{mb}}}\}$ or for $L \subseteq \mathcal{A}$ if $\mathcal{P} \in \{\mathrm{SBSNNI}_{\approx_{\mathrm{mw}}}, \mathrm{P\_BNDC}_{\approx_{\mathrm{mw}}}, \mathrm{SBNDC}_{\approx_{\mathrm{mw}}}, \mathrm{SBNDC}_{\approx_{\mathrm{mb}}}\}$.
4. $P \in \mathcal{P} \Longrightarrow P \setminus L \in \mathcal{P}$ for all $L \subseteq \mathcal{A}$.
5. $P \in \mathcal{P} \Longrightarrow P\,/\,L \in \mathcal{P}$ for all $L \subseteq \mathcal{A}_\mathcal{L}$. ∎

4.2 Taxonomy of Security Properties

First of all, similar to the nondeterministic and probabilistic settings [26, 25, 24] the properties in Definition 5 turn out to be increasingly finer. This result holds for both those based on $\approx_{\mathrm{mw}}$ and those based on $\approx_{\mathrm{mb}}$.

Theorem 3. Let $\approx \in \{\approx_{\mathrm{mw}}, \approx_{\mathrm{mb}}\}$. Then:

$$\mathrm{SBNDC}_\approx \subsetneq \mathrm{SBSNNI}_\approx = \mathrm{P\_BNDC}_\approx \subsetneq \mathrm{BNDC}_\approx \subsetneq \mathrm{BSNNI}_\approx$$

∎

Secondly, we observe that all the $\approx_{\mathrm{mb}}$-based noninterference properties imply the corresponding $\approx_{\mathrm{mw}}$-based ones, due to the fact that $\approx_{\mathrm{mb}}$ is finer than $\approx_{\mathrm{mw}}$.

Theorem 4. The following inclusions hold:

1. $\mathrm{BSNNI}_{\approx_{\mathrm{mb}}} \subsetneq \mathrm{BSNNI}_{\approx_{\mathrm{mw}}}$.
2. $\mathrm{BNDC}_{\approx_{\mathrm{mb}}} \subsetneq \mathrm{BNDC}_{\approx_{\mathrm{mw}}}$.
3. $\mathrm{SBSNNI}_{\approx_{\mathrm{mb}}} \subsetneq \mathrm{SBSNNI}_{\approx_{\mathrm{mw}}}$.
4. $\mathrm{P\_BNDC}_{\approx_{\mathrm{mb}}} \subsetneq \mathrm{P\_BNDC}_{\approx_{\mathrm{mw}}}$.
5. $\mathrm{SBNDC}_{\approx_{\mathrm{mb}}} \subsetneq \mathrm{SBNDC}_{\approx_{\mathrm{mw}}}$. ∎

All the inclusions above are strict by virtue of the following result; for an example of P_1 and P_2 below, see Fig. 1.

Theorem 5. Let $P_1, P_2 \in \mathbb{P}$ be such that $P_1 \approx_{\mathrm{mw}} P_2$ but $P_1 \not\approx_{\mathrm{mb}} P_2$. If no high-level actions occur in P_1 and P_2, then $Q \in \{P_1 + h \,.\, P_2, P_2 + h \,.\, P_1\}$ is such that:

1. $Q \in \mathrm{BSNNI}_{\approx_{\mathrm{mw}}}$ but $Q \notin \mathrm{BSNNI}_{\approx_{\mathrm{mb}}}$.
2. $Q \in \mathrm{BNDC}_{\approx_{\mathrm{mw}}}$ but $Q \notin \mathrm{BNDC}_{\approx_{\mathrm{mb}}}$.
3. $Q \in \mathrm{SBSNNI}_{\approx_{\mathrm{mw}}}$ but $Q \notin \mathrm{SBSNNI}_{\approx_{\mathrm{mb}}}$.
4. $Q \in \mathrm{P\_BNDC}_{\approx_{\mathrm{mw}}}$ but $Q \notin \mathrm{P\_BNDC}_{\approx_{\mathrm{mb}}}$.
5. $Q \in \mathrm{SBNDC}_{\approx_{\mathrm{mw}}}$ but $Q \notin \mathrm{SBNDC}_{\approx_{\mathrm{mb}}}$. ∎

The diagram in Fig. 2 summarizes the inclusions among the various noninterference properties based on the results in Theorems 3 and 4, where $\mathcal{P} \to \mathcal{Q}$ means that $\mathcal{P}$ is strictly included in $\mathcal{Q}$. These inclusions follow the same pattern as the nondeterministic and probabilistic settings [25, 24].

The arrows missing in the diagram, witnessing incomparability, are justified by the following counterexamples:

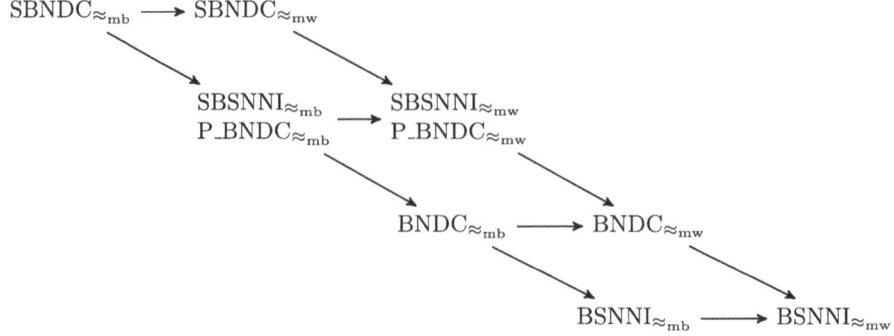

Fig. 2. Taxonomy of security properties based on Markovian bisimilarities

- $\text{SBNDC}_{\approx_{mw}}$ vs. $\text{SBSNNI}_{\approx_{mb}}$. The process $\tau.l.\underline{0}+l.l.\underline{0}+h.l.\underline{0}$ is $\text{BSNNI}_{\approx_{mb}}$ as $(\tau.l.\underline{0}+l.l.\underline{0}+h.l.\underline{0}) \setminus \{h\} \approx_{mb} \tau.l.\underline{0}+l.l.\underline{0} \approx_{mb} \tau.l.\underline{0}+l.l.\underline{0}+\tau.l.\underline{0} \approx_{mb} (\tau.l.\underline{0}+l.l.\underline{0}+h.l.\underline{0})/\{h\}$. It is also $\text{SBSNNI}_{\approx_{mb}}$ because every reachable process does not enable further high-level actions. However, it is not $\text{SBNDC}_{\approx_{mw}}$ because after executing the high-level action h it can perform a single l-action, while the original process with the restriction on high-level actions can go along a path where it performs two l-actions. On the other hand, the process Q mentioned in Theorem 5 is $\text{SBNDC}_{\approx_{mw}}$ but neither $\text{BSNNI}_{\approx_{mb}}$ nor $\text{SBSNNI}_{\approx_{mb}}$.
- $\text{SBSNNI}_{\approx_{mw}}$ vs. $\text{BNDC}_{\approx_{mb}}$. The process $l.h.l.\underline{0}+l.\underline{0}+l.l.\underline{0}$ is $\text{BSNNI}_{\approx_{mb}}$ as $(l.h.l.\underline{0}+l.\underline{0}+l.l.\underline{0}) \setminus \{h\} \approx_{mb} l.\underline{0}+l.\underline{0}+l.l.\underline{0} \approx_{mb} l.\tau.l.\underline{0}+l.\underline{0}+l.l.\underline{0} \approx_{mb} (l.h.l.\underline{0}+l.\underline{0}+l.l.\underline{0})/\{h\}$. The same process is $\text{BNDC}_{\approx_{mb}}$ too as it includes only one high-level action, hence the only possible high-level strategy coincides with the check conducted by $\text{BSNNI}_{\approx_{mb}}$. However, it is not $\text{SBSNNI}_{\approx_{mw}}$ because of the reachable process $h.l.\underline{0}$, which is not $\text{BSNNI}_{\approx_{mw}}$. On the other hand, the process Q mentioned in Theorem 5 is $\text{SBSNNI}_{\approx_{mw}}$ but not $\text{BSNNI}_{\approx_{mb}}$ and, therefore, not even $\text{BNDC}_{\approx_{mb}}$.
- $\text{BNDC}_{\approx_{mw}}$ vs. $\text{BSNNI}_{\approx_{mb}}$. The process $l.(2 \cdot \lambda).\underline{0}+l.((\lambda).h_1.l_1.\underline{0}+(\lambda).h_1.l_1.\underline{0}+l.((\lambda).l_1.\underline{0}+(\lambda).l_2.\underline{0}))$ is $\text{BSNNI}_{\approx_{mb}}$ but not $\text{BNDC}_{\approx_{mw}}$ as discussed in Sect. 3. In contrast, the process Q mentioned in Theorem 5 is both $\text{BSNNI}_{\approx_{mw}}$ and $\text{BNDC}_{\approx_{mw}}$, but not $\text{BSNNI}_{\approx_{mb}}$.

[25, 24] Like in the nondeterministic and probabilistic settings [25, 24], the strongest property based on weak Markovian bisimilarity ($\text{SBNDC}_{\approx_{mw}}$) and the weakest property based on Markovian branching bisimilarity ($\text{BSNNI}_{\approx_{mb}}$) are incomparable too. The former is a very restrictive property because it requires a local check every time a high-level action is performed, while the latter requires a check only on the initial state. On the other hand, as shown in Theorem 5, it is very easy to construct processes that are secure under properties based on $\approx_{mw}$ but not on $\approx_{mb}$, due to the minimal number of high-level actions in Q.

5 Relating Nondeterministic, Probabilistic, and Markovian Taxonomies

Let us compare our Markovian taxonomy with the nondeterministic one of [25]. In the following, we assume that $\approx_w$ denotes the weak nondeterministic bisimilarity of [49] and $\approx_b$ denotes the nondeterministic branching bisimilarity of [33]. These can also be derived from the corresponding definitions in Sect. 2.2 by ignoring the clause involving the *rate* function. Since we are abstracting from time, given a process $P \in \mathbb{P}$ we can obtain its nondeterministic variant, denoted by $nd(P)$, by replacing every occurrence of $(\lambda) . P'$ with $\tau . P'$. However, to respect maximal progress, first we have to eliminate every subprocess starting with a rate prefix that is alternative to a subprocess starting with a τ-prefix. To accomplish this transformation syntactically, we focus on the set $\mathbb{P}_{seq}$ of sequential processes, i.e., without parallel composition; this is not too restrictive because, in the absence of recursion, parallel composition can be eliminated by repeatedly applying a Markovian variant of the expansion law [38].

The next proposition states that if two sequential processes are equivalent according to any of the weak bisimilarities in Sect. 2.2, then their nondeterministic variants are equivalent according to the corresponding nondeterministic weak bisimilarity. The inverse does not hold; e.g., processes $P_1 = (1) . a . \underline{0}$ and $P_2 = (2) . a . \underline{0}$ are such that $P_1 \not\approx_{mw} P_2$ and $P_1 \not\approx_{mb} P_2$, but their nondeterministic counterparts coincide as both of them are equal to $\tau . a . \underline{0}$.

Proposition 1. *Let $P_1, P_2 \in \mathbb{P}_{seq}$. Then:*

- $P_1 \approx_{mw} P_2 \Longrightarrow nd(P_1) \approx_w nd(P_2)$.
- $P_1 \approx_{mb} P_2 \Longrightarrow nd(P_1) \approx_b nd(P_2)$. ∎

An immediate consequence is that if a sequential process is secure under any of the Markovian noninterference properties of Sect. 3, then its nondeterministic variant is secure under the corresponding nondeterministic property. The taxonomy of Fig. 2 thus extends to the left the one in [25], as each of the properties of Sect. 3 is finer than its nondeterministic counterpart.

Corollary 1. *Let $\mathcal{P}_{mk} \in \{BSNNI_{\approx_{mk}}, BNDC_{\approx_{mk}}, SBSNNI_{\approx_{mk}}, P\_BNDC_{\approx_{mk}}, SBNDC_{\approx_{mk}}\}$ and $\mathcal{P}_{nd} \in \{BSNNI_{\approx_{nd}}, BNDC_{\approx_{nd}}, SBSNNI_{\approx_{nd}}, P\_BNDC_{\approx_{nd}}, SBNDC_{\approx_{nd}}\}$ for $\approx_{mk} \in \{\approx_{mw}, \approx_{mb}\}$ and $\approx_{nd} \in \{\approx_w, \approx_b\}$, where $\mathcal{P}_{nd}$ is meant to be the nondeterministic variant of $\mathcal{P}_{mk}$. Then $P \in \mathcal{P}_{mk} \Longrightarrow nd(P) \in \mathcal{P}_{nd}$ for all $P \in \mathbb{P}_{seq}$.* ∎

We now compare our Markovian taxonomy with the probabilistic one of [24], which relies on the weak probabilistic bisimilarity $\approx_{pw}$ of [54] and the probabilistic branching bisimilarity $\approx_{pb}$ of [6], also derivable from the corresponding definitions in Sect. 2.2 by replacing the clause involving cumulative rates with a clause involving cumulative probabilities. We focus on the set $\mathbb{P}_{alt,seq}$ of processes in which action prefixes and rate prefixes alternate – to comply with the strictly alternating model of [36] adopted for probabilistic processes – that are sequential – as rate transitions, as opposed to probabilistic ones, do not synchronize. Since we are abstracting from time, given a process $P \in \mathbb{P}_{\text{alt,seq}}$ we can obtain its probabilistic variant, denoted by $pr(P)$, by replacing every occurrence of $\sum_{i \in I}(\lambda_i) . P_i$ with $\bigoplus_{i \in I}[p_i] pr(P_i)$ where $\bigoplus$ is the probabilistic choice operator and $p_i = \lambda_i / \sum_{j \in I} \lambda_j$. It is worth noting that over $\mathbb{P}_{\text{alt,seq}}$ the weak bisimilarities $\approx_{\text{mw}}$ and $\approx_{\text{mb}}$ boil down to the strong bisimilarity $\sim_{\text{m}}$ of Definition 2. This is due to the strict alternation between action prefixes and rate prefixes and the fact that the two weak bisimilarities do not abstract from rate transitions ($\approx_{\text{pw}}$ and $\approx_{\text{pb}}$ can instead abstract from probabilistic transitions).

The next proposition states that if two sequential alternating processes are equivalent according to any of the weak bisimilarities in Sect. 2.2, then their probabilistic variants are equivalent according to the corresponding probabilistic weak bisimilarity. The inverse does not hold; e.g., the probabilistic counterparts of the two inequivalent processes $(1) . a . \underline{0}$ and $(2) . a . \underline{0}$ coincide as both of them are equal to $[1]a . \underline{0}$.

Proposition 2. Let $P_1, P_2 \in \mathbb{P}_{\text{alt,seq}}$. Then:

- $P_1 \approx_{\text{mw}} P_2 \implies pr(P_1) \approx_{\text{pw}} pr(P_2)$.
- $P_1 \approx_{\text{mb}} P_2 \implies pr(P_1) \approx_{\text{pb}} pr(P_2)$. ∎

An immediate consequence is that if a sequential alternating process is secure under any of the Markovian noninterference properties of Sect. 3, then its probabilistic variant is secure under the corresponding probabilistic property. The taxonomy of Fig. 2 thus extends to the left also the one in [24], as each of the properties of Sect. 3 is finer than its probabilistic counterpart.

Corollary 2. Let $\mathcal{P}_{\text{mk}} \in \{\text{BSNNI}_{\approx_{\text{mk}}}, \text{BNDC}_{\approx_{\text{mk}}}, \text{SBSNNI}_{\approx_{\text{mk}}}, \text{P\_BNDC}_{\approx_{\text{mk}}}, \text{SBNDC}_{\approx_{\text{mk}}}\}$ and $\mathcal{P}_{\text{pr}} \in \{\text{BSNNI}_{\approx_{\text{pr}}}, \text{BNDC}_{\approx_{\text{pr}}}, \text{SBSNNI}_{\approx_{\text{pr}}}, \text{P\_BNDC}_{\approx_{\text{pr}}}, \text{SBNDC}_{\approx_{\text{pr}}}\}$ for $\approx_{\text{mk}} \in \{\approx_{\text{mw}}, \approx_{\text{mb}}\}$ and $\approx_{\text{pr}} \in \{\approx_{\text{pw}}, \approx_{\text{pb}}\}$, where $\mathcal{P}_{\text{pr}}$ is meant to be the probabilistic variant of $\mathcal{P}_{\text{mk}}$. Then $P \in \mathcal{P}_{\text{mk}} \implies pr(P) \in \mathcal{P}_{\text{pr}}$ for all $P \in \mathbb{P}_{\text{alt,seq}}$. ∎

6 Reversibility via Weak Markovian Back-and-Forth Bisimilarity

In [22] it was shown that, for nondeterministic processes, weak back-and-forth bisimilarity coincides with branching bisimilarity. We now extend that result so that Markovian branching bisimilarity can be employed in the noninterference analysis of reversible processes featuring nondeterminism and stochastic time.

An MLTS $(\mathcal{S}, \mathcal{A}_\tau, \longrightarrow)$ represents a reversible process if each of its transitions is seen as bidirectional. When going backward, it is of paramount importance to respect causality, i.e., the last performed transition must be the first one to be undone. Following [22] we set up an equivalence that enforces not only causality but also history preservation. This means that, when going backward, a process can only move along the path representing the history that brought the process to the current state even in the presence of concurrency. To accomplish this, the equivalence has to be defined over computations, not over states, and the notion of transition has to be suitably revised. We start by adapting the notation of the nondeterministic setting of [22] to our nondeterministic and stochastically timed setting. We use ℓ for a label in $\mathcal{A}_\tau \cup \mathbb{R}_{>0}$.

Definition 6. *A sequence $\xi = (s_0, \ell_1, s_1)(s_1, \ell_2, s_2) \ldots (s_{n-1}, \ell_n, s_n) \in \longrightarrow^*$ is a path of length n from state s_0. We let $first(\xi) = s_0$ and $last(\xi) = s_n$; the empty path is indicated with ε. We denote by $path(s)$ the set of paths from s.* ∎

Definition 7. *A pair $\rho = (s, \xi)$ is called a* run *from state s iff $\xi \in path(s)$, in which case we let $path(\rho) = \xi$, $first(\rho) = first(\xi) = s$, $last(\rho) = last(\xi)$, with $first(\rho) = last(\rho) = s$ when $\xi = \varepsilon$. We denote by $run(s)$ the set of runs from state s. Given $\rho = (s, \xi) \in run(s)$ and $\rho' = (s', \xi') \in run(s')$, their composition $\rho\rho' = (s, \xi\xi') \in run(s)$ is defined iff $last(\rho) = first(\rho') = s'$. We write $\rho \stackrel{\ell}{\longrightarrow} \rho'$ iff there exists $\rho'' = (\bar{s}, (\bar{s}, \ell, s'))$ with $\bar{s} = last(\rho)$ such that $\rho' = \rho\rho''$; note that $first(\rho) = first(\rho')$. Moreover rate is lifted in the expected way.* ∎

In the considered MLTS we work with the set $\mathcal{U}$ of runs in lieu of $\mathcal{S}$. Following [22], given a run ρ, we distinguish between *outgoing* and *incoming* action transitions of ρ during the weak bisimulation game. Like in [16], this does not apply to rate transitions, in the sense that the cumulative rates of incoming rate transitions are not compared. If this were not the case, states like $(\lambda_1).(\underline{0}\backslash\emptyset)+(\lambda_2).(\underline{0}/\emptyset)$ and $(\lambda_1+\lambda_2).\underline{0}$ – which are indistinguishable in the forward direction – would be told apart because the incoming cumulative rate from the class formed by those two states is λ_1, λ_2, or $\lambda_1 + \lambda_2$ depending on whether $\underline{0}\backslash\emptyset$, $\underline{0}/\emptyset$, or $\underline{0}$ is considered. When comparing the cumulative rates of outgoing transitions, we slightly deviate from the corresponding clause in Definition 4 to set up a more symmetric clause inspired by an alternative characterization of $\approx_{\text{mw}}$ in [38] that is helpful to prove the forthcoming Lemma 2.

Definition 8. *Let $(\mathcal{S}, \mathcal{A}_\tau, \longrightarrow)$ be an MLTS. We say that $s_1, s_2 \in \mathcal{S}$ are* weakly Markovian back-and-forth bisimilar, *written $s_1 \approx_{\text{mbf}} s_2$, iff $((s_1, \varepsilon), (s_2, \varepsilon)) \in \mathcal{B}$ for some weak Markovian back-and-forth bisimulation $\mathcal{B}$. An equivalence relation $\mathcal{B}$ over $\mathcal{U}$ is a* weak Markovian back-and-forth bisimulation *iff, whenever $(\rho_1, \rho_2) \in \mathcal{B}$, then:*

- *For each $\rho_1 \stackrel{a}{\longrightarrow}_a \rho_1'$ there exists $\rho_2 \stackrel{\hat{a}}{\Longrightarrow}_a \rho_2'$ such that $(\rho_1', \rho_2') \in \mathcal{B}$.*
- *For each $\rho_1' \stackrel{a}{\longrightarrow}_a \rho_1$ there exists $\rho_2' \stackrel{\hat{a}}{\Longrightarrow}_a \rho_2$ such that $(\rho_1', \rho_2') \in \mathcal{B}$.*
- *For each $\rho_1 \stackrel{\tau^*}{\Longrightarrow}_a \rho_1'$ with $\rho_1' \stackrel{\tau}{\not\longrightarrow}_a$ there exists $\rho_2 \stackrel{\tau^*}{\Longrightarrow}_a \rho_2'$ with $\rho_2' \stackrel{\tau}{\not\longrightarrow}_a$ such that $(\rho_1', \rho_2') \in \mathcal{B}$ and $rate(\rho_1', C) = rate(\rho_2', C)$ for all equivalence classes $C \in \mathcal{U}/\mathcal{B}$.*
- *For each $\rho_1' \stackrel{\lambda_1}{\longrightarrow}_r \rho_1$ with $\rho_1' \stackrel{\tau}{\not\longrightarrow}_a$ there exists $\rho_2' \stackrel{\tau^*}{\Longrightarrow}_a \bar{\rho}_2' \stackrel{\lambda_2}{\longrightarrow}_r \bar{\rho}_2 \stackrel{\tau^*}{\Longrightarrow}_a \rho_2$ with $\bar{\rho}_2' \stackrel{\tau}{\not\longrightarrow}_a$ such that $(\rho_1, \bar{\rho}_2) \in \mathcal{B}$, $(\rho_1', \bar{\rho}_2') \in \mathcal{B}$, and $(\rho_1', \rho_2') \in \mathcal{B}$.* ∎

We show that weak Markovian back-and-forth bisimilarity over runs coincides with $\approx_{\mathrm{mb}}$, the forward-only Markovian branching bisimilarity over states. We proceed by adopting the proof strategy followed in [22] to show that their weak back-and-forth bisimilarity over runs coincides with the forward-only branching bisimilarity over states of [33]. Therefore we start by proving that $\approx_{\mathrm{mbf}}$ satisfies the *cross property*. This means that, whenever two runs of two $\approx_{\mathrm{mbf}}$-equivalent states can perform a sequence of finitely many τ-transitions such that each of the two target runs is $\approx_{\mathrm{mbf}}$-equivalent to the source run of the other sequence, then the two target runs are $\approx_{\mathrm{mbf}}$-equivalent to each other as well.

Lemma 2. *Let $s_1, s_2 \in \mathcal{S}$ with $s_1 \approx_{\mathrm{mbf}} s_2$. For all $\rho_1', \rho_1'' \in run(s_1)$ such that $\rho_1' \stackrel{\tau^*}{\Longrightarrow}_a \rho_1''$ and for all $\rho_2', \rho_2'' \in run(s_2)$ such that $\rho_2' \stackrel{\tau^*}{\Longrightarrow}_a \rho_2''$, if $\rho_1' \approx_{\mathrm{mbf}} \rho_2''$ and $\rho_1'' \approx_{\mathrm{mbf}} \rho_2'$ then $\rho_1'' \approx_{\mathrm{mbf}} \rho_2''$.* ∎

Theorem 6. *Let $s_1, s_2 \in \mathcal{S}$. Then $s_1 \approx_{\mathrm{mbf}} s_2 \iff s_1 \approx_{\mathrm{mb}} s_2$.* ∎

Therefore the properties $\mathrm{BSNNI}_{\approx_{\mathrm{mb}}}$, $\mathrm{BNDC}_{\approx_{\mathrm{mb}}}$, $\mathrm{SBSNNI}_{\approx_{\mathrm{mb}}}$, $\mathrm{P\_BNDC}_{\approx_{\mathrm{mb}}}$, and $\mathrm{SBNDC}_{\approx_{\mathrm{mb}}}$ do not change if $\approx_{\mathrm{mb}}$ is replaced by $\approx_{\mathrm{mbf}}$. This allows us to study noninterference properties for reversible systems featuring nondeterminism and stochastic time by using $\approx_{\mathrm{mb}}$ in a standard Markovian process calculus like the one of Sect. 2.3, without having to resort to external memories [20], communication keys [55], or executed action decorations [17].

7 Use Case: DBMS Obfuscation and Permission Mechanisms

In [25] we have modeled the authentication mechanism of a database management system (DBMS) in which the database can be used to feed a machine learning (ML) module for training purposes, where reversible transactions are supported [23]. Due to privacy issues, DBMS users are not allowed to know which data are actually chosen to train the ML module [7]. Hence, for analysis purposes, the interactions between users and the DBMS are considered to be low level, while the interactions between the DBMS and the ML module are considered to be high level. The aim of the noninterference analysis is thus to check whether users can infer the utilization of their data in the ML dataset. In this section we present two novel examples for that scenario, which show the nature of the interferences emerging in a stochastically timed setting and the greater expressive power of branching bisimulation semantics in this setting.

Let l_w be a low-level action expressing the execution of a write transaction and l_ow be an analogous action that includes also the additional application of an obfuscation mechanism over written data for privacy purposes [1]. We assume that only obfuscated data can feed the ML module. Given the high-level actions h and h' denoting interactions between the DBMS and the ML module, consider the following process:

$$DBMS = h \, . \, \tau \, . \, (l_\mathrm{w} \, . \, \underline{0} + l_\mathrm{ow} \, . \, h' \, . \, \underline{0}) + \\ \tau \, . \, (\tau \, . \, (l_\mathrm{w} \, . \, \underline{0} + l_\mathrm{ow} \, . \, \underline{0}) + l_\mathrm{w} \, . \, \underline{0})$$

The subprocess guarded by the high-level action h represents the behavior of the DBMS whenever the ML module is activated through the h-based interaction. After an internal activity, the DBMS offers a choice between the two available transaction mechanisms, by assuming that only in the second case the transaction data will feed the ML module (through the h'-based interaction). The alternative subprocess guarded by a τ-action describes the behavior of the DBMS whenever the ML module is not involved. Note that this subprocess replicates the behavior above to simulate the presence of the ML module and, thus, makes it transparent from the viewpoint of users. In addition, the subprocess immediately enables also action l_w for efficiency reasons and because, in any case, the transaction data will not feed the ML module.

Since the two low views $\tau . (l_w . \underline{0} + l_{ow} . \tau . \underline{0})$ and $\tau . (l_w . \underline{0} + l_{ow} . \underline{0}) + l_w . \underline{0}$ are both weakly bisimilar and branching bisimilar, we immediately derive that all the noninterference properties of the nondeterministic taxonomy are satisfied. In particular, note that $DBMS \setminus \{h, h'\}$ and $DBMS / \{h, h'\}$ enable weakly/branching bisimilar behaviors by virtue of the observation above. However, if we add to the model the time spent by the DBMS in the internal activity before the choice about the possible obfuscation, we obtain:

$$DBMS_{\text{stoch\_timed}} = h . (\lambda_1) . (l_w . \underline{0} + l_{ow} . h' . \underline{0}) + \\ \tau . ((\lambda_2) . (l_w . \underline{0} + l_{ow} . \underline{0}) + l_w . \underline{0})$$

where the rates λ_1 and λ_2 govern the delays discussed above for the ML module being involved or not respectively (note that $DBMS$ is the nondeterministic version of $DBMS_{\text{stoch\_timed}}$). In this enriched process, the equivalence between the two low views $(\lambda_1) . (l_w . \underline{0} + l_{ow} . \tau . \underline{0})$ and $(\lambda_2) . (l_w . \underline{0} + l_{ow} . \underline{0}) + l_w . \underline{0}$ does not hold for the Markovian versions of the two bisimilarities. This means that no noninterference property of the Markovian taxonomy is satisfied. Note that this negative result holds also in the case $\lambda_1 = \lambda_2$, because only in the second subprocess it is possible to observe action l_w with no delay.

Let us consider a more sophisticated variant of the system above, including an explicit permission mechanism involving users. Let $l_{\text{no\_auth}}$ be a low-level action expressing that users do not authorize the DBMS to feed the ML module with the data of their transaction, $l_{\text{no\_auth\_o}}$ be a low-level action expressing that users do not authorize the obfuscation of the data of their transaction, and l_{commit} be a low-level action expressing the execution of the transaction. Then in the following process:

$$DBMS' = h . (l_{\text{no\_auth}} . l_{\text{commit}} . \underline{0} + \tau . (l_{\text{no\_auth\_o}} . l_{\text{commit}} . \underline{0} + \tau . l_{\text{commit}} . h' . \underline{0})) + \\ \tau . ((l_{\text{no\_auth}} . l_{\text{commit}} . \underline{0} + \tau . (l_{\text{no\_auth\_o}} . l_{\text{commit}} . \underline{0} + \tau . l_{\text{commit}} . \underline{0})) + \\ \tau . l_{\text{commit}} . \underline{0})$$

the subprocess guarded by the high-level action h – call it P – expresses the behavior of the system whenever the ML module is active. In particular, in such a case, once that no authorization has been forbidden, the committed data are transferred to the training set (through the h'-based interaction). Now, consider the alternative subprocess guarded by a τ-action and modeling the absence of the ML module – call it Q. This subprocess simulates the same behavior as P in the absence of the ML module and, in addition, enables the branch $\tau . l_{\text{commit}} . \underline{0}$ expressing the immediate execution of the transaction, which does not require any authorization because the ML module is not active. The two subprocesses $P / \{h'\}$ and Q are weakly bisimilar but not branching bisimilar. In fact, $P / \{h'\}$ cannot respond to the τ-action of Q leading to $l_{\text{commit}} . \underline{0}$ in a way that complies with the branching bisimulation semantics.

From the back-and-forth perspective, consider executing the run $\tau . l_{\text{commit}} . \underline{0}$ of Q and the run $\tau . \tau . l_{\text{commit}} . \tau . \underline{0}$ of $P / \{h'\}$. By undoing the actions of the Q-run it is not possible to go back to a state enabling action $l_{\text{no\_auth\_o}}$ before enabling action $l_{\text{no\_auth}}$. Instead, this is possible by undoing the other run. This is enough to distinguish $P / \{h'\}$ and Q in the setting of reversible transactions. Therefore, by following the same observations as the previous example, it turns out that the weak-bisimilarity-based noninterference properties are satisfied, while those based on branching bisimilarity are not. Finally, if we add the same rate λ just before the execution of any action l_{commit} – thus yielding $DBMS'_{\text{stoch\_timed}}$ – the same considerations continue to hold, thereby confirming the greater expressive power of branching bisimulation semantics even in the Markovian setting.

8 Conclusions

In this paper we have extended to a stochastically timed setting our previous preservation, compositionality, and classification results about a selection of noninterference properties for (irreversible and) reversible systems developed in a nondeterministic setting [25] and in a probabilistic one [24]. The two behavioral equivalences for those noninterference properties are the weak Markovian bisimilarity of [38] and a newly defined Markovian branching bisimilarity. Both equivalences are designed to comply with the assumption of maximal progress.

Since we have shown that Markovian branching bisimilarity coincides with a Markovian variant of the weak back-and-forth bisimilarity of [22], noninterference properties based on this equivalence can be applied to reversible Markovian systems. This extends the analogous result in [25] for nondeterministic systems as well as the one in [24] for systems featuring nondeterminism and probabilities.

Regarding future extensions, we are working on incorporating recursion into the process language under consideration, which will enable us to model systems that may not terminate. This requires identifying an adequate Markovian variant of the up-to technique for weak and branching bisimilarities [31,60], to be used in the proof of some results where we can now proceed by induction on the depth of the tree-like MLTS underlying the considered process term.

Another direction to pursue is the comparison of our work with those, based on an integrated-time Markovian model, of [3], addressing stochastic variants of BSNNI and SBNDC, and [41], which studies a stochastic variant of P_BNDC.

Finally, we would like to develop a taxonomy for deterministically timed systems, in which action execution is separated from time passing according to the model of [50,51] governed by time determinism and time additivity.

Acknowledgment. This research has been supported by the PRIN 2020 project *NiRvAna – Noninterference and Reversibility Analysis in Private Blockchains*.

References

1. Al-Rubaie, M., Chang, J.M.: Privacy-preserving machine learning: threats and solutions. IEEE Secur. Priv. **17**, 49–58 (2019)
2. Aldini, A.: Classification of security properties in a Linda-like process algebra. Sci. Comput. Program. **63**, 16–38 (2006)
3. Aldini, A., Bernardo, M.: A general framework for nondeterministic, probabilistic, and stochastic noninterference. In: Proceedings of the 1st Joint Workshop on Automated Reasoning for Security Protocol Analysis and Issues in the Theory of Security (ARSPA/WITS 2009), LNCS, vol. 5511, pp. 18–33. Springer (2009)
4. Aldini, A., Bernardo, M.: Component-oriented verification of noninterference. J. Syst. Architect. **57**, 282–293 (2011)
5. Aldini, A., Bravetti, M., Gorrieri, R.: A process-algebraic approach for the analysis of probabilistic noninterference. J. Comput. Secur. **12**, 191–245 (2004)
6. Andova, S., Georgievska, S., Trcka, N.: Branching bisimulation congruence for probabilistic systems. Theoret. Comput. Sci. **413**, 58–72 (2012)
7. Bai, Y., Fan, M., Li, Y., Xie, C.: Privacy risk assessment of training data in machine learning. In: Proceedings of the 34th IEEE Int. Conf. on Communications (ICC 2022), pp. 1015–1015. IEEE-CS Press (2022)
8. Barbuti, R., Tesei, L.: A decidable notion of timed non-interference. Fund. Inform. **54**, 137–150 (2003)
9. Bennett, C.H.: Logical reversibility of computation. IBM J. Res. Dev. **17**, 525–532 (1973)
10. Bernardo, M.: A survey of Markovian behavioral equivalences. In: Bernardo, M., Hillston, J. (eds.) SFM 2007. LNCS, vol. 4486, pp. 180–219. Springer, Heidelberg (2007). https://doi.org/10.1007/978-3-540-72522-0_5
11. Bernardo, M.: On the tradeoff between compositionality and exactness in weak bisimilarity for integrated-time Markovian process calculi. Theoret. Comput. Sci. **563**, 99–143 (2015)
12. Bernardo, M., Bravetti, M.: Performance measure sensitive congruences for Markovian process algebras. Theoret. Comput. Sci. **290**, 117–160 (2003)
13. Bernardo, M., Corradini, F., Tesei, L.: Timed process calculi with deterministic or stochastic delays: commuting between durational and durationless actions. Theoret. Comput. Sci. **629**, 2–39 (2016)
14. Bernardo, M., Gorrieri, R.: A tutorial on EMPA: a theory of concurrent processes with nondeterminism, priorities, probabilities and time. Theoret. Comput. Sci. **202**, 1–54 (1998)
15. Bernardo, M., Lanese, I., Marin, A., Mezzina, C.A., Rossi, S., Sacerdoti Coen, C.: Causal reversibility implies time reversibility. In: Proceedings of the 20th International Conference on the Quantitative Evaluation of Systems (QEST 2023), LNCS, vol. 14287, pp. 270–287. Springer (2023)
16. Bernardo, M., Mezzina, C.A.: Bridging causal reversibility and time reversibility: a stochastic process algebraic approach. Logical Methods Comput. Sci. **19**(2), 6:1–6:27 (2023)

17. Bernardo, M., Rossi, S.: Reverse bisimilarity vs. forward bisimilarity. In: Proceeding of the 26th International Conference on Foundations of Software Science and Computation Structures (FOSSACS 2023), LNCS, vol. 13992, pp. 265–284. Springer (2023)
18. Brookes, S.D., Hoare, C., Roscoe, A.W.: A theory of communicating sequential processes. J. ACM **31**, 560–599 (1984)
19. Buchholz, P.: Markovian process algebra: composition and equivalence. In: Proceeding of the 2nd International Workshop on Process Algebra and Performance Modelling (PAPM 1994), pp. 11–30. University of Erlangen, Technical Report 27-4 (1994)
20. Danos, V., Krivine, J.: Reversible communicating systems. In: Gardner, P., Yoshida, N. (eds.) CONCUR 2004. LNCS, vol. 3170, pp. 292–307. Springer, Heidelberg (2004). https://doi.org/10.1007/978-3-540-28644-8_19
21. Danos, V., Krivine, J.: Transactions in RCCS. In: Abadi, M., de Alfaro, L. (eds.) CONCUR 2005. LNCS, vol. 3653, pp. 398–412. Springer, Heidelberg (2005). https://doi.org/10.1007/11539452_31
22. De Nicola, R., Montanari, U., Vaandrager, F.: Back and forth bisimulations. In: Baeten, J., Klop, J.W. (eds.) CONCUR 1990. LNCS, vol. 458, pp. 152–165. Springer, Heidelberg (1990). https://doi.org/10.1007/BFb0039058
23. Engblom, J.: A review of reverse debugging. In: Proceeding of the 4th System, Software, SoC and Silicon Debug Conference (S4D 2012), pp. 1–6. IEEE-CS Press (2012)
24. Esposito, A., Aldini, A., Bernardo, M.: Noninterference analysis of reversible probabilistic systems. In: Proceeding of the 44th International Conference on Formal Techniques for Distributed Objects, Components, and Systems (FORTE 2024), LNCS, vol. 14678, pp. 39–59. Springer (2024)
25. Esposito, A., Aldini, A., Bernardo, M., Rossi, S.: Noninterference analysis of reversible systems: an approach based on branching bisimilarity. Logical Methods Comput. Sci. **21**(1), 6:1–6:28 (2025)
26. Focardi, R., Gorrieri, R.: Classification of security properties. In: Proceeding of the 1st International School on Foundations of Security Analysis and Design (FOSAD 2000), LNCS, vol. 2171, pp. 331–396. Springer (2001)
27. Focardi, R., Piazza, C., Rossi, S.: Proofs methods for bisimulation based information flow security. In: Cortesi, A. (ed.) VMCAI 2002. LNCS, vol. 2294, pp. 16–31. Springer, Heidelberg (2002). https://doi.org/10.1007/3-540-47813-2_2
28. Focardi, R., Rossi, S.: Information flow security in dynamic contexts. J. Comput. Secur. **14**, 65–110 (2006)
29. Giachino, E., Lanese, I., Mezzina, C.A.: Causal-consistent reversible debugging. In: Gnesi, S., Rensink, A. (eds.) FASE 2014. LNCS, vol. 8411, pp. 370–384. Springer, Heidelberg (2014). https://doi.org/10.1007/978-3-642-54804-8_26
30. Giacobazzi, R., Mastroeni, I.: Abstract non-interference: a unifying framework for weakening information-flow. ACM Trans. Privacy Secur. **21**(2), 9:1–9:31 (2018)
31. van Glabbeek, R.J.: A complete axiomatization for branching bisimulation congruence of finite-state behaviours. In: Borzyszkowski, A.M., Sokołowski, S. (eds.) MFCS 1993. LNCS, vol. 711, pp. 473–484. Springer, Heidelberg (1993). https://doi.org/10.1007/3-540-57182-5_39
32. van Glabbeek, R.J.: The linear time – branching time spectrum I. In: Handbook of Process Algebra, pp. 3–99. Elsevier (2001)
33. van Glabbeek, R.J., Weijland, W.P.: Branching time and abstraction in bisimulation semantics. J. ACM **43**, 555–600 (1996)

34. Goguen, J.A., Meseguer, J.: Security policies and security models. In: Proceeding of the 2nd IEEE Symposium on Security and Privacy (SSP 1982), pp. 11–20. IEEE-CS Press (1982)
35. Götz, N., Herzog, U., Rettelbach, M.: Multiprocessor and distributed systems design: the integration of functional specification and performance analysis using stochastic process algebras. In: Proceeding of the 16th International Symposium on Computer Performance Modelling, Measurement and Evaluation (PERFORMANCE 1993), LNCS, vol. 729, pp. 121–146. Springer (1993)
36. Hansson, H., Jonsson, B.: A calculus for communicating systems with time and probabilities. In: Proceeding of the 11th IEEE Real-Time Systems Symposium (RTSS 1990), pp. 278–287. IEEE-CS Press (1990)
37. Hedin, D., Sabelfeld, A.: A perspective on information-flow control. In: Software Safety and Security – Tools for Analysis and Verification, pp. 319–347. IOS Press (2012)
38. Hermanns, H.: Interactive Markov Chains. Springer (2002), volume 2428 of LNCS
39. Hermanns, H., Rettelbach, M.: Syntax, semantics, equivalences, and axioms for MTIPP. In: Proceeding of the 2nd International Workshop on Process Algebra and Performance Modelling (PAPM 1994), pp. 71–87. University of Erlangen, Technical Report 27-4 (1994)
40. Hillston, J.: A Compositional Approach to Performance Modelling. Cambridge University Press (1996)
41. Hillston, J., Marin, A., Piazza, C., Rossi, S.: Persistent stochastic non-interference. Fund. Inform. **181**, 1–35 (2021)
42. Keller, R.M.: Formal verification of parallel programs. Commun. ACM **19**, 371–384 (1976)
43. Landauer, R.: Irreversibility and heat generation in the computing process. IBM J. Res. Dev. **5**, 183–191 (1961)
44. Lanese, I., Lienhardt, M., Mezzina, C.A., Schmitt, A., Stefani, J.-B.: Concurrent flexible reversibility. In: Felleisen, M., Gardner, P. (eds.) ESOP 2013. LNCS, vol. 7792, pp. 370–390. Springer, Heidelberg (2013). https://doi.org/10.1007/978-3-642-37036-6_21
45. Lanese, I., Nishida, N., Palacios, A., Vidal, G.: CauDEr: a causal-consistent reversible debugger for erlang. In: Gallagher, J.P., Sulzmann, M. (eds.) FLOPS 2018. LNCS, vol. 10818, pp. 247–263. Springer, Cham (2018). https://doi.org/10.1007/978-3-319-90686-7_16
46. Laursen, J.S., Ellekilde, L.P., Schultz, U.P.: Modelling reversible execution of robotic assembly. Robotica **36**, 625–654 (2018)
47. Mantel, H.: Information flow and noninterference. In: Encyclopedia of Cryptography and Security, pp. 605–607. Springer (2011)
48. Martinelli, F.: Analysis of security protocols as open systems. Theoret. Comput. Sci. **290**, 1057–1106 (2003)
49. Milner, R.: Communication and Concurrency. Prentice Hall (1989)
50. Moller, F., Tofts, C.: A temporal calculus of communicating systems. In: Baeten, J., Klop, J.W. (eds.) CONCUR 1990. LNCS, vol. 458, pp. 401–415. Springer, Heidelberg (1990). https://doi.org/10.1007/BFb0039073
51. Moller, F., Tofts, C.: Behavioural abstraction in TCCS. In: Kuich, W. (ed.) ICALP 1992. LNCS, vol. 623, pp. 559–570. Springer, Heidelberg (1992). https://doi.org/10.1007/3-540-55719-9_104
52. Park, D.: Concurrency and automata on infinite sequences. In: Deussen, P. (ed.) GI-TCS 1981. LNCS, vol. 104, pp. 167–183. Springer, Heidelberg (1981). https://doi.org/10.1007/BFb0017309

53. Perumalla, K.S., Park, A.J.: Reverse computation for rollback-based fault tolerance in large parallel systems - evaluating the potential gains and systems effects. Clust. Comput. **17**, 303–313 (2014)
54. Philippou, A., Lee, I., Sokolsky, O.: Weak Bisimulation for probabilistic systems. In: Palamidessi, C. (ed.) CONCUR 2000. LNCS, vol. 1877, pp. 334–349. Springer, Heidelberg (2000). https://doi.org/10.1007/3-540-44618-4_25
55. Phillips, I., Ulidowski, I.: Reversing algebraic process calculi. J. Logic Algebraic Program. **73**, 70–96 (2007)
56. Phillips, I., Ulidowski, I., Yuen, S.: A reversible process calculus and the modelling of the ERK signalling pathway. In: Proceeding of the 4th International Workshop on Reversible Computation (RC 2012), LNCS, vol. 7581, pp. 218–232. Springer (2012)
57. Pinna, G.M.: Reversing steps in membrane systems computations. In: Proceeding of the 18th International Conference on Membrane Computing (CMC 2017), LNCS, vol. 10725, pp. 245–261. Springer (2017)
58. Priami, C.: Stochastic π-calculus. Comput. J. **38**, 578–589 (1995)
59. Sabelfeld, A., Sands, D.: Probabilistic noninterference for multi-threaded programs. In: Proceeding of the 13th IEEE Computer Security Foundations Workshop (CSFW 2000), pp. 200–214. IEEE-CS Press (2000)
60. Sangiorgi, D., Milner, R.: The problem of "weak bisimulation up to". In: Proceeding of the 3rd International Conference on Concurrency Theory (CONCUR 1992), LNCS, vol. 630, pp. 32–46. Springer (1992)
61. Schordan, M., Oppelstrup, T., Jefferson, D.R., Barnes, P.D., Jr.: Generation of reversible C++ code for optimistic parallel discrete event simulation. N. Gener. Comput. **36**, 257–280 (2018)
62. Siljak, H., Psara, K., Philippou, A.: Distributed antenna selection for massive MIMO using reversing Petri nets. IEEE Wirel. Commun. Lett. **8**, 1427–1430 (2019)
63. Vassor, M., Stefani, J.B.: Checkpoint/rollback vs causally-consistent reversibility. In: Proceeding of the 10th International Conference on Reversible Computation (RC 2018), LNCS, vol. 11106, pp. 286–303. Springer (2018)
64. Volpano, D., Smith, G.: Probabilistic noninterference in a concurrent language. In: Proceeding of the 11th IEEE Computer Security Foundations Workshop (CSFW 1998), pp. 34–43. IEEE-CS Press (1998)
65. de Vries, E., Koutavas, V., Hennessy, M.: Communicating transactions. In: Gastin, P., Laroussinie, F. (eds.) CONCUR 2010. LNCS, vol. 6269, pp. 569–583. Springer, Heidelberg (2010). https://doi.org/10.1007/978-3-642-15375-4_39
66. Ycart, B.: The philosophers' process: an ergodic reversible nearest particle system. Ann. Appl. Prob. **3**, 356–363 (1993)
67. Zheng, L., Myers, A.: Dynamic security labels and noninterference. In: Proceeding of the 2nd IFIP Workshop on Formal Aspects in Security and Trust (FAST 2004), IFIP AICT, vol. 173, pp. 27–40. Springer (2004)

Attribute-Based Communication over Pub/Sub: Transactional Coordination for Smart Systems

Marco Comini, Luca Gemolotto(✉), and Marino Miculan

Dept. of Mathematics, Computer Science and Physics, University of Udine,
Udine, Italy
{marco.comini,luca.gemolotto,marino.miculan}@uniud.it

Abstract. IoT and smart systems frequently rely on *publish-subscribe* (pub/sub) middlewares like MQTT or DDS. However, current coordination solutions often lack formal rigour, posing risks in mission-critical applications, or suffer from excessive complexity, hindering practical deployment and increasing the likelihood of errors. This paper addresses these challenges by integrating AbU, a recently introduced formal model based on *Event-Condition-Action* (ECA) rules and *attribute-based communication*, with standard pub/sub middlewares. We present a synchronization protocol that leverages pub/sub primitives to implement AbU's transactional communication semantics. We prove the correctness of this protocol, demonstrating that it accurately reflects the underlying system dynamics. This integration of a formal ECA-based programming model with pub/sub offers a compelling balance between rigorous guarantees and practical applicability for coordinating IoT and smart systems.

Keywords: Autonomic systems · Distributed coordination · ECA rules · Attribute-based communication

1 Introduction

The growing complexity of interactions in Collective Adaptive Systems (CAS), like the Internet of Things (IoT) and smart systems, demands effective coordination between distributed nodes. Effective coordination within these systems is crucial for realizing desired system-wide behaviors, especially in critical situations. Still, traditional imperative programming approaches often struggle to capture the event-driven and reactive nature of IoT and smart systems, leading to code that is difficult to understand, maintain, scale and debug.

To address this problem, AbU [10,12] has been recently proposed as a programming model for CAS. AbU merges the simplicity of *Event-Condition-Action* (ECA) rules with a powerful distributed coordination mechanism inspired by *attribute-based communication* [3]. On one hand, ECA rules provide a natural and intuitive way to specify complex reactive behaviour by explicitly separating event detection, condition evaluation, and action execution. On the other hand,

AbU allows a rule on a node to update at once the states of many nodes which are selected by means of their attributes without the need for central coordination.

Correctly implementing AbU presents significant challenges. The collective local states of devices can be viewed as a *distributed database*, with communication resembling a distributed commit. This necessitates a robust mechanism for updating these states. While prior work [11] demonstrated a Go implementation using ad-hoc libraries for cluster management and failure detection, this approach is ill-suited for the majority of IoT and smart system deployments that rely on *publish-subscribe* (pub/sub) for communication. In fact, CAS frequently leverage pub/sub middleware, such as MQTT and DDS, for their flexibility, scalability, and decoupled communication.

This paper bridges this gap by presenting a pub/sub-based implementation of the AbU runtime engine. We introduce a novel synchronization protocol that leverages pub/sub primitives to implement AbU's transactional communication semantics, ensuring consistent and predictable message delivery and processing to prevent race conditions and maintain data integrity. We provide a formal proof of correctness for this protocol, demonstrating its adherence to the intended system dynamics and guaranteeing key properties like atomicity and consistency. This integration of a formal, ECA-based approach with widely adopted pub/sub technologies offers a compelling balance, combining rigorous behavioural guarantees with the practical applicability and scalability required for coordinating complex IoT and smart systems.

Synopsis. In Sect. 2 we review the syntax and semantics of AbU, including an illustrative example. Section 3 details the implementation of the AbU runtime using pub/sub primitives. The formal correctness of this implementation, modeling agents as DFAs, is proved in Sect. 4. Finally, Sect. 5 concludes the paper, recalls some related work, and outlines directions for future work.

2 AbU: Attribute-Based Memory Updates

In this Section we recall AbU [10,12], a calculus which combines ECA rules with attribute-based communication mechanism introduced by [3].

2.1 Syntax and Semantics

Formally, an AbU system S is a list of *nodes* which execute in parallel:

$$S ::= R, \iota \langle \Sigma, \Theta \rangle \mid S \parallel S$$

where each *node* $R, \iota \langle \Sigma, \Theta \rangle$ consists of:

- a set R of ECA rules, whose format is described below;
- a *state* $\Sigma \in \mathbb{X} \to \mathbb{V}$, mapping *attributes* $x \in \mathbb{X}$ to *values* $v \in \mathbb{V}$;
- an *execution pool* $\Theta \subseteq (\mathbb{X} \times \mathbb{V})^*$, that is, a set $\Theta = \{\mathsf{upd}_1, \ldots, \mathsf{upd}_n\}$ of lists of pairs of the form $((x_1, v_1) \ldots (x_m, v_m))$. Each list, called an *update*, represents a simultaneous multiple update waiting to be applied to the state;

$$\begin{aligned}
&\text{rule} ::= \text{evt} \vartriangleright \text{task} & &\text{cnd} ::= \varphi \mid @\varphi \\
&\text{evt} ::= \text{x} \mid \text{evt evt} & &\varphi ::= \text{ff} \mid \text{tt} \mid \neg\varphi \mid \varphi \wedge \varphi \mid \varphi \vee \varphi \mid \varepsilon \bowtie \varepsilon \mid (\varphi) \\
&\text{task} ::= \text{cnd} : \text{act} & &\varepsilon ::= v \mid \text{x} \mid \overline{\text{x}} \mid \varepsilon \otimes \varepsilon \\
&\text{act} ::= \epsilon \mid \text{x} \leftarrow \varepsilon \text{ act} \mid \overline{\text{x}} \leftarrow \varepsilon \text{ act} & &\text{x} \in \mathbb{X} \quad v \in \mathbb{V}
\end{aligned}$$

Fig. 1. Grammar of ECA rules in the AbU calculus.

- an *invariant* ι, that is, a boolean expression that the node's state must satisfy at runtime. When $\iota = \text{tt}$ we simply write $R\langle \Sigma, \Theta \rangle$ instead of $R, \text{tt}\langle \Sigma, \Theta \rangle$. Invariants are useful to avoid erroneous or dangerous states, like inconsistent or out-of-range values and forbidden trajectories in planning.

The grammar of AbU rules is in Fig. 1. Each ECA rule evt ▷ task comprises an *event* evt, which is a list of attributes the rule monitors. A modification to any attribute in evt triggers the rule, causing its task to be evaluated. Evaluation does not immediately modify the node's state; instead, it generates update operations that are added to the execution pool for later application. A task consists of a condition cnd and an action act. Conditions are boolean expressions, optionally prefixed with the @ modifier. Actions are a finite (possibly empty) list of assignments of value expressions ε to local or remote resources. Tasks without @ are *local*; those with @ are *remote*. For local tasks, the condition is evaluated locally, and if true, the action is evaluated, generating an update which is added to the local node's pool. For remote tasks, the action is evaluated on *every* node where the condition cnd holds, with the resulting update added to each such remote node's pool. In remote tasks, remote attributes are denoted by overlined names (e.g., $\overline{\text{x}}$) to distinguish them from local attributes (e.g., x).

AbU operational semantics is modeled as a labeled transition system $S_1 \xrightarrow{\alpha} S_2$ whose labels α are given by the following grammar:

$$\alpha ::= T \mid \vartriangleright T \mid \blacktriangleright T$$

where T is a (possibly empty) finite list of tasks. Intuitively, label $\vartriangleright T$ denotes that one node of the system is executing an update which induces the list T of remote tasks. Dually, label T denotes the fact that all the nodes are *receiving* the list of tasks T. The label $\blacktriangleright T$ is similar to $\vartriangleright T$ but denotes that one node of the system is receiving an update from some sensors which induces the list T of remote tasks. Execution is interleaving, which means that at each step only one node of the system can perform $\vartriangleright T$ or $\blacktriangleright T$, while all the others can perform T.

More formally, the semantic rules of AbU are in Fig. 2. Rule (EXEC) executes an update picked from the pool, while rule (INPUT) models an external modification of some attributes. In both cases, the change of attributes may trigger some rules of the nodes. Hence, after updating its state, the node launches a *discovery phase*, for finding new updates to add to the local pool or some pools of remote nodes, given by the activation of some rules.

$$\text{(Exec)} \frac{\begin{array}{c}\text{upd} \in \Theta \quad \text{upd} = (x_1, v_1)\ldots(x_k, v_k) \quad \Sigma' = \Sigma[v_1/x_1 \ldots v_k/x_k] \\ \Sigma' \models \iota \quad X = \{x_i \mid i \in [1..k] \wedge \Sigma(x_i) \neq \Sigma'(x_i)\} \\ \Theta' = (\Theta \setminus \{\text{upd}\}) \cup \text{LocalUpds}(R, X, \Sigma') \quad T = \text{ExtTasks}(R, X, \Sigma')\end{array}}{R, \iota\langle \Sigma, \Theta\rangle \xrightarrow{\triangleright T} R, \iota\langle \Sigma', \Theta'\rangle}$$

$$\text{(Exec-F)} \frac{\text{upd} \in \Theta \quad \text{upd} = (x_1, v_1)\ldots(x_k, v_k) \quad \Sigma[v_1/x_1 \ldots v_k/x_k] \not\models \iota \quad \Theta' = \Theta \setminus \{\text{upd}\}}{R, \iota\langle \Sigma, \Theta\rangle \xrightarrow{\triangleright \epsilon} R, \iota\langle \Sigma, \Theta'\rangle}$$

$$\text{(Input)} \frac{\begin{array}{c}v_1, \ldots, v_k \in \mathbb{V} \quad \Sigma' = \Sigma[v_1/x_1 \ldots v_k/x_k] \quad X = \{x_1, \ldots, x_k\} \\ \Theta' = \Theta \cup \text{LocalUpds}(R, X, \Sigma') \quad T = \text{ExtTasks}(R, X, \Sigma')\end{array}}{R, \iota\langle \Sigma, \Theta\rangle \xrightarrow{\blacktriangleright T} R, \iota\langle \Sigma', \Theta'\rangle}$$

$$\text{(Disc)} \frac{\Theta'' = \{\llbracket \text{act} \rrbracket \Sigma \mid \exists i \in [1..n] \,.\, \text{task}_i = \varphi : \text{act} \wedge \Sigma \models \varphi\} \quad \Theta' = \Theta \cup \Theta''}{R, \iota\langle \Sigma, \Theta\rangle \xrightarrow{\text{task}_1 \ldots \text{task}_n} R, \iota\langle \Sigma, \Theta'\rangle}$$

$$\text{(StepL)} \frac{S_1 \xrightarrow{\alpha} S_1' \quad S_2 \xrightarrow{T} S_2'}{S_1 \parallel S_2 \xrightarrow{\alpha} S_1' \parallel S_2'} \alpha \in \{\triangleright T, \blacktriangleright T\} \qquad \text{(StepR)} \frac{S_1 \xrightarrow{T} S_1' \quad S_2 \xrightarrow{\alpha} S_2'}{S_1 \parallel S_2 \xrightarrow{\alpha} S_1' \parallel S_2'} \alpha \in \{\triangleright T, \blacktriangleright T\}$$

$\text{Active}(R, X) \triangleq \{(\text{evt} \succ \text{task}) \in R \mid \text{evt} \cap X \neq \varnothing\}$

$\text{LocalUpds}(R, X, \Sigma) \triangleq \{\llbracket \text{act} \rrbracket \Sigma \mid (\text{evt} \succ \varphi : \text{act}) \in \text{Active}(R, X) \,.\, \Sigma \models \varphi\}$

$\text{ExtTasks}(R, X, \Sigma) \triangleq \{\!|\text{task}_1|\!\} \Sigma \ldots \{\!|\text{task}_n|\!\} \Sigma$

where $\forall i \in [1..n] . \exists (\text{evt}_i \succ \text{task}_i) \in \text{Active}(R, X) \,.\, \text{task}_i = (@\varphi : \text{act})$

Fig. 2. LTS semantics of the AbU calculus.

The discovery phase is composed by two parts, the local and the external one. Locally, the node $R, \iota\langle \Sigma, \Theta\rangle$ adds to the local pool Θ all local updates originated by the activation of some rules in R; these updates are calculated by the function LocalUpds, where $\llbracket \text{act} \rrbracket \Sigma$ denotes the evaluation of the right-hand side expressions in act in the current state Σ.

For the external part, the node computes a list T of tasks that may update remote nodes by means of the function ExtTasks. In this function, $\{\!|\text{task}|\!\}\Sigma$ denotes the task obtained from task where each occurrence of an attribute x in the condition and the right-hand sides in the action is replaced with the value $\Sigma(x)$; then each instance of $\overline{x}$ is replaced with x and the modifier @ is dropped. For instance, if $\Sigma(x) = 42$ then $\{\!|@\overline{x} < x : \overline{x} \leftarrow x + 1|\!\} \Sigma =$ "$x < 42 : x \leftarrow 42 + 1$".

A node receives a task list T by executing the (Disc) rule. During this step, the node evaluates the conditions of each task in T and adds the actions of those with satisfied conditions to its local execution pool. The (StepL) and (StepR) rules synchronize a discovery phase across all nodes, triggered by a state change on any node. Although actions within individual execution pools are processed asynchronously, inter-node interaction during discovery remains synchronous: the node performing the next update is chosen non-deterministically, while all other nodes block until the discovery phase completes. Consequently, concurrent (Exec) or (Input) operations on different nodes are effectively sequentialized.

The semantics also checks the fulfillment of invariants on each node. The rule (EXEC) is applied only when the state modified by the update satisfies the invariant (i.e., $\Sigma' \models \iota$); otherwise, rule (EXEC-F) is applied. In this case, the update that would lead to a "bad" state is discarded and removed from the pool.

2.2 Example 1: Swarm of Rovers

Consider a scenario where a swarm of terrestrial rovers is in charge of taking specific measurements, randomly picked in a large uninhabited area. Each rover is equipped with a battery that periodically needs to be recharged by returning to a docking station. It may happen that a rover runs out of energy before returning to the charging spot. In this case, the low-battery rover asks for help from its neighbors. If a rover has some energy to share and it is close enough to the requester, it will enter the 'rescue mode' which starts a rover-to-rover charging protocol. We can represent in AbU the core coordination aspects of this scenario (previously modeled in AbC in [9]), as follows.

Suppose to have four rovers $R_1, \ldots, R_4$. For each rover we have an AbU node with four attributes: battery, indicating the battery level of the rover; position, indicating the rover position; mode, indicating in which operative state is the rover; and helpPos, indicating the position of a rover that needs help.

Formally, the AbU system modeling the rover-swarm scenario is

$$\mathsf{S} = R\langle \Sigma_1, \varnothing \rangle \parallel R\langle \Sigma_2, \varnothing \rangle \parallel R\langle \Sigma_3, \varnothing \rangle \parallel R\langle \Sigma_4, \varnothing \rangle$$

where R contains the following two AbU rules:

$$\text{battery} \succ @(\text{battery} < 5 \wedge \overline{\text{battery}} > 80) : \overline{\text{helpPos}} \leftarrow \text{position} \quad \text{(R1)}$$
$$\text{helpPos} \succ (|\text{position} - \text{helpPos}| < 7.0) : \text{mode} \leftarrow \text{'rescue'} \quad \text{(R2)}$$

The rule (R1) says that when a rover's battery level is low (i.e., battery < 5), then the rover sends to all neighbors with some energy to share (i.e., $\overline{\text{battery}} > 80$) its position, performing a remote update: $\overline{\text{helpPos}} \leftarrow \text{position}$. The rule (R2), instead, is fired when a rover receives a help request (i.e., when its attribute helpPos changes) and basically checks if the current rover position is close to the requester position (i.e., $|\text{position} - \text{helpPos}| < 7.0$). If it is the case, the current rover enters the rescue mode performing a local update: mode $\leftarrow$ 'rescue'.

Now suppose that the execution states of the rovers are the following:

$\Sigma_1 = [\,\text{battery} \mapsto 4 \quad \text{position} \mapsto 2.0 \quad \text{mode} \mapsto \text{'measure'} \quad \text{helpPos} \mapsto 0.0\,]$
$\Sigma_2 = [\,\text{battery} \mapsto 81 \quad \text{position} \mapsto 15.0 \quad \text{mode} \mapsto \text{'measure'} \quad \text{helpPos} \mapsto 0.0\,]$
$\Sigma_3 = [\,\text{battery} \mapsto 97 \quad \text{position} \mapsto 6.0 \quad \text{mode} \mapsto \text{'measure'} \quad \text{helpPos} \mapsto 0.0\,]$
$\Sigma_4 = [\,\text{battery} \mapsto 65 \quad \text{position} \mapsto 8.0 \quad \text{mode} \mapsto \text{'measure'} \quad \text{helpPos} \mapsto 0.0\,]$

In the example, rover R_1 can fire the rule (R1), since its battery level is low. Then, it pre-evaluates the task condition, yielding $4 < 5 \wedge \overline{\text{battery}} > 80$, which is sent to the other rovers, together with the pre-evaluation of the task action, i.e., helpPos ← 2.0. Among all receivers, only rovers R_2 and R_3 are interested in the communication, since they are the only with battery level greater than 80. So they both add to their pool the update (helpPos, 2.0). This ends the discovery phase originated by R_1. When rovers R_2 and R_3 execute the update (helpPos, 2.0), the task of the rule (R2) may be executed. For rover R_2 this does not happen, since $|15.0 - 2.0| < 7.0$ does not hold (the rover is too far from the distressed one). Instead rover R_3 can execute the rule task (since $|6.0 - 2.0| < 7.0$), adding to its pool the update (mode, 'rescue').

2.3 Example 2: Smart Building Alarm System

To illustrate the significance of AbU's transactional semantics, consider a smart building equipped with a security system that arms alarms on its windows and doors. To permit authorized door openings without triggering the alarm, the door's sensor can be preemptively disabled. Furthermore, the entire alarm system can be disabled at any time. Let us examine a simple building with one door, two windows, and a central alarm panel, where each entryway (door and windows) is also fitted with a local siren. The AbU system modeling this scenario is

$$S = D\langle \Sigma_1, \varnothing \rangle \parallel W\langle \Sigma_2, \varnothing \rangle \parallel W\langle \Sigma_3, \varnothing \rangle \parallel P\langle \Sigma_4, \varnothing \rangle$$

where D, W are the rule sets for doors and windows respectively, both containing:

$$\text{doorOpen} \triangleright @(\text{alarmOn} \wedge \text{doorOpen}) : \overline{\text{siren} \leftarrow true} \quad (R3)$$
$$\text{doorOpen} \triangleright (\text{alarmOn} \wedge \text{doorOpen}) : \text{siren} \leftarrow true \quad (R4)$$

Rule (R3) says that whenever the door is opened while the alarm is on, all sirens should turn on, while rule (R4) is the same but only for the local siren.
   On the other hand, P is the rule set for the alarm panel containing:

$$\text{alarmSwitch} \triangleright @(\text{alarmSwitch}) : \overline{\text{alarmOn} \leftarrow true} \quad (R5)$$
$$\text{alarmSwitch} \triangleright @(!\text{alarmSwitch}) : \overline{\text{siren} \leftarrow false}, \overline{\text{alarmOn} \leftarrow false} \quad (R6)$$

Rule (R5) activates the alarm system when the alarmSwitch is switched on. When it is turned off, (R6) disables the alarm system and turns off all sirens.
   Suppose that the initial execution states are as follows:

$$\Sigma_1 = [\,\text{alarmOn} \mapsto true \quad \text{doorOpen} \mapsto false \quad \text{siren} \mapsto false\,]$$
$$\Sigma_2 = [\,\text{alarmOn} \mapsto true \quad \text{doorOpen} \mapsto false \quad \text{siren} \mapsto false\,]$$
$$\Sigma_3 = [\,\text{alarmOn} \mapsto true \quad \text{doorOpen} \mapsto false \quad \text{siren} \mapsto false\,]$$
$$\Sigma_4 = [\,\text{alarmSwitch} \mapsto true\,]$$

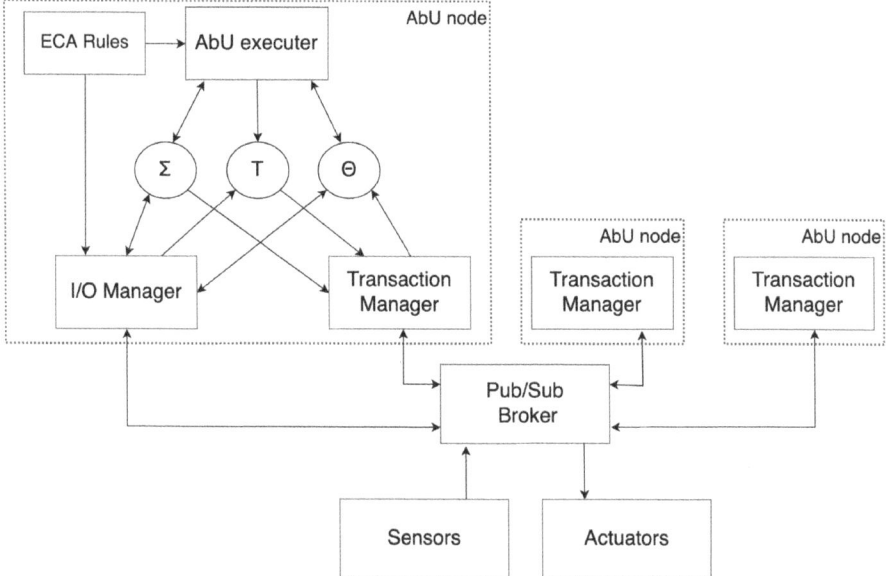

Fig. 3. Architecture of an AbU system on a generic Pub/Sub middleware.

Suppose that, at this moment, the doorOpen variable in the state Σ_1 becomes *true*. Consequently, rules (R3) and (R4) will trigger on the device $D\langle \Sigma_1, \varnothing \rangle$, activating all sirens throughout the system. Subsequently, we can disable the alarm and silence all sirens by switching off the alarmSwitch, thereby triggering rule (R6). However, if AbU semantics permitted interleaved execution of rules, it would be possible for some nodes to execute the updates from rule (R6) before those from rule (R3), leaving the siren on those nodes active despite the alarm being disabled. To prevent such inconsistencies, guaranteeing transactional execution of communications between AbU nodes is crucial.

3 Integrating AbU with Pub/Sub Middleware

In this Section we describe the implementation of AbU on a pub/sub middleware. The architecture is presented in Fig. 3.

An AbU node $R, \iota \langle \Sigma, \Theta \rangle$ is composed by three main modules: *Executer*, *Transaction Manager*, and *I/O Manager*. These modules execute in parallel (i.e., they are parallel processes or threads), and access the node's state given by attribute state Σ and execution pool Θ.

Intuitively, the Executer selects the next update from Θ to apply to the system state Σ, first verifying that this update maintains the system invariant. Upon application, it executes the rules triggered by the update, possibly generating local updates that are added to Θ and creating tasks for other nodes. These

Function executer (T, Θ, Σ):
  while *true* do
    while $T \neq NIL$ do
      $\llcorner$; // wait for potentially initiated transaction to end
    $U \leftarrow \text{selectUpdate}(\Theta)$; // select next update from Θ; blocks if $\Theta = \emptyset$
    $\text{lock}(T); \text{lock}(\Theta)$;
    $\Theta \leftarrow \Theta \setminus \{U\}$; // remove it from pool
    $(X, \Sigma') \leftarrow \text{applyUpdate}(U, \Sigma)$;
    if $\Sigma' \models \iota$ then
      $\Sigma \leftarrow \Sigma'$;
      $\Theta \leftarrow \Theta \cup \text{localUpdates}(R, X, \Sigma)$;
      $T \leftarrow \text{externalUpdates}(R, X, \Sigma)$;
    $\text{unlock}(\Theta); \text{unlock}(T)$;

Algorithm 1: Pseudocode for the AbU executer.

inter-node tasks are stored in a shared buffer T, managed by the Transaction Manager. Concurrently, the I/O Manager handles sensor inputs and actuator outputs, also interacting through the pub/sub broker and accessing the shared data structures Σ, Θ, and T in a manner similar to the Executer.

To guarantee AbU's transactional communication semantics, the Transaction Managers of different nodes communicate by exchanging messages over the underlying pub/sub middleware, utilizing specifically designated topics. Topics can be conceptualized as named, abstract *broadcast* channels: publishers transmit messages on a topic, and all subscribed nodes receive every message published on that topic. We assume the pub/sub middleware provides First-In, First-Out (FIFO) delivery per publisher: if a node publishes messages M_1 and then M_2, all subscribers will receive them in the same sequence. However, we do not rely on causal or total ordering of messages across different publishers.

We proceed with a description of the three threads.

Executer (Algorithm 1). Each Executer iteration begins by checking if the task buffer T is empty; if T is non-empty, a pending external update requires transaction completion. The Executer then acquires a lock on T to prevent concurrent access by the I/O thread. Adhering to AbU semantics, the Executer selects an update from the execution pool (according to some defined policy) and removes it. This update is applied to the current state, generating a new state and a list of modified variables. If the new state satisfies the invariants, it becomes the current state, and the execution pool is updated with any generated local updates. Finally, if any modified variables triggered remote tasks, T is populated with these tasks, and the lock on T is released.

Input Manager (Algorithm 2). The Input manager behaves similarly to the Executer, with the only two differences being that the updates are generated by reading the device's sensors (i.e., receiving data from suitable subscriptions) and not from the execution pool, and that the invariants are not checked.

Function inputManager(T, Θ, Σ):
　while *true* **do**
　　while $T \neq NIL$ **do**
　　　$\lfloor$; // wait for potentially initiated transaction to end
　　$U \leftarrow$ receiveSensors();
　　lock(T); lock(Θ);
　　$(X, \Sigma) \leftarrow$ applyUpdate(U, Σ);
　　$\Theta \leftarrow \Theta \cup$ localUpdates(R, X, Σ);
　　$T \leftarrow$ externalUpdates(R, X, Σ);
　　unlock(Θ); unlock(T);

Algorithm 2: Pseudocode for the AbU input manager.

Transaction Manager (Algorithm 3). Finally, the Transaction Manager handles the transactional propagation of tasks for all connected nodes.

As detailed in Sect. 2, AbU semantics mandates system-wide synchronization during the discovery phase. Considering the states of AbU nodes as a distributed database, updates can be viewed as distributed transactions necessitating a coordinated commit. While the traditional two-phase commit (2PC) protocol [7] offers a standard solution, its reliance on point-to-point message exchanges makes it inefficient for pub/sub middleware. Consequently, we introduce a variant of the non-blocking 2PC [4], drawing inspiration from the decentralized commit protocol presented in [8], which is designed for broadcast networks.

Although [4] introduces broadcasts, it still depends on a central coordinator. In contrast, [8] eliminates the coordinator after the vote request phase; however, it restricts initiation to a single node within the system. This limitation prevents parallel transaction initiation, simplifying conflict management but resulting in a more static system. Furthermore, the protocol in [8] assumes a non-anonymous network, making it less suitable for implementation in pub/sub systems where nodes might not have explicit knowledge of other participants' identities.

Our variant strategically leverages broadcast messages for participant coordination and enables nodes to dynamically participate in different transactions. Crucially, it extends the decentralized nature of commit protocols by allowing any node within the system to initiate a transaction.

The Transaction Manager (Algorithm 3) can initiate a new transaction if it is not currently participating in another transaction ($tid = NIL$) and there is a task list in its shared buffer T awaiting propagation ($T \neq NIL$). Upon these conditions being met, a globally unique transaction identifier (tid) is generated. This identifier is constructed by combining the node's unique ID with a local transaction counter ($lTid$), which is incremented for each transaction initiated by that node. This combination ensures global uniqueness, as no other node can generate the same identifier. Subsequently, the initiating Transaction Manager queries the pub/sub broker to determine the number n of currently connected AbU nodes. It then publishes a *PRECOMMIT* message on the appropriate topic, including the generated transaction identifier, the total number of participants n, and the contents of the task list T. In the sequel, unless explicitly stated

Function transactionManager *(T, Θ, Σ, nodeId)*:
  isInitiator ← **false**; *tid* ← *NIL*; *U* ← *NIL*; *lTid* ← 0; // state p0
  while *true* **do**
    if $T \neq NIL$ **and** $tid = NIL$ **then**
      tid ← getTransId(*nodeId, lTid*); // go from p0 to i0
      nParticipants ← getParticipants();
      publish(*PRECOMMIT, tid, nParticipants, T*);
      isInitiator ← **true**; // state i1
    msg ← receiveFromTopic();
    switch *msg* **do**
      case *(PRECOMMIT, transId, n, T')* **do**
        if $tid = NIL$ **then** // we are not involved in a transaction,
          tid ← *transId*; // so we join this one, and go to state p1
          counter ← *n*;
          U ← selectValid(T', Σ);
          publish(*OK, tid*); // state p2
        else if $transId \geq tid$ **then**
          // we can ignore the message, as it's either about the active
          //   transaction or one with lower priority and that has to wait
        else // transId is lower than tid, so we have to switch
          publish(*ABORT, tid*); // we abort the active transaction
          U ← selectValid(T', Σ); // and switch to the new one
          tid ← *transId*;
          isInitiator ← **false**; // state p1
          publish(*OK, tid*); // state p2
      case *(OK, transId)* **do**
        if $transId = tid$ **and** *not isInitiator* **then**
          // we are currently in state p2, so we decrease the counter
          counter ← *counter* − 1;
          if *counter* == 0 **then** // we go from state p2 to state p3
            publish(*COMMIT, tid*)
      case *(COMMIT, transId)* **do**
        if $transId = tid$ **then** // the transaction has finished
          if *isInitiator* **then**
            T ← *NIL*; // we do not need to commit
            isInitiator ← **false**; // since we are the initiator
            lTid ← *lTid* + 1;
          else // we commit the transaction
            lock(Θ); Θ ← Θ ∪ *U*; unlock(Θ);
          tid ← *NIL*; // we can go back to state p0
      case *(ABORT, transId)* **do**
        if $transId = tid$ **and not** *isInitiator* **then**
          tid ← *NIL*; // we abort the transaction and go back to state p0;
          //   otherwise we go from i1 to i2 and wait for a precommit do
          //   decide what to do

Algorithm 3: Pseudocode for the AbU Transaction Manager.

otherwise, any mention of publishing a message implicitly includes the identifier of the currently active transaction.

If the node has no task list to propagate, it checks its incoming message queue for any received messages, processing them in a FIFO order. If no messages are pending, the node loops back to check for new tasks or messages.

Upon receiving a $(PRECOMMIT, transId, n, T')$ message, the node evaluates two scenarios:

1. *The node is not currently involved in any transaction ($tid = NIL$).* In this situation, the node joins the transaction identified by $transId$. It updates its local transaction ID (tid), initializes its participant counter ($counter$), evaluates the conditions of each update within the received task list T', and adds those updates whose conditions are satisfied in the current state Σ to its local update set U. Finally, the node publishes an acknowledgement message (OK) to the relevant topic, including $transId$.
2. *The node is already participating in another transaction ($tid \neq NIL$).* This situation represents a conflict between the ongoing transaction and a newly proposed transaction with ID $transId$. This conflict is resolved by prioritizing the transaction with the lower ID. Consequently, if the received $transId$ is greater than or equal to the current transaction's ID, the new transaction is disregarded. Conversely, if $transId$ is lower, the current transaction is aborted. The node then joins the transaction identified by $transId$, updating its tid, initializing its $counter$, and adding the applicable updates from T' to U, followed by publishing an OK message for $transId$. Importantly, the local task list T remains unchanged, ensuring that its propagation will be re-attempted once the newly joined transaction $transId$ concludes.

The OK message plays a vital role in achieving transaction completion. Upon receiving an (OK, tid) message, each node participating in the transaction identified by tid decrements its local $counter$. When a node's $counter$ reaches zero, it indicates that all expected participants have acknowledged the $PRECOMMIT$ message, thus concluding the first phase of the commit protocol for that node. At this point, any participant that has reached this zero count can initiate the second phase by broadcasting a $COMMIT$ message associated with tid.

Upon receiving a $COMMIT$ message bearing the correct transaction identifier, a node acknowledges that system-wide consensus has been achieved, regardless of whether its local $counter$ reached zero. If the receiving node initiated the transaction, it clears its task buffer T and increments its local transaction counter ($lTid$) in preparation for future transactions. If the node was a participant but not the initiator, it applies the accumulated updates in its local set U to its execution pool Θ.

Conversely, upon receiving an $ABORT$ message (typically due to a higher-priority conflicting transaction), the Transaction Manager aborts the currently active transaction if its identifier indicates a lower priority. If the aborted transaction was initiated by this node, the contents of its task buffer T are preserved, ensuring that the intended tasks will be re-attempted in a subsequent transac-

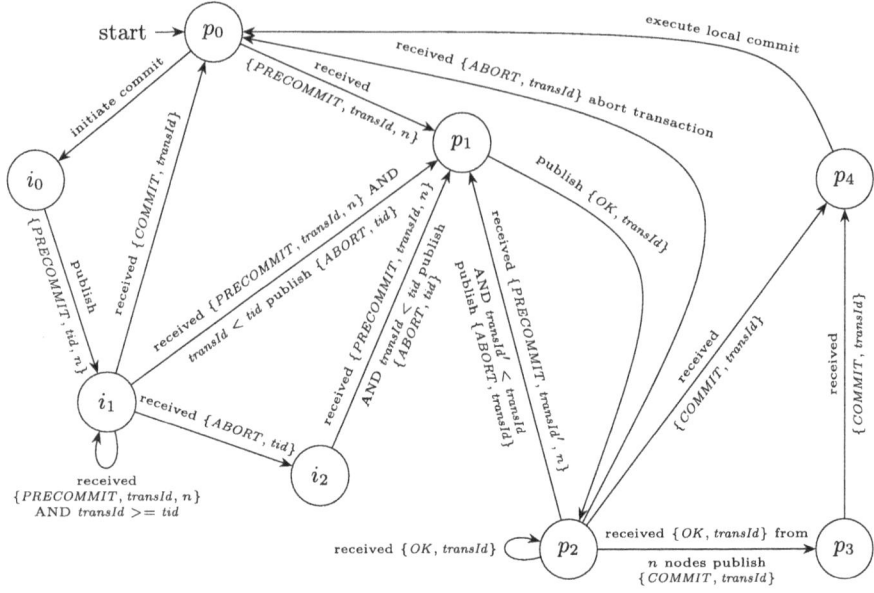

Fig. 4. Finite state automaton for the commit protocol.

tion. Notice that the local transaction counter ($lTid$) is not incremented in this scenario, as the aborted transaction did not successfully commit.

4 Correctness of the Commit Protocol

This section provides a correctness proof for the Commit protocol implemented by the Transaction Managers. We model the protocol (Algorithm 3) as the Deterministic Finite Automaton (DFA) illustrated in Fig. 4, where the DFA's states directly correspond to specific points annotated in the pseudocode comments.

Although all nodes execute the same underlying DFA, their transitions and roles differ based on whether they initiate or participate in a transaction. To emphasize that a node assumes only one role at any given time within a specific transaction - it cannot be both initiator and participant simultaneously for the same tid - we define a single DFA that encompasses both initiator and participant behaviors. State p_0 represents the initial state where a node is not engaged in any transaction. States p_1, p_2, p_3, and p_4 capture the participant's progression through the protocol, while states i_0, i_1, and i_2 represent the initiator's lifecycle. Communication between these DFA instances occurs via a designated pub/sub topic, effectively providing a broadcast communication channel.

Upon receiving a *PRECOMMIT* message (containing the expected total number of participants, n) while not currently involved in a transaction, a node moves to participant states, sends an *OK* acknowledgement, and begins listening for subsequent messages. Once a participant has received n *OK* acknowledgements (inclusive of its own implicit acknowledgement), it broadcasts a *COMMIT* message and proceeds with its local commit action. Although causal ordering of messages across different publishers cannot be guaranteed, the protocol ensures that at least one participant will eventually gather all n acknowledgements and broadcast the *COMMIT* message. Consequently, if a node receives a *COMMIT* message before it has completed its acknowledgement count, it can safely proceed with its local commit, as the reception of the *COMMIT* implicitly confirms that all participants have agreed to the transaction.

During this phase, an *ABORT* message can also be received. Upon receiving an *ABORT* message associated with the current transaction, the DFA transitions back to its initial state, effectively aborting the local participation in that transaction. While it is possible for an *ABORT* message to arrive before the initial *PRECOMMIT* and thus be initially disregarded, this scenario is addressed by the initiator's continuous propagation of *ABORT* messages upon detecting a conflict. Given the FIFO delivery guarantee from each publisher provided by the pub/sub middleware, we are assured that participants will eventually receive and correctly process any relevant *ABORT* messages, as discussed below.

We can now state the properties for this synchronization protocol.

SP1 *Eventual Transaction Termination*: Every transaction will eventually be committed.

SP2 *Absence of Deadlocks*: The Executer thread will always be released from its wait on T.

Before proving these properties let us summarize the assumptions we make on the system.

SA1 *Reliable Broadcast*: Each published message will be delivered to all subscribers within a bounded amount of time.

SA2 *Transaction identifiers uniqueness and ordering* : Transaction identifiers are generated locally on each node by combining a local counter t with the node's unique identifier id, denoted as $Id(t, id)$. This construction ensures global uniqueness. We assume a strict total order $<$ exists for node identifiers, such that $id < id'$. This ordering is then extended to transaction identifiers, resulting in a strict total order $<$ for transaction identifiers with the following properties:
– For any local counter values t and t' and node identifiers id and id', if $t < t'$, then $Id(t, id) < Id(t', id')$.
– For any local counter value t and node identifiers id and id', if $id < id'$, then $Id(t, id) < Id(t, id')$.

Specifically, the provided conditions imply that a transaction identifier generated later by the same node will always be greater, and transactions generated by a node with a smaller ID will have a smaller identifier given the same local counter value. This strict total order is crucial for resolving conflicts during concurrent transactions.

SA3 *Scheduling Fairness*: Each node implements a fair scheduler such that no thread can be infinitely often enabled and never executed.

SA4 *FIFO Ordering* : Two messages m_1 and m_2 sent by the same node will also be delivered in the same order.

Given that our only ordering guarantee is FIFO per publisher, and specifically not causal ordering across different publishers, it is possible for an OK acknowledgement message for transaction t originating from one participant to arrive at another participant (or the initiator) before the corresponding $PRECOMMIT$ message from the initiator. This out-of-order arrival could lead to the OK being discarded by a node not yet aware of the transaction, potentially preventing any node from reaching the required n acknowledgements needed to initiate the $COMMIT$. However, we will now demonstrate that despite this potential for out-of-order delivery, *at least* one node will be able to correctly accumulate the acknowledgements and subsequently broadcast the $COMMIT$ message.

Proposition 1 (Reachability of the commit state). *For a given transaction t among n participants, if no faults occur, at least one node will eventually be able to count n "OK" messages.*

Proof. Because of property SA1 (all subscribers receive all messages published on a topic), every node in the system will eventually receive the $PRECOMMIT$ message for transaction t. A node can only fail to count all n acknowledgements if one or more OK messages arrive before the corresponding $PRECOMMIT$ and are consequently discarded by nodes not yet participating in the transaction. However, a node N_i can only send an OK acknowledgement *after* it has received and processed the $PRECOMMIT$ message. This implies that at least one other node, say N_j, must have received the $PRECOMMIT$ before N_i could have sent its acknowledgement. Let N_f be the first node in the system to receive the $PRECOMMIT$ message for transaction t. Since N_f is the first to receive it, no other node could have sent an OK for t yet, thus no acknowledgements for t could have been discarded before N_f received the $PRECOMMIT$. Given the reliable nature of the pub/sub middleware (SA1) and our assumption of no node failures, N_f will subsequently receive all n acknowledgements (including its own) in the order they are sent. This will eventually cause N_f's local counter to reach zero, at which point N_f will broadcast the $COMMIT$ for transaction t. □

Let us now proceed to prove property SP1 (Eventual Termination). Since the Transaction Manager process can operate continuously, "termination" in this context does not refer to the cessation of the automaton's execution; instead, it signifies the eventual completion of each initiated transaction instance, specifically reaching the commit phase where the $COMMIT$ message is broadcast.

Theorem 1. *The protocol satisfies property SP1.*

Proof. First, consider the case where no transaction conflicts occur. By Proposition 1, at least one participating node will eventually send a COMMIT message, transitioning all nodes from state p_2 to p_4, and subsequently to p_0, effectively completing the transaction for those nodes. Similarly, in the absence of conflicts, the initiator remains in state i_1 and, upon receiving the COMMIT message, transitions to p_0, also completing the transaction.

The only potential issue arises when transaction conflicts occur. If two transactions t_1 and t_2, with $t_1 < t_2$, conflict, t_1 is prioritized and t_2 is aborted and postponed. As we can see from the pseudocode, the transaction identifier is modified and the payload T consumed *only* after the transaction is committed. This means that when the node completes transaction t_1, it will restart the transaction t_2, that could not be completed earlier, with the same identifier as before.

A potential issue could arise if another transaction repeatedly conflicts with t_2 each time t_2 attempts to commit, potentially preventing t_2 from ever reaching the commit state. Property SA2 prevents this scenario. The transaction identifier assigned to t_2 remains constant throughout its lifetime. Since each node increments its local counter with every successful transaction, eventually, all transactions initiated by nodes with lower node IDs will acquire a local counter value at least as large as t_2's. Consequently, due to the ordering defined in SA2 (prioritizing lower local counters and then lower node IDs), t_2's identifier will eventually become the globally lowest among all currently active transactions in the system, thus ensuring that no other transaction can preempt it.

Another potential issue that could prevent reaching the commit state is if a *COMMIT* message were received and discarded by a node before it had even processed the corresponding *PRECOMMIT* message. However, this scenario is impossible due to the protocol's logic. If a node were to process a *PRECOMMIT* message *after* already receiving a *COMMIT* for the same transaction, it implies that this node could not have sent its *OK* acknowledgement *before* processing the *PRECOMMIT*. Consequently the initiating node (or any other participant counting acknowledgements) would not have reached the necessary count to broadcast the *COMMIT* message in the first place. Therefore, a *COMMIT* message cannot be validly broadcast and received before the corresponding *PRECOMMIT* has been processed by at least one participant. □

From this theorem immediately follows property SP2 for the Executer.

Corollary 1. *The Executer thread will never indefinitely wait for T to become empty (i.e., loop indefinitely in lines 2–3 of Algorithm 1), thus avoiding deadlock.*

Proof. This follows directly from Theorem 1 and the lock-based access control to the shared memory T. □

Finally, we can demonstrate the absence of race conditions, meaning it is impossible for two different nodes to simultaneously reach their commit phases for distinct, conflicting transactions.

Corollary 2. *At any time, all automata which are in state p_4 (local commit) have the same transId.*

Proof. As established in Theorem 1, when two or more transactions enter a conflict, the protocol ensures that only the transaction with the lowest identifier will proceed towards commitment, while all others involved in the conflict will be aborted. Consequently, if an automaton reaches the state p_4 (local commit), it signifies that the $transId$ associated with its current transaction must be the lowest among all transaction attempts currently active within the system. Given the total ordering of transaction identifiers (SA2), the lowest $transId$ is unique at any given moment of conflict resolution. □

Remark 1. A potential issue arises in state p_2 if the pub/sub middleware does not guarantee the absence of duplicate messages. Because acknowledgements are anonymous, duplicates could lead to premature COMMIT messages: a node might decrement its counter to zero before all participants have actually consented. If the underlying system suffers of frequent duplicate messages, we recommend augmenting acknowledgements with the sender's unique ID. Upon receiving an acknowledgment, instead of simply decrementing a counter, the node updates a bitmap, setting the bit corresponding to the sender's ID. Only when all expected acknowledgements have been received (indicated by all bits in the bitmap being set) the node can proceed with the commit.

5 Conclusions

This paper presented the integration of AbU, a recent calculus combining ECA rules with attribute-based communication, with pub/sub middleware commonly used in IoT systems, such as MQTT and DDS. We introduced a novel approach for implementing distributed transactions between nodes by leveraging pub/sub primitives. This approach treats the system as a distributed database requiring synchronized commits, enabling decentralized coordination without a central authority, thus promoting scalability and robustness. Our work provides both automata and pseudocode representations, establishing a theoretical and practical foundation for future development and real-world applications. We formally proved that our proposed protocol guarantees transaction termination and the absence of deadlocks and race conditions in parallel threads.

This integration offers several key advantages: it combines the expressiveness of ECA rules for defining complex interactions with the efficiency and scalability of pub/sub communication; it provides formal guarantees of correctness, crucial for reliable system operation; and it offers a practical implementation framework readily deployable in existing IoT infrastructures and smart systems.

Related Work. Previous work has been carried out about the implementation of attribute-based communications in Erlang [5], Java [2] and Go [1]. AbaCus and GoAt, namely the implementations in Java and Go, while implementing AbC's semantics, rely on a centralised broker, leading to an undesirable single point-of-failure. AErlang can be seen as an extension of the Erlang language with some AbC ingredients. A more recent work, ABEL [6] makes another attempt at encoding AbC into Erlang, with a provably correct implementation. ABEL shares the same tree-shaped infrastructure proposed in [1] as GoAt, although the latter also offers ring and cluster shaped infrastructures, which ABEL lacks.

Furthermore, GoAt's proofs of correctness [1] prove that components converge to correct values, while with ABEL it can be proven that there is a correct correspondence between its transitions and AbC's lock-step evolution.

Future Work. We plan to perform an evaluation of our implementation's performance and scalability in real-world IoT deployments, especially with resource-constrained devices which could require specific optimizations. Furthermore, we will investigate the broader applicability of our approach, particularly the presented pub/sub-based distributed commit protocol, to other distributed systems relying on anonymous, reliable pub/sub communication. An especially interesting avenue for future research involves guaranteeing global invariants through coordinated local updates, following the principles outlined in [13].

Acknowledgments. This work has been partially supported by the M4C2 I1.3 "SEcurity and RIghts In the CyberSpace - SERICS" (PE00000014 - CUP H73C2200089001), under the National Recovery and Resilience Plan (NRRP) funded by NextGenerationEU, and by the Project BRIGANTINE - *Chemico-physical and multispectral data fusion for Adriatic Sea monitoring by autonomous vessel* (INTERREG Italy-Croatia Program 2021–2027, grant number ITHR0200237), funded by the European Union.

References

1. Abd Alrahman, Y., De Nicola, R., Garbi, G., Loreti, M.: A distributed coordination infrastructure for attribute-based interaction. In: Formal Techniques for Distributed Objects, Components, and Systems (FORTE 2018), LNCS, vol. 10854, pp. 1–20. Springer (2018)
2. Abd Alrahman, Y., De Nicola, R., Loreti, M.: Programming of CAS systems by relying on attribute-based communication. In: Margaria, T., Steffen, B. (eds.) Leveraging Applications of Formal Methods, Verification and Validation: Foundational Techniques - 7th Int. Symposium, ISoLA 2016, Proceedings, Part I, LNCS, vol. 9952, pp. 539–553 (2016). https://doi.org/10.1007/978-3-319-47166-2_38
3. Abd Alrahman, Y., De Nicola, R., Loreti, M., Tiezzi, F., Vigo, R.: A calculus for attribute-based communication. In: Proceeding of 30th SAC, pp. 1840–1845. ACM (2015)
4. Babaoglu, O., Toueg, S.: Understanding non-blocking atomic commitment. Technical Report (1993)
5. De Nicola, R., Duong, T., Inverso, O., Trubiani, C.: AErlang at work. In: Steffen, B., Baier, C., van den Brand, M., Eder, J., Hinchey, M., Margaria, T. (eds.) SOFSEM 2017: Theory and Practice of Computer Science, pp. 485–497. Springer, Cham (2017)
6. De Nicola, R., Duong, T., Loreti, M.: Provably correct implementation of the AbC calculus. Sci. Comput. Program. **202**, 102567 (2021), http://www.sciencedirect.com/science/article/pii/S0167642320301751
7. Gray, J.: Notes on data base operating systems, vol. 6, pp. 393–481. Springer, Berlin, Germany (1978). https://doi.org/10.1007/3-540-08755-9_9

8. Guerraoui, R., Schiper, A.: The decentralized non-blocking atomic commitment protocol. In: Proceedings Seventh IEEE Symposium on Parallel and Distributed Processing. pp. 2–9. IEEE, Los Alamitos, CA, USA (1995). https://doi.org/10.1109/SPDP.1995.530658
9. Inverso, O., Trubiani, C., Tuosto, E.: Abstractions for collective adaptive systems. In: Margaria, T., Steffen, B. (eds.) Leveraging Applications of Formal Methods, Verification and Validation: Engineering Principles - 9th Int. Symposium, ISoLA 2020, Proceedings, Part II. Lecture Notes in Computer Science, vol. 12477, pp. 243–260. Springer (2020). https://doi.org/10.1007/978-3-030-61470-6_15
10. Miculan, M., Pasqua, M.: A calculus for attribute-based memory updates. In: Cerone, A., Ölveczky, P.C. (eds.) ICTAC 2021. LNCS, vol. 12819, pp. 366–385. Springer, Cham (2021). https://doi.org/10.1007/978-3-030-85315-0_21
11. Pasqua, M., Comuzzo, M., Miculan, M.: The AbU language: IoT distributed programming made easy. IEEE Access **10**, 132763–132776 (2022). https://doi.org/10.1109/ACCESS.2022.3230287
12. Pasqua, M., Miculan, M.: AbU: A calculus for distributed event-driven programming with attribute-based interaction. Theor. Comput. Sci. 1–32 (2023). https://doi.org/10.1016/j.tcs.2023.113841
13. Pasqua, M., Miculan, M.: Local reasoning and attribute-based memory updates for enforcing global invariants in collective adaptive systems. In: Margaria, T., Steffen, B. (eds.) Leveraging Applications of Formal Methods, Verification and Validation. Rigorous Engineering of Collective Adaptive Systems - 12th Int. Symposium, ISoLA 2024, Proceedings, Part II, LNCS, vol. 15220, pp. 351–367. Springer (2024). https://doi.org/10.1007/978-3-031-75107-3_21

Probabilistic Safety Verification of Distributed Systems: A Statistical Approach for Monitoring

Bineet Ghosh[1](✉) and Étienne André[2,3]

[1] The University of Alabama, Tuscaloosa, AL, USA
bineet@ua.edu
[2] Université Sorbonne Paris Nord, LIPN, CNRS UMR 7030, Villetaneuse, France
[3] Institut universitaire de France (IUF), Paris, France
https://lipn.univ-paris13.fr/~andre/

Abstract. With the increasing autonomous capabilities of distributed cyber-physical systems, the complexity of their models also increases significantly, thus continually posing challenges to existing formal methods for safety verification. In contrast to model checking, monitoring emerges as an effective lightweight, yet practical verification technique capable of delivering results of practical importance with better scalability. Monitoring involves analyzing logs from an actual system to determine whether a specification (such as a safety property) is violated. Monitoring techniques, such as those using reachability methods, may fail to produce results when dealing with complex models like Deep Neural Networks (DNNs). We propose here a novel statistical approach for monitoring that is able to generate results with high probabilistic guarantees. We evaluate our monitoring technique on three case studies.

Keywords: Autonomous Systems · Monitoring · Statistical Verification

1 Introduction

Over the past decade, there has been a swift increase in the deployment of distributed autonomous systems across various domains. While formal methods have proven successful in various safety-critical domains, several existing techniques have been unable to cope with the growing complexity of these models. Formal verification requires an accurate model, which may not often be available, because some components are black-box, or because the entire system has no formal model. Despite some success in verifying formal models from the industry (e.g., [3,9,20,22]), formal verification techniques for autonomous systems are often subject to state space explosion and conservative analysis.

This work is partially supported by ANR BisoUS (ANR-22-CE48-0012). Artifacts available in https://doi.org/10.5281/zenodo.15190263.

Monitoring. Contrary to model checking, monitoring is an effective lightweight, yet feasible verification technique, that can bring practical results for systems with relatively high complexity. Monitoring involves analyzing the log of a system to determine if a given specification has been violated [7]. Deterministic monitoring—where safety guarantees that are not probabilistic but formally ensured—encounters challenges in dealing with complex models like black-box systems, DNN-based models, and Simulink models. These challenges include limited adaptability to complex models, difficulties in achieving black-box transparency, and scalability issues [7,8,15,24,25,30].

Proposed Approach and Statistical Hypothesis Testing. This work, on the other hand, aims to ensure that autonomous systems are *trustworthy*, which means they are safe for most practical purposes with a high level of confidence. This approach contrasts with approaches that strive for formal safety, which might not be practical for complex systems. As such, we propose a statistical monitoring approach that employs Bayesian hypothesis testing [13,21,36]. By trading-off formal safety guarantees with statistical guarantees, our technique has the following advantages: i) Our method is versatile and can handle various system types, including non-linear and DNNs models. This is achieved merely by leveraging the knowledge of the system's input/output execution behavior (with detailed explanations provided later). In simpler terms, our approach simply assumes that random executions (i.e., trajectories) of the system can be generated from a specified initial state. We refer to this representation as *I/O execution*. ii) The user can adjust the confidence level needed for the analysis based on the specific use case. For example, in a safety critical scenario, a high confidence level (e.g., 0.99) may be chosen, while in less critical situations, a lower confidence level can be selected. Our method requires less time for monitoring as the desired confidence level decreases. iii) If the I/O execution is computationally efficient for a given system model, this method scales well even when the system model is complex.

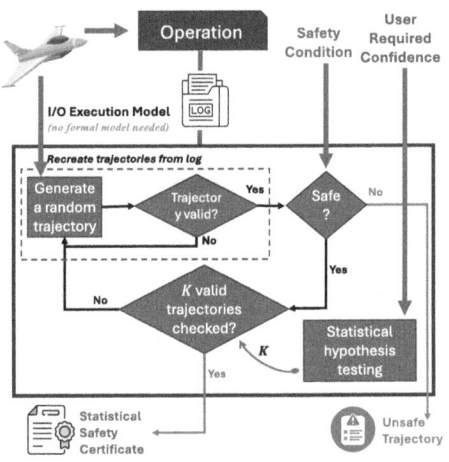

Fig. 1. Proposed Monitoring Approach

Our approach is illustrated in Fig. 1. After the system completes its real-world operation, it produces a log that comprises of both noisy and missing records. The noise in the log may result from sensor uncertainties, while missing records could be attributed to transmission losses over a shared network or the system's energy-saving policies (especially in intermittently powered devices). The task of monitoring is to analyze this log for possible safety violations. Once the inputs are received (I/O execution model, log, safety condition), the proposed approach performs a series of steps to analyze the log for safety violation. Before discussing the steps of the proposed approach, it is worth recalling that our approach is statistical, and as such, the assurances it offers are inherently probabilistic. Specifically, if the approach identifies a trajectory breaching the safety condition, it is reported as a counterexample. Upon discovering such a counterexample, the intrinsic nature of our method ensures that it is concrete—meaning it is a real execution of the actual system, reconstructed from the available logs, that indeed violates the safety condition. Consequently, the system is confirmed to be unsafe. However, if no violating trajectory is found, it infers that the system is safe *with probabilistic guarantees*. The key challenge in monitoring a given uncertain system log with missing records lies in efficiently recreating the missing records from the available noisy records of the log. In essence, recreating missing records amounts to generating complete trajectories (i.e., records available at all time steps) of the system from the given log. These recreated trajectories are regarded as a valid recreation of the behavior of the system from the given log. As the available records of the given log are noisy (i.e., not reduced to a point), there could be an infinite number of potential trajectories that can be recreated from the available records of the given log. That is, any trajectory of the system that passes through (i.e., intersects) all the available noisy records of the log, is considered a valid recreation of the behavior of the system from the given log. We refer to such a trajectory as a valid sample trajectory (or simply a valid trajectory) w.r.t. the given log (formally defined in Definition 3). Recreating all possible valid trajectories from a given noisy log usually requires reachability analysis, which often results in conservative estimates, suffers from scalability problems, and may be completely unavailable for complex systems. In contrast, our method overcomes this issue by trading-off formal guarantees with statistical guarantees, and thus only requiring to check a finite number of valid sample trajectories generated from the log. To do so, the user configures the proposed monitoring approach by specifying the desired confidence level for the analysis. This is typically chosen to be high, e.g., $c = 0.99$, where c stands for the desired confidence. Based on the required pre-set user confidence, our method computes the value of K, which is the number of random valid trajectories (recreated from the records in the log) that must be checked for safety in order to infer the system to be safe with the required confidence c. It is worth noting, in our approach, to generate a valid trajectory (w.r.t. to the given log), we simply proceed to generate a random trajectory of the system (from the given initial set), and then check if it intersects with all the records in the given log (see Fig. 1). If the trajectory intersects with every record of the log, we classify it as one of the valid trajectories among the K valid trajectories to be checked for safety. Otherwise, we discard it and generate a new trajectory. While checking K random valid trajectories for safety, if a trajectory is found to be violating the safety condition, then it is returned as concrete counterexample, and the system is inferred as unsafe. If all the K random valid trajectories are safe, our method guarantees the system is safe with the required the probabilistic confidence c. An overview of the propsoed approach is given in Fig. 1.

Contributions. The main contributions of this work are:

1. An SHT (statistical hypothesis testing)-based framework, using Jefferies Bayes factor, for monitoring (proposed in Sect. 4).
2. A monitoring algorithm—that leverages the SHT-based framework—to detect safety violations from a given input log with noisy and missing records (proposed in Sect. 5).
3. We implemented our method as prototype tool, named `Posto`. Further, using this tool, we evaluated the proposed algorithm on three case studies, with two non-linear models and one DNN-based model. Our tool successfully monitored all the systems under 250 s.

Outline. Section 2 reviews related works. Section 3 recalls necessary preliminaries. Section 5 and 4 introduce our approach, and Sect. 6 discusses implementation and experiments. Section 7 outlines future works.

2 Related Work

Deterministic Monitoring. Signal Temporal Logic (STL) formalizes real-valued signal properties in dense-time contexts. In practical scenarios with continuous dynamics and numerical parameters, simple yes/no answers are insufficient, requiring quantitative satisfaction details for informed decision-making. Existing methods like [14,18] handle complex safety specifications but often need formal models or direct signal access, which can be overly complex or unavailable. In addition to STL-based monitoring, recent attention has shifted towards monitoring using automata-based specifications. Notably, advancements have been made in the study of complex, quantitative extensions of automata. Techniques such as timed pattern matching on timed regular expressions [6,29] have emerged, particularly in the context of deterministic offline monitoring. The concept of *model-bounded monitoring*, introduced in [30], deviates from the conventional approach of monitoring a black-box system solely against a specification. Instead, it incorporates a limited, over-approximated understanding of the system to mitigate false positives. The over-approximated knowledge takes the form of a *linear hybrid automaton*. Model-bounded monitoring was extended in the framework of uncertain linear systems in [15]. Unlike all these deterministic approaches, our proposed monitoring approach does not require any formal model—and can handle complex models such as non-linear models, DNNs etc.—of the system. It trades off formal safety guarantees with high confidence probabilistic guarantees.

Statistical Verification. Statistical verification has found extensive application across various domains, such as [12,19,28,34] (see a survey in [23]). The method proposed in [35] uses statistical model checking which relies on Clopper-Pearson confidence levels (see [27]). This approach is used for verification of sample specifications in a Neural Network-based controller, captured through STL formulas. The work in [13] also uses the *Jeffries Bayes factor* test but tackles a fundamentally different problem. While they analyze falsifying traces in cyber-physical systems to identify input regions responsible for property violations, we apply the same statistical method for monitoring complex systems with noisy and missing logs. Our goal is to detect safety violations, rather than characterize counterexample neighborhoods. Further, privacy implications of statistical model checking algorithms through the lens of differential privacy has also been explored [31]. Specifically, it focuses on sequential algorithms that draw samples until a specified condition is satisfied. It shows that disclosing the number of samples drawn can compromise privacy and highlights the inadequacy of the standard exponential mechanism in achieving differential privacy for sequential algorithms. Statistical methods have also been applied to learn simpler models of systems, that can offer probabilistic guarantees, using a limited number of samples. These models, known as *Probabilistic Approximately Correct (PAC)* models, have been used in various works, such as [4,11,26]. One commonly used approach for learning PAC models is through *scenario optimization* [10]. Additionally, techniques based on scenario optimization have been employed to identify safe inputs for black box systems, as discussed in [32,33].

3 Background and Problem Statement

The autonomous system under consideration evolves in discrete time in $\mathbb{R}^n$, called state space, where n is the dimension of the system. A state is $x \in \mathbb{R}^n$. It is worth noting that a formal model of the system is not explicitly required to apply our proposed monitoring approach. Essentially, all that is needed is a knowledge of the I/O execution described by $f_{sys}(x_0, t, [\epsilon]_{t-1}) = x_t$, where $x_0 \in \mathbb{R}^n$ represents the initial state, $x_t \in \mathbb{R}^n$ represents the system's state at time t, and $[\epsilon]_{t-1} = \{\epsilon_0, \epsilon_1, \ldots, \epsilon_{t-1}\}$ is a set of environmental inputs (i.e., disturbances experienced) to the system up to time t where $\forall_i \epsilon_i \in \mathbb{R}^n$. In simpler terms, $f_{sys}(x_0, t, [\epsilon]_{t-1})$ represents the behavior of the system from an initial state x_0 over time t to yield the state x_t, with environmental inputs $[\epsilon]_{t-1}$. The benefit of this formulation lies in its agnosticism towards the specific details of the system's internal workings. The proposed monitoring approach operates effectively as long as the output state x_t can be generated from the given input parameters $(x_0, t, [\epsilon]_{t-1})$. No constraints are imposed on the nature of the discrete-time system model; it can be non-linear, utilize DNNs, or exhibit various other characteristics. This flexibility in accommodating diverse system models underscores the versatility of the proposed method. In other words, this allows for our method to be applied on a wide range of autonomous systems, making it a suitable approach for handling complex and diverse scenarios where detailed knowledge of the internal system dynamics may not be readily accessible. In our experiments, we evaluated our proposed approach on both non-linear models and a model employing a DNN-based controller, all of which was successfully monitored under 250 s.

Definition 1 (Reachable Set). *We overload the function $f_{sys}(\cdot)$ to take set values as follows. Given an initial set θ_0, and environmental inputs $[\mathcal{O}]_{t-1} = \{o_1, o_2, \cdots, o_{t-1}\}$, the reachable set at time step t is given as θ_t. Formally, the*

I/O execution of the system is given as follows: $f_{sys}(\theta_0, t, [\mathcal{O}]_{t-1}) = \theta_t$; where $\theta_0, \theta_t \subset \mathbb{R}^n$, and $\forall_{i \in [0, t-1]} o_i \subset \mathbb{R}^n$.

Definition 2 (Log). *Given a system I/O execution model as in Definition 1, a finite size (uncertain) log of the system is defined as follows:* $\ell = \{(\hat{\theta}_t, t) \mid \theta_t \subseteq \hat{\theta}_t, t \leq H\}$, *where* $H \in \mathbb{N}$ *is a given time bound.*

Properties and Notations for Logs. Each tuple $(\hat{\theta}_t, t)$ is called a *record*. It is worth noting that the records are not necessarily reduced to a *point*. The size of the log ℓ, indicating the number of records it contains, is denoted by $|\ell|$. In a log ℓ, the k-th record is denoted as $\ell_k = (\hat{\theta}_{t_k}, t_k)$, where $\hat{\theta}_{t_k}$ over-approximates the system's state at time step t_k. It is worth highlighting that the size of a log may not necessarily be equal to H, but rather, $|\ell| \leq H$. In other words, the logs are considered *scattered*, implying that they may not contain a record for every t in the range of $1, \ldots, H$. We assume that each record of the log contains the true state of the system at a given time step, i.e., it is an over-approximation of the system's state. In practical scenarios, this assumption is generally valid. Physical sensors, as employed in applications like medical devices and cars, record values within an acceptable margin of error, providing a range of values that encompass the actual state.

Definition 3 (Valid Trajectory). *A trajectory τ of the system is an ordered sequence of states given as follows:* $\tau = \{x_0, x_1, \cdots, x_H\}$; *where* $\forall_{t \in [0, H]} f_{sys}(x_0, t, [\epsilon]_{t-1}) = x_t$. *A trajectory* $\tau = \{x_0, x_1, \cdots, x_H\}$ *is said to be valid w.r.t. a given log* $\ell = \{(\hat{\theta}_t, t) \mid \theta_t \subseteq \hat{\theta}_t, t \leq H\}$ *(of the same system) if:* $\forall_{(\hat{\theta}_t, t) \in \ell} \ x_t \in \hat{\theta}_t$.

In other words, a valid trajectory is a valid "recreation" of the behavior of the system from the given uncertain log.

Definition 4 (Random Trajectory). *Given a log* ℓ, *let* $\bar{\tau}_{val}$ *denote the set of all valid trajectories of the system w.r.t.* ℓ, *with environmental inputs* $[\mathcal{O}]_H$ *(see Definition 3). We assume that the trajectories* $\tau \in \bar{\tau}_{val}$ *are distributed according to a given probability distribution* $\mathcal{D}$. *Let a trajectory* τ *be randomly chosen from the set of all valid trajectories* $\bar{\tau}_{val}$ *(w.r.t. to* ℓ *and environmental inputs* $[\mathcal{O}]_H$*). This is randomly drawn according to the distribution* $\mathcal{D}$, *and formally expressed as* $\tau = \texttt{Sample}(f_{sys}(\cdot), \ell, [\mathcal{O}]_H, \mathcal{D})$.

For all our experiments, we assume $\mathcal{D}$ to be a uniform distribution. However, our method is compatible with any distribution $\mathcal{D}$ provided that an implementation of $\texttt{Sample}(\cdot)$ is available.

We aim here at performing safety monitoring of systems, from an uncertain log, utilizing an I/O execution model.

Problem 1. **INPUTS**:

1. the system I/O execution model $f_{sys}(\cdot)$;

2. an uncertain log $\ell = \{(\hat{\theta}_t, t) \mid \theta_t \subseteq \hat{\theta}_t, t \leq H\}$;
3. environmental inputs $[\mathcal{O}]_H$;
4. the probability distribution $\mathcal{D}$ followed by the set of valid trajectories;
5. an unsafe set $\mathcal{U}$; and
6. a confidence $c \in (0,1)$ desired on the required safety verification.

PROBLEM: perform monitoring to ensure safety of the system with confidence c as defined by Jefferies Bayes factor based SHT.

4 SHT for Probabilistic Monitoring

In this section, we outline the statistical framework using Jeffries Bayes factor for hypothesis testing. The goal is to derive the value of K, representing the number of valid trajectories. These trajectories must be examined for safety to confirm that the system meets the required guarantee c. Let us first provide a brief overview of SHT. Our SHT framework formulates two hypotheses: the null hypothesis H_0 and the alternate hypothesis H_1. These hypotheses aim to determine if the system violated the safety condition based on the provided log. The null hypothesis H_0 asserts that a randomly chosen valid trajectory is safe (i.e., it does not intersect with the unsafe set), with a probability of *at most c*. On the other hand, the alternate hypothesis H_1 asserts that a randomly chosen valid trajectory is safe with a probability of *at least c*. After formulating the hypotheses, we collect evidence through random sampling of a finite number of valid trajectories. The algorithm concludes when enough evidence is gathered to validate either hypothesis (H_0 or H_1). The supported hypothesis, determined by observed random samples, is accepted, while the opposing one is rejected. Subsequently, we employ a Bayesian hypothesis test to make a decision between these two hypotheses [21]. An important consequence of our test is, when the samples we have drawn do not support the alternate hypothesis, they will contain a *counterexample* (also a valid trajectory) that violates safety. Within our statistical hypothesis framework, we not only incorporate the probabilistic guarantee c but also set bounds for the so called type I and type II errors. The type I error denotes the likelihood of incorrectly concluding the alternate hypothesis when, in reality, the null hypothesis is true. Similarly, the type II error denotes the probability of incorrectly concluding the null hypothesis when in reality the alternate hypothesis holds. We choose the relevant parameters such that the type I error is kept significantly low (as desired). Type II error, which refers to the probability of incorrectly selecting the null hypothesis when the alternative hypothesis is true, is not relevant in our setting. This is because we never select the null hypothesis, which would claim the system is safe with a probability less than c. Instead, we only conclude that the system is probabilistically safe when the alternative hypothesis is selected, which asserts that the system is safe with probability is greater than or equal to c. If the alternative hypothesis is rejected, we provide a concrete counterexample. Thus, type II error does not apply in this context. Next, we describe how the hypothesis test is carried for a given value of $c \in (0,1)$. We use Bayesian hypothesis testing based on Jefferies Bayes factor [13]. Accordingly, we first formulate the null and alternate hypotheses:

$$H_0 : \mathcal{P}rob\,[f_{sys}(\cdot),\ell,\mathcal{D},\mathcal{U}] < c, \quad (1) \qquad H_1 : \mathcal{P}rob\,[f_{sys}(\cdot),\ell,\mathcal{D},\mathcal{U}] \geq c. \quad (2)$$

Here, $\mathcal{P}rob\,[f_{sys}(\cdot),\ell,\mathcal{D},\mathcal{U}]$ denotes the probability that a randomly drawn valid trajectory is safe. In other words, it represents the probability that a given random trajectory τ (of the system $f_{sys}(\cdot)$), that is valid w.r.t. the log ℓ does not intersect with the unsafe set $\mathcal{U}$. Our goal is to determine if the alternate hypothesis is accepted with the given parameters. We begin by setting a sufficiently high value (say 10^5) for the *Bayes factor* B, a term we will define shortly [16]. Using this Bayes factor B and the probability c, we compute K, the number of valid trajectories needed to decide between the null and alternate hypotheses. Next, we draw K samples $X = \{\tau_1, \tau_2, \ldots, \tau_K\}$ according to the given distribution $\mathcal{D}$ over the set of all valid trajectories. That is, for each i, τ_i is randomly selected as follows: $\tau_i = \texttt{Sample}(f_{sys}(\cdot), \ell, [\mathcal{O}]_H, \mathcal{D})$. Then, we check if *each* member of X does not intersect with the unsafe set $\mathcal{U}$, i.e., $\forall_i \tau_i \cap \mathcal{U} = \emptyset$. If this is true for every trajectory, we accept the alternate hypothesis, concluding that the system is (probabilistically) safe. If not—there is at least one trajectory that violates safety—we consider the first such trajectory as a counterexample, i.e., $\tau_j \cap \mathcal{U} \neq \emptyset$. This counterexample is then returned as a result, leading to the conclusion that the system is unsafe.

Now, we will present the connection between the Bayes factor B, confidence c, and the number of valid trajectories to be generated, denoted as K. Consider $X = \{\tau_1, \tau_2, \ldots, \tau_K\}$ as a set of randomly selected valid trajectories, all of which are deemed *safe*. The probability that all these trajectories are safe, assuming the null hypothesis, is expressed as (similar to the treatment in [13]):

$$\mathbf{Pr}\,[\forall \tau \in X : \tau \cap \mathcal{U} = \emptyset \,|\, H_0] = \int_0^c q^K \, dq. \quad (3)$$

Similarly, the probability that all the trajectories are safe, given the alternate hypothesis, is expressed as:

$$\mathbf{Pr}\,[\forall \tau \in X : \tau \cap \mathcal{U} = \emptyset \,|\, H_1] = \int_c^1 q^K \, dq. \quad (4)$$

The *Bayes factor* is the ratio of the above two probabilities:

$$\frac{\mathbf{Pr}\,[\forall \tau \in X : \tau \cap \mathcal{U} = \emptyset \,|\, H_1]}{\mathbf{Pr}\,[\forall \tau \in X : \tau \cap \mathcal{U} = \emptyset \,|\, H_0]} = \frac{1 - c^{K+1}}{c^{K+1}} \quad (5)$$

The Bayes factor serves as a measure of the strength of evidence supporting the alternate hypothesis in comparison to the null hypothesis. In Jeffries Bayes factor test, we ensure that the ratio calculated in Eq. (5) exceeds the Bayes factor B specified by the user. Hence, a sufficiently high Bayes factor value indicates that the evidence favors the alternate hypothesis over the null hypothesis.

Algorithm 1: Proposed Statistical Monitoring

input : $f_{sys}(\cdot)$, ℓ, $[\mathcal{O}]_H$, $\mathcal{D}$, $\mathcal{U}$, c
output : Return *probabilistic-safe* (resp. *unsafe*) if the system behavior is probabilistically safe (resp. unsafe with a counterexample).

```
/* f_sys(): System input/output execution (see Definition 1);          */
/* ℓ: Uncertain log (see Definition 2);                                 */
/* [O]_H: Environmental inputs experienced by the system up to time H;  */
/* D: Probability distribution followed by the set of all valid trajectories (see
     Definition 4);                                                     */
/* U: Unsafe set;                                                       */
/* c: Required probabilistic confidence (see Section 4);                */
1 K ← Compute using Eq. (6) with given c;
2 for k ∈ [1, K] do
3     τ ← Sample(f_sys(·), ℓ, [O]_H, D);     // generate a random valid trajectory
4     if τ ∩ U ≠ ∅    // check if trajectory is unsafe
5     then
6         return (unsafe, τ);
7 return probabilistic-safe;
```

We note that, for the sake of clarity in presentation, we do not treat it as an input to our method, but rather assume that it is preset by the user. However, Bayes factor is indeed a parameter chosen by the user. With B given, we can now compute the required number of samples K in the following manner:

$$\frac{1 - c^{K+1}}{c^{K+1}} > B \iff K > -\log_c(B + 1) \tag{6}$$

We conclude this subsection by bounding type I error, i.e., where the alternate hypothesis accepted but in reality the null hypothesis is true. According to [13], the type I error rate is bounded by: $err(B, c) = c/(c + (1 - c)B)$. The detailed steps of our monitoring procedure are discussed in Sect. 5. We note that while, in theory, one can explore other hypothesis testing methods (including sequential hypothesis testing), this framework (using Jeffries Bayes factor) offers several advantages [16], notably: 1) ability to work with any distribution $\mathcal{D}$; and 2) the value of K can be pre-computed and is independent of the sample size, etc.

5 Methodology

The structure of our algorithm is in Fig. 1. The formalization of the main algorithm is presented in Algorithm 1. Let us discuss its primary components:

Computing K. We use the formula specified in Eq. (6) to calculate the value of K based on the provided c in line 1.

Checking safety of K random valid trajectories. Within the `for` loop in line 2, we generate K random valid trajectories and check its safety.

Generate a random valid trajectory. In line 3, a random valid trajectory $\tau = \{x_0, x_1, \cdots, x_H\}$ is generated according to the distribution $\mathcal{D}$ (see Definition 3).

Checking safety of τ. In line 5, we check if the trajectory τ intersects with the unsafe set $\mathcal{U}$, i.e., $\exists_t x_t \cap \mathcal{U} \neq \emptyset$. If there exists such a t at which the trajectory τ intersects with unsafe set $\mathcal{U}$, we return the trajectory τ as a counterexample, and infer the system as unsafe, in line 6. If none of the K generated random valid trajectories are unsafe, we infer the system as probabilistically safe (with the desired confidence c) in line 7.

Theorem 1 (Probabilistic Soundness of Algorithm 1). *If Algorithm 1 infers the system as probabilistic-safe (in line 7), then the system is safe with the required probabilistic confidence c.*

The proof of Theorem 1 follows from the hypothesis testing framework discussed in Sect. 4. While our method (Algorithm 1) is compatible with any distribution $\mathcal{D}$ provided that the implementation of Sample($\cdot$) is available, we specifically discuss a method to implement Sample($\cdot$) tailored for a uniform distribution, named **UNIFORM SAMPLING**. This adaptation is made because, for our experiments, we assume that $\mathcal{D}$ is a uniform distribution. This is incorporated into Fig. 1, providing an integrated overview of the proposed monitoring approach (see also Algorithm 1). Given a log $\ell = \{(\hat{\theta}_t, t)\}$ and environmental inputs $[\mathcal{O}]_H = \{o_1, o_2, \cdots, o_H\}$, where $\forall_{t \in [0,H]} \hat{\theta}_t, o_t \subset \mathbb{R}^n$, the **UNIFORM SAMPLING** algorithm proceeds as follows:

Selecting the initial set. The initial log record, denoted as $\ell_0 = (\hat{\theta}_0, t = 0)$, is considered to be the starting point for monitoring, assuming this occurs at time step $t = 0$. Consequently, $\hat{\theta}_0$ is presumed to be the over-approximated initial set of the system, serving as the starting point for monitoring.

Generating a random trajectory. The first step in generating a random valid trajectory, is to generate a trajectory of the system (not necessarily valid yet) from the given initial set $\hat{\theta}_0$ and environmental inputs $[\mathcal{O}]_H$. To do so, we first sample a state $x_0 (\in \mathbb{R}^n)$ uniformly at random from the initial set $\hat{\theta}_0$. Next, we sample the environmental inputs $[\epsilon]_H = \{\epsilon_0, \epsilon_1, \cdots, \epsilon_H\}$, such that, for all $t \in [0, H]$ $\epsilon_t (\in \mathbb{R}^n)$ is drawn uniformly at random from the set o_t. Once the initial state x_0 and the environmental inputs $[\epsilon]$ are sampled, we compute the trajectory as follows: $\tau = \{x_0, x_1, \cdots, x_H\}$, where $\forall_{t \in [0,H]} x_t = f_{sys}(x_0, [\epsilon]_{t-1}, t)$.

Check if τ is valid. A trajectory is considered valid when it meets the conditions outlined in Definition 3. In order for τ to be valid, all the records in ℓ must intersect with the points in τ at their respective time steps. Encountering a record in ℓ that fails to intersect with τ at a given time step implies that the trajectory τ was not observed during the real execution of the system.

Discussion. Our technique is applicable whenever the I/O execution of a system is available, which is a reasonable assumption in most cases. When designing autonomous systems, models are often created within a framework or simulations, which are also used for testing and performance evaluation. Additionally, the bounds on the initial set and environmental inputs, along with their corresponding probabilistic distributions, are typically known. In practice, these distributions are usually uniform or concentrated around a central value. This makes it reasonable to assume that the I/O execution model and the probabilistic distributions of trajectories are known in most real-world scenarios.

6 Case Studies

We illustrate the effectiveness and practicality of our method through its application to three benchmarks. The first two benchmarks involve non-linear models with added environmental uncertainties (namely jet model and van der Pol Oscillator discussed in Sects. 6.1 and 6.2 respectively), while the third benchmark incorporates a DNN-based controller (namely mountain car discussed in Sect. 6.2). We implemented the proposed statistical monitoring approach (Algorithm 1) as a prototype tool developed in Python, named Posto[1][2].

Input/Output Execution Model. We recall that our monitoring approach requires only the I/O execution of the system, which is capable of generating output trajectories from the inputs (and not a detailed formal model). In our experiments, we simulated such an execution behavior using the known system formal models (without the need to explicitly provide them as input to our monitoring approach) while incorporating additional uncertainties.

Generating Logs. We simulate a trajectory according to **UNIFORM SAMPLING**, by randomly selecting an initial state from the initial set and a set of environmental inputs. Following the generation of this trajectory, we simulate logging on it, as per specified probability p. In essence, at each time step along the trajectory, we gather a record with a probability of p. After collecting these records, we introduce random uncertainty δ_{log} to each record, replicating sensor noise in the system. In the end, we get an uncertain log as in Definition 2.

Implementation Details. Next, we highlight certain implementation details of our proposed statistical monitoring approach (Algorithm 1): i) We set the value of $B = 10^5$ as a default in our implementation. Unless otherwise stated, for all our experiments, we use $c = 0.99$. ii) Since we assume a uniform distribution of valid trajectories (Definition 4), we implemented the Sample(·) method (in line 3 of Algorithm 1) according to **UNIFORM SAMPLING**. However, our proposed approach can work with any distribution.

---

[1] The code, binaries, models, and scripts for stochastic result recreation are open-sourced on GitHub https://github.com/bineet-coderep/posto.
[2] Experiments were performed on a Lenovo ThinkPad with i7-8750H CPU with 2.20 GHz and 32 GiB memory on Ubuntu 20.04 LTS (64 bit).

Research Questions (RQ). We consider the following research questions in our case studies:

1. The impact of varying the logging probability p (i.e., the number of records in the log) on the frequency of discovering a counterexample or inferring the system as probabilistically safe.
2. The impact of varying the amount of uncertainties δ_{log} in the log records (i.e., the volume of records in the log) on the frequency of discovering a counterexample or inferring the system as probabilistically safe.
3. Impact of varying the probabilistic confidence c.
4. In the UNIFORM SAMPLING algorithm, the effect of various parameters (logging probability and the amount of uncertainty present in the log records) on the chances of identifying valid trajectories.

6.1 Jet Model

System Description. The dynamics of the jet model we employed to simulate the I/O execution corresponds with a Moore-Greitzer model of a jet engine with a stabilizing feedback control while operating in the no-stall mode [5]. We discretized the system with additional environmental uncertainties (inputs), ϵ_x, ϵ_y, on states x and y respectively. In this model, the origin is translated to a desired no-stall equilibrium. The state variables correspond to $x = \mathcal{X} - 1$, $y = \mathcal{Y} - \mathcal{Y}_{co} - 2$, where $\mathcal{X}$ is the mass flow, $\mathcal{Y}$ is the pressure rise and $\mathcal{Y}_{co}$ is a constant.

Safety. The system is considered safe if the mass flow of the jet model is maintained at all time steps as follows: $x \geq -0.10$. Imagine a crash scenario where the only available data for analysis is the log recorded by the jet prior to the crash. Conducting an analysis with our monitoring algorithm can be beneficial for investigating agencies, manufacturers, and others. It enables the detection of safety condition violations during the jet's execution and the identification of trajectories that breached safety conditions.

Experiments. The initial set and the environmental inputs considered for this example are as follows: $x \in [0.8, 1], y \in [0.8, 1], \epsilon_x, \epsilon_y \in [0, 0.002]$ (see [1] for initial sets). Some random trajectories of the system are shown in Fig. 2a. In Fig. 3, the plots in the bottom row (Figs. 3c and 3d) and upper row (Figs. 3a and 3b) have logging probabilities (p) of 3% and 5% respectively. Additionally, the logs in the left column (Figs. 3a and 3c) and right column ((Figs. 3b and 3d) have log uncertainty (δ_{log}) values of 0.02 and 0.04 respectively. We also conduct an analysis of our monitoring algorithm using logging probabilities (p) set at 7%, 9%, and 11%, each with a log uncertainty value of $\delta_{log} = 0.02$. Due to the similarity of the plots to those in Fig. 3, we have omitted them from the paper. For Figs. 2b and 2c, log uncertainty was set to $\delta_{log} = 0.02$. We now answer RQs (1)-(4), using Figs. 2b, 2c ,3.

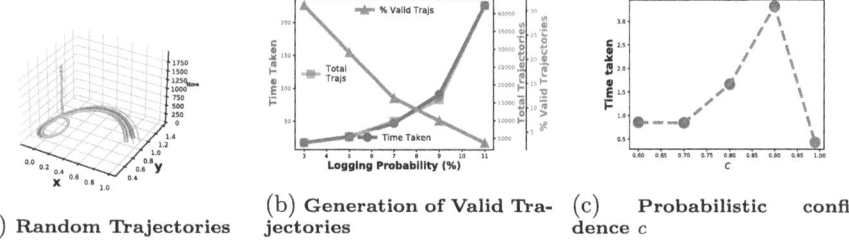

(a) **Random Trajectories** (b) **Generation of Valid Trajectories** (c) **Probabilistic confidence** c

Fig. 2. Jet Model Case Study. *Random Trajectories (Fig. 2a).* x- and y- axis represents state variables, and z-axis represents time step. *Impact of Logging Probability on Generation of Valid Trajectories (Fig. 2b).* We illustrate how varying the logging probability affects the monitoring execution time (Algorithm 1) and the percentage of valid trajectories out of the total number of generated trajectories. *Impact of Probabilistic confidence c (Fig. 2c).* We illustrate the impact of logging probability on the time taken to perform monitoring (Algorithm 1) and safety inferences. The red dot denotes an instance where the system was inferred to be unsafe with a counterexample, and green dots denote instances where the system was inferred to be probabilistically safe (with the corresponding confidence value indicated in the x-axis.

Answer to RQ 1 (impact of logging probability p) We address this by comparing two sets of figures in Fig. 3. In the left column, with a smaller record size, Fig. 3c took 17.26 s to conclude that the system is probabilistically safe. Increasing the probability of logging (i.e., incorporating more records) as shown in Fig. 3a, also inferred the system to be probabilistically safe. However, the inference of safety took longer, requiring 26.07 s. This increase in monitoring time will be discussed in detail in RQ 4. In the right column, with larger record size, the analysis in Fig. 3d concluded in 0.51 s, determining the system behavior as unsafe and generating a counterexample (dotted red trajectory). The behavior of the system in Fig. 3b, with a logging probability of 5%, resulted in inferring the system behavior as unsafe, as three records in the input log were unsafe. In this case, the main statistical monitoring process did not initiate; instead, it concluded by merely verifying the safety of the logs, and this process took 0.006 s. We additionally assess the influence of logging probability through Fig. 2b. We further incrementally increase the logging probability to 7%, 9%, and 11%. In each of these cases, although the conclusion about the system being probabilistically safe remained consistent, the duration for performing the monitoring varied: 47.5 s, 90.88 s, and 226.43 s, respectively. Figure 2b further illustrates how the time required for monitoring increases quite noticeably with the increase in logging probability.

Answer to RQ 2 (impact of log uncertainty δ_{log}) We address this question by comparing two sets of figures in Fig. 3. In the bottom row, with a smaller logging probability: Increasing the uncertainty in the log leads to a change in the inference from safe (Fig. 3c) to unsafe with a counterexample (Fig. 3d). Similarly, in the top row (with higher logging probability): Increasing the uncertainty in the

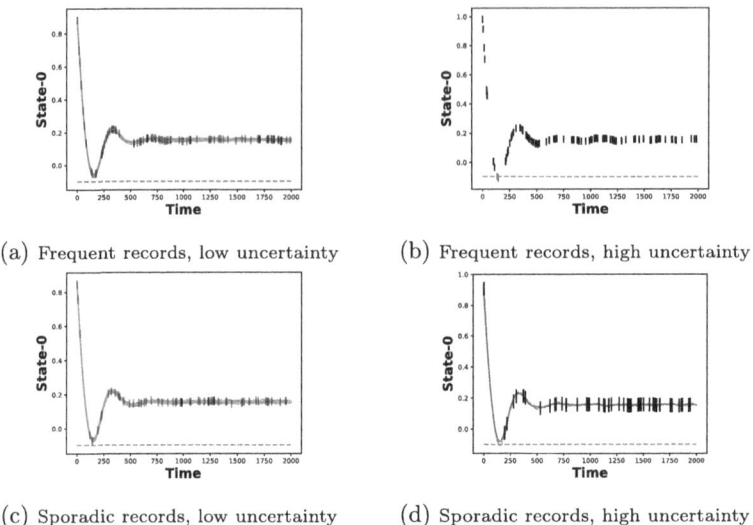

Fig. 3. Statistical Monitoring. Evolution of the state—x for the jet model—with time. The volume of the records increases from left to right, and the probability of logging increases from bottom to top. The colored trajectories are the generated random valid trajectories during the process of monitoring, the dotted trajectory in red is an unsafe trajectory discovered during the process of monitoring (see Fig. 3d), the black regions are records in the log given as an input to the monitoring algorithm, and the dark-brown regions are unsafe-records in the log (Fig. 3b). The red dotted line represents the safe range for the variable.

log results in rendering some of the log records unsafe, leading to the system being inferred as unsafe (Fig. 3b).

Answer to RQ 3 (impact of probabilistic confidence c) We address this question by using Fig. 2c. By varying the probabilistic confidence c through $0.6, 0.7, 0.8, 0.9$ and 0.99, we witness a drastic increase in the time taken by the monitoring approach: 0.85 s, 0.85 s, 1.66 s, 3.31 s and 0.42 s respectively. This is natural, as the value K (i.e., number of valid trajectories) required to infer the system as safe, with the respective confidence c, also increases drastically as per Eq. (6). Also, note that increasing the value c increases the chances of finding a counterexample that violates safety. The plot illustrates this trend, demonstrating that although no counterexamples were discovered at c values of 0.6, 0.7, and 0.8, a counterexample violating the system's safety was discovered when $c = 0.99$.

Answer to RQ 4 (Chances of Finding Valid Trajectories). We investigate this question by using Fig. 2b. When we increase the logging probability (p), even with the same level of confidence (c), it takes more time to perform monitoring. To put it simply, even if the number of valid trajectories needed to infer the system's safety (as defined by c) stays the same, increasing the number of records in the log (due to an increase in the value of p) results in a longer monitoring time. This behavior results from the implementation, which involves generating random valid trajectories based on a uniform distribution, as outlined in **Uniform Sampling**. To elaborate, when we increase the logging probability p by increments of 3%, 5%, 7%, 9%, and 11%, the proportion of valid trajectories among all randomly generated trajectories is observed to be 31.08%, 21.3%, 11.9%, 7.26%, and 2.71%, respectively.

6.2 Other Benchmarks and General Observations

Let us briefly discuss the other two case studies (namely van der Pol and mountain car). Given the similar trends observed in these two case studies with respect to RQs (1)-(4), and further owing to space limitations, we cumulate the observations from all the experiments and discuss them in detail here as general observations. The details of the mountain car model are discussed next, while the van der Pol oscillator model is presented in Sect. 6.2, due to its similarity to the previously discussed jet model (Sect. 6.1) and space limitations.

Mountain Car. We now evaluate our proposed approach on a mountain car model with a DNN-based controller. Given the complexity of a DNN-based controller and the increasing deployment of such controllers in safety-critical scenarios, it is important to scalably investigate such systems in the event of a crash. This helps us to determine the cause of the crash and identify the trajectory that violated safety by analyzing the system's log. Thus, making this model an ideal candidate to evaluate our monitoring approach.

System Description. We consider a scenario where an under-powered car needs to climb a steep hill. Because the car lacks sufficient power to directly go up the hill, it has to drive up the hill in the opposite direction first to build up enough momentum to reach its destination. The DNN-based controller $f_{DNN}(\cdot)$ uses the car's position (p) and velocity (v) as inputs and provide an acceleration command as output (refer to [17] for the discrete time dynamics).

Experiments. The system is considered safe if the velocity of mountain car is maintained at all time steps as follows: $v \leq 0.055$. The initial set considered for this example are as follows: $p \in [-1.2, -1], v \in [-0.07, 0.07]$ (see [17]). To assess our monitoring approach in this case study, we conducted four distinct analyses, categorized into two sets (similar to the other case studies): one involving varying logging probabilities p (20% and 40%), and the other involving varying log uncertainties δ_{log} (0.004 and 0.008). As the observed plots closely resemble those depicted in Figs. 3 and 4, we have not included them here. We additionally conducted analysis using c values of 0.7, 0.7, 0.8, and 0.99, while keeping $\delta_{log} = 0.004$. We have not included the corresponding plot since it closely resembles Fig. 2c.

Van Der Pol Oscillator. In this case study, the dynamics of the van der Pol model (as in [2]) was discretized with additional environmental uncertainties ($\epsilon_x, \epsilon_y, \epsilon_\mu$) to simulate the I/O execution. Here, the state variables x and y represent position and velocity, respectively, while μ denotes the damping strength that remains constant in the system.

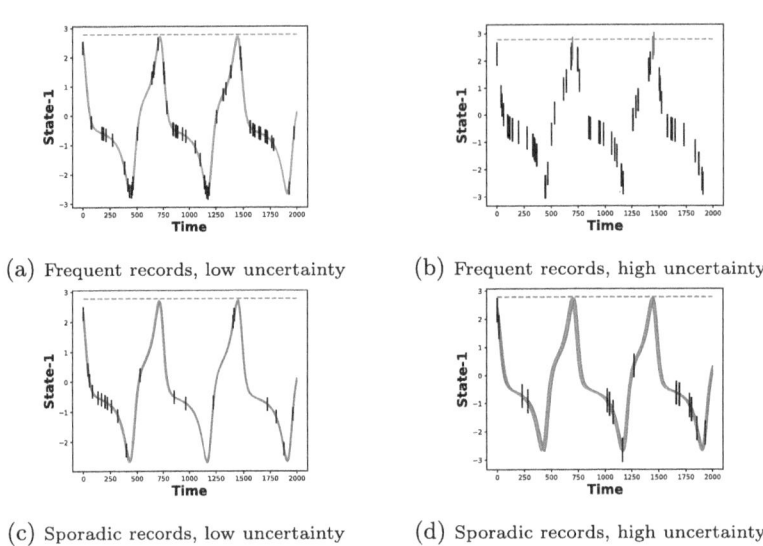

(a) Frequent records, low uncertainty (b) Frequent records, high uncertainty

(c) Sporadic records, low uncertainty (d) Sporadic records, high uncertainty

Fig. 4. Van der Pol Oscillator Monitoring. Evolution of the state—y for the Van der Pol model—with time. The volume of the records increases from left to right, and the probability of logging increases from bottom to top. The colored trajectories are the generated random valid trajectories during the process of monitoring, the dotted trajectory in red is an unsafe trajectory discovered during the process of monitoring (see Fig. 4d), the black regions are records in the log given as an input to the monitoring algorithm, and the dark-brown regions are unsafe-records in the log (Fig. 4b). The red dotted line represents the safe range for the variable.

Experiments. The system is considered safe if the velocity is maintained at all time steps as follows: $y \leq 2.78$. The initial set and the environmental inputs considered for this example are as follows: $x \in [1.25, 1.45], y \in [2.25, 2.35], \epsilon_x, \epsilon_y \in [0, 0.004], \epsilon_\mu \in [0, 0.01]$ (see [1,2] for initial sets). The illustration of random trajectories of this system is omitted as it is similar in essence to that of the jet model. In Fig. 4, the plots in the bottom row (Figs. 4c and 4d) and upper row (Figs. 4a and 4b) have logging probabilities (p) of 1% and 3% respectively. Additionally, the logs in the left column (Figs. 4a and 4c) and right column (Figs. 4b and 4d) have log uncertainty (δ_{log}) values of 0.2 and 0.4 respectively. We additionally conducted analysis using c values of 0.6, 0.7, 0.8, and 0.99, while keeping $\delta_{log} = 0.2$. We omit the plot as it similar to Fig. 2c.

General Observations.

Answer to RQ 1. As evidenced across nearly all three benchmarks (with the exception of a single sub case in van der Pol), increasing the logging probability shows no significant effect on the inference of system's safety by the proposed monitoring approach. However, there is a noticeable increase in the computational time required for the monitoring algorithm as the logging probability increases. This can primarily be attributed to the decreasing chances of discovering valid trajectories with higher logging probabilities, which will be elaborated in RQ 4.

Answer to RQ 2. As observed in the first two benchmarks, increasing the uncertainty in the log, increases the chances of discovering a counterexample (while the third benchmark remained probabilistically safe in all cases). With an increase in log uncertainty, we observed noticeable decrease in monitoring time in some sub-cases. This could again be attributed to increasing chances of finding valid trajectories with an increase in log uncertainties. See RQ 4.

Answer to RQ 3. Increasing the probabilistic confidence increases the chances of finding a counterexample that violates safety, and also the compute time by the monitoring algorithm increases. This outcome is to be expected, given that the value of K (i.e., number of valid trajectories) required to infer the system as safe, with the respective confidence c, also increases drastically as per Eq. (6). Specifically, for c values of 0.6, 0.7, 0.8, 0.9, and 0.99, the computed values of K are 23, 33, 52, 110, and 1146, respectively.

Answer to RQ 4. As observed in several of the cases across the three benchmarks, the chances of finding valid trajectories increases with: i) decrease in logging probability p, and ii) increase in log uncertainty δ_{log}. This behavior arises from how random valid trajectories are generated in **UNIFORM SAMPLING**. Nevertheless, it is worth noting that across all our benchmarks (including all subcases), which includes nonlinear and DNN-based controllers, the monitoring was completed within 250s on a standard laptop.

7 Conclusion and Perspectives

This work opts to trade-off formal safety guarantees with high-confidence probabilistic assurances to ensure trustworthy monitoring suitable for most practical applications. To this end, we propose an SHT-based framework for monitoring to detect safety violations from an input log with noisy and missing records. Our implementation into a prototype tool `Posto` showed that we can successfully monitor non-linear and DNN based benchmarks under 250s. Given the scalability of our method and the observations it offer, this work paves the way for several future research directions. Our ultimate aim is to adopt a fully representation-free strategy, where the I/O execution representation will be co-designed with the monitoring approach. The goal of this synergy is to mutually enhance both the I/O execution representation and the monitoring process, to achieve a better scalability for complex models and are tuned towards finding counterexamples faster.

References

1. Jet Model. https://ths.rwth-aachen.de/research/projects/hypro/benchmarks-of-continuous-and-hybrid-systems/
2. Althoff, M., Stursberg, O., Buss, M.: Reachability analysis of nonlinear systems with uncertain parameters using conservative linearization. In: CDC, pp. 4042–4048. IEEE (2008). https://doi.org/10.1109/CDC.2008.4738704
3. André, É., Coquard, E., Fribourg, L., Jerray, J., Lesens, D.: Parametric schedulability analysis of a launcher flight control system under reactivity constraints. FI **182**(1), 31–67 (2021). https://doi.org/10.3233/FI-2021-2065
4. Ashok, P., Křetínský, J., Weininger, M.: PAC statistical model checking for Markov decision processes and stochastic games. In: Dillig, I., Tasiran, S. (eds.) CAV 2019. LNCS, vol. 11561, pp. 497–519. Springer, Cham (2019). https://doi.org/10.1007/978-3-030-25540-4_29
5. Aylward, E.M., Parrilo, P.A., Slotine, J.: Stability and robustness analysis of nonlinear systems via contraction metrics and SOS programming. Automatica **44**(8), 2163–2170 (2008). https://doi.org/10.1016/J.AUTOMATICA.2007.12.012
6. Bakhirkin, A., Ferrère, T., Nickovic, D., Maler, O., Asarin, E.: Online timed pattern matching using automata. In: Jansen, D.N., Prabhakar, P. (eds.) FORMATS 2018. LNCS, vol. 11022, pp. 215–232. Springer, Cham (2018). https://doi.org/10.1007/978-3-030-00151-3_13
7. Bartocci, E., et al.: Specification-based monitoring of cyber-physical systems: a survey on theory, tools and applications. In: Bartocci, E., Falcone, Y. (eds.) Lectures on Runtime Verification. LNCS, vol. 10457, pp. 135–175. Springer, Cham (2018). https://doi.org/10.1007/978-3-319-75632-5_5
8. Basin, D.A., Klaedtke, F., Zalinescu, E.: The MonPoly monitoring tool. In: Reger, G., Havelund, K. (eds.) RV-CuBES. Kalpa Publications in Computing, vol. 3, pp. 19–28. EasyChair (2017)
9. Burch, J.R., Clarke, E.M., McMillan, K.L., Dill, D.L., Hwang, L.J.: Symbolic model checking: 10^{20} states and beyond. Inf. Comput. **98**(2), 142–170 (1992). https://doi.org/10.1016/0890-5401(92)90017-A
10. Calafiore, G.C., Campi, M.C.: The scenario approach to robust control design. IEEE Trans. Autom. Control **51**(5), 742–753 (2006). https://doi.org/10.1109/TAC.2006.875041
11. Chen, Y., et al.: PAC learning-based verification and model synthesis. In: Dillon, L.K., Visser, W., Williams, L.A. (eds.) ICSE, pp. 714–724. ACM (2016). https://doi.org/10.1145/2884781.2884860
12. Clarke, E.M., Zuliani, P.: Statistical model checking for cyber-physical systems. In: Bultan, T., Hsiung, P.-A. (eds.) ATVA 2011. LNCS, vol. 6996, pp. 1–12. Springer, Heidelberg (2011). https://doi.org/10.1007/978-3-642-24372-1_1
13. Diwakaran, R.D., Sankaranarayanan, S., Trivedi, A.: Analyzing neighborhoods of falsifying traces in cyber-physical systems. In: Martínez, S., Tovar, E., Gill, C., Sinopoli, B. (eds.) ICCPS, pp. 109–119. ACM (2017). https://doi.org/10.1145/3055004.3055029

14. Donzé, A., Ferrère, T., Maler, O.: Efficient robust monitoring for STL. In: Sharygina, N., Veith, H. (eds.) CAV 2013. LNCS, vol. 8044, pp. 264–279. Springer, Heidelberg (2013). https://doi.org/10.1007/978-3-642-39799-8_19
15. Ghosh, B., André, É.: Offline and online energy-efficient monitoring of scattered uncertain logs using a bounding model. LMCS **20**(1), 2:1–2:33 (J2023). https://doi.org/10.46298/lmcs-20(1:2)2024
16. Ghosh, B., et al.: Statistical hypothesis testing of controller implementations under timing uncertainties. In: RTCSA, pp. 11–20. IEEE (2022). https://doi.org/10.1109/RTCSA55878.2022.00008
17. Ivanov, R., Weimer, J., Alur, R., Pappas, G.J., Lee, I.: Verisig: verifying safety properties of hybrid systems with neural network controllers. In: Ozay, N., Prabhakar, P. (eds.) HSCC, pp. 169–178. ACM (2019). https://doi.org/10.1145/3302504.3311806
18. Jakšić, S., Bartocci, E., Grosu, R., Nguyen, T., Ničković, D.: Quantitative monitoring of STL with edit distance. Formal Methods Syst. Des. **53**(1), 83–112 (2018). https://doi.org/10.1007/s10703-018-0319-x
19. Jha, S.K., Clarke, E.M., Langmead, C.J., Legay, A., Platzer, A., Zuliani, P.: A Bayesian approach to model checking biological systems. In: Degano, P., Gorrieri, R. (eds.) CMSB 2009. LNCS, vol. 5688, pp. 218–234. Springer, Heidelberg (2009). https://doi.org/10.1007/978-3-642-03845-7_15
20. Kaivola, R., et al.: Replacing testing with formal verification in Intel CoreTM i7 processor execution engine validation. In: Bouajjani, A., Maler, O. (eds.) CAV 2009. LNCS, vol. 5643, pp. 414–429. Springer, Heidelberg (2009). https://doi.org/10.1007/978-3-642-02658-4_32
21. Kass, R., Raftery, A.: Bayes factors. J. Am. Stat. Assoc. **90**(430), 773–795 (1995)
22. Larsen, K.G., Lorber, F., Nielsen, B.: 20 years of UPPAAL enabled industrial model-based validation and beyond. In: Margaria, T., Steffen, B. (eds.) ISoLA, Part IV. LNCS, vol. 11247, pp. 212–229. Springer, Cham (2018). https://doi.org/10.1007/978-3-030-03427-6_18
23. Legay, A., Delahaye, B., Bensalem, S.: Statistical model checking: an overview. In: Barringer, H., et al. (eds.) RV. LNCS, vol. 6418, pp. 122–135. Springer, Cham (2010). https://doi.org/10.1007/978-3-642-16612-9_11
24. Maler, O., Nickovic, D.: Monitoring temporal properties of continuous signals. In: Lakhnech, Y., Yovine, S. (eds.) FORMATS and FTRTFT. LNCS, vol. 3253, pp. 152–166. Springer, Cham (2004). https://doi.org/10.1007/978-3-540-30206-3_12
25. Mamouras, K., Chattopadhyay, A., Wang, Z.: A compositional framework for quantitative online monitoring over continuous-time signals. In: Feng, L., Fisman, D. (eds.) RV. LNCS, vol. 12974, pp. 142–163. Springer, Cham (2021). https://doi.org/10.1007/978-3-030-88494-9_8
26. Park, S., Bastani, O., Matni, N., Lee, I.: PAC confidence sets for deep neural networks via calibrated prediction. In: ICLR. OpenReview.net (2020). https://openreview.net/forum?id=BJxVI04YvB
27. Roohi, N., Wang, Y., West, M., Dullerud, G.E., Viswanathan, M.: Statistical verification of the Toyota powertrain control verification benchmark. In: Frehse, G., Mitra, S. (eds.) HSCC, pp. 65–70. ACM (2017). https://doi.org/10.1145/3049797.3049804
28. Sen, K., Viswanathan, M., Agha, G.: On statistical model checking of stochastic systems. In: Etessami, K., Rajamani, S.K. (eds.) CAV. LNCS, vol. 3576, pp. 266–280. Springer, Cham (2005). https://doi.org/10.1007/11513988_26

29. Waga, M., Akazaki, T., Hasuo, I.: A Boyer-Moore type algorithm for timed pattern matching. In: Fränzle, M., Markey, N. (eds.) FORMATS. LNCS, vol. 9884, pp. 121–139. Springer, Cham (2016). https://doi.org/10.1007/978-3-319-44878-7_8
30. Waga, M., André, É., Hasuo, I.: Model-bounded monitoring of hybrid systems. ACM Trans. Cyber-Phys. Syst. **6**(4), 30:1–30:26 (2022). https://doi.org/10.1145/3529095
31. Wang, Y., Sibai, H., Yen, M., Mitra, S., Dullerud, G.E.: Differentially private algorithms for statistical verification of cyber-physical systems. IEEE Open J. Control Syst. **1**, 294–305 (2022). https://doi.org/10.1109/OJCSYS.2022.3207108
32. Xue, B., Liu, Y., Ma, L., Zhang, X., Sun, M., Xie, X.: Safe inputs approximation for black-box systems. In: Pang, J., Sun, J. (eds.) ICECCS, pp. 180–189. IEEE (2019). https://doi.org/10.1109/ICECCS.2019.00027
33. Xue, B., Zhang, M., Easwaran, A., Li, Q.: PAC model checking of black-box continuous-time dynamical systems. IEEE Trans. Comput. Aided Des. Integr. Circuits Syst. **39**(11), 3944–3955 (2020). https://doi.org/10.1109/TCAD.2020.3012251
34. Younes, H.L.S., Simmons, R.G.: Probabilistic verification of discrete event systems using acceptance sampling. In: Brinksma, E., Larsen, K.G. (eds.) CAV. LNCS, vol. 2404, pp. 223–235. Springer, Cham (2002). https://doi.org/10.1007/3-540-45657-0_17
35. Zarei, M., Wang, Y., Pajic, M.: Statistical verification of learning-based cyber-physical systems. In: Ames, A.D., Seshia, S.A., Deshmukh, J. (eds.) HSCC, pp. 12:1–12:7. ACM (2020). https://doi.org/10.1145/3365365.3382209
36. Zuliani, P., Platzer, A., Clarke, E.M.: Bayesian statistical model checking with application to simulink/stateflow verification. In: HSCC, pp. 243–252. Association for Computing Machinery, New York, NY, USA (2010). https://doi.org/10.1145/1755952.1755987

Towards Efficient Verification of Parallel Applications with Mc SimGrid

Mathieu Laurent[✉][iD], Thierry Jéron[iD], and Martin Quinson[iD]

Univ Rennes, Inria, CNRS, Irisa, Rennes, France
mathieu.laurent@ens-rennes.fr

Abstract. Assessing the correctness of distributed and parallel applications is notoriously difficult due to the complexity of the concurrent behaviors and the difficulty to reproduce bugs. In this context, Dynamic Partial Order Reduction (DPOR) techniques have proved successful in exploiting concurrency to verify applications without exploring all their behaviors. However, they may lack of efficiency when tracking non-systematic bugs of real size applications. In this paper, we suggest two adaptations of the Optimal Dynamic Partial Order Reduction (ODPOR) algorithm with a particular focus on bug finding and explanation. The first adaptation is an out-of-order version called RFS ODPOR which avoids being stuck in uninteresting large parts of the state space. Once a bug is found, the second adaptation takes advantage of ODPOR principles to efficiently find the origins of the bug.

1 Introduction

We consider parallel applications made of interacting actors that can share the memory of a single computer, or can be geographically distributed across the network. These actors interact through message passing over the network, or through classical synchronization mechanisms such as mutexes or semaphores. This class of applications encompasses a large amount of real-world programs, such as message-passing ones that are commonly built upon the MPI standard [11] in High-Performance Computing, or classical multithreaded applications built for example upon the POSIX `pthread` standard [19]. These applications are notoriously difficult to get right as they add the challenges of concurrent and multithreaded applications (race conditions, deadlocks, livelocks) to the challenges linked to asynchronous message passing (communication mismatch), and memory coherency in distributed settings.

The main challenge to the correctness of these applications lays in the fact that the ordering of events changes the behavior. Moreover, triggering existing bugs also becomes challenging in such complex applications. The purpose of our work is therefore to design automatic verification methods that are both complete for a fixed input, and efficient for finding bugs in applications whose behaviors are supposed to be finite but possibly non-deterministic.

Testing can be efficient for detecting bugs in software. It can be made formal, in particular by synthesizing tests and their verdicts automatically from a model of the system. Unfortunately, it suffers from non-completeness and its difficulty to reproduce bugs for distributed applications. Among formal verification techniques, model checking is complete. In its classical form it requires building a formal model by abstraction of the system behavior. Completeness is then relative to this model, not necessarily the real system. Moreover, it often does not scale to real size programs, which hampers completeness in practice. Software model checking is an alternative which focuses on the software code itself, releasing the user from the burden of building a formal model. This approach encompasses a set of techniques inspired from static analysis, model checking or automated proving, and proved to be scalable [12].

Among these, dynamic partial order reduction (DPOR) [10] comprises techniques that are complete (under some hypothesis), and exploit the independence of actions of concurrent actors to avoid explicitly traversing all behaviors. DPOR is stateless, meaning that system states are not stored, since they are too large. In the last decade, new developments proposed optimal solutions (see *e.g.* [1,2,23]). In the same time, those techniques have been tuned for relaxed memory models where even local actions may be independent (see *e.g.* [14,25]).

Our goal is to verify real parallel programs, for which we do not dispose of a model, but can execute their code. We build upon Mc SimGrid [22], a stateless model checker targeting parallel distributed applications that interact through message passing or through synchronization mechanisms (mutex, barrier, etc.). We use this tool as an experimental platform for the study of model checking techniques in this domain.Underneath, Mc SimGrid leverages the SimGrid simulator [7] to observe and control the execution of the applications under scrutiny.

In this paper, we propose adaptations of the ODPOR algorithm [1]. We want to improve the practical efficiency of ODPOR when searching for bugs. Indeed, even if ODPOR is complete and optimal, its depth-first search (DFS) nature may make it inefficient at detecting bugs by forcing the full exploration of uninteresting parts of the state space before reaching a bug. Our first contribution propose a variant of ODPOR based on an out-of-order traversal that increases the chance to detect bugs quickly. We also aim at increasing the usefulness of counter-examples when bugs are found, when the usually long sequences of actions reveal hard to analyze by humans. We define a notion of *critical transition*, which separates correct from incorrect executions in an execution path to a bug. It is thus part of the bug root cause. Our second contribution is to further adapt the ODPOR algorithm so that, when a bug is found, it efficiently searches this critical transition. All algorithms are implemented in the prototype Mc SimGrid and experimented on some benchmarks. The analysis of the experiments show promising results.

The rest of this article is organized as follows. Section 2 provides some background information about the considered class of applications, the limits of the programming model, and how classical DPOR techniques are leveraged to verify real distributed applications. Section 3 presents the contributions of this work, while Sect. 4 provides some preliminary experiments to evaluate these contributions. Section 5 concludes this paper by sketching possible future works.

2 Adapting Model Checking Techniques to the Verification of Parallel Applications

In this section, we first sketch the programming model for parallel applications implemented in Mc SimGrid. We then introduce the formalism necessary for DPOR algorithms, and then explain the principles of the ODPOR algorithm.

2.1 Extended Programming Model

Real parallel systems can be built with many programming interfaces, each containing many primitives. The amount of primitives makes it impractical to reason at that level to verify the resulting applications [20]. Instead, we build upon an abstract model entailing only about 20 actions. This reduced set of primitives are used at the core of the SimGrid simulator to mediate all interactions between interacting actors[1], with the exception of direct memory sharing between actors. Over the years, this set of primitives was proven sufficient to represent a large class of parallel applications: [9] presents a SimGrid implementation of the MPI standard [11], that prevails in High-Performance Computing. [8] presents a SimGrid implementation of the POSIX pthread library, that is used by multithreaded UNIX applications. These near-complete reimplementations of the standards allow most of the applications written with these interfaces to run unmodified on top of SimGrid.

This programming model is composed of several subsystems, each proposing specific actions allowing actors to interact through shared objects: The *network subsystem* proposes *mailbox objects* allowing receiving actors to be matched with sending ones. The corresponding actions are asynchronous and non-blocking to meet the needs of the MPI interface: ASYNC_SEND and ASYNC_RECV (receive) represent the start of a background communication. The usual asynchronous communication pattern becomes the combination of an ASYNC_SEND and of an ASYNC_RECV immediately followed by a WAIT. This extension is mandatory to precisely model the MPI semantics as with the MPI_Isend, MPI_Irecv and MPI_Wait primitives. The *synchronization subsystem* proposes four classical types of objects: *mutex, semaphore, barrier,* and POSIX *condition variable*. The corresponding actions implement classical operations such as lock/unlock, test and signal/broadcast for condition variables. Although the POSIX standard describes only synchronous versions of these operations, we refine them into an asynchronous action followed by a WAIT for symmetry with the network subsystem. Finally, WAITALL can be used to wait atomically for the completion of all actions in a given set while WAITANY blocks until the completion of an arbitrary

---

[1] We use actor and process interchangeably to designate an entity interacting with others either by message passing or shared memory.

action among a given set. This last action is *non-deterministic* in the sense that an actor executing it returns *any* of the terminated actions in the set. Similarly, RANDOM can be used to explore several alternate outcomes. For example, RANDOM($\{1, 2\}$) can return either 1 or 2.

This programming model refines the one described in [21], enriched with the pthread semantics. It is probably sufficient to encode the semantics of other libraries such as the BSD sockets that base almost all Internet communications. The main limitation of this model is that it does not capture direct memory accesses. Memory reads and writes are not observable in our model for sake of verification efficiency. This implies that data races, for instance, are out of the scope of our study. Instead, we focus on bugs triggered by specific orderings of actions, such as deadlocks or assertion errors due to communication mismatch or synchronization misuses. Previous work have shown the importance of this class of bugs in real applications [6].

2.2 Notations and Definitions

Formally, we consider a parallel system composed of n programs $p_1, \ldots, p_n \in \mathbb{P}$. The global behaviour of this system can be described by a *labelled transition system* (LTS) $\mathcal{M} = (S, \mathsf{Act}, s_0, \mathcal{T})$ where S is a *set of states* encoding local states of processes, contents of communication channels and status of synchronization objects, $s_0 \in S$ is the *initial state* where each process p is in its initial state, communication channels are empty and synchronization objects free, $\mathsf{Act} = \bigcup_{i=1}^{n} \mathsf{Act}_i$ is the alphabet of *actions*, the disjoint union of local alphabets, $\mathcal{T} \subseteq S \times \mathsf{Act} \times S$ is the *transition relation*, each *transition* $(s, a, s') \in \mathcal{T}$ sometimes written $s \xrightarrow{a} s'$. We note $\mathsf{proc}((s, a, s')) = \mathsf{proc}(a) = p_i$ if $a \in \mathsf{Act}_i$ meaning that $s \xrightarrow{a} s'$ is executed by process p_i. We denote by *enabled*(s) the set of transitions that can be taken from state s. In the following, we assume that actors are *deterministic*, i.e., for each $s \in S$, if $t_1, t_2 \in enabled(s)$, then $\mathsf{proc}(t_1) \neq \mathsf{proc}(t_2)$. This allows one to identify the transitions in a given state by their actors. Our results and implementation hold for non-deterministic actors, but distinguishing the transitions outcomes of a given actor in a given state would make the notations artificially complex.

We restrict our study to acyclic LTS. An *execution* of $\mathcal{M}$ is a finite sequence of transitions starting in the initial state $E := t_1 \cdot t_2 \cdots t_n = (s_0, a_1, s_1) \cdot (s_1, a_2, s_2) \cdots (s_{n-1}, a_n, s_n) \in \mathcal{T}^*$ also written $s_0 \xrightarrow{a_1 \cdot a_2 \cdots a_n} s_n$. With the remark above, E can also be written by its sequence of processes $\mathsf{proc}(t_1) \cdots \mathsf{proc}(t_n)$. E is *maximal* when $enabled(\mathsf{last}(E)) = \emptyset$. The following notations are introduced:

- $\mathsf{dom}(E) := \{1, \ldots, n\}$, the range of transitions in E,
- $E_i := t_i$ for $i \in \mathsf{dom}(E)$, the ith transition of E,
- $E \cdot t := t_1 \cdots t_n \cdot t$, for $t = (s_n, a_{n+1}, s_{n+1})$, the concatenation of E with t,
- $E \vdash t$ (or equivalently $E \vdash p$ where $p = \mathsf{proc}(t)$), for $t \in T$, the fact that $E \cdot t$ is a valid execution,
- $\mathsf{sub}(E, t_i) := t_1 \cdots t_i$ for $i \in \mathsf{dom}(E)$, the prefix of E, up to t_i included,

- $\mathsf{pre}(E, i) := s_{i-1}$ for $i \in \mathsf{dom}(E)$, the state reached before executing t_i,
- $\mathsf{last}(E) := s_n$, the last state of the execution E.

For sake of algorithmic simplicity, we assume a property called *persistency*: an enabled process cannot be disabled before it executes some action. Formaly, for any execution E, any process $p \in \mathbb{P}$, if $E \vdash p$, then for any other process $q \neq p$, $E \vdash q$ implies $E \cdot q \vdash p$. Notice that in the programming model, persitency justifies to split blocking calls such as MUTEX_LOCK into a non-blocking MUTEX_ASYNC_LOCK, that adds the caller's ID to the list of actors requesting this mutex, followed by a blocking MUTEX_WAIT, that becomes enabled only when the caller's ID is first in that list. While an atomic MUTEX_LOCK would not be persistent (it gets disabled if another actor gets the lock), both MUTEX_ASYNC_LOCK and MUTEX_WAIT are actually persistent.

2.3 State Space Reduction Using ODPOR

Dynamic partial order reduction (DPOR) [10] is a software model checking technique that exploits the independence between concurrent actions. To avoid the exploration of the full state space, it relies on the equivalence of executions by commutation of adjacent transitions carrying independent actions.

Intuitively, two actions are independent if firing one cannot enable or disable the other, and they commute, *i.e.* their execution order does not impact the final result. Formaly, a valid *independency* relation for $\mathcal{M}$ is an irreflexive and symmetric relation $\mathcal{I} \subseteq \mathsf{Act} \times \mathsf{Act}$ such that, for any state $s \in S$ and any pair of *independent* actions $(a_1, a_2) \in \mathcal{I}$, we have:

- if there exists $s' \in S$ such that $s \xrightarrow{a_1} s'$, then $a_2 \in enabled(s)$ if and only if $a_2 \in enabled(s')$,
- if $a_1, a_2 \in enabled(s)$, then there exists $s' \in S$ such that $s \xrightarrow{a_1 a_2} s'$ and $s \xrightarrow{a_2 a_1} s'$.

The *dependency* relation $\mathcal{D} = \mathsf{Act} \times \mathsf{Act} \setminus \mathcal{I}$ is the complementary relation. In this paper we only consider a statically defined valid dependency relation, *i.e.*, based on the semantics of the programming model of Mc SimGrid. For instance, we can state that ASYNC_SEND and ASYNC_RECV actions are always independent, while two MUTEX_LOCK concerned by the same mutex are dependent [21].

P1	P2	P3
ASYNC_SEND(P3)	ASYNC_SEND(P3)	ASYNC_RECV(from any); WAIT()
		ASYNC_RECV(from P2) ; WAIT()

Fig. 1. A communication pattern using the *any* wildcard.

For a sequence of transitions $E = t_1 \cdots t_n$, the *happens-before* [17] relation $\to_E$ is the smallest transitively closed relation on $\mathsf{dom}(E)$ such that if $i < j$ and the actions carried by t_i and t_j are dependent then $i \to_E j$.

Example 1. Consider the execution $E = P_1 \cdot P_2 \cdot P_3 \cdot P_3$ from Fig. 1 (remember that a transition can be identified with its actor). We have that $E_1 \to_E E_2$ because two ASYNC_SEND actions to the same actor are dependent, and $E_3 \to_E E_4$ because actions from the same actors are causally ordered.

Let $\simeq$ be the equivalence relation on executions such that $E \simeq E'$ if $\mathsf{dom}(E) = \mathsf{dom}(E')$ and $\to_E = \to_{E'}$. A *Mazurkiewicz's trace* $[E]_\simeq$, is the class of executions equivalent for $\simeq$ and containing E.

DPOR algorithms aim at exploring the smallest number of executions while ensuring soundness of the exploration. This is ensured by exploring at least one execution per Mazurkiewicz's trace. To that extend, reduction algorithms aim at finding *reversible races*, *i.e.*, identifying pairs of dependent transitions which inversion leads to a distinct Mazurkiewicz's trace. Formally, t_i and t_j with $i < j \in \mathsf{dom}(E)$ are in reversible race, noted $i \precsim_E j$, when:

- $\mathsf{proc}(t_i) \neq \mathsf{proc}(t_j)$, and $i \to_E j$,
- there is no k such that $i < k < j$, $i \to_E k$ and $k \to_E j$,
- for any $E' \in [E]_\simeq$ of the form $E' = F \cdot t_i \cdot t_j \cdot F'$, then $F \vdash t_j$.

The first condition states that t_i and t_j belong to different actors and are dependent, ensuring that their inversion produces a different Mazurkiewicz's trace. The second condition ensures that there is no intermediate transition that would be in reversible race with both of them. The last one ensures that t_i does not enable t_j. We then get that if $i \precsim_E j$, there exists $E' \not\simeq E$ with $j \to_{E'} i$. The satisfaction of properties such as absence of deadlock or assertion violation is consistent with Mazurkiewicz's traces [10], meaning that for any such property φ, if $E \simeq E'$ then $\varphi \models E \iff \varphi \models E'$. The principle of a DPOR algorithm is then to verify those properties by building a so called "reduced LTS", where each Mazurkiewicz's trace is represented by at least one execution.

Optimal Dynamic Partial Order Reduction (ODPOR) [1] is a recent DPOR technique. Like other DPOR algorithms, ODPOR is based on a stateless depth-first exploration of a reduced state space. The exploration also uses a set of processes called *sleep set* to avoid exploring executions equivalent to already traversed ones. The original DPOR algorithm stores in each traversed execution E a *persistent set*, *i.e.* a set of processes that should be visited later when backtracking, populated when a reversible race just after E is detected in some continuation execution. The optimality of ODPOR is gained by associating to each traversed execution E a more precise information called *wakeup tree*, a set of initial sequences that should be visited later when backtracking to E.

The crucial notion of wakeup tree is detailed now. First, we define *weak initials* of a sequence w after a prefix E: $WI_{[E]}(w)$ is the set of processes p s.t. there exists sequences w' and v satisfying $E \cdot w \cdot v \simeq E \cdot p \cdot w'$. Intuitively, $WI_{[E]}(w)$ are the processes in $\mathsf{enabled}(E)$ that have no happens-before predecessor in w. Let an *ordered tree* $(B, \prec)$ be a prefix-closed set of executions, each *node* being an execution and the *root* is the empty one $\langle\rangle$. A *wakeup tree* after a prefix E written $WuT(E)$, relative to a set of processes P (the sleep set in E) is then an ordered tree $(B, \prec)$ s.t.:

- for every leaf node $w \in B$, $WI_{[E]}(w) \cap P = \emptyset$,
- for every node $u.p$ and leaf $u.w$ in B, if $u.p \prec u.w$ then $p \notin WI_{[E.u]}(w)$.

Both conditions are necessary to achieve optimality of ODPOR, meaning that each Mazurkiewicz's trace is explored exactly once by the algorithm and no sleep-set-blocked (SSB) execution is visited (an SSB execution is an execution equivalent to an already explored one, but discovered lately when already partially explored). In fact, if P above is the sleep set computed when backtracking to E, the first condition ensures that no SSB will be visited. The second condition prevents inserting a sequence for which a possibly equivalent prefix already exists in a given wakeup tree. We skip most details here, and report to [1] for the explanations on how to construct wakeup trees and the corresponding insertion and suppression operations. Simply remember that $WuT(E)$ is populated each time a reversible race at E is detected on a complete continuation of E, and consists in inserting in order an initial execution sequence needed to reverse the race from E.

Example 2. The example shown in Fig. 1 contains a deadlock: if the ASYNC_SEND from P_2 is executed first and matches the ASYNC_RECV (from any) of P_3 then the second ASYNC_RECV of P_3 can never be fulfiled, and process P_3 can never make progress. On this simple example, both DPOR and ODPOR behave the same. They explore a first execution, *e.g.* $P_1 \cdot P_2 \cdot P_3 \cdot P_3$. After discovering a reversible race between the first and the second transitions (the two ASYNC_SEND), they try an execution with those two transitions reversed. While the DPOR will only force the execution of P_2 before P_1 (at the start of the program), ODPOR will force the whole sequence $P_2 \cdot P_3 \cdot P_3$ also before P_1. By further restricting the degree of freedom in the exploration, ODPOR achieves optimality.

Applying ODPOR to our programming model requires defining a valid static dependence relation [21]. It consists in a set of boolean functions, one for each pair of action types, that are used extensively during the ODPOR exploration of the application. The number of functions being quadratic in the number of actions types, covering the full API of both MPI and pthread with only 20 action types dramatically simplifies the definition of the dependence relation and is a serious argument over working directly at the API level (like in [24]).

3 Making Verification Efficient and Practical

This section details our two contributions, both being adaptations of ODPOR. In the first subsection we propose an out-of-order traversal of the reduced LTS aimed at improving the efficiency of ODPOR. In the second subsection, we further adapt ODPOR to better explain bugs exhibited during the traversal.

3.1 Directed Verification

In the last decade, DPOR variants have been developed with the objective of either reaching optimality, or improving the efficiency in a complete but suboptimal exploration of the reduced LTS. However, for real size programs, even reduced LTS may be too large to be explored exhaustively. The challenge that we adress is then to increase the chance to quickly find bugs when they exist, while preserving optimality and completeness in the absence of bug.

We first notice that one of the main pitfalls of DPOR techniques, which may hamper their ability to quickly discover bugs, lays in their depth-first search nature. Indeed, depending on the first explored sequence, there is a risk that algorithms start in a region of the state space and spend a huge amount of time unsuccessfuly trying to find bugs there, while a single try in a different area would perhaps immediately yield an answer. This problem is examplified by slightly modifying the program of Fig. 1 as follows.

Example 3. Let us consider the program composed of the same P_1 and P_2, ending with the same actor P_3, but with some amount of synchronizations added in between. If (O)DPOR first explores $P_1 \cdot P_2$, it will then have to explore all its continuations before considering a (possibly faulty) run starting with $P_2 \cdot P_1$.

We thus want to maximize the likelihood of detecting undesired behaviors in real size applications that are too large even for reduction techniques to terminate. The idea behind our random-first search ODPOR (RFS ODPOR— presented in Algorithm 1) is then to abandon the depth-first search nature of ODPOR. After encountering a maximal execution and computing reversible races, ODPOR would backtrack to a state of this execution with non-empty wakeup tree, *i.e.* from which some unexplored Mazurkiewicz trace remains. Instead, in RFS ODPOR we authorize to jump to any other state with non-empty wakeup tree. This gives much more flexibility to the algorithm in the order in which the reduced state space is built. We could use some heuristics to select the best candidate to continue the exploration.

As we explain now, since ODPOR is tight to the DFS traversal, the modifications are not immediate. We detail the changes required by the algorithm while preserving soundness and optimality.

WuT and Tree: as a DFS algorithm, the ODPOR algorithm only stored the stack of currently explored abstract states. Each such state is populated with a wakeup tree, eventually grown by sequences allowing to reverse races at this state. Wakeup trees are later explored when backtracking and then forgotten. This raises an issue in random-first order since starting to unfold wakeup trees before having fully populating them could lead to exploring a same trace twice, thus loosing optimality.

We store currently explored executions in a tree-like structure *Tree*, as a counterpart to the call stack of the ODPOR DFS. It helps us traverse the state space at will and preserves optimality by its combination with wakeup trees. When a race is detected (line 17 of RFS ODPOR), a sequence v is inserted at a node E' in *Tree*, as described by Algorithm 2. The insertion generalizes the insertion in the *WuT* to the *Tree*. It finds the leftmost (in the exploration order) and longest non-contradictory prefix in *Tree*, and continues to the current *WuT* if necessary: when a weak initial p of v is found in the current node of the tree

Algorithm 1. RFS ODPOR(s_0)

1: initialize *exploration-heads* with the empty sequence $\langle \rangle$;
2: choose some $t \in enabled(s_0)$;
3: initialize $WuT(\langle\rangle)$ with t;
4: **while** *exploration-heads* $\neq \emptyset$ **do**
5:      choose $E \in$ *exploration-heads*;
6:      choose p among nodes of height one in $WuT(E)$;
7:      $done(E).add(p)$;
8:      add p as a child of E in *Tree*;
9:      $sleep(E \cdot p) := \{q \in sleep(E) \cup done(E) \mid (p,q) \notin \mathcal{D}\}$;
10:     move the subtree of $WuT(E)$ rooted after p to $WuT(E \cdot p)$;
11:     **if** $WuT(E)$ is empty **then**
12:         remove E from *exploration-heads*;
13:     **if** $E \cdot p$ is maximal **then**
14:         **for all** $i, j \in \mathrm{dom}(E \cdot p)$ such that $i \precsim_{E \cdot p} j$ **do**
15:            $E' := \mathsf{sub}(E, E_{i-1})$;
16:            $v := notdep(E_i, E).\mathsf{proc}(E_j)$;
17:            **if** $(sleep(E') \cup done(E')_{<\mathsf{proc}(E_i)}) \cap WI_{[E']}(v) = \emptyset$ **then**
18:                $E'' := Tree[E'].insert(v)$;
19:                *exploration-heads*.add(E'');
20:         $GarbageCollect(E \cdot p)$;
21:     **else**
22:         **if** $WuT(E \cdot p)$ is empty **then**
23:            choose $p' \in enabled(\mathsf{last}(E \cdot p)) \setminus sleep(E \cdot p)$;
24:            initialize $WuT(E \cdot p)$ with p';
25:         *exploration-heads*.add$(E.p)$;

E, a recursive call at node $E \cdot p$ is done with sequence $v \setminus p$, i.e. v where the first occurence of p in v, if any, is removed; when the algorithm fails to find such an action, it inserts v in the WuT of the current node E, and returns E so that ODPOR knows where to explore later.

Sleep Sets: similar to ODPOR, we use sleep sets to memorize transitions that should not be taken by future explorations, because they start sequences equivalent to already explored ones. In RFS ODPOR, we would need to update sleep sets as soon as some children state is explored, not only when a left subtree is fully explored like in ODPOR. Unfortunately, directly adding those to the sleep set could result in missed executions, as illustrated by the following example.

Algorithm 2. $Tree[E].insert(v)$

1: **for all** p in order of $done(E)$ **do**
2:     **if** $p \in WI_{[E]}(v)$ **then**
3:        **return** $Tree[E \cdot p].insert(v \setminus p)$;
4: insert v in $WuT(E)$;
5: **return** E;

Example 4. Consider an execution E leading to state s, from which we first explore p_1. Suppose that this exploration detects a race leading to insert a sequence starting with p_2 in $WuT(E)$. The algorithm then decides to explore that race without completing the exploration of the subtree $E \cdot p_1$, hence we need to add p_1 to the sleep set so that explorations after $E \cdot p_2$ do not execute p_1 right away. Now when we go back to $E \cdot p_1$ and discover another race after E starting with p_2, if p_2 was already in the sleep set, the race would not be inserted in the WuT.

To tackle this issue, we must add some order information to the sleep sets. In fact, we separate each sleep set into an inherited part, called $sleep(E)$ in the algorithm, and the set of processes explored from E ordered according to insertion time, $done(E)$. When checking for a *weak initial* at line 17, we need to intersect with the union of $sleep(E')$ and those elements of $done(E')$ inserted before the considered one for the race, denoted $done(E')_{<\mathsf{proc}(E_i)}$.

Memory Management: we implement a procedure $GarbageCollect(E)$ which keeps in *Tree* only nodes that could be useful in future explorations. Indeed, due to the ordering of $done(E)$, only explorations on the left of E may impact $WuT(E)$. Thus we need to detect when explored nodes cannot be impacted anymore and remove them. A leftmost leaf explored in *Tree* can thus be removed, which triggers $GarbageCollect(E)$. Recursively, a parent node E' with no remaining child in *Tree* and in $WuT(E')$ is removed. When a parent node with children in *Tree* is found, the procedure recursively tries to close its remaining leftmost leaf. The recursion stops when called from a node with non-empty WuT, since it will be triggered again in a future exploration of a leaf in that WuT. RFS ODPOR memory comsuption remains higher than its DFS counterpart as we need to keep in memory a subtree instead of a single stack. However, thanks to the *GarbageCollect* procedure, the random choice of an element in *exploration-heads* can be biased so that the total memory consumption remains under a given threshold. In fact, if the threshold is nearly reached, the exploration can be biased to leftmost nodes in order to release memory.

Theorem 1. *The RFS ODPOR algorithm is sound and optimal in the sense that its explores a unique execution per Mazurkiewicz's trace and explores no sleep-set-blocked execution.*

Sketch of Proof. For the following proof we consider that $GarbageCollect(E)$ is disabled so that *Tree* contains all explored sequences, Considering *Tree* at the end of the algorithm, proving soundness boils down to proving that it contains all Mazurkiewicz trace. By contradiction, let us suppose that there exists some execution E uncovered by *Tree*, i.e. $\forall E' \in Tree, E \notin [E']_\simeq$. Consider lg_E the longest sequence equivalent with a prefix of E which has an equivalent execution in *Tree*. Formaly, lg_E is the longest sequence such that there exists $v, v' \in \mathcal{T}^*$ and $E' \in Tree$ satisfying $E \simeq lg_E \cdot v$ and $E' \cdot v' \simeq lg_E \cdot v'$. Among such sequences E, consider now the one with lg_E of maximal length. By definition of lg_E, there exists some E' equivalent to lg_E in *Tree*, such that after E', RFS ODPOR explored some transitions $t_1, \ldots, t_k$, but did not explore a transition t that would have led to E. In particular, for each i, $t_i \notin WI_{[E']}(v)$ and there is a transition t'_i in v such that $D(t_i, t'_i)$, and each transition $v_1, \ldots, v_l$ in v before t'_i is independent with t_i. Hence, due to independences, $E' \cdot v_1 \cdots v_l t_i t'_i$ is a possible prefix of a trace of the programm. If the RFS ODPOR explored that prefix at some point, the race between t_i and t'_i would lead to exploring their inversion. Therefore this prefix must not have been explored. But $|lg_{E' \cdot v_1 \cdots v_l t_i t'_i}| \geq |E' \cdot t_i| > |lg_E|$ contradicts the fact that E is maximal for the length of lg_E.

To prove optimality, we show that "*Tree* $\cup \{WuT(E)|E \in \text{\textit{Tree}}\}$ is a wakeup tree" is an invariant for RFS ODPOR, which is similar to the proof of optimality for ODPOR. The invariant is preserved thanks to the way insertion is done inside *Tree* and its prolongation in the *WuT*. In particular, respecting the order in *done* is crucial for verifying that if $u.p \prec u.w$ then $p \notin WI_{[E.u]}(w)$. Once the invariant is shown, if we suppose that two sequences in *Tree* are equivalent, we reach a contradiction with the properties of wakeup trees.

Example of Use: Busy-Waiting. Another interest of RFS ODPOR is its ability to tackle programs that use busy-waiting. This classical pattern in asynchronous parallel programming allows a process to perform computations while waiting for another process, typically through a while loop guarded by a test on a reception or a condition variable. In its extreme form, this pattern consists of an empty loop guarded by a test on an asynchronous action. This is commonly used in HPC to reduce the latency by ensuring that the communication thread remains executed on this empty loop rather than descheduled by the operating system. That way, incoming messages get handled immediately.

Unfortunately, this construct poses a challenge to verification. Indeed, the application has an unbounded behavior consisting of an infinite number of tests. However, this behaviors cannot arise in real systems, as it would imply that the process in a busy-waiting loop executes infinitely often without the other processes to execute at all. The natural fairness provided by real systems without failures prevents such behaviors. A classical DFS ODPOR could find its way out of the infinite loop by randomly trying other processes once in a while, but it may waste time in the recursive exploration of nearby subtrees that also have that infinite loop behavior. On the other hand, RFS ODPOR allows the exploration to backtrack in a completely different area of the code where the busy-waiting never occurs, hence spending more time effectively looking for a bug.

In [15], the authors propose a specific answer to this problem in the case of spin loops for weak memory models. They transform busy-waiting into `assume` statements (as explained in [16]) and perform important computations to determine whether a given execution could be blocked before effectively visiting it. This solution is not possible in our case since it requires access to variable values, which is too costly in our context.

Other works propose to use techniques based on randomization to find bugs. These techniques goes from randomizing the scheduler to injecting randomly generated Byzantine behaviors [5]. Using random in those approaches helps cover a certain part of the program state space and returns results with certain probabilistic guarantees. Those differ from our work in the sense that randomness only helps us to order the exploration in the hope of finding a bug faster. In particular, the exploration remains sound and will give a certain result, not a probabilistic one.

3.2 Counter-Example Explainability

In this section, we focus on refinning counter-examples found by previous algorithm.

Counter-examples are helpful for developers to understand the flaws and better correct them. Surprisingly, few work deal with explanability of counter-examples [13]. Moreover, most work related to model checking need the full state space to identify actions that cause bugs (see *e.g.* [3]). These techniques cannot be applied in stateless model checking, the transition system of the application is never explicitly built. We propose to perform some sort of root cause analysis as an extension of the ODPOR algorithm, and show how it also adapts to our RFS ODPOR. Our notion of critical transition is close to the notion of neighbourhood of [3] but contrary to their solution, our algorithm can be adapted to ODPOR.

The principle is the following. In a run E that fails a property, we call *critical transition* (CT) the last transitions γ after which the bug inevitably occurs. Formaly, let φ be a safety property, E such that $E \nvDash \varphi$. The *critical transition* of E, is the unique transition $\gamma = (s, a, s') \in E$ such that, calling E' the prefix of E ending in s, all maximal continuations of $E' \cdot \gamma$ violate φ and there exists a maximal continuation of E' satisfying φ.

Example 5. Let us recall that example 1 contains a deadlock, and that a possible counterexample is $P_2 \cdot P_1 \cdot P_3 \cdot P_3$. Now, if actors 1 and 2 have more code to execute, the counterexamples can become much longer. In fact, they can execute anything that does not interact with actor 3, and the deadlock will only be found when there are done. On the other hand, any execution starting with the action of actor 2 will lead to the deadlock. This is the critical transition to this bug, no matter what the other actions of actor 1 and 2 are.

We propose an algorithm to find the CT that takes advantage of the reduction operated by ODPOR. We illustrate the principles by Fig. 2. After finding a first faulty execution E, we switch to the CT mode and keep exploring the reduced state space until finding a correct execution. We then need to decide whether transitions in E, some of them with unexplored siblings, lead to correct or incorrect executions. Let $E = F \cdot b_1 \cdots b_n$ with F the prefix from which all alternative traces to E (the subtree rooted in c_1) have been explored and are correct, by definition. The critical transition is necessarily among $b_1, \ldots, b_n$. The set of states $\{s_1, \ldots, s_n\}$ can always be partitionned into older ones $S_1 = \{s_1, \ldots, s_k\}$ with non-empty sleep sets, and the younger ones $S_2 = \{s_{k+1}, \ldots, s_n\}$ with empty sleep sets. We can prove that states in S_1 belong to correct executions, so that the critical section lead to a state in S_2. Starting from s_n, the ODPOR algorithm then backtracks in S_2, using wakeup trees to explore alternatives, until finding a correct execution. The adaptation to RFS ODPOR is similar but requires special attention when the underlying program crashes as explained in the appendix.

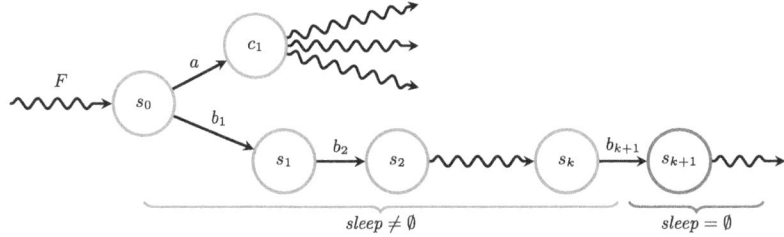

Fig. 2. An exploration tree at some point during CTF+ODPOR algorithm.

It is worth noting that the CT only identifies the last action that leads to an issue. For instance, in the case of a four-actor deadlock, where P_1 and P_2 are blocking each other while P_3 and P_4 are doing the same, the CT is not enough. It captures only the last occurring pair of deadlock. Furthermore, one can look at the causal past of the CT, *i.e.* the set of transitions executed before the CT, causally related to it. This is interesting since in most cases, it allows replicating the found bug with a much smaller counterexample. But again, the same four-actor deadlock shows this is not enough, and that, in the general case, the causal past does not fully reproduce the bug. In the future, we plan to refine the notion in order to tackle those cases where bugs are caused by apparently unrelated actions. This is mandatory in order to fully take advantage of the information conveyed by the CT.

4 Evaluation

We implemented a prototype of our algorithm in Mc SimGrid v3.36.1 to serve as a proof of concept. All experiments were run on Intel Xeon E5-2630 v3 at max 2.40GHz. Programs were compiled using gcc-10.2.1 with -O3 parameter.

4.1 Evaluating RFS Overhead

In this first experiment, we compare the performance of our implementation of RFS with two state-of-the-art software model checker Nidhugg [1] and DPU [18] over examples taken from the latter evaluation. Nidhugg is an implementation of source-DPOR, a slightly different version of ODPOR that can encounter SSB executions. It is tuned to search pthread code for data races under weak memory models. DPU is a proof of concept implementing unfolding DPOR, an optimal reduction algorithm based on partial event systems. DPU can only verify mutexes

Table 1. Performance comparison for exhaustive exploration. TO means the execution did not finish in 10 min while ERR reports a runtime error.

Benchmark		DPU		Nidhugg		McSimGrid RFS	
Name	Traces	Time	Mem	Time	Mem	Time	Mem
DISP(5,3)	1482	0.629	55M	6.314	65M	2.665	50M
DISP(5,4)	15282	6.285	135M	65.034	65M	28.445	442M
DISP(5,5)	151032	203.785	973M	TO	65M	289.361	4191M
DISP(5,6)		ERR	1016M	TO	65M	TO	10798M
MPAT(5)	3840	1.860	80M	1.203	64M	7.210	144M
MPAT(6)	46080	51.283	420M	16.273	64M	94.917	1770M
MPAT(7)	645120	TO	1553M	255.109	64M	TO	12951M
MPAT(8)		TO	1603M	TO	64M	TO	17055M
MPC(3,5)	2958	0.937	61M	37.662	65M	4.709	75M
MPC(4,5)	313683	ERR	63M	TO	65M	521.814	6383M
MPC(5,5)		TO	1344M	TO	65M	TO	15693M
PI(7)	5040	1.950	66M	ERR	66M	6.019	71M
PI(8)	40320	28.748	273M	ERR	66M	50.453	555M
PI(9)	362880	TO	1128M	ERR	65M	505.053	5172M
POKE(8)	3700	1.934	99M	146.232	65M	11.427	186M
POKE(9)	5332	2.913	124M	458.337	65M	18.004	292M
POKE(10)	7384	4.479	152M	TO	64M	26.799	446M
POKE(11)	9904	6.674	193M	TO	65M	38.861	656M
POKE(12)	12940	9.969	242M	TO	65M	53.417	874M
POKE(13)	16540	14.506	310M	ERR	64M	72.032	1214M

operations. The benchmark against which we are testing is composed of examples taken from the SV-COMP [4] repository. These examples are bug-free, and scalable in terms of number of processes.

The results are presented in Table 1. Experiments have a ten minutes timeout. For each run, we report the time in seconds and the peak of memory consumption by the applications. Nidhugg can not run on example PI as it involves C primitives it does not cover. Overall, we observe that our RFS implementation performs in the same order of magnitude as the state-of-the-art tools regarding time. On the other hand, the memory consumption is higher. This was intended as the algorithm may require to keep a tree rather than only a stack in memory. As a conclusion, the overhead of the RFS approach is not a bottleneck for these examples. If memory consumption becomes an issue on bigger examples, it is still possible to tailor the order of exploration. For example when the memory usage reaches a given threshold, the exploration could focus on leftmost states so that the *GarbageCollect* procedure reclaims memory.

4.2 Evaluating RFS Benefits for Bug Finding

To evaluate the benefits of changing the order of exploration, we ran our algorithm over three bugged codes that can be scaled at will either in the number of synchronizations or in the number of processes:

- *MPI-any* is the MPI code of the program in Fig. 1 The scaling factor is the number of *rendezvous* (MPI_Barrier) between the sendings and the receptions. Those synchronizations consist of broadcasts. Hence, adding one *rendezvous* effectively doubles the number of interleaving to consider.
- *philosophers-mutex-deadlock* is an implementation of the dining philosophers using one mutex per fork, scaling with the number of philosophers. A deadlock occurs if all philosopher pick their first fork before a philosopher considers its second fork.
- *philosophers-semaphore-deadlock* is a variant of the same program, with an additional semaphore restricting the number of philosophers allowed to pick forks A deadlock occurs since the initial number of tokens in the semaphore equals the number of philosophers.

We ran four variants of ODPOR over these examples: DFS, Uniform-DFS, Uniform-RFS Branch and Uniform-RFS Step. DFS is the classical ODPOR algorithm from [1] running in an arbitrary depth-first search manner. When confronted to a choice, it picks the process with the smaller identifier. The Uniform-DFS variant resolves those choices with a uniform random pick. The last two variants both resolve choices with a uniform pick: the "Step" variant picks any element in *exploration-heads* at each step, while the "Branch" variant completes a branch before choosing any element in *exploration-heads*. Randomized explorations are run 100 times each, with 100 different seeds. The results depicted in Fig. 3 show the number of states explored before finding a deadlock when the scaling factor varies.

All runs of *MPI-any* (1st table) and *philosophers-mutex-deadlock* (2nd table) terminate in less than 5mn, while for *philosophers-semaphore-deadlock* (3rd table) some runs timeout after 10mn without finding a bug. For these runs, the number of states explored before timeout is used, allowing the box plots to depict the success rate of a given strategy for large applications. The number of timeouted runs (over 100) is written above each box plot.

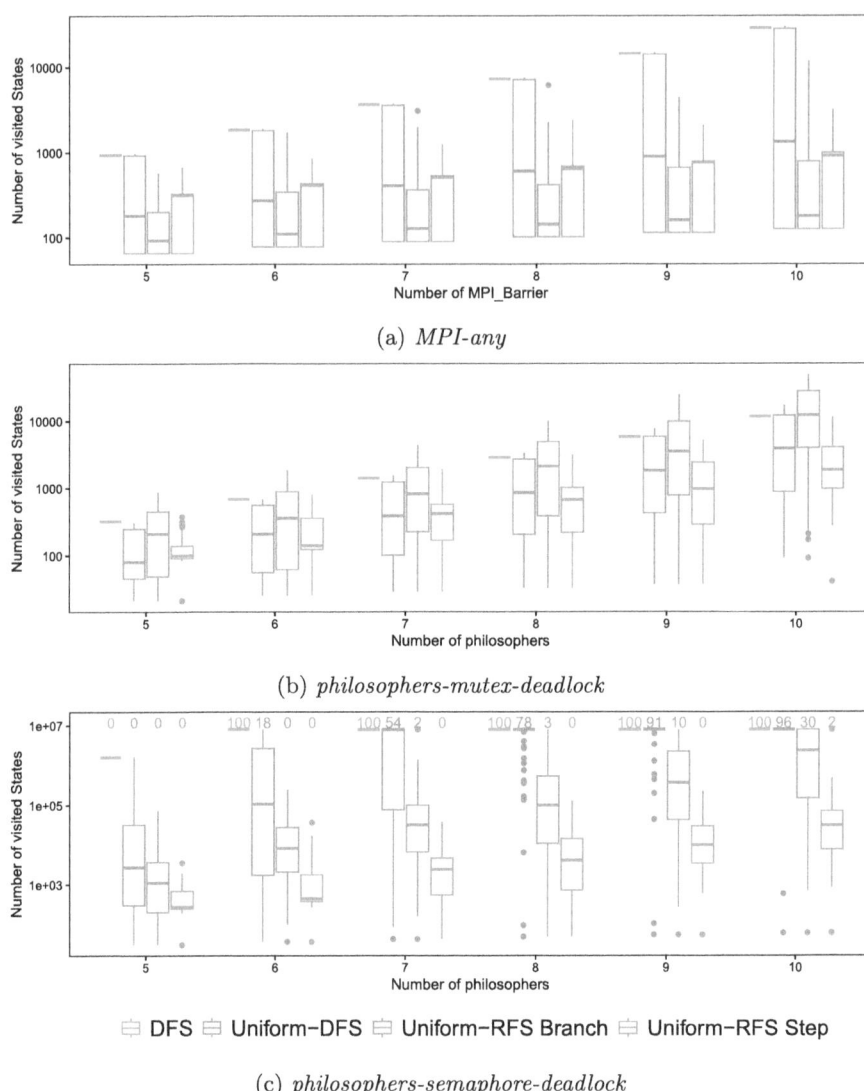

Fig. 3. Number of states explored before finding the deadlock at various scales.

The first experiment with *MPI-any* illustrates an example where the scaling is in number of operations per actor. In this case, randomizing the original DFS algorithm with Uniform-DFS helps keep the average time on a linear scale, but at least 25% of the executions still behave as badly as the worst-case scenario. On the opposite, both Step-RFS and Branch-RFS runs 75% of the time faster than the average for Uniform-DFS, with Branch-RFS behaving a bit better in that example. This is because Branch-DFS has the opportunity to explore a faulty execution each time it backtracks.

The other experiments are examples of scaling in the number of actors, with the semaphore variant having many more interleaving to consider. On the smaller example of *philosophers-mutex-deadlock*, it is hard to conclude to any trend. By trying whole sequence and never a few steps, Branch-RFS is in average slower, while Step-RFS tends to explore in parallel different sequences step-by-step, and faster reaches deadlocks that are located somewhere in the middle of the state space. The trend is more visible on the biggest example *philosophers-semaphore-deadlock*. In that case, for ten philosophers, only 4 executions out of 100 finished in under 10 min with Unfirom-DFS while other executions visit more than 10 millions nodes without finishing. Our solution performs better with Step-RFS finishing 98% of the times, visiting an average of only 12,000 nodes before finding the bug. Step-RFS does not behave like a BFS exploration as one could expect. This is due to the high restriction the reduction has on the state space. By extensively limiting the number of parallel branches opened at the same time, the reduction turns a simple random step variation into a working trade-off over the various situations. These preliminary experimental results are promising for the efficiency of our techniques to detect bugs in real-size applications.

In all these experiments, we also evaluated the CT overhead. The worst case is when the first explored execution leads to a fault, in which case CT must explore entirely the sub-tree around that run while it can reuse previously explored traces otherwise. That exploration is very fast in the two *philosophers* benchmarks as the critical transition is one of the last trace's actions, but takes more time for the first benchmark where the critical transition is the very first action in the trace. This is indeed the worst case for the CT algorithm, as it needs to exhaustively explore the reduced LTS searching for a correct execution which does not exist.

5 Conclusion and Future Work

In this paper, we proposed two adaptations of ODPOR, a state-of-the-art Dynamical Partial Order Reduction technique, focused on bug finding and explanation, implemented in Mc SimGrid. First, the RFS ODPOR variant allows arbitrary orderings of the state space exploration. This degree of freedom shows promising results in discovering faulty behaviors early. Second, we adapted further the ODPOR technique with a novel algorithm for counter-example explainability, based on the notion of critical transition, which requires minimal computation overhead. In the future, we plan to search for model specific heuristics in order to further accelerate RFS ODPOR in the presence of faults in the program. Thanks to its design, RFS ODPOR also paves the way for intensive parallelization through producer-consumer patterns. Finally, we aim at refining our notion of critical transition in order to explain counter-examples a step further.

Acknowledgment. Experiments presented in this paper were carried out using the Grid'5000 testbed, supported by a scientific interest group hosted by Inria and including CNRS, RENATER and several Universities as well as other organizations (see https://www.grid5000.fr/

References

1. Abdulla, P.A., Aronis, S., Jonsson, B., Sagonas, K.: Optimal dynamic partial order reduction. In: Jagannathan, S., Sewell, P. (eds.) The 41st Annual ACM SIGPLAN-SIGACT Symposium on Principles of Programming Languages, POPL '14, pp. 373–384. ACM (2014)
2. Abdulla, P.A., Aronis, S., Jonsson, B., Sagonas, K.: Source sets: a foundation for optimal dynamic partial order reduction. J. ACM **64**(4), 25:1–25:49 (2017)
3. Barbon, G., Leroy, V., Salaün, G.: Debugging of behavioural models using counterexample analysis. IEEE Trans. Softw. Eng. **47**(6), 1184–1197 (2021)
4. Beyer, D.: Software verification with validation of results. In: Legay, A., Margaria, T. (eds.) TACAS 2017. LNCS, vol. 10206, pp. 331–349. Springer, Heidelberg (2017). https://doi.org/10.1007/978-3-662-54580-5_20
5. Burckhardt, S., Kothari, P., Musuvathi, M., Nagarakatte, S.: A randomized scheduler with probabilistic guarantees of finding bugs. SIGPLAN Not. **45**(3), 167–178 (2010)
6. Cai, Y., Yao, P., Ye, C., Zhang, C.: Place your locks well: understanding and detecting lock misuse bugs. In: 32nd USENIX Security Symposium (USENIX Security 23), pp. 3727–3744. USENIX Association, Anaheim (2023)
7. Casanova, H., Giersch, A., Legrand, A., Quinson, M., Suter, F.: Versatile, scalable, and accurate simulation of distributed applications and platforms. J. Parallel Distrib. Comput. **74**(10), 2899–2917 (2014)
8. Cooperman, G., Quinson, M.: Sthread: In-Vivo Model Checking of Multithreaded Programs. The Art, Science, and Engineering of Programming (2020)
9. Degomme, A., Legrand, A., Markomanolis, G.S., Quinson, M., Stillwell, M., Suter, F.: Simulating MPI applications: the SMPI approach. IEEE Trans. Parallel Distrib. Syst. **28**(8), 2387–2400 (2017)

10. Flanagan, C., Godefroid, P.: Dynamic partial-order reduction for model checking software. In: Palsberg, J., Abadi, M. (eds.) Proceedings of the 32nd ACM SIGPLAN-SIGACT Symposium on Principles of Programming Languages, POPL 2005, pp. 110–121. ACM (2005)
11. Forum, T.M.: MPI: a message passing interface. In: Borchers, B., Crawford, D. (eds.) Proceedings Supercomputing '93, pp. 878–883. ACM (1993)
12. Jhala, R., Majumdar, R.: Software model checking. ACM Comput. Surv. (CSUR) **41**(4), 1–54 (2009)
13. Kaleeswaran, A.P., Nordmann, A., Vogel, T., Grunske, L.: A systematic literature review on counterexample explanation. Inf. Softw. Technol. **145**, 106800 (2022)
14. Kokologiannakis, M., Marmanis, I., Gladstein, V., Vafeiadis, V.: Truly stateless, optimal dynamic partial order reduction. Proc. ACM Program. Lang. **6**(POPL), 1–28 (2022)
15. Kokologiannakis, M., Marmanis, I., Vafeiadis, V.: Unblocking dynamic partial order reduction. In: Enea, C., Lal, A. (eds.) Computer Aided Verification, pp. 230–250. Springer, Cham (2023)
16. Kokologiannakis, M., Ren, X., Vafeiadis, V.: Dynamic partial order reductions for spinloops. In: 2021 Formal Methods in Computer Aided Design (FMCAD), pp. 163–172 (2021)
17. Lamport, L.: Time, clocks, and the ordering of events in a distributed system. Commun. ACM **21**(7), 558–565 (1978)
18. Nguyen, H., Rodríguez, C., Sousa, M., Coti, C., Petrucci, L.: Quasi-optimal partial order reduction. In: Chockler, H., Weissenbacher, G. (eds.) CAV 2018. LNCS, vol. 10982, pp. 354–371. Springer, Cham (2018). https://doi.org/10.1007/978-3-319-96142-2_22
19. Nichols, B., Buttlar, D., Farrell, J.: Pthreads Programming: A POSIX Standard for Better Multiprocessing. O'Reilly Media Inc, Newton (1996)
20. Palmer, R., Gopalakrishnan, G., Kirby, R.M.: Semantics driven dynamic partial-order reduction of MPI-based parallel programs. In: Proceedings of the 2007 ACM Workshop on Parallel and Distributed Systems: Testing and Debugging, PADTAD '07, pp. 43–53. ACM (2007)
21. Pham, T.A.: Efficient state-space exploration for asynchronous distributed programs: Adapting unfolding-based dynamic partial order reduction to MPI programs. PhD thesis, École normale supérieure de Rennes, France (2019)
22. Pham, T.A., Jéron, T., Quinson, M.: Verifying MPI applications with SimGridMC. In: Correctness 2017 - First International Workshop on Software Correctness for HPC Applications, Denver, United States, pp. 28–33 (2017)
23. Rodríguez, C., Sousa, M., Sharma, S., Kroening, D.: Unfolding-based partial order reduction. In: Aceto, L., de Frutos-Escrig, Eds. 26th International Conference on Concurrency Theory, CONCUR 2015, Madrid, Spain, 1–4 September 2015, , vol. 42 of LIPIcs, pp. 456–469 . Schloss Dagstuhl - Leibniz-Zentrum für Informatik (2015)

24. Yang, Yu., Chen, X., Gopalakrishnan, G., Kirby, R.M.: Distributed dynamic partial order reduction based verification of threaded software. In: Bošnački, D., Edelkamp, S. (eds.) SPIN 2007. LNCS, vol. 4595, pp. 58–75. Springer, Heidelberg (2007). https://doi.org/10.1007/978-3-540-73370-6_6
25. Zhang, N., Kusano, M., Wang, C.: Dynamic partial order reduction for relaxed memory models. In: Proceedings of the 36th ACM SIGPLAN Conference on Programming Language Design and Implementation, pp. 250–259 (2015)

Revisited Convergence of a Self-stabilizing BFS Spanning Tree Algorithm

Karine Altisen[ ] and Marius Bozga[✉][ ]

Univ. Grenoble Alpes, CNRS, Grenoble INP, VERIMAG, 38000 Grenoble, France
{Karine.Altisen,Marius.Bozga}@univ-grenoble-alpes.fr
http://www-verimag.imag.fr/

Abstract. We provide a constructive proof for the convergence of Dolev *et al.* BFS spanning tree algorithm running under the general assumption of an unfair daemon. Already known proofs of this algorithm are either using non-constructive principles (*e.g.*, proofs by contradiction) or are restricted to less general execution daemons (*e.g.*, weakly fair). In this work, we address these limitations by defining the well-founded orders and potential functions ensuring convergence in the general case. The proof has been fully formalized in PADEC, a Coq/Rocq-based framework for certification of self-stabilization algorithms.

Keywords: spanning tree algorithm · self-stabilization · constructive proof · proof assistant · Coq/Rocq

1 Introduction

To obtain properties about distributed systems is a difficult task. Indeed, such systems generally involve an arbitrary number of participants, interconnected and communicating according to arbitrary or specific topologies. Their execution could be subject to various assumptions about the degree of asynchronism between participants. The context in which those systems are considered is increasingly complex, for example, large scale distributed systems, made of heterogeneous devices, running in highly dynamic networks. Above all, every distributed system nowadays requires some fault tolerance properties which are particularly difficult to handle. Therefore, the proofs for distributed algorithms quickly become complex and may lead to errors [24].

In this context, the common practice for establishing the correctness of distributed algorithms was to provide proofs on paper. But, computer-aided validation tools are being developed as a method to improve those practices. In particular, many approaches are based on model-checking (see *e.g.*, [8,28]) or controller synthesis (see *e.g.*, [19,29]). However, those methods usually face the large execution space, restricting their applicability. Furthermore, they either

---

Grenoble INP—Institute of Engineering Univ. Grenoble Alpes
This research has been partially supported by the French ANR projects Adapt ANR-23-ce25-0004, SkyData ANR-22-ce25-0008 and PaVeDyS ANR-23-ce48-0005.

© IFIP International Federation for Information Processing 2025
Published by Springer Nature Switzerland AG 2025
C. Ferreira and C. A. Mezzina (Eds.): FORTE 2025, LNCS 15732, pp. 154–170, 2025.
https://doi.org/10.1007/978-3-031-95497-9_9

require a complete definition of the full context of execution (such as the number of participants, the topology of the network, etc.) or provide parametric solutions (*e.g.*, for N participants where N is a parameter) which are often restricted due to undecidability limitations [9].

On the other hand, the use of a proof assistant such as Coq/Rocq [27] allows to formalize the proofs and automatically check (or certify) their correctness for a given distributed algorithm, for every instantiation of the parameters such as the topology or the number of participants. Note that a proof assistant is not meant to derive any proof: the proof designer comes with (at least) a sketch of the proof and the tool is used as a guidance to enumerate cases, avoid flaws and clarify the assumptions. Once completed, the proof has been fully checked by the tool and its soundness is guaranteed. Many frameworks have been developed to certify the proof of some distributed algorithms using various proof assistant such as Coq/Rocq [1,6,13], TLA+ [15,23] or Isabelle/HOL [11,21,22].

We focus here on distributed self-stabilizing algorithms. Self-stabilization [17] is a lightweight fault tolerance property to withstand transient faults: once such faults hit a self-stabilizing system, it is guaranteed to recover a correct behavior within finite time. Note that no assumption is made on the nature of the transient faults (memory corruption, topology changes, etc.). But, once those faults cease, there is a finite period—the stabilization time—during which the system may misbehave (notably its safety guarantees are no longer ensured during this recovery period). In this paper, we are interested in the proof of self-stabilization of a BFS spanning tree algorithm by Dolev *et al.* [18].

Related Work. The correctness of several non fault-tolerant distributed algorithms has been certified, (see *e.g.*, [10,20]). Certification of fault-tolerant, yet non self-stabilizing, distributed systems has been addressed using various proof assistants, *e.g.*, in Isabelle/HOL [11,12,21,22], TLA+ [15,16], Coq/Rocq [26], NuPRL [25]. This approach is called *robust* fault tolerance; it masks the effect of the faults (whereas self-stabilization is non-masking by essence). In the robust approach, many results are related to agreement problems, such as consensus or state-machine replication, in fully connected networks. Moreover, many works only certify the safety property of the considered problem (see *e.g.*, [15,16,25,26]). However, both liveness and safety properties are certified in [11,12,22]. Finally, robust fault tolerance has also been considered in the context of mobile robot computing: using the PACTOLE Coq/Rocq framework, impossibility results for swarms of robots that are subjected to Byzantine faults have been certified [6,14].

Several frameworks to certify self-stabilizing algorithms using the Coq/Rocq proof assistant have been proposed, *e.g.*, [1,13]. In particular, the PADEC Coq/Rocq library provides a framework to develop proofs of self-stabilizing algorithms written in the atomic state model [17], and allows various assumptions defined in the literature. For instance, the asynchronism of the system can be defined using several levels of fairness. Notably, it includes use cases and support to prove the composition of self-stabilizing algorithms [2], their time complexity in steps [3] and rounds [4] (Rounds provide a measure of time taking into account the parallelism of the system whereas steps provide a sequential measure).

The research on proving termination (*i.e.* convergence) of distributed algorithms is extremely vast. Usually, formal techniques such as ranking/potential functions (*e.g.*, [3]), well-founded orders (*e.g.*, [1]) provide direct means to prove the termination over all executions. Alternatively, by the principle of the excluded middle, termination follows from a proof of the absence of non-terminating runs. That is, proofs of termination by contradiction usually exhibit contradictions in the case non-terminating executions are presumed possible. The principle of the excluded middle is, however, not allowed in intuitionistic logics and hence impossible to use in the constructive proof assistant Coq/Rocq [7] (unless changing the basic set of axioms).

Contributions. In this paper, we revisit the proof of convergence of the self-stabilizing Dolev *et al.* BFS spanning tree algorithm [18]. The first proof of convergence of this algorithm has been provided in [18], that is, the same paper where the algorithm has been introduced; but this proof is restricted to some restricted fairness assumptions. Since then, other proofs have been proposed. As [5, 18] proves the self-stabilization of the algorithm under the mild assumption of a weakly fair daemon, that is, by restricting the asynchronism along the executions of the algorithm; this proof has been formalized, developed and mechanically checked in PADEC [4]. While relaxing the fairness assumption, [5] also provides a non-constructive proof, by contradiction, working under the explicit assumption that the diameter of the graph is a priori known and used as a bound on some of the variables of the algorithm.

In this paper, still with no fairness assumption, we provide, a contrario, a constructive proof of the result which has been fully formalized and mechanically checked in PADEC. Our contribution is twofold:

- We provide the first constructive proof of the convergence of the Dolev *et al.* BFS spanning tree algorithm under the most general execution assumptions (*i.e.*, unfair daemon, unbounded variables). The proof exploits a novel potential function, allowing for a more refined understanding of the system executions towards convergence.
- The convergence proof has been fully formalized and automatically checked using the PADEC framework. The result can therefore be fully trusted and moreover, illustrates the capabilities of the PADEC framework to formally handle distributed algorithms and their properties.

Coq/Rocq Development. The development for this contribution represents about 5,155 lines of Coq/Rocq code (#loc, as measured by coqwc), precisely #loc: spec = 1,111; proof = 3,662; comments = 382. It is available as an online browsing documentation at https://www-verimag.imag.fr/PADEC-1063.html. We encourage the reader to visit this web-page for a deeper understanding of our work.

Organization. The paper is organized as follows. Section 2 recalls the Dolev *et al.* algorithm for the construction of BFS spanning trees. Section 3 provides a brief overview of the PADEC framework and the formal encoding of the abovementioned algorithm. Section 4 provides the proof of convergence. Section 5 elaborates on the definition of the potential function over system configurations, that is, the key ingredient ensuring that the proof is constructive and therefore representable in PADEC. Finally, Sect. 6 concludes and provides directions for future work.

2 Dolev *et al.* BFS Spanning Tree Algorithm

The Dolev *et al.* BFS spanning tree algorithm [18] is a self-stabilizing distributed algorithm that computes a BFS spanning tree in an arbitrary rooted, connected, and bidirectional network. By "bidirectional", we mean that each node can both transmit and acquire information from its adjacent nodes in the network topology, *i.e.*, its neighbors. The algorithm being distributed, these are the only possible direct communications. "Rooted" indicates that a particular node, called the root and denoted by r, is distinguished in the network. As in the present case, algorithms for rooted networks are usually semi-anonymous: all nodes have the same code except the root.

This algorithm was initially written in the Read/Write atomicity model. We study, here, a straightforward translation into the *atomic-state model*, denoted hereafter by *BFS*, and presented as Algorithm 1. Notice that, as in the original presentation [18] and contrarily to other adaptations (see *e.g.*, [5]), the variables are not assumed to be bounded.

In the *atomic-state model*, nodes communicate through locally shared variables: a node can read its variables and the ones of its neighbors, but can only write to its own variables. Every node can access the variables of its neighbors through local channels, denoted by the set *Channels* in Algorithm 1. The network is locally defined at each node p using constant local inputs. The fact that the network is rooted is implemented using a constant Boolean input called $p.root$ which is false for every node except r. The input $p.neighbors$ is the set of channels linking p to its neighbors. When it is clear from the context, we do not distinguish a neighbor from the channels to that neighbor.

The code of Algorithm 1 is given as three locally-mutually-exclusive actions written as: **if** *condition* **then** *statement*. We say that an action is *enabled* when its condition is true. By extension, a node is said to be enabled when at least one of its actions is enabled. The *semantics of the system* defines an execution as follows. The system current *configuration* is given by the current value of all variables at each node. If no node is enabled in the current configuration, then the configuration is said to be *terminal* and the execution is over. Otherwise, a *step* is performed: a *daemon* (an oracle that models the asynchronism of the system) *activates* a non-empty set of enabled nodes. All activated nodes choose one of their enabled actions in the current configuration and then, *atomically execute* the associated statements, leading the system to a new configuration.

Algorithm 1. Algorithm $\mathcal{BFS}$, code for each node p.

Constant Local Inputs:
$p.neighbors \subseteq Channels$; $p.root \in \{true, false\}$
/* $p.neighbors$, as other sets below, are implemented as lists */

Local Variables:
$p.d \in \mathbb{N}$; $p.par \in Channels$

Macros:
$Dist_p = \min\{q.d + 1 \mid q \in p.neighbors\}$
Par_{dist} returns the first channel in the list $\{q \in p.neighbors \mid q.d + 1 = p.d\}$

Action for the root, *i.e.*, for p such that $p.root = true$
Action *Root*: **if** $p.d \neq 0$ **then** $p.d := 0$

Actions for any non-root node, *i.e.*, for p such that $p.root = false$
Action CD: **if** $p.d \neq Dist_p$ **then** $p.d := Dist_p$
Action CP: **if** $p.d = Dist_p$ and $p.par.d + 1 \neq p.d$ **then** $p.par := Par_{dist}$

Assumptions can be made about the daemon. Here, we consider the most general asynchrony assumption, namely the *unfair* daemon, meaning that it can choose any non-empty subset of the enabled nodes for execution. In contrast, *fair* daemons would guarantee additional properties. For example, a *strongly* (resp. *weakly*) *fair* daemon ensures that every node that is enabled infinitely (resp. continuously) often is eventually chosen for execution by the daemon.

In Algorithm $\mathcal{BFS}$, each node p maintains two variables. First, it evaluates in $p.d$ its distance to the root. Then, it maintains $p.par$ as a pointer to its *parent* in the tree under construction: $p.par$ is assigned to a neighbor that is closest to the root (*n.b.*, $r.par$ is meaningless). Algorithm $\mathcal{BFS}$ is a self-stabilizing BFS spanning tree construction in the sense that, regardless the initial configuration, it makes the system converge to a terminal configuration where par-variables describe a BFS spanning tree rooted at r. To that goal, nodes first compute into their d-variable their distance to the root. The root simply forces the value of $r.d$ to be 0; see Action *Root*. Then, the d-variables of other nodes are gradually corrected: every non-root node p maintains $p.d$ to be the minimum value of the d-variables of its neighbors incremented by one; see $Dist_p$ and Action CD. In parallel, each non-root node p chooses as parent a neighbor q such that $q.d = p.d - 1$ when $p.d$ is locally correct *i.e.*, $p.d = Dist_p$) but $p.par$ is not correctly assigned *i.e.*, $p.par.d$ is not equal to $p.d - 1$); see Action CP.

3 The PADEC Framework

PADEC [1] is a general framework, written in Coq/Rocq [7], to develop mechanically checked proofs of self-stabilizing algorithms. It includes the definition of the atomic-state model and its semantics, tools for the definition of the algorithms and their properties, lemmas for common proof patterns, and case studies. Definitions in PADEC are designed to be as close as possible to what is common practice in the self-stabilizing research community. Moreover, it is made general enough to encompass many usual hypothesis (*e.g.*, about topologies or daemons).

In PADEC, the finite network is described using types *Nodes* and *Channels*, which respectively represent the nodes and the links between nodes. The distributed algorithm is defined by providing a local algorithm at each node. This latter is defined using a type *States* that represents the local state of a node *i.e.*, the values of its local variables and a function *run* that encodes the local algorithm itself and computes a new state depending on the current state of the node and that of its neighbors.[1]

The model semantics defines a *configuration* as a function from *Nodes* to *States* that provides the local state of each node. The type of a configuration is given by $\Gamma \stackrel{def}{=} Nodes \to States$. An *atomic step* of the distributed algorithm is encoded as a binary relation over configurations, denoted by Step $\subseteq \Gamma \times \Gamma$, that checks the conditions given in the informal model; see Sect. 2. An *execution* e is a finite or infinite stream of configurations, which models a *maximal* sequence of configurations where any two consecutive configurations are linked by the Step relation. "Maximal" means that e is finite if and only if its last configuration is terminal. We use the coinductive[2] type *Exec* to represent an execution stream along with a coinductive predicate *isExec* to check the above condition. Daemons are also defined as predicates over executions (in the case of the unfair daemon, this predicate is simply equal to *true*).

Self-stabilization in PADEC is defined according to the usual practice: the property is formalized as a predicate (*selfStabilization SPEC*) where *SPEC* is a predicate over executions that models the specification of the algorithm. An algorithm is *self-stabilizing w.r.t. the specification SPEC* if there exists a set of legitimate configurations that satisfies the following three properties in every execution e:

- <u>Closure</u>: if e starts in a legitimate configuration then e contains only legitimate configurations;
- <u>Convergence</u>: e eventually reaches a legitimate configuration; and
- <u>Specification</u>: if e starts in a legitimate configuration then e satisfies the intended specification w.r.t. *SPEC*.

An algorithm is said to be *silent* when each of its executions eventually reaches a terminal configuration; in such a case, the set of legitimate configurations can be chosen as the set of terminal configurations. The closure, convergence, and silent properties are expressed using Linear Time Logic operators provided in the PADEC library.

The BFS Algorithm in PADEC

For the BFS Algorithm and its specification, we use the formal encoding provided in [4]; in particular, the algorithm is a straightforward faithful translation in Coq/Rocq of Algorithm 1. Notably, an element of *States*, namely a state of a given node, is a tuple $(d, par, root, neighbors)$ representing the variables of the node as in Algorithm 1.

---

[1] Note that PADEC is restricted to deterministic local algorithms.
[2] Coinduction allows to define and reason about potentially infinite objects.

As the constant variables *root* and *neighbors* represent the network, the assumptions that this network is static, rooted, bidirected and connected is encoded in a predicate on a configuration using only those variables. This predicate, in particular uses the set of edges of the network $Edges \stackrel{def}{=} \{(p,q) \mid p, q \in Nodes \land (p \in q.neighbors \lor q \in p.neighbors)\}$. Globally in this predicate, the neighbor links represent a bidirected connected graph and the Boolean *root* should be true for a unique node. We will assume moreover that this predicate holds for any configuration, even if this is no more mentioned in the sequel.

In [4], the *BFS* Algorithm was proven using PADEC to be self-stabilizing and silent for the specification *SPEC* of a BFS spanning tree, *under the assumption of a weakly fair daemon*. We extend here this result to the *unfair daemon*. Note that, the properties of closure and specification hold regardless the type of the daemon. The property of convergence is however lost when relaxing the assumption from a weakly fair to an unfair daemon. The rest of the paper therefore focuses on proving the convergence of the *BFS* Algorithm under an unfair daemon in PADEC, *i.e.*, providing a constructive proof under the form of a potential function and its corresponding order.

4 Overview of the Proof

An execution is fully defined by the Step relation, as the unfair daemon does not add any other restriction. As a consequence, the convergence property can be expressed by the fact that the Step relation is well-founded:

$$\text{WellFounded Step} \tag{1}$$

This means that any execution $e \stackrel{def}{=} \gamma_0 \xrightarrow{\text{Step}} \gamma_1 \xrightarrow{\text{Step}} \ldots$ is finite. WellFounded comes from the Coq/Rocq standard library where it is expressed as

$$(\text{WellFounded } R) \stackrel{def}{=} (\forall x.\ \text{Acc } R\ x)$$

for a given relation R. Acc is an inductive predicate from the Coq/Rocq standard library as well, and (Acc $R\ x$) means that every sequence of elements starting from x and linked by R is finite.

In the following, we will prove the assertion (1). To this end, we will consider the partitioning of the Step relation as $\text{Step}^{(r)} \cup \text{Step}^{(d)} \cup \text{Step}^{(p)}$ denoting respectively *root steps*, *d-steps* and *par-steps* defined as follows:

- $\text{Step}^{(r)}$ holds for any step $\gamma \xrightarrow{\text{Step}} \gamma'$ in which the root executes *i.e.*, such that $\gamma.r.d \neq \gamma'.r.d$. Note that any subset of non-root nodes may also execute during this step.
- $\text{Step}^{(d)}$ holds for any step $\gamma \xrightarrow{\text{Step}} \gamma'$ in which the root does not execute and at least one non-root node executes a CD-action *i.e.*, $\gamma.r.d = \gamma'.r.d$ and $\exists p.\ \gamma.p.d \neq \gamma'.p.d$. Note that any subset of non-root nodes may also execute either Action CD or CP.

– Step$^{(p)}$ holds for any step $\gamma \xrightarrow{\text{Step}} \gamma'$ where d variables are left unchanged *i.e.*, $\forall p.\ \gamma.p.d = \gamma'.p.d$. This implies that a node which executes is not the root and executes its CP-action.

In addition, we will use the following general result, (developed as a tool in PADEC), which gives sufficient conditions ensuring the union of two relations is well-founded. This tool has first been developed in PADEC for algorithms with prioritized rules (as Actions CD and CP) and has been enhanced for this proof.

Proposition 1. *Let R_1, R_2 be relations, x an element. Assume that (1) R_2 is well-founded and (2) there exist a set B_1 and relations R'_1 well-founded, E_1 transitive such that*

(2.i) $x \in B_1$ and for all elements a, b if $a \in B_1$ and $a \xrightarrow{R_1 \cup R_2} b$ then $b \in B_1$,

(2.ii) for all elements a, b if $a \in B_1$ and $a \xrightarrow{R_1} b$ then $a \xrightarrow{R'_1} b$,

(2.iii) for all elements a, b, c, if $a \xrightarrow{R'_1} b$ and $b \xrightarrow{E_1} c$ then $a \xrightarrow{R'_1} c$,

(2.iv) for all elements a, b if $a \xrightarrow{R_2} b$ then $a \xrightarrow{E_1} b$.

We can conclude that $(\text{Acc}\ (R_1 \cup R_2)\ x)$ holds.

Proof. Intuitively, the set B_1 represents an over-approximation of the elements reachable from x through $R_1 \cup R_2$ (2.i). The relation R'_1 represents an abstraction of the relation R_1 when restricted to the set B_1 (2.ii). The relation E_1 can be understood as an equality with respect to R'_1 (2.iii) which moreover abstracts the relation R_2 (2.iv). Usually, R'_1 and E_1 can be derived from a potential function on the set of elements and its induced partial order and equality.

The result is then directly obtained by considering the relation $<_{lex}$ defined on pairs of elements by

$$(a, b) <_{lex} (c, d) \stackrel{def}{=} a \xrightarrow{R'_1} c \text{ or } (a \xrightarrow{E_1} c \text{ and } b \xrightarrow{R_2} d)$$

and the key observations that:

– $<_{lex}$ is a well-founded lexicographic order since R'_1 and R_2 are well-founded;
– for all elements a, b, if $a \in B_1$ and $a \xrightarrow{R_1 \cup R_2} b$ then $(a, a) <_{lex} (b, b)$.

□

As a corollary, using the same notations as in Proposition 1, being given two relations R_1 and R_2, if for every x we can effectively construct the set B_1 and the relations R'_1, E_1 such that all assumptions are met (1, 2.i to 2.iv), then we can conclude that $R_1 \cup R_2$ is well-founded.

We now proceed to the core of the convergence proof and show progressively that Step$^{(p)}$, Step$^{(d)} \cup$ Step$^{(p)}$ and Step$^{(r)} \cup$ Step$^{(d)} \cup$ Step$^{(p)}$ are well-founded.

Lemma 1. WellFounded Step$^{(p)}$.

Proof. We use the potential function denoted $\#CP(\gamma)$ which counts for a given configuration γ the number of nodes for which the guard of their CP-action is enabled. We say that such a node is CP-enabled, otherwise it is CP-disabled.

Considering *par*-steps only *i.e.*, the values of d-variables are left unchanged then either (i) a node is CP-disabled and will remain so or (ii) it is CP-enabled and if it executes, it becomes CP-disabled, otherwise it remains CP-enabled. Hence, for every two configurations γ and γ' such that $\gamma \xrightarrow{\mathsf{Step}^{(p)}} \gamma'$ we have $\#CP(\gamma') < \#CP(\gamma)$, namely $\#CP$ is decreasing. As $\#CP$ is obviously lower-bounded by 0, this ensures that $\mathsf{Step}^{(p)}$ is well-founded. $\square$

To proceed on the next phase of the convergence proof, we will use a result about executions consisting of d-steps only. The next proposition guarantees the well-foundedness of the relation $\mathsf{Step}^{(d)}$ through the existence of an effectively constructive potential function and its ordering:

Proposition 2. *Given a configuration γ_0, we can effectively construct:*

(a) a set of configurations $B(\gamma_0)$ containing γ_0 and closed by taking d- or par-steps,

(b) a potential function on configurations from Γ to a domain $D(\gamma_0)$, $\pi_{\gamma_0} : \Gamma \to D(\gamma_0)$, independent of par-variables, and

(c) a well-founded order $\prec_d$ on $D(\gamma_0)$, such that for all $\gamma \in B(\gamma_0)$ and $\gamma \xrightarrow{\mathsf{Step}^{(d)}} \gamma'$, it holds that $\pi_{\gamma_0}(\gamma') \prec_d \pi_{\gamma_0}(\gamma)$.

The technical details and the proof of Proposition 2 are presented in Sect. 5.

Lemma 2. WellFounded $(\mathsf{Step}^{(d)} \cup \mathsf{Step}^{(p)})$.

Proof. We must prove $(\mathsf{Acc}\ (\mathsf{Step}^{(d)} \cup \mathsf{Step}^{(p)})\ \gamma_0)$ for an arbitrary configuration γ_0. Therefore, we use Proposition 1 by taking $R_1 \stackrel{def}{=} \mathsf{Step}^{(d)}$, $R_2 \stackrel{def}{=} \mathsf{Step}^{(p)}$ and $x \stackrel{def}{=} \gamma_0$. First, Lemma 1 ensures that R_2 is well-founded. Using the Proposition 2 above, we define the set B_1, and the relations R'_1 and E_1 as follows:

$$B_1 \stackrel{def}{=} B(\gamma_0)$$
$$\gamma \xrightarrow{R'_1} \gamma' \stackrel{def}{=} \pi_{\gamma_0}(\gamma') \prec_d \pi_{\gamma_0}(\gamma)$$
$$\gamma \xrightarrow{E_1} \gamma' \stackrel{def}{=} \pi_{\gamma_0}(\gamma') = \pi_{\gamma_0}(\gamma)$$

The guarantees of Proposition 2 allow to fulfill the assumptions of Proposition 1. Indeed, the relation R'_1 is well-founded, see Proposition 2(*c*). The relation E_1 is transitive by its definition (based on equality of potentials). The assumption (*2.i*), that is, B_1 contains x and is closed by R_1 or R_2 steps follows from Proposition 2(*a*). Assumption (*2.ii*), that is, R'_1 is an abstraction of $\mathsf{Step}^{(d)}$ on the set B_1 holds because of Proposition 2(*c*). Assumption (*2.iii*) holds trivially by the construction of R'_1 and E_1. Last, assumption (*2.iv*) holds as the potential function π_{γ_0} is not depending on the *par* variables, that is, remains insensitive to *par*-steps. This proves $(\mathsf{Acc}\ (\mathsf{Step}^{(d)} \cup \mathsf{Step}^{(p)})\ \gamma_0)$ and finally, as the choice of γ_0 was arbitrary, we prove that WellFounded $(\mathsf{Step}^{(d)} \cup \mathsf{Step}^{(p)})$. $\square$

It remains to take into account the root steps from $\mathsf{Step}^{(r)}$. Recall that the root r can execute at most once in any execution: either its d-variable is 0 from the beginning and r never executes; or it is positive and then r is enabled. If it executes, the variable is set to 0 and r is then disabled forever. The fact that $\mathsf{Step}^{(r)}$ is well-founded is therefore trivial to obtain.

Theorem 1. WellFounded ($\mathsf{Step}^{(r)} \cup \mathsf{Step}^{(d)} \cup \mathsf{Step}^{(p)}$).

Proof. We use Proposition 1 by taking $R_1 \stackrel{def}{=} \mathsf{Step}^{(r)}$, $R_2 \stackrel{def}{=} \mathsf{Step}^{(d)} \cup \mathsf{Step}^{(p)}$, and an arbitrary configuration γ_0. First, Lemma 2 ensures that R_2 is well-founded. Second, we define the set $B_1 \stackrel{def}{=} \Gamma$ and the relations R'_1 and E_1 as follows:

$$\gamma \xrightarrow{R'_1} \gamma' \stackrel{def}{=} \gamma'.r.d < \gamma.r.d$$
$$\gamma \xrightarrow{E_1} \gamma' \stackrel{def}{=} \gamma'.r.d = \gamma.r.d$$

Obviously, R'_1 is well-founded as observed above, and E_1 is transitive by definition. Since B_1 contains all configurations, the assumption (*2.i*) is trivially satisfied. Also, $R_1 \subseteq R'_1$ holds by definition of R'_1, hence, it implies assumption (*2.ii*). Assumption (*2.iii*) follows from definitions as well and assumption (*2.iv*) holds because $\gamma.r.d$ is not changing for any non-root step. $\square$

5 A Decreasing Potential Function for d-Steps

This section is concerned with the proof of Proposition 2 stated in Sect. 4. To this end, we proceed in three steps. First, we establish a finite over-approximation on the set of the d values that could be possibly reached in an execution involving d-steps only from some initial configuration γ_0. Second, we introduce a partitioning of edges and prove some preservation properties on this partitioning along d-steps. Third, we combine the above results to effectively construct a potential function for d-steps and a well-founded order on the co-domain of this function, ultimately proving Proposition 2.

For the sake of readability, we denote d-steps $\gamma \xrightarrow{\mathsf{Step}^{(d)}} \gamma'$ shortly by $\gamma \to_d \gamma'$.

5.1 Bounds on Distance Values

For a configuration γ, we define the non-negative integers $\max_d \gamma \stackrel{def}{=} \max\{\gamma.q.d \mid q \in \mathsf{Nodes}\}$, $\min_d \gamma \stackrel{def}{=} \min\{\gamma.q.d \mid q \in \mathsf{Nodes}\}$, $\mathsf{sum}_d \gamma \stackrel{def}{=} \sum\{\gamma.q.d \mid q \in \mathsf{Nodes}\}$.[3] We also define $\gamma^\perp$, $\gamma^\top$ respectively a *bottom* and a *top* configuration associated to γ. These are identical to γ except for d values, defined for every node p as follows:

$$\gamma^\perp.p.d \stackrel{def}{=} \min_d \gamma$$

$$\gamma^\top.p.d \stackrel{def}{=} \begin{cases} \gamma.p.d & \text{if } p = r \\ \max\{\gamma.p.d, 1 + \min\{\gamma^\top.q.d \mid \\ \quad (p,q) \in \mathsf{Edges}, \mathsf{dist}(p, r) = 1 + \mathsf{dist}(q, r)\}\} & \text{otherwise,} \end{cases}$$

---
[3] The sum is taken on the multiset of d values.

where dist(q, r) represents the distance of some node q to the root r. Note that the recursive definition of $\gamma^\top.p.d$ is well-defined as the recursion is limited to neighbors q of p located at a smaller distance to the root r than p. Intuitively, the maximal d value of a non-root node p in some configuration reachable from γ is either its value in γ (*i.e.*, it can be the case when p does not execute) or 1 plus the minimum of the maximal d values of its neighbors q closer to the root (see Action CD when p executes). We define the partial order $\leq_d$ on configurations by taking

$$\gamma_1 \leq_d \gamma_2 \stackrel{def}{=} \forall q \in Nodes : \gamma_1.q.d \leq \gamma_2.q.d$$

The next lemma states basic properties of the $(.)^\perp, (.)^\top$ operators, namely their idempotence and their monotonicity with respect to $\leq_d$. The proof follows from definitions and uses induction on nodes according to their distance to the root.

Lemma 3. *For all configurations $\gamma, \gamma_1, \gamma_2$:*

(i) $\gamma^\perp \leq_d \gamma \leq_d \gamma^\top, (\gamma^\perp)^\perp = \gamma^\perp, (\gamma^\top)^\top = \gamma^\top,$
(ii) if $\gamma_1 \leq_d \gamma_2$ then $\gamma_1^\perp \leq_d \gamma_2^\perp, \gamma_1^\top \leq_d \gamma_2^\top$.

The next lemma relates the bottom and top configurations to d-steps. The proof is done by induction respectively, on the set of nodes according to their distance to the root (i) and on the length of an execution sequence from γ_0 (ii).[4]

Lemma 4. *For all configurations $\gamma, \gamma', \gamma_0$:*

(i) if $\gamma \to_d \gamma'$ then $\gamma^\perp \leq_d \gamma'^\perp, \gamma'^\top \leq_d \gamma^\top,$
(ii) if $\gamma_0 \to_d^* \gamma$ then $\gamma_0^\perp \leq_d \gamma \leq_d \gamma_0^\top$.

5.2 Smooth and Non-smooth d-Steps

We say that an edge $(p, q) \in Edges$ is *smooth* (resp. *non-smooth*) in a configuration $\gamma \in \Gamma$ if the difference (in absolute value, abs) between the d-values at its endpoints p, q is at most 1 (resp. at least 2). Formally, consider the predicate

$$smooth_\gamma((p,q)) \stackrel{def}{=} (abs(\gamma.p.d - \gamma.q.d) \leq 1).$$

We say that a d-step $\gamma \to_d \gamma'$ is *smooth* if all the nodes p changing their values from γ to γ' are connected to smooth edges only in γ, formally:

$$smooth(\gamma \to_d \gamma') \stackrel{def}{=}$$
$$\forall p \in Nodes : (\gamma'.p.d \neq \gamma.p.d) \Rightarrow (\forall q \in p.neighbors : smooth_\gamma((p,q)))$$

We define the rank of an edge $(p, q) \in Edges$ in a configuration $\gamma \in \Gamma$ as $rank_\gamma((p,q)) \stackrel{def}{=} \min(\gamma.p.d, \gamma.q.d).$

For illustration, consider the three configurations $\gamma_1, \gamma_2, \gamma_3$ depicted in Fig. 1. We represented the d values of the nodes by their positioning on the horizontal

---

[4] $\gamma_0 \to_d^* \gamma$ means that γ is reachable from γ_0 using a finite number of d-steps.

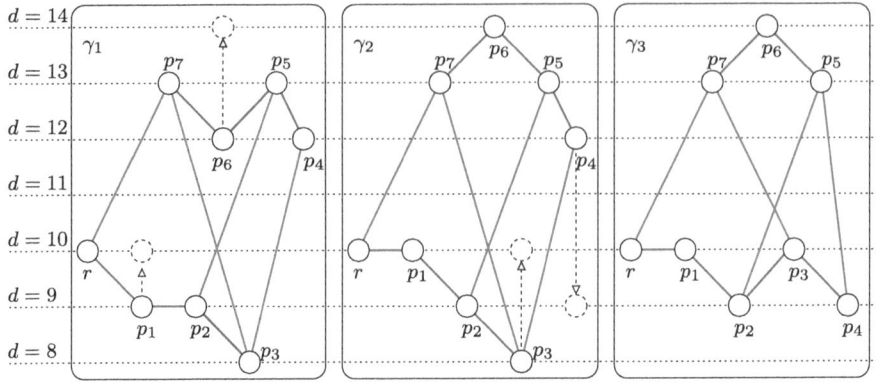

Fig. 1. Smooth and non-smooth steps (Color figure online)

lines e.g., $\gamma_1.r.d = 10$, $\gamma_1.p_1.d = 9$, $\gamma_2.p_1.d = 10$, etc. Edges are represented by lines connecting nodes: smooth (resp. non-smooth) edges are depicted in blue (resp. red). Configuration γ_2 is the successor of γ_1 by a smooth step. That is, only p_1 and p_6 have been executed and these nodes were connected only to smooth (blue) edges in γ_1. Configuration γ_3 is the successor of γ_2 by a non-smooth step. That is, p_3 and p_4 have been executed along the step, and these nodes were connected to some non-smooth edges.

The next lemmas provide key properties for understanding the execution of d-steps, depending if they are smooth or not. Lemma 5 basically states that partitioning between smooth and non-smooth, as well as the rank of every non-smooth edge is preserved by smooth steps. In addition, the total sum of d values is increasing along such a step.

Lemma 5. *Consider a smooth d-step $\gamma \rightarrow_d \gamma'$. Then,*

(i) $\forall e \in Edges : \neg smooth_\gamma(e) \Leftrightarrow \neg smooth_{\gamma'}(e)$,
(ii) $\forall e \in Edges : \neg smooth_\gamma(e) \Rightarrow (rank_\gamma(e) = rank_{\gamma'}(e))$,
(iii) $\text{sum}_d \gamma' > \text{sum}_d \gamma$.

Proof. The proof follows immediately from the definition of smooth steps and/or edges. First, the fact that non-smooth edges are preserved along with their rank in a smooth d-step directly comes from the definition of a smooth step: since no node connected to a non-smooth edge can execute, non-smooth edges remain unchanged. Second, we obtain the increasing of the sum of all d-values by observing that when a node executes in a smooth d-step, its d value increases by one or two (due to its neighbors which are either above by one or at the same level of d value). As a smooth d-step involves at least one such executing node, sum_d necessarily increases (since nodes that do not increase d leave it unchanged). □

For illustration, consider the smooth step depicted in Fig. 1, *i.e.*, between γ_1 and γ_2. It is rather trivial that, as long as the nodes executing were connected to smooth edges only (in blue), their execution has no impact on the non-smooth edges i.e., they remain non-smooth and preserve their rank. Yet, the overall sum of the d values increases, here because at least the values of the two moving nodes have increased (by 1 for p_1 and by 2 for p_6).

Lemma 6 provides a similar preservation result for non-smooth steps. In this case, the key property is that one can effectively compute a bound k^* such that (i) all non-smooth edges with rank lower than k^* remain non-smooth and preserve their rank and (ii) the set of non-smooth edges with rank k^* is strictly decreasing along the step. The lemma provides both the explicit definition of k^* as well as the identification of a non-smooth edge at level k^* which either becomes smooth or gets a reduced rank after the step, that is, some edge (p,q) for which the minimum is achieved in the definition of k^*.

Lemma 6. *Consider a non-smooth d-step $\gamma \to_d \gamma'$. Let*

$$k^* \stackrel{def}{=} \min\{rank_\gamma((p,q)) \mid (p,q) \in Edges : \neg smooth_\gamma((p,q)),\\ \gamma'.p.d \neq \gamma.p.d \text{ or } \gamma'.q.d \neq \gamma.q.d\}$$

Then,

(i) $\forall e \in Edges : (rank_{\gamma'}(e) \leq k^* \land \neg smooth_{\gamma'}(e)) \Rightarrow (rank_\gamma(e) = rank_{\gamma'}(e) \land \neg smooth_\gamma(e))$,
(ii) $\forall e \in Edges : (rank_\gamma(e) < k^* \land \neg smooth_\gamma(e)) \Rightarrow (rank_{\gamma'}(e) = rank_\gamma(e) \land \neg smooth_{\gamma'}(e))$,
(iii) $\exists e \in Edges : (rank_\gamma(e) = k^* \land \neg smooth_\gamma(e)) \land (\neg smooth_{\gamma'}(e) \Rightarrow rank_{\gamma'}(e) > rank_\gamma(e)))$.

Proof. (i) The proof is done by case splitting, considering which endpoints of non-smooth edges e execute. In fact, the only feasible case is when none of them executes. In all other cases, by choosing the node which gives a new value to its d variable, we obtain a contradiction, either with the minimality of k^* or with the non-smoothness of e in γ'.

(ii) By definition of k^*, no node involved in a non-smooth edge can execute if the rank is below k^*, hence rank and non-smoothness are left unchanged.

(iii) Note here that, using Coq/Rocq, to be able to prove "$\exists e \in Edges : ...$", we have to effectively construct such an edge. In our case, it is chosen as one of the edges that achieves the minimum rank value when computing k^*: a non-smooth edge e^* such that $rank_\gamma(e^*) = k^*$, and one of its end nodes executes during the step (such an edge can be computed using the computation of the minimum value over a finite set). Now, consider the case where e^* remains non-smooth in γ'. We note $e^* = (p,q)$ with $rank_\gamma((p,q)) = \gamma.p.d$. We can prove that if p executes then $\gamma'.p.d > \gamma.p.d$ and that if q executes then $\gamma'.q.d = \gamma.p.d + 1$ (see Fig. 2 for an illustration). In any case, we obtain $rank_{\gamma'}(e) > rank_\gamma(e)$ and the result is then easy to conclude. □

For illustration also, consider the non-smooth step depicted in Fig. 1 between γ_2 and γ_3. In this case, the bound value is $k^* = 8$. The lemma ensures that the

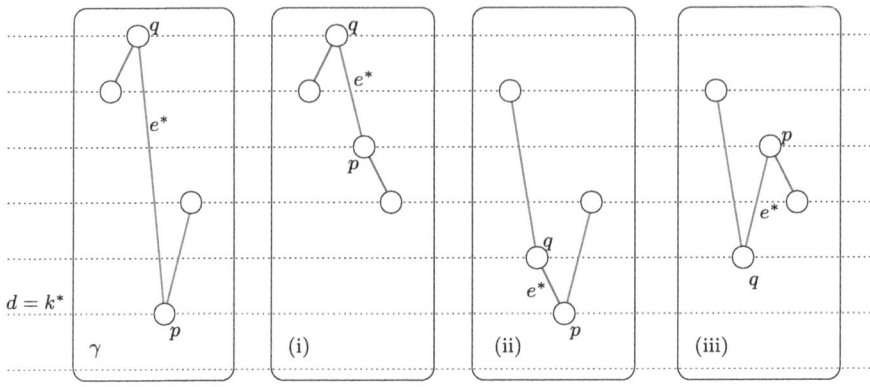

Fig. 2. Possible evolutions of a non-smooth edge $e^* = (p,q)$ with minimal rank k^*: (i) only p executes, (ii) only q executes (iii) p and q executes.

set of non-smooth edges of rank strictly lower than 8 are unchanged. No such edges actually exist in the configurations γ_2 or γ_3. But, actually, it is not hard to imagine that if such edges would exist and are not related to p_3 and p_6, they would not be impacted by the move. Also, the lemma guarantees that the set of edges at level 8 is strictly decreasing. That is, the set of non-smooth edges at level 8 is $\{(p_3, p_7), (p_3, p_4)\}$ in γ_2, respectively $\emptyset$ in γ_3.

Finally, we define $E_{\gamma,k} \stackrel{def}{=} \{e \in Edges \mid \neg smooth_\gamma(e) \land rank_\gamma(e) = k\}$, that is, the set of non-smooth edges of rank k in γ. The next lemma simply reformulates the results of Lemma 5 in point (i) and Lemma 6 in point (ii) into a single statement about the sets $E_{\gamma,k}$ to facilitate their use in the definition of the potential function in the next subsection.

Lemma 7. *Consider a d-step $\gamma \to_d \gamma'$. Then*

(i) if the step $\gamma \to_d \gamma'$ is smooth then $E_{\gamma,k} = E_{\gamma',k}$ for all non-negative integer k,
(ii) if the step $\gamma \to_d \gamma'$ is non-smooth then (a) $E_{\gamma,k} = E_{\gamma',k}$ for all non-negative integer $k < k^*$ and (b) $E_{\gamma',k^*} \subsetneq E_{\gamma,k^*}$.

5.3 Potential Function and Proof of Proposition 2

Given a finite interval of non-negative integers K, and two finite sequences of K-indexed finite sets $\mathcal{X} \stackrel{def}{=} (X_k)_{k \in K}$, $\mathcal{Y} \stackrel{def}{=} (Y_k)_{k \in K}$ we write $\mathcal{X} = \mathcal{Y}$ whenever $X_k = Y_k$ for all $k \in K$, and $\mathcal{X} \prec_{setlex} \mathcal{Y}$ whenever there exists a non-negative integer $k^* \in K$ such that $X_k = Y_k$ for all $k \in K$, $k < k^*$ and $X_{k^*} \subsetneq Y_{k^*}$. Note that $\prec_{setlex}$ is a well-founded lexicographic order on the set of finite sequences of K-indexed finite sets.

We are now ready to complete the proof of Proposition 2, restated hereafter for the sake of readability.

Proposition 2. *Given a configuration γ_0, we can effectively construct:*

(a) a set of configurations $B(\gamma_0)$ containing γ_0 and closed by taking d- or par-steps,

(b) a potential function on configurations from Γ to a domain $D(\gamma_0)$, $\pi_{\gamma_0} : \Gamma \to D(\gamma_0)$, independent on par-variables, and

(c) a well-founded order $\prec_d$ on $D(\gamma_0)$, such that for all $\gamma \in B(\gamma_0)$ and $\gamma \xrightarrow{\text{Step}^{(d)}} \gamma'$, it holds that $\pi_{\gamma_0}(\gamma') \prec_d \pi_{\gamma_0}(\gamma)$.

Proof. (a) We define $B(\gamma_0) \stackrel{def}{=} \{\gamma \mid \gamma_0^\perp \leq_d \gamma \leq_d \gamma_0^\top\}$. From Lemma 3(i) we obtain immediately $\gamma_0 \in B(\gamma_0)$. The set $B(\gamma_0)$ is obviously closed by taking *par*-steps, as these steps do no change the values of *d*-variables. The closure of $B(\gamma_0)$ by *d*-steps can be understood by the $\leq_d$ inequalities depicted below:

$$\gamma_0^\perp \leq_d \gamma^\perp \leq_d \gamma \leq_d \gamma^\top \leq_d \gamma_0^\top$$

$$\gamma'^\perp \leq_d \gamma' \leq_d \gamma'^\top$$

Knowing $\gamma \in B(\gamma_0)$, that is, $\gamma_0^\perp \leq_d \gamma \leq_d \gamma_0^\top$ we obtain the inequalities from the top line by using the idempotence and monotonicity of $(.)^\perp$, $(.)^\top$ with respect to $\leq_d$ (Lemma 3). The same lemma ensures the inequalities of the bottom line. Finally, the inequalities across the two lines hold because of Lemma 4. All over, they ensure that $\gamma_0^\perp \leq_d \gamma' \leq_d \gamma_0^\top$ for any *d*-step $\gamma \to_d \gamma'$.

(b) We define the interval of non-negative integers $K_0 \stackrel{def}{=} [\min_d \gamma_0^\perp, \max_d \gamma_0^\top]$, that is, the interval of possible *d*-values in the configurations reachable from γ_0. We define the domain $D(\gamma_0) \stackrel{def}{=} (2^{Edges})^{K_0} \times [\text{sum}_d \gamma_0^\perp, \text{sum}_d \gamma_0^\top]$. That is, $D(\gamma_0)$ consists of pairs $(\mathcal{E}, s)$ where $\mathcal{E} : K_0 \to 2^{Edges}$ is a K_0-indexed sequence of sets of edges and s is a bounded non-negative integer. In particular, note that $D(\gamma_0)$ is finite. We define the potential function $\pi_{\gamma_0} : \Gamma \to D(\gamma_0)$ by taking $\pi_{\gamma_0}(\gamma) \stackrel{def}{=} ((E_{\gamma,k})_{k \in K_0}, \text{sum}_d \gamma)$. Remark that π_{γ_0} is not dependent on *par* variables in γ.

(c) We define the relation $\prec_d$ on $D(\gamma_0)$ by taking $(\mathcal{E}_1, s_1) \prec_d (\mathcal{E}_2, s_2) \stackrel{def}{=} \mathcal{E}_1 \prec_{setlex} \mathcal{E}_2 \vee (\mathcal{E}_1 = \mathcal{E}_2 \wedge s_2 < s_1)$. That is, $\prec_d$ is actually a strict lexicographic order on pairs $(\mathcal{E}, s)$ which combines the well-founded order $\prec_{setlex}$ on finite sequences of finite sets and a well-founded order $<$ on bounded integers. It remains to prove that

$$\forall \gamma, \gamma' \in \Gamma, \; \gamma \in B(\gamma_0) \text{ and } \gamma \to_d \gamma' \Rightarrow \pi_{\gamma_0}(\gamma') \prec_d \pi_{\gamma_0}(\gamma)$$

Let respectively $(\mathcal{E}, s) \stackrel{def}{=} \pi_{\gamma_0}(\gamma)$, $(\mathcal{E}', s') \stackrel{def}{=} \pi_{\gamma_0}(\gamma')$. Note that from $\gamma \in B(\gamma_0)$ and the previous point (a) we obtain that $\gamma' \in B(\gamma_0)$ as well. In particular, this ensures the ranks of non-smooth edges of γ, γ' are contained in K_0 and respectively s, s' are contained in the interval $[\text{sum}_d \gamma_0^\perp, \text{sum}_d \gamma_0^\top]$. Lemma 7 and Lemma 5(*iii*) provide the conditions ensuring that π_{γ_0} is indeed a decreasing potential function with respect to $\prec_d$ as expected. For non-smooth steps, we observe the strict inequality $\mathcal{E}' \prec_{setlex} \mathcal{E}$. For smooth *d*-steps we observe the equality $\mathcal{E} = \mathcal{E}'$ and the strict inequality $s < s'$. $\square$

6 Conclusion

In this paper, we provide the first constructive proof for the convergence of the Dolev *et al.* BFS spanning tree algorithm under the most general execution assumptions (*i.e.*, unfair daemon, unbounded variables). The convergence proof has been fully formalized and automatically checked using the PADEC framework. Contrarily to many papers about formal certified proofs of distributed algorithms, we do not formalize and validate an existing proof. Rather, due to the constructive aspect of the proofs allowed in Coq/Rocq, we had to develop a new proof: we have defined a novel potential function, allowing a finer comprehension of the system executions towards terminal configurations. We believe that, even though the algorithm time complexity is exponential, this potential function will open the door to a tighter complexity analysis.

References

1. Altisen, K., Corbineau, P., Devismes, S.: A framework for certified self-stabilization. Log. Methods Comput. Sci. **13**(4) (2017)
2. Altisen, K., Corbineau, P., Devismes, S.: Squeezing streams and composition of self-stabilizing algorithms. In: Pérez, J.A., Yoshida, N. (eds.) FORTE 2019. LNCS, vol. 11535, pp. 21–38. Springer, Cham (2019). https://doi.org/10.1007/978-3-030-21759-4_2
3. Altisen, K., Corbineau, P., Devismes, S.: Certification of an exact worst-case self-stabilization time. In: ICDCN, pp. 46–55. ACM (2021)
4. Altisen, K., Corbineau, P., Devismes, S.: Certified round complexity of self-stabilizing algorithms. In: DISC. LIPIcs, vol. 281, pp. 2:1–2:22. Schloss Dagstuhl - Leibniz-Zentrum für Informatik (2023)
5. Altisen, K., Devismes, S., Dubois, S., Petit, F.: Introduction to Distributed Self-Stabilizing Algorithms. Synthesis Lectures on Distributed Computing Theory. Morgan & Claypool Publishers (2019)
6. Auger, C., Bouzid, Z., Courtieu, P., Tixeuil, S., Urbain, X.: Certified impossibility results for byzantine-tolerant mobile robots. In: Higashino, T., Katayama, Y., Masuzawa, T., Potop-Butucaru, M., Yamashita, M. (eds.) SSS 2013. LNCS, vol. 8255, pp. 178–190. Springer, Cham (2013). https://doi.org/10.1007/978-3-319-03089-0_13
7. Bertot, Y., Castéran, P.: Interactive Theorem Proving and Program Development - Coq'Art: The Calculus of Inductive Constructions. Texts in Theoretical Computer Science. An EATCS Series. Springer (2004)
8. Bertrand, N., Konnov, I., Lazic, M., Widder, J.: Verification of randomized consensus algorithms under round-rigid adversaries. Int. J. Softw. Tools Technol. Transf. **23**(5), 797–821 (2021)
9. Bloem, R., et al.: Decidability of Parameterized Verification. Synthesis Lectures on Distributed Computing Theory. Morgan & Claypool Publishers (2015)
10. Castéran, P., Filou, V.: Tasks, types and tactics for local computation systems. Stud. Inform. Univ. **9**(1), 39–86 (2011)
11. Charron-Bost, B., Debrat, H., Merz, S.: Formal verification of consensus algorithms tolerating malicious faults. In: Défago, X., Petit, F., Villain, V. (eds.) SSS 2011. LNCS, vol. 6976, pp. 120–134. Springer, Heidelberg (2011). https://doi.org/10.1007/978-3-642-24550-3_11

12. Charron-Bost, B., Merz, S.: Formal verification of a consensus algorithm in the heard-of model. Int. J. Softw. Inform. **3**(2–3), 273–303 (2009)
13. Courtieu, P.: Proving self-stabilization with a proof assistant. In: IPDPS. IEEE Computer Society (2002)
14. Courtieu, P., Rieg, L., Tixeuil, S., Urbain, X.: Impossibility of gathering, a certification. Inf. Process. Lett. **115**(3), 447–452 (2015)
15. Cousineau, D., Doligez, D., Lamport, L., Merz, S., Ricketts, D., Vanzetto, H.: TLA + proofs. In: FM. Lecture Notes in Computer Science, vol. 7436, pp. 147–154. Springer (2012)
16. Delporte-Gallet, C., Fauconnier, H., Gafni, E., Lamport, L.: Adaptive register allocation with a linear number of registers. In: Afek, Y. (ed.) DISC 2013. LNCS, vol. 8205, pp. 269–283. Springer, Heidelberg (2013). https://doi.org/10.1007/978-3-642-41527-2_19
17. Dijkstra, E.W.: Self-stabilizing systems in spite of distributed control. Commun. ACM **17**(11), 643–644 (1974)
18. Dolev, S., Israeli, A., Moran, S.: Self-stabilization of dynamic systems assuming only Read/Write atomicity. Distrib. Comput. **7**(1), 3–16 (1993)
19. Ebnenasir, A.: Synthesizing self-stabilizing parameterized protocols with unbounded variables. In: FMCAD, pp. 245–254. IEEE (2022)
20. Hesselink, W.H.: Mechanical verification of Lamport's Bakery algorithm. Sci. Comput. Program. **78**(9), 1622–1638 (2013)
21. Jaskelioff, M., Merz, S.: Proving the correctness of disk paxos. Archive of Formal Proofs **2005** (2005)
22. Küfner, P., Nestmann, U., Rickmann, C.: formal verification of distributed algorithms. In: Baeten, J., Ball, T., de Boer, F.S. (eds.) TCS 2012. LNCS, vol. 7604, pp. 209–224. Springer, Heidelberg (2012). https://doi.org/10.1007/978-3-642-33475-7_15
23. Lamport, L.: Specifying Systems: The TLA+ Language and Tools for Hardware and Software Engineers. Addison-Wesley Longman Publishing Co. Inc., Boston (2002)
24. Lamport, L.: How to write a 21st century proof. J. fixed point theory appl. **11**(1), 43–63 (2012)
25. Rahli, V., Guaspari, D., Bickford, M., Constable, R.L.: EventML: specification, verification, and implementation of crash-tolerant state machine replication systems. Sci. Comput. Program. **148**, 26–48 (2017)
26. Rahli, V., Vukotic, I., Völp, M., Esteves-Verissimo, P.: Velisarios: byzantine fault-tolerant protocols powered by Coq. In: Ahmed, A. (ed.) ESOP 2018. LNCS, vol. 10801, pp. 619–650. Springer, Cham (2018). https://doi.org/10.1007/978-3-319-89884-1_22
27. Rocq Team: The Rocq Prover (2025). https://rocq-prover.org/
28. Tsuchiya, T., Nagano, S., Paidi, R.B., Kikuno, T.: Symbolic model checking for self-stabilizing algorithms. IEEE TPDS **12**(1), 81–95 (2001)
29. Volk, M., Bonakdarpour, B., Katoen, J., Aflaki, S.: Synthesizing optimal bias in randomized self-stabilization. Distributed Comput. **35**(1), 37–57 (2022)

Short/Tool Papers

Choreographies for Program Understanding

Gabriele Genovese[1,2], Ivan Lanese[3(✉)], Cinzia Di Giusto[2],
Emilio Tuosto[4], and Germán Vidal[5]

[1] University of Bologna, Bologna, Italy
[2] Université Côte d'Azur, CNRS, I3S, Nice, France
[3] Olas Team, University of Bologna & Inria - Université Côte d'Azur, Bologna, Italy
ivan.lanese@gmail.com
[4] Gran Sasso Science Institute, L'Aquila, Italy
[5] VRAIN, Universitat Politècnica de València, Valencia, Spain

Abstract. Current choreography-based approaches to the specification and implementation of distributed systems lack support when it comes to program understanding. In particular, we miss systematic methodologies and algorithms to take a message-passing program written in a mainstream programming language and automatically produce a global description of all its communication behaviors. This helps understanding the program interaction patterns and also highlights possible unexpected behaviors to support debugging. We discuss the requirements and difficulties of the approach we envisage. Through concrete examples we outline the kind of global descriptions we want to obtain.

1 Context and Vision

The impetus of service-oriented computing and, more recently, of microservices has determined a radical shift from monolithic applications to distributed components cooperating through message-passing. In this domain, *choreographic* coordination [17] allows designers to focus on the so-called *application-level protocols*, i.e., a description of the *communication interactions*[1] among the system's components (hereafter called *participants*). This focus is typically expressed by two distinct, yet related views of distributed computations: the so-called *global* and *local* views. The former view abstracts away from the actual communication

---

This work has been partially supported by French ANR project SmartCloud ANR-23-CE25-0012, by INdAM - GNCS 2024 project MARVEL, code CUP E53C23001670001, by the project FREEDA (CUP: I53D23003550006), funded by the frameworks PRIN (MUR, Italy) and Next Generation EU, by the PRIN PNRR project DeLICE (F53D23009130001), by the MUR dipartimento di eccellenza 2023-2027, and by *Generalitat Valenciana* under grant CIPROM/2022/6 (FassLow).

[1] With interaction, we refer to a full message-passing communication, comprised of both a send of a message and the corresponding receive.

infrastructure in order to give a blueprint of the communication protocol. The latter view provides the description of the communication behavior of participants in isolation and can guide their implementation. Choreographies can be expressed in modelling languages or formalisms (like WS-CDL [17], BPMN diagrams [26]), multiparty session types [15], message-sequence charts [1,22,28], multiparty contracts [4,5,8,18], and many others (see also the survey in [16]).

Besides offering a development methodology[2] for message-passing systems, global views yield a high-level description of application-level protocols. It is therefore crucial that global views faithfully capture all the interactions in the system. While this is relatively simple when participants' implementations are driven by the global view (e.g., in the top-down approach), the correspondence can be easily spoiled when software evolves or dynamic composition takes place (as advocated in microservice architectures). The classical top-down approach is then of little help: one needs to write a global description of the desired behavior and then use type checking or monitoring to find possible discrepancies.

In this paper, we advocate bottom-up approaches that "extract" global views from code to understand the actual, possibly bugged, behavior of the program. Note that bottom-up approaches exist [9,11,19,20,25], but they have several limitations. Firstly, they produce global views out of abstract models of local views (such as communicating-finite state machines [7] or some kind of behavioral types [16]) and not from actual code written in a mainstream programming language. Secondly, the extracted global views do faithfully capture the behavior of a local view only under some "well-formedness" conditions (e.g., multiparty compatibility in [20]). Parts of the choreography that do not respect the conditions are just dropped, hiding buggy or unexpected behavior that they may contain. We claim that this is exactly the case where a global view would be most useful: the program is buggy and, in order to fix the bug, we need to understand the application-level protocol via a global abstract description.

We claim that the full potential of choreographic approaches in building tools for program understanding can only be unleashed if top-down and bottom-up techniques are married. In particular, we advocate the need of developing bottom-up debugging tools to support the work of programmers.

2 Requirements & Difficulties

Let us discuss a few requirements that we deem decisive to realise our vision.

Push-Button Technique: the extraction of the choreography should be fully automatic, to be applicable to existing code without the need to add special annotations or any other input from the programmer.

Always Capture the Good Behaviors: even if the system is not well-behaved, hence its behavior can not be described by a choreography in the classical sense

---

[2] According to the so-called top-down approach, a global view (formalised, e.g., as a multiparty session type) can be algorithmically projected on a local view preserving relevant properties.

(since choreographies enforce properties such as race and deadlock freedom), a choreography should be extracted. It should contain at least all the good behaviors.

Highlight Misbehaviors: debugging is our key reason to extract choreographies from code; therefore, choreographies for ill-behaved systems, beyond describing the correct behaviors as mentioned above, should flag, as much as possible, misbehaviors due to communications such as deadlocks, orphan messages, unspecified receptions, etc.

Applicable to Mainstream Languages: one should be able to extract the choreography from a real program written in a mainstream language. Natural targets are languages with a clean concurrency/distribution model and dedicated primitives for message-passing such as Erlang, Go, and Scala.

Support Creation and Termination of Participants: in real message-passing systems new processes can be spawned, and some processes may terminate. Hence, a choreographic description should allow for a dynamic number of participants.

Support Races: often choreographic models do not admit races, yet races are commonplace in concurrent programs. Therefore, races should not be forbidden, but possibly flagged as potentially wrong in line with the requirement of highlighting misbehaviors, since they could lead to unexpected behavior.

Accessible yet Precise Notation: choreographies should be represented with an intuitive, possibly graphical, formalism to improve readability. Instead of the usual algebraic formalisms one should appeal to graph-like notations such as labelled transition systems or finite state automata that pair a graphical representation with a well-defined mathematical definition.

We have given above a number of requirements that the approach we envisage should satisfy, but the reader familiar with the topic may have already found a number of potential difficulties. Indeed, we are aware of a few problems that need to be solved in order to make such an approach feasible. We describe them below, together with possible mitigation measures:

Undecidability: extracting a precise description of all the behaviors of a system is in general impossible, since it would require, e.g., deciding termination. Hence, one can focus on extracting a precise choreography in simple cases and giving approximations of the behavior otherwise (e.g., when the system is infinite state). An over-approximation may exhibit spurious behavior w.r.t. the actual behavior of the system. Thus, one can understand the actual behavior, including bugs; however, it is necessary to verify if the reported bugs are false positives. Therefore, care should be taken to limit the number of false positives, since a too high number would make the approach not viable. Over-approximations can be too coarse; e.g., if it is not possible to statically determine which is the expected recipient of a message, an over-approximation may yield a huge number of spurious communications by adding an interaction for each participant in the system. When, as in the case discussed above, over-approximations are not suitable, an under-approximation may be more useful, possibly paired with warnings highlighting issues. The problem in this case is to ensure that false negatives, i.e., cutting off misbehavior from extracted choreographies, are avoided.

Huge descriptions: choreographies of real programs may be huge, thus hindering their usefulness for program understanding. We believe this issue should be tackled by providing tools to abstract, explore, or better visualize the choreography. For instance, one may decide that in order to understand a particular behavior interaction, some participants are immaterial, hence they can be abstracted away (e.g., like ϵ-transitions in automata based approaches). Another option to reduce the size of the description could be to collapse behaviors which are equal up to swap of concurrent actions (as in partial order reduction techniques within model checking [14]), or collapse the behaviors of multiple processes executing the same code.

3 Motivating Examples

In order to better illustrate our point, we consider two simple examples. We use Erlang-like pseudocode for which we provide a global view in terms of choreography automata [3], a formal model of global views featuring a graphical representation akin to finite-state automata. Here, a *global view* is an abstract description of all the possible behaviors of the full system. We consider a language where receive statements are blocking operations. A state where each participant has completed its task and terminated is called *final*. As such, a state that is not final and has no outgoing transitions is a *deadlock*.

The first example is a concise reproduction of the dining philosophers problem, which highlights a possible deadlock. The second example shows a possible mutual exclusion error when operating a simple bank account. Both examples are available online [12]; the corresponding choreography automata have been obtained with the help of our prototype tool Chorer [10].

In the examples, we exploit two operations for sending and receiving messages, respectively. More precisely, send msg to proc sends message msg to process proc, while receive pat_1 from $proc_1 \to e_1$; ... ; pat_n from $proc_n \to e_n$ represents a branching point where the process receives the first message that matches a pattern pat_i and continues with the execution of e_i. As in Erlang, pattern matching is tried from top to bottom. When a receive has only one clause, we abbreviate it as receive pat from proc (and continues with the execution of the next sentence).

3.1 Dining Philosophers Example

Let us consider a program with two participants playing the role of a dining philosopher who shares two forks with the other participant. The behavior of the philosophers is given by the pseudocode on the right while pseudocode for the behavior of the forks is discussed below. Each philosopher first acquires the forks (starting with the one on its right, that is the

```
philosopher(Fork1, Fork2) →
    send req to Fork1,
    receive ack from Fork1,
    send req to Fork2,
    receive ack from Fork2,
    eat(),
    send release to Fork1,
    send release to Fork2,
    philosopher(Fork1, Fork2).
```

one with the same index), then eats (with the function call eat() representing some terminating local computation), and finally releases the forks before recurring.

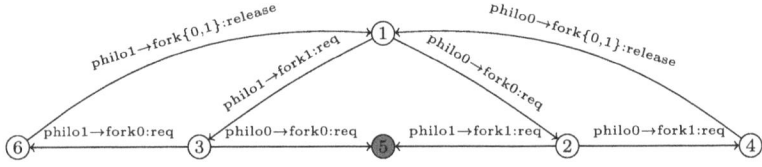

Fig. 1. Global view of the dining philosophers example.

```
fork() →
    receive req from Phil,
    send ack to Phil,
    receive release from Phil,
    fork().
```

Parameters Fork1 and Fork2 are references to processes executing the behavior of forks described by the pseudocode on the left that repeatedly waits for the request from process Phil, ack the request, and waits for the release message from Phil.

There are two possible behaviors of the system. The first (good) one where the philosophers alternate eating infinitely and a second (bad) behavior where both philosophers manage to take only one fork each resulting in a deadlock. Figure 1 depicts the global Choreography Automaton representing the program above. We have two recursive executions where both philosophers eat, represented as loops, and two executions which end in the same deadlock state. The deadlock is visible since State 5 is not final, and it has no outgoing transitions. The automaton is simplified as it does not display the ack messages, and the release messages are merged since their order is irrelevant. The focus here is solely on the order of the req messages. One can imagine to first extract the full choreography automaton, and then merge equivalent behaviors and abstract away from uninteresting transitions.

3.2 Bank Account Example

We now consider a system where a bank account is accessed by two clients, dubbed C1 and C2.

The pseudocode on the right yields the behavior of the bank account, where Value represents its current balance. This process waits for requests from a client. A request can either be a read access to know the current balance or an update request of such value to a NewValue.

```
account(Value) →
  receive
    read from Client →
      send Value to Client,
      account(Value);
    NewValue from Client →
      account(NewValue).
```

Symmetrically, client processes C1 and C2 behave according to the pseudocode on the left: the process reads the current balance from the account, performs some internal operations based on such value, and updates the balance. The global view of the communicating system is depicted in Fig. 2. We can observe two correct executions where the operations are performed in a read-update-read-update order (taking the path via states 1-2-4-7-11 or the one via states 1-3-6-10-14). However, there is also a read-read-update-update order on the highlighted paths. Although the choreography is not inherently incorrect, these highlighted paths could represent a violation of mutual exclusion which may be undesirable for developers in certain contexts. The choreography automaton in Fig. 2 helps in spotting this issue.

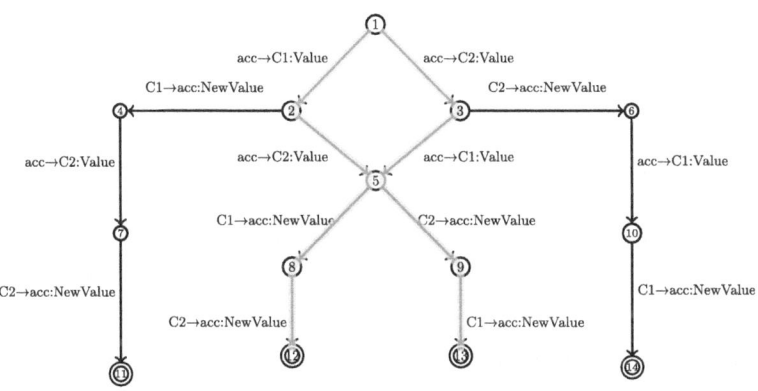

Fig. 2. Global view of the bank account example.

```
client() →
  send read to Acc,
  receive Value from Acc,
  send NewValue to Acc.
```

As for the Dining Philosophers example, the automaton is simplified as we omit the read requests since they are not relevant to spot the undesired behavior (but may be needed for further analysis of its causes).

4 Related Work and Conclusion

Software industry is increasingly devoting attention to choreographic approaches [2,6,13,26] because they naturally support modularization and decoupling. In fact, distributed components coordinate according to a global description without the need of an explicit coordinator. In this context, global specifications are crucial for guaranteeing correctness (since they are blueprints of complex distributed systems and feature model-driven development) as well as for program understanding. To the best of our knowledge, the first attempts to distil global specifications for message-passing systems goes back to [19, 21, 25]. These approaches aim to identify "meaningful" global specifications according to general properties such as deadlock-freedom or absence of orphan messages [7]. A limitation of these approaches is that they do not start from components written in a full-fledged programming language. Rather, distributed components are specified in [19, 21] as abstract models (respectively, π-calculus processes [23, 24, 27] and communicating finite-state machines [7]).

In this paper we have discussed the use of choreographies for program understanding, highlighting both the requirements of such an approach and contrasting them with the more common approaches we are aware of. We have also discussed challenges to be overcome and shown some examples to make our discussion more concrete.

Tool support is paramount to successfully employ choreographies for program understanding. Indeed, we are working on a tool, called Chorer, to extract choreographies from programs written in the Erlang programming language [10], which follows the ideas outlined above.

Chorer. The tool is currently under active development. At this stage, it is capable of parsing relatively simple Erlang programs, such as those presented in Sect. 3. It exploits *static analysis* techniques to construct a best-effort global view of the system, formalized as an extension of choreography automata [3]. This is achieved through a bottom-up approach, as discussed in detail in Sect. 2. Chorer can be used via a Command Line Interface. Upon execution, the tool generates automata that represent both local and global behaviors. These automata are represented in Graphviz's DOT language format [29], facilitating their easy visualization. Chorer is also able to identify and highlight potential deadlock states. However, the correctness of these results has not yet been formally proven, and further verification steps are required to establish the overall soundness of the approach.

Chorer relies on an over-approximation algorithm. This technique should preserve correct behaviors in the analyzed system but may also introduce spurious behaviors that would not occur in actual executions. Over-approximation is required for instance when it is not possible to decide statically whether a given message matches a given pattern (currently, approximation on values of variables is quite rough): the algorithm then considers both the options of matching succeeding and failing, while in practice maybe only one of them can actually happen. Creation and termination of participants are analyzed statically. The tool is currently unable to analyze programs that dynamically spawn actors within recursive functions, since this may result in an infinite state space.

Despite these constraints, the tool satisfies the majority of the requirements outlined in Sect. 2, e.g., it considers (a subset of) the mainstream language Erlang, it is a push-button technique, and it is based on the accessible yet precise notion of finite state automata. Beyond improving the coverage of the language construct and patterns, a main item of future work is studying abstraction techniques to make the resulting choreography automata easier to understand.

Acknowledgements. We thank the anonymous reviewers for their useful comments and suggestions.

References

1. Alur, R., Etessami, K., Yannakakis, M.: Realizability and verification of MSC graphs. Theor. Comput. Sci. **331**(1), 97–114 (2005)
2. Autili, M., Inverardi, P., Tivoli, M.: Automated synthesis of service choreographies. IEEE Softw. **32**(1), 50–57 (2015)
3. Barbanera, F., Lanese, I., Tuosto, E.: Choreography automata. In: Bliudze, S., Bocchi, L. (eds.) COORDINATION 2020. LNCS, vol. 12134, pp. 86–106. Springer, Cham (2020). https://doi.org/10.1007/978-3-030-50029-0_6
4. Bartoletti, M., Tuosto, E., Zunino, R.: Contracts in distributed systems. In: Silva, A., Bliudze, S., Bruni, R., Carbone, M., (eds.) ICE, vol. 59, 130–147 (2011)
5. Bartoletti, M., Tuosto, E., Zunino, R.: On the realizability of contracts in dishonest systems. In: Sirjani, M., (ed.) COORDINATION, pp. 245–260 (2012)
6. Bonér, J.: Reactive Microsystems - The Evolution Of Microservices At Scale. O'Reilly, Sebastopol (2018)
7. Brand, D., Zafiropulo, P.: On communicating finite-state machines. J. ACM **30**(2), 323–342 (1983)
8. Bravetti, M., Zavattaro, G.: A theory of contracts for strong service compliance. Math. Struct. Comput. Sci. **19**(3), 601–638 (2009)
9. Carbone, M., Montesi, F., Schürmann, C.: Choreographies, logically. Distri. Comput. **31**, 51–67 (2018)
10. Chorer github repository. https://github.com/gabrielegenovese/chorer
11. Cruz-Filipe, L., Larsen, K.S., Montesi, F.: The paths to choreography extraction. In: Esparza, J., Murawski, A.S. (eds.) FoSSaCS 2017. LNCS, vol. 10203, pp. 424–440. Springer, Heidelberg (2017). https://doi.org/10.1007/978-3-662-54458-7_25
12. Two simple examples. Dining example and Account example, https://github.com/gabrielegenovese/chorer/tree/master/examples/dining. https://github.com/gabrielegenovese/chorer/tree/master/examples/account
13. Frittelli, L., Maldonado, F., Melgratti, H., Tuosto, E.: A choreography-driven approach to APIs: the OpenDXL case study. In: Bliudze, S., Bocchi, L. (eds.) COORDINATION 2020. LNCS, vol. 12134, pp. 107–124. Springer, Cham (2020). https://doi.org/10.1007/978-3-030-50029-0_7
14. Godefroid, P.: Model checking for programming languages using verisoft. In: POPL, pp. 174–186 (1997)

15. Honda, K., Yoshida, N., Carbone, M.: Multiparty asynchronous session types. J. ACM **63**(1), 9:1-9:67 (2016)
16. Hüttel, H., et al.: Foundations of session types and behavioural contracts. ACM Comput. Surv. **49**(1), 3:1-3:36 (2016)
17. Kavantzas, N., Burdett, D., Ritzinger, G., Fletcher, T., Lafon, Y., Barreto, C.: Web services choreography description language version 1.0. Technical report, W3C (2005). http://www.w3.org/TR/ws-cdl-10/
18. Lange, J., Scalas, A.: Choreography synthesis as contract agreement. In: Proceedings 6th Interaction and Concurrency Experience, ICE 2013, pp. 52–67 (2013)
19. Lange, J., Tuosto, E.: Synthesising choreographies from local session types. In: Koutny, M., Ulidowski, I. (eds.) CONCUR 2012. LNCS, vol. 7454, pp. 225–239. Springer, Heidelberg (2012). https://doi.org/10.1007/978-3-642-32940-1_17
20. Lange, J., Tuosto, E., Yoshida, N.: From communicating machines to graphical choreographies. In: Rajamani, S.K., Walker, D., (eds.) POPL, pp. 221–232. ACM (2015)
21. Lange, J., Tuosto, E., Yoshida, N.: From communicating machines to graphical choreographies. In: POPL15, pp. 221–232 (2015)
22. Lohrey, M.: Realizability of high-level message sequence charts: closing the gaps. Theor. Comput. Sci. **309**(1–3), 529–554 (2003)
23. Milner, R.: Communicating and Mobile Systems: the π-calculus. Cambridge University Press, Cambridge (1999)
24. Milner, R., Parrow, J., Walker, D.: A calculus of mobile processes, I and II. Inf. Comp. **100**(1), 1–40 (1992)
25. Mostrous, D., Yoshida, N., Honda, K.: Global principal typing in partially commutative asynchronous sessions. In: Castagna, G. (ed.) ESOP 2009. LNCS, vol. 5502, pp. 316–332. Springer, Heidelberg (2009). https://doi.org/10.1007/978-3-642-00590-9_23
26. OMG. Business Process Model and Notation (BPMN), Version 2.0, January 2011. https://www.omg.org/spec/BPMN
27. Sangiorgi, D., Walker, D.: The π-Calculus: a Theory of Mobile Processes. Cambridge University Press, Cambridge (2002)
28. Stutz, F.: Asynchronous multiparty session type implementability is decidable - lessons learned from message sequence charts. In: Ali, K., Salvaneschi, G., (eds.) 37th European Conference on Object-Oriented Programming, ECOOP 2023, July 17-21, 2023, Seattle, Washington, United States, vol. 263, LIPIcs, pp. 32:1–32:31. Schloss Dagstuhl - Leibniz-Zentrum für Informatik (2023)
29. The Graphviz Authors. Dot format. https://graphviz.org/doc/info/lang.html

An Approach to Formalize Information-Theoretic Security of Multiparty Computation Protocols

Cheng-Hui Weng[1](✉), Reynald Affeldt[2], Jacques Garrigue[1], and Takafumi Saikawa[1]

[1] Nagoya University, Nagoya, Japan
weng.cheng.hui.c4@math.nagoya-u.ac.jp
[2] National Institute of Advanced Industrial Science and Technology, Tokyo, Japan

Abstract. Secure multiparty computation (hereafter, SMC) refers to cryptographic protocols that allow multiple parties to jointly compute a function over their inputs while keeping them private. The main security property of SMC protocols is information leakage freedom, whose proofs can be found in the scientific literature for idealized models. But how does one guarantee that information leakage freedom still holds once SMC is implemented as a concrete piece of software? As a step toward solving this problem, we use the proof assistant ROCQ to formalize the security claims of an SMC stack. We develop a method based on an interpreter for a subset of the π-calculus in which protocols can be modeled as programs and then input traces verified for correctness and information leakage freedom. Thanks to this approach, the properties of SMC can be established in a clearly defined trusted base that can be reused to verify other SMC stacks.

1 Introduction

Secure multiparty computation (SMC, also known as MPC) refers to cryptographic protocols that allow multiple parties to jointly compute a function over their inputs while keeping the inputs private [25,26]. Usually there are other upper-level components in the computation stack (hereafter, *SMC stack*) that wrap the fundamental SMC protocols to provide user-friendly functionalities for real-world applications, like online auctions [15], medical data categorization [3], face recognition [18], data mining [13], GDPR compliance [11], medical networks and databases [17], and federated machine learning [23]. Therefore, it is important to verify the fundamental SMC protocols to assure the correctness of software based on SMC.

By leveraging the proof assistant ROCQ (renamed from COQ in 2025), we develop an interpreter-based method to provide a mechanized formalization of SMC protocols. The first goal for the formalization is to have a clearly defined trusted base instead of multiple trusted bases from many pen-and-paper proofs.

C.-H. Weng—Supported by the mercari R4D Support Program.

The second goal is to express the properties of algorithm correctness and information leakage freedom in the same language, while the language used in pen-and-paper work for the former is far different from the mathematical language used in the latter.

To showcase our method, we focus on a series of work that provides computation components for real-world applications [8,9,19,20]. We formalize its fundamental protocol: the scalar product protocol between two parties and one commodity server (hereafter, *SMC scalar product*) [9]. We summarize our contributions as follows:

- We introduce the interpreter-based formalization method as a general method to formalize SMC protocols in ROCQ (Sect. 3). The main ingredient is a subset language of the π-calculus [14]. We apply it to the SMC scalar product protocol.
- In this framework, we prove the correctness of the protocol and information leakage freedom properties using input traces (Sect. 4), which provide a direct connection between the specification and implementation. In the process, we expose a number of implicit hypotheses in the original pen-and-paper work, which leads to clarification of intermediate steps with new lemmas that enrich the ROCQ framework.

2 Background: the SMC Scalar Product Protocol

The SMC scalar product protocol [9] is the fundamental building block of our target SMC stack. The distinctive feature of this protocol is that the authors introduced a commodity server to reduce the complexity of cryptography of common two-party SMC protocols. The authors assume protocol participants are *semi-honest (honest-but-curious)*: corrupted players follow the protocol specifications, but also try to gather as much information as possible in order to deduce some private inputs.

During protocol execution, the commodity server issues random vectors ($\mathbf{s_a}$, $\mathbf{s_b}$) and random scalars (r_a, $\mathbf{s_a} \cdot \mathbf{s_b} - r_a$) to the two parties. We use bold font to denote vectors and italic font for scalars. The two parties use the random values to disguise their secret inputs ($\mathbf{x_a}$, $\mathbf{x_b}$) before sending them to each other. After execution, *Party#1* holds y_a and *Party#2* holds y_b, which is a random scalar generated by *Party#2* itself. The protocol is correct if and only if $\mathbf{x_a} \cdot \mathbf{x_b} = y_a + y_b$. Depending on the requirements, they may need to deliver the results to an external examiner. The examiner can add both results to get the scalar product result, or, like in other arithmetic protocols [19] in the stack, the two parties may be instructed to continue the following computations with the partial protocol results.

In Sect. 3 we introduce a π-calculus sublanguage to model this protocol. Before diving into it, we depict the protocol in polyadic π-calculus. Note that here we omit the initialization of random variables and secret inputs, and three parallel components in the program represent the commodity server, *Party#1* and *Party#2*, from top to bottom. Also, we assume that new channel operations are performed all at the beginning:

$$\overline{C_A}\langle s_a, r_a\rangle.\ \overline{C_B}\langle s_b, s_a \cdot s_b - r_a\rangle.\ 0$$
$$|\ C_A(s_a, r_a).\ B_A(x'_b).\ \overline{A_B}\langle x_a + s_a\rangle.\ B_A(t).\ \overline{E_A}\langle t - x'_b \cdot s_a + r_a\rangle.\ 0$$
$$|\ C_B(s_b, r_b).\ \overline{B_A}\langle x_b + s_b\rangle.\ A_B(x'_a).\ \overline{B_A}\langle x'_a \cdot x_b + r_b - y_b\rangle.\ \overline{E_B}\langle y_b\rangle.\ 0$$

For the information leakage freedom property, it was defined formally in the pen-and-paper work of protocol security proofs [20]:

$$H(x_i \mid VIEW_j^\pi) = H(x_i) \quad \text{whenever} \quad i \neq j. \tag{1}$$

In Eq. 1, x_i denotes the secret input of *Party#i*, while $VIEW_j^\pi$ denotes all variables the *Party#j* can gain during protocol execution, which matches the generic definition of "view" by Iwamoto [12, §5.1]. Thus, the Eq. 1 denotes that executing the SMC scalar product protocol does not increase *Party#j*'s knowledge of its counterpart's secret input x_i. This information leakage freedom property was proved by Shen et al. [20]. We formalize their pen-and-paper result in the proof of Theorem 2 in Sect. 4.

3 An Interpreter-Based Specific Methodology for SMC

In ROCQ, we introduce a simple protocol description language to express SMC protocols as programs [24, file `smc_interpreter.v`]:

```
Inductive proc : Type :=
| Init : data → proc → proc        (* Register input to trace *)
| Recv : N → (data → proc) → proc  (* Receive from nth process *)
| Send : N → data → proc → proc    (* Send to nth process *)
| Ret  : data → proc               (* Return result *)
| Finish : proc                    (* Finish successfully *)
| Fail : proc.                     (* Finish with failure *)
```

Here, each protocol participant is represented by one process, in type `proc`. Then an interpreter executes programs to capture *which* process knows *what* data during the execution. In particular, payloads in terms `Init`, `Recv` and `Ret` are recorded in *input traces* of processes for later verifications. The method allows us to achieve the goals mentioned in Sect. 1. Furthermore, formalization based on the captured input traces avoids the risk of providing theorems restricted to any specific implementation and language.

All payloads in the input traces are recorded under the same wrapper type, `data`. Therefore, instead of identifying operations in the traces by types, one can trace back to the corresponding operation by the recording order. While typing operations can distinguish operations explicitly, it complicates following proofs.

In the language, the `Init` term represents that a local variable is initialized. In real-world implementations, variable initialization may involve complicated processes like I/O reading or random number generation, but such details are not necessary for protocol correctness and information leakage freedom verifications. The `Ret` term represents that a protocol participant completes its computation with a result. After `Ret`, the process finishes its computation by moving

An Approach to Formalize Information-Theoretic Security of MPC Protocols

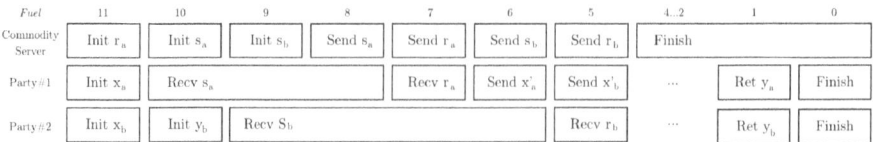

Fig. 1. The SMC interpreter execution sequence for the SMC scalar product protocol.

to Finish. If a protocol participant completes its computation without a result (e.g., the commodity server in the SMC scalar product protocol), it will directly move to Finish. Since there is no result to be recorded and used in verification. Finally, a process immediately moves to the Fail term whenever it receives an unexpected value. The programmer can use Rocq functionalities to define what are unexpected values to Fail the process. It can be a trivial type check like in the SMC scalar product, but it also can be used to implement the security with abort, like the DSDP protocol with zero-knowledge proofs [10, §5.2].

As in the π-calculus, computation can be described through rules rewriting a configuration, i.e. a non-ordered list of tagged channels. The label on top of the arrow indicates a datum to be added to the input trace.

$$i : \text{Init } x.\, p \mid C \xrightarrow{i \leftarrow x} i : p \mid C$$
$$i : \text{Send } j\, x.\, p \mid j : \text{Recv } i\, f.\, \mid C \xrightarrow{j \leftarrow x} i : p \mid j : f\, x \mid C$$
$$i : \text{Ret } x \mid C \xrightarrow{i \leftarrow x} i : \text{Finish} \mid C$$

Naturally, evaluation terminates when no further rewriting can be done. However, due to Rocq's requirements for function termination, the interpreter must have a parameter h for the quantity *fuel* left for interpretation. If the fuel reaches zero, the interpretation stops even if there are further rewritings to be done.

Note that while there may be several possible reductions in a configuration, there is only one possible reduction per process. Whenever all processes reach the Finish state, the trace obtained from each process is finite and deterministic.

Here we describe the SMC scalar product in the language as three processes[1]. Details are omitted here for brevity. We plot the actual interpretation sequence in Fig. 1

$C : \text{Init } r_a\, s_a\, s_b.\text{Send}_A(s_a).\text{Send}_A(r_a).\text{Send}_B(s_b).\text{Send}_B(s_a \cdot s_b - r_a).\text{Finish}$
$\mid A : \text{Init } x_a.\text{Recv}_C \lambda s_a r_a.\text{Recv}_B \lambda x_b'.\text{Send}_B(x_a + s_a).\text{Recv}_B \lambda t.\text{Ret } t - x_b' \cdot s_a + r_a$
$\mid B : \text{Init } x_b\, y_b.\text{Recv}_C \lambda s_b r_b.\text{Send}_A(x_b + s_b).\text{Recv}_A \lambda x_a'.\text{Send}_A(x_a' \cdot x_b + r_b - y_b).\text{Ret } y_b$

Our language's limitations compared to π-calculus are that processes are choice-free, sequential, and non-recursive. This naturally precludes replication. Also, due to the fact that Rocq requires all functions to be terminating, a receiver process cannot extend itself infinitely by the continuation[2]. Lastly, since

---
[1] Function smc_scalar_product_traces in the file [24, scalar_product_program.v].
[2] The finite repetitions is available for protocols like the zn-to-z2 protocol [19].

one Recv exactly waits for one Send from a specific process, communications either continue with a fixed Recv-Send pair, or get stuck due to an incomplete pair. In either case, the program execution is deterministic.

For protocols with branches, the programmer can already write ordinary pattern matching code in the continuation of Recv term to indicate which counterpart process to send to and receive from. For protocols require dynamic channels, we need to unify the data type (*data*) and party type ($\mathbb{N}$). In both cases, integrating with the MONAE framework [2] can provide a more expressive monadic interface for programs with branches, instead of writing all branches in the continuation.

4 Formalization Using Interpretation

The SMC scalar product protocol is deterministic, and the correctness of its input traces is also stated and proved as deterministic equalities. We begin with a basic lemma:

Lemma 1 (Correctness of SMC Scalar Product Traces). *The input traces generated from the SMC scalar protocol (Fig. 1) are*

$$\mathtt{smc\_scalar\_product\_traces} :=$$
$$((r_a, s_b, s_a), (y_a, t_a, x'_b, r_a, s_a, x_a), (y_b, x'_a, r_b, s_b, y_b, x_b))$$

and satisfy the following equations:

$$r_b = s_a \cdot s_b - r_a, \qquad x'_a = x_a + s_a, \qquad x'_b = x_b + s_b,$$
$$t_a = x'_a \cdot x_b + r_b - y_b, \qquad y_a = t_a - x'_b \cdot s_a + r_a.$$

In Lemma 1, *commodity server's* input trace is (r_a, s_b, s_a), while *Party#1's* and *Party#2's* input traces are $(y_a, t_a, x'_b, r_a, s_a, x_a)$ and $(y_b, x'_a, r_b, s_b, y_b, x_b)$. As we mentioned earlier in Sect. 3, traces represent *which* process knows *what* data during the protocol execution. Intuitively, the primitive variables $x_a, x_b, s_a, s_b, r_a,$ and y_b are initialized by I/O operations or random number generator, and other variables are the results of computation on the primitive variables. Lemma 1 shows that the communications among participants are correct because input traces match the protocol specification. Since our interpreter is computable, Lemma 1 is proved by evaluation, which is intrinsic in the type theory of RoCQ (see conversion rules in the RoCQ manual [22]).

The correctness of the final result of the computation, $x_a \cdot x_b = y_a + y_b$ (see Sect. 2), is an easy corollary thanks to the RoCQ tactic `ring` [6] that automatically decides ring equations:

Theorem 1 (Correctness of SMC Scalar Product). *Let x_a, x_b, y_a and y_b be variables from* `smc_scalar_product_traces`, *then $x_a \cdot x_b = y_a + y_b$.*

Proof. Lemma 1 allows for expanding y_a so that only primitive variables remain. Further rewriting it by the commutativity and distributivity laws for dot products, we get:

$$\mathbf{x_a} \cdot \mathbf{x_b} = \overbrace{\mathbf{x_a} \cdot \mathbf{x_b} + \mathbf{s_a} \cdot \mathbf{x_b} + (\mathbf{s_a} \cdot \mathbf{s_b} - r_a) - y_b}^{y_a} - (\mathbf{s_a} \cdot \mathbf{x_b} + \mathbf{s_a} \cdot \mathbf{s_b}) + r_a + y_b$$

This is a valid ring equation that can be automatically proved by the `ring` tactic. □

After formalizing the correctness proofs of the SMC scalar product protocol, we formalize the information leakage freedom proofs [20, §II]. The formal definition of this property is Eq. 1. To use input traces for both kinds of proofs, we need to reconcile their different requirements for the types of variables. Unlike the deterministic variables in the correctness proofs, those used to discuss information leakage are random variables, which are yet to be measured and obey some distribution. Such random variables can be used to formulate an amount of information in terms of entropy, as in the original pen-and-paper proof [20, §III.C]:

$$H(\mathbf{x_2} \mid VIEW_1^\pi) = H(\mathbf{x_2} \mid \langle\, x_1, s_1, r_1, \mathbf{x_2'}, t_1, \mathbf{y_1}\rangle) = H(\mathbf{x_2} \mid \langle\, x_1, s_1, r_1, \mathbf{x_2'}, t_1\rangle)$$
$$= \cdots = H(\mathbf{x_2})$$

Note that we use the notation $\langle \ldots \rangle$ for a compound random variable valued in a tuple. We use the same name for corresponding random and deterministic variables but with numeric and alphabetical subscripts respectively, e.g.,

$r_1 : \{\text{RV } P \to T\}$ random variable with distribution P and valued in T

$r_a : T$ deterministic value in the range of the random variable

To connect these two types, we *lift* input traces to random variables, which means to compose the random variables with the `smc_scalar_product_traces` function (Lemma 1). The general definition of such a composition is as follows:

Definition 1 (Composition of a Function with a Random Variable). *Let X be a random variable of type $\{RV\ P \to T_a\}$ and $f : T_a \to T_b$ be a function. Then we define the function `comp_RV` [1] (denoted by $\underset{RV}{\circ}$) to compose a function f with X as follows:*

$$f \underset{RV}{\circ} X := \lambda x.\ f(X\ x) : \{RV\ P \to T_b\}$$

Lifting the input traces in Lemma 1 results in the random counterpart of the equations between the variables:

Lemma 2 (The Lifted SMC Scalar Product Traces). *Let s_1, s_2, r_1, y_2, x_1, x_2 be random variables, then:*

$$\langle\langle r_1, s_1, s_1\rangle, \langle y_1, t_1, \mathbf{x_2'}, r_1, s_1, \mathbf{x_1}\rangle, \langle y_2, \mathbf{x_1'}, r_2, s_2, y_2, \mathbf{x_2}\rangle\rangle =$$
$$\textit{uncurry smc\_scalar\_product\_traces} \underset{RV}{\circ} \langle s_1, s_2, r_1, y_2, \mathbf{x_1}, \mathbf{x_2}\rangle$$

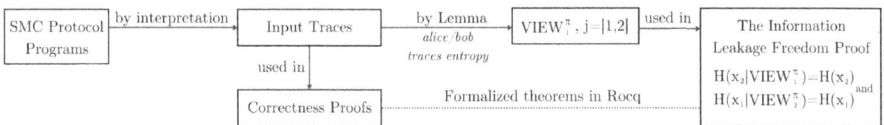

Fig. 2. Overview of the formalization of the SMC scalar product protocol

and satisfies the following equations:

$$r_2 = s_1 \odot s_2 \ominus r_1, \quad \mathbf{x}'_1 = \mathbf{x}_1 \oplus \mathbf{s}_1, \quad \mathbf{x}'_1 = \mathbf{x}_2 \oplus \mathbf{s}_2,$$
$$t_1 = \mathbf{x}'_1 \odot \mathbf{x}_2 \oplus r_2 \ominus y_2, \quad y_1 = t_1 \ominus \mathbf{x}'_2 \odot \mathbf{s}_1 \oplus r_1,$$
where $\oplus$ $\ominus$ $\odot$ denote lifted addition, subtraction and dot product.

Thus, the lifting establishes a connection between the interpretation, correctness and information leakage freedom (Fig. 2), and allows us to prove the Eq. 1 in ROCQ:

Theorem 2 (SMC Scalar Product Is Information Leakage Free).
Let $\langle y_1, t, \mathbf{x}'_2, r_1, \mathbf{s}_1, \mathbf{x}_1 \rangle$ and $\langle y_2, \mathbf{x}'_1, r_2, \mathbf{s}_2, y_2, \mathbf{x}_2 \rangle$ be input traces of Party#1 and Party#2 from the lifted `smc_scalar_product_traces`*, then*

$$H(\mathbf{x}_1 \mid \langle y_2, \mathbf{x}'_1, r_2, \mathbf{s}_2, y_2, \mathbf{x}_2 \rangle) = H(\mathbf{x}_1) \quad \text{and} \quad H(\mathbf{x}_2 \mid \langle y_1, t_1, \mathbf{x}'_2, r_1, \mathbf{s}_1, \mathbf{x}_1 \rangle) = H(\mathbf{x}_2).$$

To prove this theorem, we formalize steps [20, §III.B] and [20, §III.C] by applying the *graphoid axioms* [16] (as formalized in the INFOTHEO library [1]). Thanks to the rigor of ROCQ, we were led to make all the hypotheses explicit, leaving no space to ambiguity. One instance is in the following theorem quoted from [20]:

Theorem 3 (Masked Condition Removal [20, Theorem 3.7]). *Let R, X_1, ..., X_n be random variables defined on $\mathbb{Z}_p$. If R follows a uniform distribution and is independent of $(X_1, \ldots, X_n)$, and $Y_1, \ldots, Y_m$ are functions of $X_1, \ldots, X_n$, then we have*

$$\Pr(Y_1 \mid Y_2, \ldots, Y_{m-1}, Y_m + R) = \Pr(Y_1 \mid Y_2, \ldots, Y_{m-1}); \; i.e., \tag{A}$$
$$H(Y_1 \mid Y_2, \ldots, Y_{m-1}, Y_m + R) = H(Y_1 \mid Y_2, \ldots, Y_{m-1}). \tag{B}$$

It turned out that the "i.e." between (A) and (B) was a gap, and we filled it by proving a generalization that is easier to use. This generalization is a genuine product of the formalization in the sense that it was revealed by refactoring:

Lemma 3 (From Conditional Probability to Conditional Entropy[3]).
Let X and Y be random variables and f be a function, such that for any x and y, $\Pr(X = x \mid Y = y) = \Pr(X = x \mid f \underset{RV}{\circ} Y = f(y))$ holds whenever $\Pr(Y = y)$ is not 0. Then $H(X \mid Y) = H(X \mid f \underset{RV}{\circ} Y)$.

---
[3] Lemma `cpr_centropy'` in [24, file `smc_entropy.v`].

5 Related Work

Butler et al. propose another approach to prove secure multiparty computation using a proof assistant [7]. Their idea is to use CRYPTHOL [4], an ISABELLE/HOL library that provides a probabilistic programming language and a notion of computational indistinguishability to formalize provable security. They use the probabilistic programming language to represent participants and they state security in terms of an equality between a "real view" and a "simulator" where the absence of leakage is obvious. The formal proof consists in showing that both the real view and the simulator are computationally indistinguishable, which implies information-theoretic security [7, §5,6]. In comparison, we capture the view from a program from its execution and we resort to information theory to prove information-theoretic security.

Despite different security notions, simple protocols like the Secure Multiplication Protocol described in [7, §5] demonstrate that the equality proofs between the real view and the simulator share a similar approach to the lifting process outlined in Lemma 2 in Sect. 4. The lifting process establishes a bijection between the deterministic values in the traces and the random variables in $VIEW_j^\pi$. This aligns with Iwamoto's findings [12, §5.4], where the author proves that various equivalent approaches—such as simulation, conditional probabilities, and information theory—can be used to express security. Consequently, we *emulate* the simulation-based security for simple protocols described by our language while still allowing for information-theoretic verifications. By examining how simulation-based proofs are conducted for more advanced protocols, we can enhance our language to formalize additional protocols effectively.

Lastly, we have not introduced a type system for our language. It was not necessary since our language is limited to choice-free sequential non-recursive processes. However, *session types* [27] would be a natural choice if we extend our language.

6 Conclusion and Future Work

We proposed a method based on the use of an interpreter to verify SMC protocols in ROCQ. Protocols are specified using a subset of the π-calculus whose interpretation captures traces of inputs that occur during execution. These traces are used (1) to prove correctness using the arithmetic properties of the protocol messages and (2) to prove information leakage freedom using (conditional) entropy. The combination of these ingredients to perform formal verification is the original aspect of our method.

We demonstrated our method by verifying the SMC scalar product protocol [9], a realistic protocol that has been used in a public health study [8]. We successfully formalized its correctness and information leakage freedom using the traces of inputs (see Fig. 2). Thanks to formalization, we uncovered implicit hypotheses and made explicit proof steps that were overlooked by the original pen-and-paper analysis [20] (e.g., Lemma 3 in Sect. 4). The formalization thus proved useful while staying manageable: to give a concrete idea, it consists of 88 lemmas and 2 theorems in 3 files for a total of 756 lines of code.

We also intend to apply our method to formalize more advanced SMC protocols to explore its advantages and limitations. As an experiment, after completing the above formalization, we started to formalize a homomorphic cryptosystem based protocol, DSDP, which is used for trust computation [10, §4]. While still a work in progress, the formalization uncovers additional hypotheses for both semi-honest and active security models. We also successfully reproduce an attack path detailed in [10, §5.2] in a purely information-theoretic approach. These findings underscore the capability of our methodology to formalize both security and insecurity scenarios for SMC protocols, addressing both semi-honest and active adversary settings. As a very rough estimation of proof overhead for more intricate protocols or cryptographic primitives, it took us just about one week to complete most of the formalization, including extending our methodology to express homomorphic cryptosystem based SMC protocols, despite this being the first protocol we formalized after the one in this paper.

In future work, we will formalize other SMC protocols related to the SMC scalar product within the SMC stack [19]. The formalization will enable us to examine how to formalize the secure composition of building block protocols. Besides that, we shall complete the proof of the *t-privacy* property of the DSDP protocol. The *t*-privacy property indicates that a group of colluding parties consisting of *t* members or fewer cannot gain any additional information about the private inputs [5].

Our ultimate goal is a framework in which the user only needs to write protocol programs and perform the main proofs. In order to achieve such a goal, we plan to work on further automation. In particular, we want to automate the proofs of lifting process in Lemma 2 by COQ-ELPI [21], an embedded language to define new commands and tactics in ROCQ.

References

1. Affeldt, R., Garrigue, J., Saikawa, T.: Reasoning with conditional probabilities and joint distributions in Coq. Comput. Softw. **37**(3), 79–95 (2020). https://doi.org/10.11309/jssst.37.3_79
2. Affeldt, R., Garrigue, J., Saikawa, T.: A practical formalization of monadic equational reasoning in dependent-type theory. J. Funct. Program. **35** (2025). https://doi.org/10.1017/S0956796824000157
3. Barni, M., Failla, P., Kolesnikov, V., Lazzeretti, R., Sadeghi, A.-R., Schneider, T.: Secure evaluation of private linear branching programs with medical applications. In: Backes, M., Ning, P. (eds.) ESORICS 2009. LNCS, vol. 5789, pp. 424–439. Springer, Heidelberg (2009). https://doi.org/10.1007/978-3-642-04444-1_26
4. Basin, D.A., Lochbihler, A., Sefidgar, S.R.: CryptHOL: game-based proofs in higher-order logic. J. Cryptol. **33**(2), 494–566 (2020). https://doi.org/10.1007/S00145-019-09341-Z
5. Blundo, C., De Santis, A., Persiano, G., Vaccaro, U.: Randomness complexity of private computation. Comput. Complex. **8**(2), 145–168 (1999). https://doi.org/10.1007/s000370050025

6. Boutillier, P., et al.: Rocq 9.0 reference manual - the ring and field tactic families (2025). https://rocq-prover.org/doc/v9.0/refman/addendum/ring.html
7. Butler, D., Aspinall, D., Gascón, A.: How to simulate it in Isabelle: towards formal proof for secure multi-party computation. In: Ayala-Rincón, M., Muñoz, C.A. (eds.) ITP 2017. LNCS, vol. 10499, pp. 114–130. Springer, Cham (2017). https://doi.org/10.1007/978-3-319-66107-0_8
8. Chen, K., Hsu, T.S., Huang, W.K., Liau, C.J., Wang, D.W.: Towards a scripting language for automating secure multiparty computation. In: First Asia-Pacific Programming Languages and Compilers Workshop (APPLC 2012), Beijing, China, 14 June 2012 (2012)
9. Du, W., Zhan, J.Z.: A practical approach to solve secure multi-party computation problems. In: Workshop on New Security Paradigms (NSPW 2002), Virginia Beach, VA, USA, 23–26 September 2002, pp. 127–135. ACM (2002). https://doi.org/10.1145/844102.844125
10. Dumas, J., Lafourcade, P., Orfila, J., Puys, M.: Dual protocols for private multi-party matrix multiplication and trust computations. Comput. Secur. **71**, 51–70 (2017). https://doi.org/10.1016/J.COSE.2017.04.013
11. Helminger, L., Rechberger, C.: Multi-party computation in the GDPR. In: Privacy Symposium 2022—Data Protection Law International Convergence and Compliance with Innovative Technologies, pp. 21–39. Springer, Heidelberg (2022). https://doi.org/10.1007/978-3-031-09901-4_2
12. Iwamoto, M.: Information-theoretic perspectives for simulation-based security in multi-party computation. IEICE Trans. Fund. **E107-A**(3), 360–372 (2024). https://doi.org/10.1587/transfun.2023TAI0001
13. Lindell, Y.: Secure computation for privacy preserving data mining. In: Wang, J. (ed.) Encyclopedia of Data Warehousing and Mining, 2nd edn, vol. 4, pp. 1747–1752. IGI Global (2009). http://www.igi-global.com/Bookstore/Chapter.aspx?TitleId=11054
14. Milner, R.: Communicating and Mobile Systems: The π-Calculus. Cambridge University Press, Cambridge (1999)
15. Naor, M., Pinkas, B., Sumner, R.: Privacy preserving auctions and mechanism design. In: First ACM Conference on Electronic Commerce (EC-99), Denver, CO, USA, 3–5 November 1999, pp. 129–139. ACM (1999). https://doi.org/10.1145/336992.337028
16. Pearl, J., Paz, A.: GRAPHOIDS: a graph-based logic for reasoning about relevance relations. Technical Report. R-53 CSD-850038, UCLA Computer Science Department (1985)
17. Rogers, J., et al.: VaultDB: a real-world pilot of secure multi-party computation within a clinical research network. arXiv preprint arXiv:2203.00146 (2022). https://doi.org/10.48550/arXiv.2203.00146
18. Sadeghi, A.-R., Schneider, T., Wehrenberg, I.: Efficient privacy-preserving face recognition. In: Lee, D., Hong, S. (eds.) ICISC 2009. LNCS, vol. 5984, pp. 229–244. Springer, Heidelberg (2010). https://doi.org/10.1007/978-3-642-14423-3_16
19. Shen, C.H., Zhan, J., Hsu, T.S., Liau, C.J., Wang, D.W.: Scalar-product based secure two-party computation. In: 2008 IEEE International Conference on Granular Computing, pp. 556–561 (2008). https://doi.org/10.1109/GRC.2008.4664775
20. Shen, C.H., Zhan, J., Wang, D.W., Hsu, T.S., Liau, C.J.: Information-theoretically secure number-product protocol. In: 2007 International Conference on Machine Learning and Cybernetics, vol. 5, pp. 3006–3011 (2007). https://doi.org/10.1109/ICMLC.2007.4370663

21. Tassi, E.: Elpi: an extension language for Coq (Metaprogramming Coq in the Elpi λProlog dialect). In: The Fourth International Workshop on Coq for Programming Languages (2018)
22. The Rocq Development Team: The Rocq Proof Assistant Reference Manual. Inria (2024). https://coq.inria.fr. Version 8.20.0
23. Wang, H., Li, Z., Ge, C., Susilo, W.: ABG: a multi-party mixed protocol framework for privacy-preserving cooperative learning. arXiv preprint arXiv:2202.02928 (2022). https://doi.org/10.48550/arXiv.2202.02928
24. Weng, C.H., Affeldt, R., Garrigue, J., Saikawa, T.: Formalization for the SMC scalar product protocol (2024). https://github.com/affeldt-aist/infotheo/pull/138
25. Yao, A.C.: Protocols for secure computations (extended abstract). In: 23rd Annual Symposium on Foundations of Computer Science, Chicago, Illinois, USA, 3–5 November 1982, pp. 160–164. IEEE Computer Society (1982). https://doi.org/10.1109/SFCS.1982.38
26. Yao, A.C.: How to generate and exchange secrets (extended abstract). In: 27th Annual Symposium on Foundations of Computer Science, Toronto, Canada, 27–29 October 1986, pp. 162–167. IEEE Computer Society (1986). https://doi.org/10.1109/SFCS.1986.25
27. Yoshida, N., Gheri, L.: A very gentle introduction to multiparty session types. In: Hung, D.V., D'Souza, M. (eds.) ICDCIT 2020. LNCS, vol. 11969, pp. 73–93. Springer, Cham (2020). https://doi.org/10.1007/978-3-030-36987-3_5

SNexpression: A New Component for SN Matrix-Based Structural Analysis

Lorenzo Capra[1], Massimiliano De Pierro[2(✉)], and Giuliana Franceschinis[3]

[1] Dip. di Informatica, Università di Milano, Milano, Italy
capra@di.unimi.it
[2] Dip. di Informatica, Università di Torino, Torino, Italy
massimiliano.depierro@unito.it
[3] DISIT, Università del Piemonte Orientale, Alessandria, Italy
giuliana.franceschinis@uniupo.it

Abstract. Symmetric nets (SN), including their stochastic extension (SSN), are a type of high-level Petri net (HLPN) known for their structured syntax, which aids in efficient analysis. Their dynamics is described by a quotient state-transition system (SRG) linked to a lumped Markov chain. State-space analysis and stochastic model checking are supported by tools like GreatSPN [4,7] and COSMOS [3,9], then a toolset has become available for structural analysis of SN: SNexpression [2,10]. This framework is based on algebraic calculi to derive properties in a symbolic manner. The paper presents a novel component for operating at the net level by manipulating matrices of structural expressions directly. This approach enables a coherent definition of stochastic parameters in SSNs with several transition priority levels and extends the analysis capabilities by identifying independent classes of transition instances. The paper illustrates the new SNexpression functionalities of matrix structural calculi on two examples.

Keywords: Symmetric Nets · Structural analysis · Matrix calculus

1 Introduction

The Symmetric Nets (SN) formalism [13] is an instance of High-Level Petri Nets designed to exploit regularities (symmetries) in concurrent systems. We briefly introduce the formalism and its semantics through a very simple model (Fig. 1) and a portion of a more complex model (Fig. 2) studied in [8] and proposed as a benchmark for the Model Checking Contest [6]: the Control Room SSN [1]. The former is an illustrative example showing a complete set of arc functions; it is used to provide examples of structural relations. The latter will be used to illustrate a more complex matrix-based structural relation: It represents the behavior of a team of technicians, employed by a utility service, responding to customer calls in case of appliance failures (the goal of the complete SSN model is to estimate the minimum number of technicians that guarantee the possibility of meeting the requirements of the Service Level Agreement). Like any other HLPN, SNs comprise places $P = \{p_1, \ldots, p_n\}$, which contain tokens defining their marking and correspond to discrete state variables, and transitions $T = \{t_1, \ldots, t_m\}$, representing activities that locally cause state changes. Places and transitions are connected by directed arcs to form a bipartite graph. The tokens in SN places carry information and are represented by tuples belonging to the place *color domain*, defined as a Cartesian product of *color classes* (nonempty finite sets, pairwise disjoint). Each SN transition represents many similar activities, characterized by different color instances to distinguish individual activities. The instances can be represented as tuples belonging to transition *color domains*: in SN, each color class in a transition domain conventionally matches a transition parameter (variable) appearing in arc expressions, and an instance defines a binding of its parameters to colors from the corresponding classes. The arcs are decorated with functions that determine the transition instances enabled in a given marking and the state change caused by their firing.

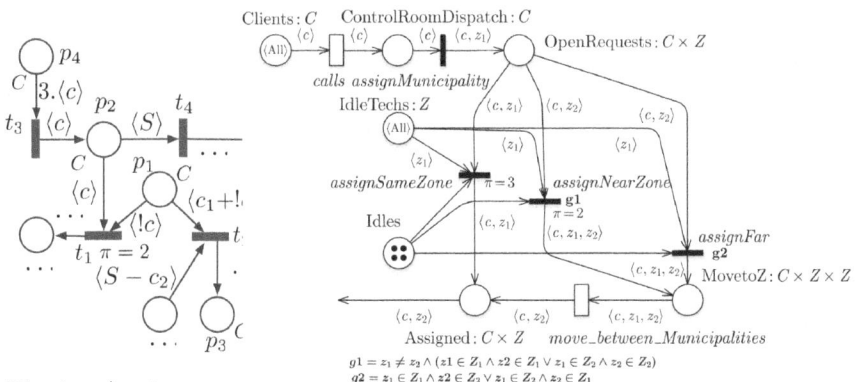

Fig. 1. A simple SN

Fig. 2. Portion of the control room SN model from [1].

The simple net in Fig. 1 has only one (circularly) ordered color class C (a successor function, denoted !, is defined in the elements of C) and the color domain of all places is just C. Several expressions appear on the net arcs: $\langle c \rangle$, $\langle S \rangle$, $\langle S - c_2 \rangle$, $\langle c_1 + !c_1 \rangle$. The variables c, c_1, and c_2 correspond to transition parameters of type C; the constant symbol S corresponds to the whole set C. The (sub)net in Fig. 2 is a portion of a larger model [8] (provided as supplementary material in [2]): It has two unordered color classes, Z and C; Z is partitioned into two subclasses Z_1 and Z_2. The places have different color domains: C, $C \times Z$, $C \times Z \times Z$. In this model, the arc functions (which apply to transition instances) are tuples of variables, e.g. $\langle c, z_1, z_2 \rangle$, or $\langle c \rangle$. Arc functions result in a multiset of tokens withdrawn/added from/to the connected input/output place. In the second model, they always result in a singleton color tuple (token), while in the model of Fig. 1 functions $\langle S \rangle$, $\langle S - c_2 \rangle$, $3.\langle c \rangle$ and $\langle c_1 + !c_1 \rangle$ result in multisets of cardinality $|C|$,

$|C|-1$, 3 and 2, respectively. The evaluation of a tuple of functions, for a given transition instance, is the Cartesian product of the evaluations of its elements.

An instance of t is a binding of its parameters to colors from the corresponding color classes (class C for symbols c, c_1 and c_2, class Z for symbols z_1 and z_2): the arc functions are evaluated on a transition instance binding and the resulting multiset is subtracted/added to the place connected to the arc. In general, weighted sums of tuples (possibly with guards) composed of linear combinations of base functions are allowed as arc expressions, and SNexpression symbolic calculus operates without restrictions on such expressions. Transitions may have guards whose terms indicate membership of a variable to a subclass or equality of two variables: the model in Fig. 2 has two guards: g_1 and g_2 which express conditions on the enabling of the corresponding transition instances.

SSNs include timed and immediate transitions: graphically, the timed transitions are white boxes, and the immediate ones are black bars; the latter may have different priorities (the default is 1): this is the case for t_1 in Fig. 1, which has priority $\pi = 2$, and for transitions assignSameZone, assignNearZone in Fig. 2 that have priority $\pi = 3$ and 2, respectively.

In the next sections, the general structure of SNexpression is recalled, showing how the new component is integrated into its architecture. Some legacy structural relations defined on transition pairs computed by the tool are first illustrated. Then an example sequence of matrix-based operations that work simultaneously on all transitions in the net is shown. Finally, the application of matrix-based calculus to the computation of a structural dependency relation on immediate transitions with different priorities is explained on the example in Fig. 2. Supplementary material is provided on the examples page of [2], which contains a more extensive presentation of the control room net along with some files that allow a user to execute the experiments discussed in the paper.

2 The SNexpression Tool

SNexpression is a tool for the symbolic structural analysis of SNs. The core of the tool is an implementation of an algebraic calculus for solving expressions built of SN arc functions and a base set of functional operators employed in structural analysis of SNs. These expressions are rewritten into normal forms, whose syntax is a slight extension of SN arc functions. The main peculiarity is that the solving engine operates without *unfolding* the high level expressions, whose terms are structured functions, into a scalar calculus. The primary advantages are enhanced efficiency, parameterization in color class sizes, and results expressed using the SN syntax.

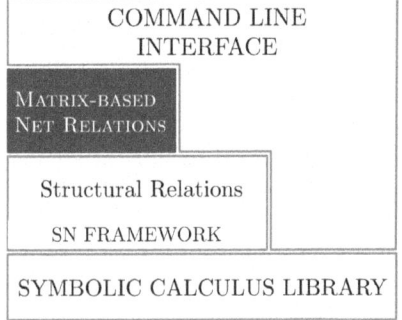

Fig. 3. SNexpression architecture.

Table 1. Main CLI's commands to compute Structural Relations.

SYMMETRIC NETS FRAMEWORK COMMAND	
DESCRIPTION	CLI COMMANDS
Conflict between t1 and t2	SC(t1,t2,p), SC(t1,t2)
Self-Conflict of t	SC(t,p), SC(t)
Causal Connection between t1 and t2	SCC(t1,t2,p), SCC(t1,t2),
Mutual Exclusion between t1 and t2	SME(t1,t2,p), SME(t1,t2)

Figure 3 depicts the layered architecture of SNexpression. At the bottom there is the Library for Symbolic Calculus (LSC), which implements a sort of Computer Algebra System (equipped with a suitable API) whose operands are the expressions of the language based on the SN arc functions. On top of LSC there is the SN framework (SNF), a middle layer that manages more abstract objects, such as structural relation formulae between nodes of the SN models loaded into the system. The new component, located on top of the SNF, provides an additional layer through which the user can effectively obtain structural relations defined in matrix form at the level of the entire SN. At the summit of the entire architecture is the Command Line Interface (CLI), a shell that enables user interaction with either the two intermediary layers or directly with the LSC for executing calculations. The reader can find a comprehensive description of the legacy functionalities of SNexpression in [10]; in Table 1 a few legacy CLI's commands implemented into SNF methods are described: they are the commands to compute structural properties between pairs of nodes of the SN: for instance the command SC(t1,t2,p) computes the expression providing the instances of transition t1 in structural conflict with a generic instance of t2 on tokens of a shared input place p.

The next section describes the new features of the *Matrix-based structural Relations* layer: the structural relations between pairs of nodes, listed in Table 1, are all extended to the entire net by the layer, using a matrix representation. The new functionalities are explained by showing the corresponding CLI commands, with particular emphasis on those interacting with the new layer.

SNexpression is entirely implemented in Java. The LSC is distributed as a standalone jar file so that programmers can use it in other projects. The tool-set and the LSC API are available at [2]. The LSC sources are available at [5].

The purpose of the suite, including the CLI, is twofold: (1) it provides the user with a tool to interactively perform basic structural analysis and calculation on a SN model; the limit of this approach is due to the not so trivial interpretation of the results; (2) it allows the user to test the validity of the new components, in particular the *Matrix-based Net Relations* layer; All components of the suite implement a public library of methods that can be integrated in complex applications and algorithms that perform high-level systematic analysis.

3 New Component's Features

The newly developed component integrates SNexpression with the capabilities for efficient large-scale computation of structural relations within an SN model. Consequently, the tool introduces several basic structural relations that are defined on the entire SN and that in the legacy release were computable only between pairs of nodes. The relations currently available are derived from those described in Table 1 and comprise SCC, SSC, SME, and **1**: They are the Structural Causal Connection, the Symmetric Structural Conflict, the Structural Mutual Exclusion, and the identity. In the new component, a net-level structural relation R is represented by a matrix R[] whose element $R[i,j]$ is the relation between the node i and the node j of the SN. The above relations are all among transitions. CLI commands to derive the built-in relations on the loaded SN are formatted as: `build` *relation-name*. For example, the command `build SCC` calculates the SCC between each pair of transitions within the loaded SN model.

In addition to the basic structural relations above, the new component implements the newly defined SD (Structural Dependency) relationship. SD captures a more general form of dependency between transitions in SN where multiple priority levels may be present. The SD derivation uses a fixed point algorithm and involves non-trivial theoretical aspects [11].

Based on the few built-in relations and with a limited set of operators discussed later, the tool allows to specify any user-defined structural relation, making it possible to perform more complex calculations. Through the symbol definition feature provided by the CLI, the user can specify, solve, and reuse structural relations that he/she has previously written.

A session of net-level structural calculations is started and ended, respectively, with the CLI commands `netcalc` and `exit`. Let us give an example of the calculation of the structural conflicts between all transition pairs of the SN in Fig. 1: the shell command `build SSC` executes the task. The solved expressions are stored in internal matrices whose elements can be queried using dedicated commands; the easiest way is through the `print SSC` shell command. Limiting ourselves to transitions `t1` and `t2` the computation gives the following results: $SSC[t_1,t_2]=\langle !^{-1}c_1 + c_1 \rangle$ and $SSC[t_2,t_2]=\langle c_1, S - c_2 \rangle + \langle S - c_1, S_C \rangle$. The first expression provides in functional form the instances of t_1 that are in the SSC with a generic instance (c_1, c_2) of t_2. The meaning of the expression is verifiable directly: the resulting t_1 instances are due to the shared place p_1 and depend only on the variable c_1 of t_2; instance $t_2(c_1, c_2)$ withdraws from p_1 the multiset of tokens $c_1 + !c_1$; the instances of t_1 withdrawing these tokens are those with $c = !^{-1}c_1$ and $c = c_1$. $SSC[t_2,t_2]$ provides the conflicts between instances of t_2: instance $t_2(c_1, c_2)$ is in conflict with any other instance of t_2.

Another interesting case of dependency is the indirect conflict. For example, t_3 is in indirect conflict with t_2. Since t_1 has priority over t_2 and t_3 is causally connected to t_1 (in turn, in conflict with t_2), some instances of t_3 might be in a form of Indirect Conflict with some instances of t_2. We can compute such instances on the whole SN by composing SCC and SSC:

$$IC := SCC.SSC.$$

The character . here denotes the composition operator between relations. With the formula on the right, the user computes the relation IC for each pair t_i and t_j of the SN model: the matrix element $IC[t_i, t_j]$ provides in symbolic form the instances of t_i that are in indirect conflict with an instance of t_j due to priority. The result is named IC, a symbol that can be used in other expressions, for example, to define all dependencies SD_1 that are conflicts or indirect conflicts:

$$\$ \text{ SD\_1} := \text{IC} + \text{SSC}$$

Let A and B be two structural relations. The operators allowed on the relations are: the sum A + B, the difference A − B, the product (composition) A.B, the transpose B', the n-th power B^n, the transitive closure A*, the symmetric closure A^s, the scalar product A.n, where $n \in Z$. Unary operators have the highest precedence, all other operators adhere to the conventions of classical algebra.

4 Practical Application of the New Features

In this section we briefly introduce the reasons that motivated us to develop the new component. As mentioned, the tool as a monolithic object, with its CLI, is just a means through which we demonstrate the potentialities given by the new layer, although in any case the results obtained through the shell can be used manually by the modeler to guide his/her choices. However, the capabilities of the underlying new layer can be integrated into and used by automatic analysis instruments according to the application. Understanding the dependencies between transitions has been our main guiding objective. Such a task is useful and critical in several applications of PN models analysis which can benefit from it. Examples of these applications are the calculation of Extended Conflict Sets (ECS) [16] in order to reduce transitions interleaving, or the implementation of techniques to efficiently compute enabled transitions [12].

The aim of this work is to disclose the new computational abilities of the added layer; investigating the application fields in detail is beyond our scope. Next we explore a bit more the practical computation of *dependencies* in SN, in [11] we used this feature to define an algorithm for the derivation of the ECS (at the current stage the algorithm is not still implemented). If all transitions have the same priority 1, it has been shown in [11] that all potential structural dependencies can be computed with the following formula:

$$SD_{pri\_1} = (SCC^* \cdot SSC + SSC) + (SCC^* \cdot SSC + SSC) \cdot (SCC^*)^t$$

The session of SNexpression to solve the above formula may be:

```
$ SCC_tclos := SCC*
$ R       := SCC_tclos.SSC + SSC
$ SDpri_1 := R+R.SCC_tclos'
```

The command **print** *relation-name* displays the relation values for each pair of transitions. Transitive and reflexive closures can then be computed as follows:

```
$ SD_rclos := SDpri_1* + 1
```

where 1 is the identity matrix, implicitly defined when the SN model is loaded. Then this relation can be used by the algorithm to compute the ECS.

In SN with many immediate transition priority levels, an ad hoc algorithm is required: this is provided as a built-in relation SD, since the new component still does not provide a structured programming language to express algorithms.

Let us show an application of the SD computation and the results that can be obtained on the subnet in Fig. 2, featuring three priority levels: the interest is in evaluating the possible dependencies relating pairs of immediate transitions that require a proper assignment of weights (needed for probabilistic conflict resolution). Multiple priorities make the study of dependencies more interesting due to indirect conflicts. We consider relation SD^*, the transitive closure of SD.

Before presenting a few examples of dependency, we summarize the meaning of the SN in Fig. 2. The partition of Z reflects the distance between zones: two zones in the same Z_i are near, two zones in different sublcasses are far. The timed transition calls represents the arrival of a customer $\langle c \rangle$ call, then assignMunicipality randomly chooses his residence zone $z_1 \in Z$: a token $\langle c, z_1 \rangle$ is therefore placed in OpenRequests. A request is assigned to an idle technician (if available in idleTechs): for efficiency reasons, a request is assigned with highest priority to a technician who is in the customer residence zone (assignSameZone, with $\pi = 3$), with medium priority to one in a nearby zone (assignNearZone, with $\pi = 2$ and guard $g1$), and with the lowest priority to one in a far zone (assignFar, with $\pi = 1$ and guard $g2$). In the last two cases, the technician must travel to reach the customer (moveBetweenMunicipalities).

The computation of the relation SD* on the SN in Fig. 2 required only a few ms on a mid-range laptop. The simplest case concerns SD* between instances of assignMunicipality, which is $\langle S_C, S_Z \rangle = C \times Z$; in fact all instances of this transition are mutually dependent because client $\langle c \rangle$ in ControlRoomDispatch can choose any zone $z_1 \in Z$ (autoconflict of instances with same client and different zone), moreover different clients, once chosen the zone, can compete to acquire the same technician (indirect conflict due to the causal connection with the transitions sharing input place IdleTechs).

The dependencies SD*[assignFar,assignMunicipality] are defined through the following constant expression $\langle S_C, S_{Z_1}, S_{Z_2} \rangle + \langle S_C, S_{Z_2}, S_{Z_1} \rangle$: Any instance of assignMunicipality potentially depends on all instances of assignFar since the firing of the latter can prevent the assignment of a technician to another call. The SD*[assignNearZone,assignNearZone] is more complex: it is a sum of mutually exclusive terms (which map to pairwise disjoint sets). For instance, let us consider the term: $[z_1! = z_2]\langle S - c_1, S_{Z_2} - z_2, S_{Z_2} - z_2\rangle[g]$, where $[z_1! = z_2]$ acts as a filter and $g = z_1 \in Z_2, z_2 \in Z_2, z_1! = z_2$ (',' is the logical conjunction). This means that there is a dependency between an instance $\langle c_1, z_1, z_2\rangle$ of assignNearZone and the instances involving a different client $(S - c_1)$ resident in a different nearby zone in the same subclass Z_2 and attended by a technician located in a nearby (in Z_2) but different zone (expressed by the filter $z_1 \neq z_2$).

5 Conclusions and Future Work

The symbolic calculus implemented in SNexpression offers a suite of operators designed to verify the structural properties of SNs without unfolding the model or imposing limitations on the formalism, as is common in related works (e.g., [14,15]). In this paper, we present a new component designed to perform matrix operations. The new capabilities improve usability and speed up the derivation of properties and relations at the net level. Some possible applications of the tool are: identification of groups of potentially interdependent immediate transitions in SSN (to reduce interleaving), the exploitation of structural conflict and causal connection relations to identify newly enabled/disabled transitions after the firing of a given transition instance. Finally, it may support a recently proposed method to generate an agent-based simulation model from an extended SN [17].

Acknowledgements. This work was partially funded by the MUR project "T-LADIES" (PRIN 2020TL3X8X).

References

1. Model checking contest models (2025). https://mcc.lip6.fr/2025/models.php
2. SNexpression home page (2025). http://www.di.unito.it/~depierro/SNexpression
3. The COSMOS tool (2025). https://cosmos.lacl.fr/
4. The GreatSPN sources (2025). https://github.com/greatspn/SOURCES
5. The Library for Symbolic Calculus (2025). https://github.com/lgcapra/SNlib-stable
6. The Model Checking Contest home page (2025). https://mcc.lip6.fr
7. Amparore, E.G., Balbo, G., Beccuti, M., Donatelli, S., Franceschinis, G.: 30 years of GreatSPN. In: Fiondella, L., Puliafito, A. (eds.) Principles of Performance and Reliability Modeling and Evaluation. SSRE, pp. 227–254. Springer, Cham (2016). https://doi.org/10.1007/978-3-319-30599-8_9
8. Amparore, E.G., Donatelli, S., Landini, E.: Modelling and evaluation of a control room application. In: van der Aalst, W., Best, E. (eds.) PETRI NETS 2017. LNCS, vol. 10258, pp. 243–263. Springer, Cham (2017). https://doi.org/10.1007/978-3-319-57861-3_15

9. Ballarini, P., Barbot, B., Duflot, M., Haddad, S., Pekergin, N.: HASL: a new approach for performance evaluation and model checking from concepts to experimentation. Perform. Eval. **90**, 53–77 (2015)
10. Capra, L., De Pierro, M., Franceschinis, G.: SNexpression: a symbolic calculator for symmetric net expressions. In: Janicki, R., Sidorova, N., Chatain, T. (eds.) PETRI NETS 2020. LNCS, vol. 12152, pp. 381–391. Springer, Cham (2020). https://doi.org/10.1007/978-3-030-51831-8_19
11. Capra, L., De Pierro, M., Franceschinis, G.: Symbolic dependency relations calculation in Symmetric Nets. Transactions on Petri Nets and Other Models of Concurrency (2025). (accepted for publication)
12. Capra, L., De Pierro, M.: Efficient enabling test in simulation of SWN. In: The 2006 European Simulation and Modelling Conference - Modelling and Simulation 2006 - ESM 2006, pp. 367–374. EUROSIS-ETI Publication (2006)
13. Chiola, G., Dutheillet, C., Franceschinis, G., Haddad, S.: Stochastic well-formed coloured nets for symmetric modelling applications. IEEE Trans. Comput. **42**(11), 1343–1360 (1993)
14. Evangelista, S., Haddad, S., Pradat-Peyre, J.-F.: Syntactical colored petri nets reductions. In: Peled, D.A., Tsay, Y.-K. (eds.) ATVA 2005. LNCS, vol. 3707, pp. 202–216. Springer, Heidelberg (2005). https://doi.org/10.1007/11562948_17
15. Evangelista, S., Pradat-Peyre, J.-F.: On the computation of stubborn sets of colored petri nets. In: Donatelli, S., Thiagarajan, P.S. (eds.) ICATPN 2006. LNCS, vol. 4024, pp. 146–165. Springer, Heidelberg (2006). https://doi.org/10.1007/11767589_9
16. Marsan, M.A., Balbo, G., Conte, G., Donatelli, S., Franceschinis, G.: Modelling with Generalized Stochastic Petri Nets. Wiley Series in Parallel Computing, John Wiley and Sons (1995)
17. Pennisi, M., Amparore, E.G., Franceschinis, G.: Exploiting structural dependency relations for efficient agent based model simulation. In: Iacono, M., Scarpa, M., Barbierato, E., Serrano, S., Cerotti, D., Longo, F. (eds.) Computer Performance Engineering and Stochastic Modelling. EPEW ASMTA 2023 2023. LNCS, vol. 14231, pp. 353–368. Springer, Cham (2023). https://doi.org/10.1007/978-3-031-43185-2_24

Assessing Code Understanding in LLMs

C. Laneve[2], A. Spanò[1], D. Ressi[1(✉)], S. Rossi[1], and M. Bugliesi[1]

[1] DAIS, Ca' Foscari University of Venice, Venice, Italy
{alvise.spano,dalila.ressi,sabina.rossi,michele.bugliesi}@unive.it
[2] DISI, University of Bologna, Bologna, Italy
cosimo.laneve@unibo.it

Abstract. We present an empirical evaluation of Large Language Models (LLMs) in understanding semantic-preserving code transformations such as copy propagation and constant folding. Our results show that LLMs fail to recognize semantic equivalence in approximately 41% of cases without additional context, and in 29% of cases even when provided with a simple, generic context. To improve performance, we propose to integrate LLMs with code optimization tools – both to enhance training and to support deeper program comprehension.

Keywords: Large Language Models · Semantic Preserving Code Transformations · Code Understanding

1 Introduction

Modern Large Language Models (LLMs) exhibit remarkable capabilities in tasks related to programming, including code generation, comprehension, processing, and analysis [3]. However, no thorough assessment appears to have been conducted on their robustness in scenarios requiring a nuanced understanding of the code. In fact, while LLMs have been tested on source-level transformations such as variable renaming or introduction of no-op instructions [10,17,18], their ability to grasp program equivalence remains underexamined when it comes to non-trivial semantic-preserving transformations and more general semantic equivalence questions.

In the present paper, we focus on transformations that guarantee identical outputs for identical inputs. In particular, we focus on source-to-source transformations inspired by standard compiler optimizations – specifically, copy propagation and constant folding of complex expressions [1] – and prompt LLMs to assess the equivalence of program variants produced by these transformations. According to our findings, LLMs fail in their assessment in 41% of the cases when no context is provided and in about 29% of the cases when given a simple additional context. The performance improves slightly when the models are prompted with variants obtained by semantically-breaking transformations, somehow reinforcing the common insight that detecting a mistake is easier than proving correctness.

The poor performance observed is likely due to insufficient training for the task, and additional training focused on semantically preserving code transformations is therefore necessary for improvement. However, traditional training methods would be slow and require costly expert supervision to assess semantic equivalence across a vast code base, even for specific transformations like constant folding. To lower both the learning curve and the associated costs, we advocate for the integration of LLMs with automatic tools that implement code transformations, such as those of our present interest. Such integration would make the tools available for self-supervised training starting from the existing code base (simply, the tools would be employed to produce semantic equivalent transformations of the existing samples in the code base). Furthermore, and more interestingly, they could be employed as general-purpose code pre-processors to eliminate "noisy" bits, thus enhancing LLMs in their code understanding task.

Due to space constraints, we omit the full details of the experiments and the formalization of the code transformations discussed here; instead, we refer the reader to [13] for a comprehensive treatment of both aspects.

2 Related Work

The integration of formal methods with AI and ML has gained traction in areas such as data augmentation [16], dataset labeling [22], network compression [19,21], and software security [20,22]. Formal tools enable rigorous semantic-preserving transformations, while ML models improve scalability [26].

LLMs are increasingly evaluated on code generation and manipulation. Tools like GitHub Copilot have been assessed on classical algorithm tasks such as sorting and data structure implementation [4,27], but deeper semantic reasoning remains underexplored. Indeed, recent studies show that even trivial edits (e.g., variable renaming) can degrade LLM performance in tasks like bug detection and code analysis [6,8]. On a related note, [2] demonstrates how unoptimized code can hinder ML-based side-channel attacks, highlighting the relevance of code transformations in security contexts.

To our knowledge, no prior work has systematically assessed the robustness of LLMs against compiler-style, semantics-preserving optimizations such as copy propagation or constant folding. This gap is partly due to the challenges of evaluation: results depend on varied prompting strategies and often ambiguous model outputs [15].

Prompt configuration plays a key role in LLM behavior. User prompts include techniques such as zero- or few-shot, chain-of-thought, and instruction-tuned prompting; system prompts allow deeper control (e.g., temperature, token limits, logit bias) [23]. We focus on user prompts for two reasons: they mirror typical use of free-tier models like ChatGPT, and they provide more reproducible results than API-dependent system prompts with opaque configurations. Additionally, we adopt a zero-shot setting [12] to assess raw model reasoning. Open-source models such as LLaMA [7], Gemma [25], and Mixtral [11] are mostly explored in academic settings and not the focus of this work.

3 Experimental Setup

To conduct our esperiments we crafted a dataset of semantically equivalent variants of a series of small Python programs, obtained by the application of two well-known compiler techniques, commonly used in intermediate code optimization: *copy propagation* of variables and *constant folding* of expressions [1]. The transformations are formalized a set of rules (noted $\overset{CP}{\Longrightarrow}$ and $\overset{CF}{\Longrightarrow}$) to be applied to the source-level Python code implementing the selected programs [13]. To illustrate, by removing copies and folding constant expression we are able to identify the following programs:

```
n = int(input())
m = 1
tmp = n
while (n>1):
    m = m * n
    tmp = n - 1
    n = tmp
print(m)
```
$\overset{CP}{\Longrightarrow}$
```
n = int(input())
m = 1
while (n>1):
    m = m * n
    n = n - 1
print(m)
```

```
n = int(input())
tmp = 1
m = 2*tmp - 1
while (n > tmp):
    tmp = tmp + 1
    m = m * n
    n = n - tmp + 1
    tmp = tmp - 1
print(m)
```
$\overset{CF}{\Longrightarrow}$
```
n = int(input())
tmp = 1
m = 1
while (n > 1):
    m = m * n
    n = n - 1
print(m)
```

The dataset comprises 11 distinct programs implementing a variety of algorithms, each differing in length, complexity, and prominence. These programs manipulate data structures such as lists and arrays, and perform mathematical computations, offering a diverse set of challenges. Some algorithms, such as Bubblesort and the Sieve of Eratosthenes, are well known, while others, like type unification and 3D point rotation, are less commonly recognized.

Each program is available in 8 variants, grouped into two classes:

- **semantically equivalent variants:** one standard implementation serving as a reference; three *unoptimized* variants generated by inverting the transformations – copy propagation, constant folding, and their combination – such that the reference program can be recovered by applying these optimizations;
- **semantically non-equivalent variants:** one bugged version of the reference implementation, and three additional versions derived from each of the unoptimized variants by introducing a bug, so that all versions are pairwise inequivalent. The bugs involve small but significant changes, e.g., index modifications or incorrect assignments, making them semantically incorrect.

To further challenge the models, the programs are obfuscated by anonymizing function names, replacing variable identifiers with short, uninformative labels, thereby reducing the models' ability to rely on superficial cues. Table 1 gives an overview of all the algorithms, while full details on the dataset are publicly available on GitHub [24].

The experiments involved collecting and analyzing responses from seven mainstream chatbots to a multi-instance binary classification task. For each program in the dataset, we designed four zero-shot prompts – varying in contextual priming and number of function variants – to evaluate the chatbot's ability to identify semantically equivalent implementations.

Table 1. Our dataset of Python programs. Colors mark the notoriety of the algorithm: green denotes classic algorithms, yellow marks notorious functions typically found in libraries, red refers to uncommon algorithms that belong to specific domains.

Arithmetics	List Manipulation	Other
Fibonacci	Remove Duplicates	Anti Aliasing
Primality Test	Find Occurrence	Unification (MGU)
Rotate 3D Point	Count Occurrences	
Fast Fourier Transform	Sieve of Eratosthenes	
	Bubblesort	

Contextless Preamble

> Are the following functions semantically equivalent to the first one?

Contextual Preamble

> You are a chatbot for comparing the semantics of small Python programs. I will provide you with multiple implementations of the same Python function. The first function is the reference version. The other functions are unoptimized with copy propagation, constant folding or a combination of the two. Tell me whether the functions are semantically equivalent to the reference version or not.

Fig. 1. Contextless vs. contextual preambles used in prompts.

Prompt 1 (single-class, contextless): brief question followed by four correct implementations (one reference, three unoptimized).
Prompt 2 (single-class, contextual): same as Prompt 1, but preceded by a contextual preamble.
Prompt 3 (multi-class, contextless): same structure as Prompt 1, but including four incorrect implementations for a total of eight functions.
Prompt 4 (multi-class, contextual): like Prompt 3, but with the contextual preamble from Prompt 2.

Prompts 1 and 2 test the model's ability to recognize semantic equivalence among correct implementations, with or without context. Prompts 3 and 4 introduce incorrect implementations, probing the model's classification skills in more ambiguous settings.

The contextual preamble combines role prompting, instruction prompting, and additional semantic information, as shown in Fig. 1. All prompts follow a zero-shot setup, with no examples provided. Each prompt was submitted 10 times per chatbot in a new session, producing a total of $11 \cdot 4 \cdot 7 \cdot 10 = 3080$ outputs. Chatbot responses were manually analyzed by two authors to evaluate consistency and semantic correctness. Rather than relying on simple yes/no answers, which degrade performance, we allowed full-text reasoning to better

Table 2. Chatbot models and versions involved in our experiments as of Jan-Feb 2025.

Company	Product	Model
Github	Copilot Pro	Claude 3.5 Sonnet
Github	Copilot Pro	GPT-4o
Google	Gemini	Gemini 2.0 Flash
OpenAI	ChatGPT	GPT-4o
DeepSeek	DeepSeek	DeepSeek-R1 V3
Amazon Web Services	Q Developer	Various
Anthropic	Claude	Claude 3.5 Sonnet

capture the models' interpretation. No automated post-processing was used to preserve the fidelity of human evaluation.

Table 2 lists the chatbots and underlying models tested. No premium or API-based access was used (except for Copilot, which requires a subscription). All evaluations were conducted via publicly available interfaces, ensuring alignment with typical usage scenarios.

Notably, Copilot and Amazon Q act as frontends for multiple models. We specifically targeted Copilot's GPT-4o and Claude Sonnet variants. Although these are technically the same models as their standalone counterparts, their behavior in Copilot differs, justifying separate analysis. Amazon Q also uses Claude 3.5 Sonnet[1] alongside custom backend models, with similarly divergent outputs.

Finally, we note that chat-based interfaces typically hide system-level settings like the *temperature* parameter [5], which affects response variability. Most models default to approximately 0.7, but this is often opaque. Since responses can vary across time, sessions, and user accounts, we spread our runs across different timeframes to obtain a robust sampling of each model's behavior.

4 Experimental Results

We collected 4,620 responses for single-class prompts (Prompts 1 and 2) and 10,780 evaluations for multi-class experiments (Prompts 3 and 4), totaling 15,400 fine-grained yes/no answers (see Tables 3 and 4). Table 3 presents the accuracy of semantically equivalent programs per prompt and chatbot. Claude Sonnet and DeepSeek achieve the best overall performance, with Claude slightly ahead (79.09% vs. 76.88%), whereas Gemini scores the lowest (43.72% overall), with Copilot Claude following at 60.19%. Contextual prompts (Prompts 2 and 4) generally improve accuracy (except for Gemini) and benefit Copilot ChatGPT and Amazon Q the most, while top performers gain only marginally.

---

[1] As of February 2025, Amazon Q Developer's blog confirms Claude Sonnet is used for code tasks: https://aws.amazon.com/it/blogs/devops/amazon-q-developer-inline-chat.

Assessing Code Understanding in LLMs   207

We also examined the performance of the models in the presence of both correct and incorrect unoptimized code (in green and yellow, respectively). Compared to the single-class prompts, performance drops by approximately 8% from Prompt 1 to Prompt 3 (with the exception of DeepSeek) and by about 3.5% from Prompt 2 to Prompt 4. Notably, ChatGPT remains largely unaffected. These results suggest that while multi-class prompts improve the detection of incorrect implementations, they do so at the cost of accurately identifying semantically equivalent programs, revealing a classification bias.

As a final remark, the overall accuracy collected for all algorithms for all unoptimized variants (CP, CF, CP+CF) shows that constant folding is the least confusing transformation across all models (76.40% accuracy), copy propagation is more challenging (69.20%), and the combination yields the lowest accuracy (49.39%).

Table 3. Performance of all chatbots on the class of semantically correct programs. Prompts 1 and 2 contain only correct implementations. To ensure a fair comparison, for Prompt 3 and Prompt 4 we report only the performance on the class of correct programs, i.e. the truly semantically equivalent ones. The best and worst performances are highlighted in bold.

| | VSCode Plugin | | | Web Interface | | | | |
| | Copilot | | Extension | | | | | |
Prompt #	Claude	ChatGPT	Amazon Q	Gemini	ChatGPT	DeepSeek	Claude	Average
#1	63.20%	53.68%	56.99%	47.62%	67.53%	70.56%	**76.77%**	62.34%
#2	71.52%	79.39%	76.36%	41.82%	61.21%	82.42%	**84.85%**	71.08%
#3 / Correct Programs	43.03%	51.52%	46.06%	45.45%	46.06%	**76.97%**	71.72%	54.40%
#4 / Correct Programs	63.03%	72.73%	65.45%	**40.00%**	70.91%	77.58%	83.03%	67.53%
Average	60.19%	64.33%	61.22%	**43.72%**	61.43%	76.88%	**79.09%**	

Table 4. Complete results on the classification of both semantically correct and incorrect programs. A comparison is made between prompts with and without contexts.

| | VSCode Plugin | | | Web Interface | | | | |
| | Copilot | | Extension | | | | | |
Prompt #	Claude	ChatGPT	Amazon Q	Gemini	ChatGPT	DeepSeek	Claude	Average
#3 / Correct Programs	**43.03%**	51.52%	46.06%	45.45%	46.06%	**76.97%**	71.72%	54.40%
#3 / Incorrect Programs	94.55%	89.55%	95.00%	**95.91%**	90.00%	95.45%	93.94%	93.48%
#3 / Overall	72.47%	73.25%	74.03%	74.29%	71.17%	**87.53%**	76.19%	75.56%
#4 / Correct Programs	63.03%	72.73%	65.45%	**40.00%**	70.91%	77.58%	83.03%	67.53%
#4 / Incorrect Programs	**98.64%**	85.45%	96.82%	93.64%	90.45%	89.55%	96.36%	92.99%
#4 / Overall	83.38%	80.00%	83.38%	**70.65%**	82.08%	84.42%	**90.65%**	82.08%

Discussion. The analysis highlights recurring issues in consistency, reasoning depth, and the understanding of programming constructs. Contradictory responses – such as reversing conclusions mid-output – suggest shallow reasoning mechanisms. This instability is particularly evident when evaluating unoptimized code involving copy propagation or constant folding, where initial judgments are often revised later on.

Copy propagation proves especially challenging when lists or arrays are involved, reflecting confusion over Python's assignment semantics. For example, the statement B = A (with A as a list) creates a reference rather than a copy, an important distinction that most models failed to handle correctly. Only Claude Sonnet and Deepseek demonstrated some awareness of this behavior.

While many models correctly identify algorithms even when function names are obfuscated, they consistently misinterpret the antialiasing algorithm, mistaking its blur-inducing downscaling for simple upscaling. Similarly, the unification algorithm poses difficulties, likely because it relies on symbolic structures and pattern matching across case-based classes, in contrast to the more familiar numerical or list-based patterns.

Algorithms that combine arithmetic and list manipulation, such as the Sieve of Eratosthenes, yield the lowest accuracy. In particular, the modulus condition within the if guard appears to be a recurring source of error, especially in unoptimized versions where distinguishing between references and actual copies becomes critical.

Finally, we observed a correlation between reduced verbosity and increased errors. While this was not formally quantified, it suggests that more verbose outputs may support more complete chains of reasoning.

5 Conclusions

We evaluated LLMs' code understanding on semantically equivalent Python functions derived by copy propagation and constant folding. Though adapted to operate directly on source code, these transformations exposed significant reasoning failures in current LLMs. Performance improved from 59% to 71% with the addition of contextual prompts, yet a 29% error rate remains unacceptably high for reliable code reasoning.

Improving performance may require both architectural and procedural innovations. Modern chatbots, such as ChatGPT and Gemini, operate within complex ecosystems that may involve multiple models or execution backends. When asked directly, only ChatGPT consistently acknowledged the ability to execute Python code, while Gemini offered contradictory responses, suggesting dynamic or opaque back-end behavior.

We contend that integrating static analysis tools or code transformation pipelines into the LLM workflow could enhance reasoning capabilities. Semantic-preserving pre-processing steps may help clarify code logic before it reaches the model. Fine-tuning also shows promise: by inverting our transformation rules, one could generate high-quality training data for learning invariant-preserving rewrites [9,14]. However, such interventions remain inaccessible to most users due to proprietary constraints.

Future work should focus on expanding benchmarks, testing across a wider range of models, and isolating specific sources of reasoning failure. Stronger integration between programming language theory and LLM design may offer a promising path toward more semantically aware and robust models.

Acknowledgments. This study was carried out within the PE0000014 - Security and Rights in the CyberSpace (SERICS) and received funding from the European Union Next-GenerationEU - National Recovery and Resilience Plan (NRRP) - MISSION 4 COMPONENT 2, INVESTIMENT 1.3 - CUP N. H73C22000890001. This work has been also partially supported by the Research Project INDAM GNCS 2024 - CUP E53C23001670001 "Modelli composizionali per l'analisi di sistemi reversibili distribuiti (MARVEL)" and by the Project PRIN 2020 - CUP N. 20202FCJMH"NiRvAna - Noninterference and Reversibility Analysis in Private Blockchains". This manuscript reflects only the authors' views and opinions, neither the European Union nor the European Commission can be considered responsible for them.

References

1. Aho, A.V., Lam, M.S., Sethi, R., Ullman, J.D.: Compilers: Principles, Techniques, and Tools, 2nd edn. Addison Wesley, Boston, MA, USA (2006)
2. Aydin, F., Aysu, A.: Leaking secrets in homomorphic encryption with side-channel attacks. Journal of Cryptographic Engineering, pp. 1–11 (2024)
3. Cao, Y., et al.: A comprehensive survey of AI-generated content (AIGC): a history of generative AI from GAN to ChatGPT. arXiv preprint arXiv:2303.04226 (2023)
4. Dakhel, A.M., Majdinasab, V., Nikanjam, A., Khomh, F., Desmarais, M.C., Jiang, Z.: GitHub copilot AI pair programmer: asset or liability? J. Syst. Softw. **203**, 111734 (2023)
5. Davis, J., Van Bulck, L., Durieux, B.N., Lindvall, C., et al.: The temperature feature of ChatGPT: modifying creativity for clinical research. JMIR Hum. Factors **11**(1), e53559 (2024)
6. Dolcetti, G., Arceri, V., Iotti, E., Maffeis, S., Cortesi, A., Zaffanella, E.: Helping LLMs improve code generation using feedback from testing and static analysis. arXiv preprint arXiv:2412.14841 (2024)
7. Dubey, A., et al.: The llama 3 herd of models. arXiv preprint arXiv:2407.21783 (2024)
8. Fang, C., et al.: Large language models for code analysis: do {LLMs} really do their job? In: 33rd USENIX Security Symposium (USENIX Security 24), pp. 829–846 (2024)
9. Han, Z., Gao, C., Liu, J., Zhang, J., Zhang, S.Q.: Parameter-efficient fine-tuning for large models: a comprehensive survey. arXiv preprint arXiv:2403.14608 (2024)
10. Henkel, J., Ramakrishnan, G., Wang, Z., Albarghouthi, A., Jha, S., Reps, T.: Semantic robustness of models of source code. In: 2022 IEEE International Conference on Software Analysis, Evolution and Reengineering (SANER), pp. 526–537. IEEE (2022)
11. Jiang, A.Q., et al.: Mixtral of experts. arXiv preprint arXiv:2401.04088 (2024)
12. Kojima, T., Gu, S.S., Reid, M., Matsuo, Y., Iwasawa, Y.: Large language models are zero-shot reasoners. Adv. Neural. Inf. Process. Syst. **35**, 22199–22213 (2022)
13. Laneve, C., Spanò, A., Ressi, D., Rossi, S., Bugliesi, M.: Assessing code understanding in LLMs. arXiv preprint arXiv:2504.00065 (2025)

14. Latif, E., Zhai, X.: Fine-tuning ChatGPT for automatic scoring. Comput. Educ. Artif. Intell. **6**, 100210 (2024)
15. Maroengsit, W., Piyakulpinyo, T., Phonyiam, K., Pongnumkul, S., Chaovalit, P., Theeramunkong, T.: A survey on evaluation methods for chatbots. In: Proceedings of the 2019 7th International Conference on Information and Education Technology, pp. 111–119 (2019)
16. Pellicer, L., Ferreira, T.M., Costa, A.: Data augmentation techniques in natural language processing. Appl. Soft Comput. **132**, 109803 (2023)
17. Pour, M.V., Li, Z., Ma, L., Hemmati, H.: A search-based testing framework for deep neural networks of source code embedding. In: 2021 14th IEEE Conference on Software Testing, Verification and Validation (ICST), pp. 36–46. IEEE (2021)
18. Rabin, M.R.I., Alipour, M.A.: Evaluation of generalizability of neural program analyzers under semantic-preserving transformations. arXiv preprint arXiv:2004.07313 (2020)
19. Ressi, D., Romanello, R., Piazza, C., Rossi, S.: Neural networks reduction via lumping. In: International Conference of the Italian Association for Artificial Intelligence, pp. 75–90. Springer (2022)
20. Ressi, D., Romanello, R., Piazza, C., Rossi, S.: Ai-enhanced blockchain technology: a review of advancements and opportunities. J. Netw. Comput. Appl. **225**, 103858 (2024)
21. Ressi, D., Romanello, R., Rossi, S., Piazza, C.: Compressing neural networks via formal methods. Neural Netw. **178**, 106411 (2024)
22. Ressi, D., Spanò, A., Benetollo, L., Piazza, C., Bugliesi, M., Rossi, S.: Vulnerability detection in Ethereum smart contracts via machine learning: a qualitative analysis. arXiv preprint arXiv:2407.18639 (2024)
23. Sahoo, P., Singh, A.K., Saha, S., Jain, V., Mondal, S., Chadha, A.: A systematic survey of prompt engineering in large language models: techniques and applications. arXiv preprint arXiv:2402.07927 (2024)
24. Spanò, A.: GitHub Repository. https://github.com/alvisespano/perturb
25. Team, G., et al.: Gemma: open models based on Gemini research and technology. arXiv preprint arXiv:2403.08295 (2024)
26. Urban, C., Miné, A.: A review of formal methods applied to machine learning. arXiv preprint arXiv:2104.02466 (2021)
27. Wermelinger, M.: Using GitHub copilot to solve simple programming problems. In: Proceedings of the 54th ACM Technical Symposium on Computer Science Education, vol. 1, pp. 172–178 (2023)

LolaPrompts: Assisting the General Public in Performing Real-Driving Emission Tests

Melane Navaratnarajah[1], Ma'ayan Armony[1], Sebastian Biewer[2], Holger Hermanns[3], and Mohammad Reza Mousavi[1](✉)

[1] King's College London, London, UK
[2] consistec GmbH, Saarbrücken, Germany
[3] Saarland University, Saarbrücken, Germany

Abstract. The Real-Driving Emissions (RDE) is a regulation set by the European Union Commission. Its main purpose is to set out the foundations for vehicle emission tests. In this paper, we present LolaPrompts, which exploits runtime monitoring to assist the drivers in performing driving scenarios that confirm to the RDE constraints. It provides the drivers with audible prompts and explanations in order to produce a valid RDE test. The purpose of our tool, LolaPrompts, is to make RDE test available for the general public and allow them to scrutinise the emission profile of their vehicles.

Keywords: formal verification · runtime monitoring · autonomous vehicles · exhaust emission test · real driving emissions

1 Introduction

The Real-Driving Emission (RDE) test [16] is put forward by the European Union Commission to serve as a uniform benchmark for vehicle emissions across the European Union [10]. The latest specification of the test is RDE-4, which was introduced in 2019, and is the benchmark currently used in EU legislation. The regulation defines constraints on which driving style makes a test *valid* and thresholds for emissions to *pass* a valid test.

Nitrogen oxide (NOx) emission levels during vehicle approval tests can be significantly different from those of tests carried out during 'on-road driving' [11]; this could be seen through Volkswagen defeat devices.

LolaDrives [3,4] is an Android application which has been developed to monitor RDE tests, and to provide the driver with run-time verification and information about the test drive. The application connects the mobile phone through Bluetooth to a publicly available and affordable dongle that connects to the on-board diagnostics (OBD) port of the vehicle. This application is freely available, allowing the public to carry out vehicle tests against the RDE standard. However, when doing so, it is challenging to keep track of the range of RDE constraints during the driving effort, and as such, is difficult to produce driving cycles that are a valid RDE test. In this work, we present LolaPrompts, which augments LolaDrives with the ability to provide the drivers with audible prompts and explanations in order to facilitate the production of valid RDE tests. For the sake of reproducibility and transparency, the tool developed and used in our study and the experiment data are all available online [14]. It also contains a video detailing the app and demos of the app.

In this paper, we report on the design of LolaPrompts and its empirical evaluation in real driving emission tests with volunteer participants.[1] Through our empirical evaluation of LolaPrompts, we discuss the research questions below:

(**RQ1**) Does the prompt system in LolaPrompts increase the ease to perform valid RDE tests?
(**RQ2**) What additional improvements do users suggest be made to improve the system further?

To answer these questions, we ask the drivers to drive an RDE test both using our system, and without, in order to evaluate the effectiveness of LolaPrompts; after the test, we interview the drivers to receive feedback for further improvements.

To summarise, the contributions of this paper are as follows:

1. We provide an augmented version of LolaDrives, in order to guide the driver on top of the verification system.
2. We show that our modifications to LolaDrives help achieve more valid RDE tests compared to those without the application.
3. We provide the data from our user study, as well as additional extensions to LolaDrives, implementing the feedback received, to further improve the usability of the app.

2 Related Work

Real Driving Emissions are expected to vary in on-road conditions, for the same vehicle model, in different conditions [10] [13]. Millions of diesel-powered cars have been fraudulently equipped with tampered emission cleaning systems [15].

A single Nitrogen Oxide cheating device in a diesel car out of 1000 cars, can contribute to about 2% increased infant mortality rate [11]. The detrimental effects of these emissions on the environment and public health are evident and as such, the development of methods to better test vehicles and reveal any cheating device or under-engineered vehicle functions is crucial.

This concern can be addressed by the development of a technology which reintroduces transparency to the system. One way to improve the system's transparency is by providing runtime verification for the state of the RDE constraints

---

[1] Ethics review process has been followed and approval has been obtained from King's College London prior to the user studies with KCL Ethics Reference LRU/DP-23/24–41035.

and emissions of the vehicle, independently of the car's internal monitor. In this way, we enable the public, as well as policy-makers, to detect cheating devices in vehicles by analysing systems' behaviour. With the integration of autonomous systems in vehicles, it is important to recognise the ability to cheat the testing systems and facilitate and assist public scrutiny.

LolaDrives utilises RTLola [8], a stream-based runtime monitoring system extending LOLA [4]. Köhl et al. [12] present a formal description of RDE constraints and their violation, by initially extending the LOLA specification language [5] and later using only an enhanced official version of RTLola [4]. The formalisation of RDE constraints is used to determine the information that is presented to the user by LolaDrives.

The existing LolaDrives app provides the user with a visual representation of the NOx emissions, the proportions for the different driving modes and their corresponding dynamics. At the end of a test, the app will provide details on whether the RDE test that has been completed was valid [3]. The app does not currently provide the user with explicit information on violation of contraints, or with suggestions that aim to help the user to complete a valid RDE test. We aim to address this gap in the LolaPrompts app. To this end, we develop our runtime monitoring module that in parallel with the validation using RTLola analyses the stream of data and generates visual and voice-based prompts.

Text to speech is being used in web contents to improve accessibility of applications. According to the W3C recommendations for web accessibility, audio may be used as a text alternative [1]. Incorporating a text-to-speech corpus provides the driver with information about the status of the test in an alternative form, reducing the frequency the driver needs to look at the screen in order to understand the state of the test.

This paper is a continuation of our long-standing effort to detect and characterise software and systems doping [2,6,7]. Through facilitating valid RDE tests, we can gather useful data that can be used through our doping detection pipeline and allow for a more accurate scrutiny of vehicle emission behaviour by the general public.

3 Tool and Methodology

We propose LolaPrompts as an extension to LolaDrives, where we build an extra layer of runtime monitoring on top of RTLola in order to generate and play a voice feedback mechanism. To provide the user with the most relevant instructions, we have created three main components: a velocity profiler, a trajectory analyser and a prompt generator.

The velocity profiler logs the vehicle's velocity regularly through interaction with RTLola. Using a similar runtime monitoring mechanism, it builds a profile according to the speed classifications of driving styles as the RDE constraints define them. This includes stopping time when the car is at $0\,\text{km/h}$, a high-speed for velocity over $100\,\text{km/h}$, and a very high-speed for at least $145\,\text{km/h}$ and up to $160\,\text{km/h}$, which is the highest allowed limit.

This data is used in the trajectory analyser, which analyses the current state of the test, and determines the latest state and violations of each of the RDE constraints accordingly. For constraints which can make the RDE test invalid, the analyser will calculate whether and how those could be remedied, considering the maximum time left. Accordingly, the analyser determines the next driving mode the driver should aim for, and provides the user with the speed they should drive in, and the time required for this driving mode to be sufficient.

The prompt handler prioritises the prompts based on their urgency, and on the current driving style, to provide the driver with an instruction that they can currently take into consideration. The prompt is then shown to the user as well as spoken to the driver. Currently, the following constraints are included in the prompts:

1. Stopping Percentage - the vehicle must be stopped for between 6% and 30% of the urban time.
2. Average Urban Speed - the average speed must be between 15 km/h and 45 km/h.
3. High driving speed (>100km/h) - must be driven for at least 5 min of the test.
4. Very-high speed (>145km/h) - must account for no more than 3% of motorway time.
5. Urban proportion - the urban distance must be between 29% and 44% of the total distance of the test.
6. Rural proportion - the rural distance must be between 23% and 43% of the total distance of the test.
7. Motorway proportion - the motorway distance must be between 23% and 43% of the total distance of the test.
8. Urban Dynamics - the 95th percentile of the vehicle's jerk is below a limit based on urban average speed, and the relative positive acceleration is above a limit based on the average speed.
9. Rural Dynamics - the 95th percentile of the vehicle's jerk is below a limit based on rural average speed, and the relative positive acceleration is above a limit based on the average speed.
10. Motorway Dynamics - the 95th percentile of the vehicle's jerk is below a limit based on motorway average speed, if it is under 94 km/h else it will be 0.025 m^2/s^3, and the relative positive acceleration is above a limit based on the average speed.

The last three dynamics are too technical for an unfamiliar driver, and we only produce general prompts about the smoothness/aggressiveness of the journey if they are being violated.

The text to speech Android package[2] is used to allow for a vocal alternative to the text. The speech is evoked on the main suggestion to improve safety and accessibility by reducing the user's need to look at the screen for instructions. To avoid unnecessary reiterations of suggestions, and allow the driver to focus

---

[2] https://developer.android.com/reference/android/speech/tts/TextToSpeech.

on the road, a suggestion is spoken out only in certain conditions, such as when the text changes as well as the type of prompt.

We use the RTLola specification to provide the driver with a reason when the RDE test is deemed invalid. Additionally, after the completion of the test, we use the final validation results from RTLola to display the final outcome of the RDE test and display the overall outcome and extract the specific reason for an invalid test. After the RDE test has been running for 90 min, a prompt indicating whether the overall test is valid or not will appear. If the test is invalid, the prompt will also provide a clear reason for its invalidity. This will interpret the value for the invalid RDE(number), which is returned from the RTLola specification, as an indicator for the appropriate prompt. For example, "The RDE test is invalid currently because the stopping percentage of 2% is too low". This provides a specific reason for the driver as to why the test might be invalid at the current state and providing actionable guidance to help adjust the test condition towards validity.

3.1 Testing

To improve the efficiency of the testing process of the app, and the reliability of the software, we have introduced Android tests of the existing fragments in the app, and Unit tests for the events and the newly added functionality.

The initial test drives have been conducted within the development team, to evaluate the usability of the app and make design decisions, such as the ideal frequency of instructions to the driver that will provide useful information without distracting them from driving.

To perform a meaningful evaluation, the car model was not known in advance of each test drive, in line with the original user experience evaluation of the LolaDrives app [3].

As opposed to the original version of the LolaDrives app [3], the updated version, which is used in LolaPrompts, allows conducting a test even if the NOx sensor provides only raw data, and no diagnosis. This increases the range of cars that can be used, and their emissions can still be recorded.

From the test drives, some improvements have been made to the design, such as providing the driver with the reason as to why the test has failed, and an explanation which includes the relevant data. We hope that providing explanations will increase the trust of the user in the system, and improve its reliability for test conductors, as well as allow them to attempt to recover the test in the time left until the maximal duration (30 min).

During simulation testing, we have found that it is useful to initially have general prompts about the overall progress, as in the early stages of the test no constraint would be exceeded. This has been set to the initial 15 min, or until the driver completes the minimal requirement for at least one driving style. An example of a prompt during this time could be, "You are driving at the speed of 30 km/h. You have completed 2% of the required urban driving, 10% of the required rural driving and 4% of the required of the required motorway driving." When testing the app in a real-world scenario, we found that 15 min is too long, the drivers were doubting whether something has gone wrong. The first 10 min of the test is the time which has been found to provide only generic information. We have also modified the initial prompt to providing them with regular but infrequent analysis of the current progression for each driving style, rather than no information at all.

Some other modifications have been made to the instructions to improve the user experience. Rather than giving an instruction to the driver to change their driving mode, the app now informs them that they have completed sufficient driving in a certain driving style. This has been found to be more beneficial, as the ability to change the driving style is often dependent on the route, and was not as helpful a recommendation. In addition to the prompt type, the time duration has also been added as a consideration for when to speak a prompt.

4 Evaluation and User Feedback

4.1 Experimental Setup

To provide a more comprehensive evaluation of the system, twelve of test drives have been conducted with six volunteer drivers. Each driver participate in two test-drives: one without using the app (called the control group) and one with the app (called the experiment group). At the experimentation stage, the model of the vehicle was not known in advance, hence it was difficult to know the available sensors in the car that the tool can get data from. As the study is testing the effectiveness of the app in helping with facilitating valid RDE tests, we adapted the app to broaden the accepting criteria to vehicle without NOx sensors. To do this, we have loosened the criteria to allowing the tests to run even without NOx data, making the app more flexible to a wider range of different cars.

Before the test, the participants were provided with general information about the project, as well as a video about RDE tests and the app to watch. They were then required to fill in a short questionnaire, to ensure their basic understanding of the RDE test constraints and how the test would be carried out. The volunteers were expected to meet at an agreed location (somewhere feasible and close to the motorway) and were given a preplanned route to accommodate for a sufficient amount of rural and motorway driving, which they were free to adjust during the drive, (according to the app's prompts, if they were not in the control group). All participants were given a simple introduction to RDE tests and the motive behind the project, and were asked to raise any questions they might have ahead of the test drive and the follow-up questionnaire.

Each test was conducted in sets of EC or CE forms (C = control, E = experiment) [9]; we performed four sets of EC tests with participants A, B, C and E and two sets of CE tests with Participants D and F. The control setup included driving with a simple assistance, such as a timer and a map, and the experiment setup used the LolaPrompts app whilst driving. This helps us mitigate the bias introduced by the order of tests and the learning experience of RDE test from the first test brought into the second one. Particularly, performing more EC than CE tests mitigates any bias in favour of our intervention E. Each participant was allocated the order of executing the two test drives. After the drives, each participant was interviewed in a semi-structured interview in the form of a questionnaire. The participants were asked about their experience in both drives, and for general feedback about the app.

4.2 Results

In this section, we analyse the performance and validity of the app, using the data collected from the test drives, by comparing the results from both control and experiment groups to determine the effectiveness of the features added to the app. Table 1 provides an overview of the results, which are explained further below.

Table 1. Comparison of RDE test validity between Control and Experiment drives

Test No.	Ordering (CE or EC)	Control		Experiment	
		Valid	Constraints Broken	Valid	Constraints Broken
A	CE	No	8	No	8
B	CE	No	8	Yes	N/A
C	CE	No	5 8	No	8
D	EC	No	8	Yes	N/A
E	CE	No	7 5 8	No	9
F	EC	No	5 8 9 10	Yes	N/A

The control tests carried out were all invalid. The primary constraints commonly violated were related to the dynamic lower boundary for urban and rural driving modes, and the proportion of urban driving mode. It is a challenging constraint and in our experience smooth driving style or enabling Eco mode in the vehicle, which bound acceleration and jerk, often leads to violating it.

The experiment tests show notable improvements when compared to the control group, with three tests out of the six being valid and only one constraint being broken in each of the invalid tests. This indicates that the app's enhancements helped the drivers navigate the constraints more effectively.

User Feedback. User feedback was gathered through a semi-structured interview after each test drive. The main points of the feedback included:

1. Positive Feedback:
   (a) Prompts were useful, especially the text to speech.
   (b) The app provided good guidance for performing tests.
2. Constructive feedback:

(a) Frequency of prompt distracting in certain portions of test.
(b) Suggestions for additional features such as imperial and metric units (mph in addition to km/h).
(c) Recommendations for enhancing visual elements, including larger and more distinguishable bars, and the use of colours or pictures for different driving modes.
(d) Need for an earlier notification if the test is invalid.
(e) Bigger text for readability.
(f) Ensuring compatibility with various car systems.

4.3 Improvements

Following the experiments, we have improved the app according to driver's feedback from the tests:

1. **Metric/imperial toggle:** added option to switch between metric and imperial units, allowing easier interpretation of speed data and region-specific testing.
2. **Enhanced Visuals:** enlarged critical on-screen elements to improve visibility and ease of use for drivers, ensuring that essential information is easily accessible at a glance.
3. **Adjustable text-to-speech:** added feature to mute text-to-speech, in case the driver does not want to receive instructions for a part of the drive (e.g., a long stretch of motorway) and modified when text to speech is alerted.
4. **Option to Increase Text Size:** to improve readability and ensure all instructions and information is clear and easy to read while driving.
5. **Invalid Test Early Notification:** implemented an early notification system to inform the driver whether the test is invalidated, enabling them to restart and achieve a valid test run.

These improvements aimed to enhance the overall user experience and address specific concerns raised by test participants. The test run with the improved functionality in addition to testing the app with the simulator helped to correct mistakes.

5 Discussion

We found through our user studies that the voice prompts improve the user experience and enables more valid RDE tests. The user studies have significantly contributed to the enhancement of the app. For example, we enhanced the prompts for the acceleration and jerk constraints, which were difficult to achieve in the previous version of the app.

Potential threats to the soundness of this work is the small sample size and limited scenarios tested due to limited number of volunteers. We plan to unroll the app publicly after further testing. Across the many tests that the team and the volunteers have performed (both for preparing the app and during the designed experiments), we have never driven a single diesel car that would satisfy the maximum allowed NOx emission of 120 mg/km. On average, across all tests (valid and invalid), we measured 307.64 mg/km of NOx emission. This underscores the importance of our next steps in unrolling the app and allowing for public scrutiny.

Acknowledgements. Mohammad Reza Mousavi has been partially supported by the UKRI Trustworthy Autonomous Systems Node in Verifiability, Grant Award Reference EP/V026801/2, EPSRC project on Verified Simulation for Large Quantum Systems (VSL-Q), grant reference EP/Y005244/1 and the EPSRC project on Robust and Reliable Quantum Computing (RoaRQ), Investigation 009 Model-based monitoring and calibration of quantum computations (ModeMCQ), grant reference EP/W032635/1 and ITEA/InnovateUK projects GENIUS and GreenCode. Furthermore, this work is partially funded by DFG grant 389792660 as part of TRR 248 – CPEC.

References

1. Accessibility Guidelines Working Group: Web content accessibility guidelines (WCAG) 2.1. https://www.w3.org/TR/WCAG21/#dfn-media-alternative-for-text
2. Biewer, S., et al.: Conformance relations and hyperproperties for doping detection in time and space. Log. Methods Comput. Sci. **18**(1) (2022). https://doi.org/10.46298/LMCS-18(1:14)2022, https://doi.org/10.46298/lmcs-18(1:14)2022
3. Biewer, S., Finkbeiner, B., Hermanns, H., Köhl, M.A., Schnitzer, Y., Schwenger, M.: RTLola on Board: testing real driving emissions on your phone. In: International Conference on Tools and Algorithms for the Construction and Analysis of Systems, pp. 365–372. Springer (2021)
4. Biewer, S., Finkbeiner, B., Hermanns, H., Köhl, M.A., Schnitzer, Y., Schwenger, M.: On the road with RTLola. Int. J. Softw. Tools Technol. Transf. **25**(2), 205–218 (2023)
5. D'Angelo, B., et al.: LOLA: runtime monitoring of synchronous systems. In: 12th International Symposium on Temporal Representation and Reasoning (TIME 2005), 23-25 June 2005, Burlington, Vermont, USA, pp. 166–174. IEEE Computer Society (2005). https://doi.org/10.1109/TIME.2005.26, https://doi.org/10.1109/TIME.2005.26
6. D'Argenio, P.R., Barthe, G., Biewer, S., Finkbeiner, B., Hermanns, H.: Is your software on dope? - Formal analysis of surreptitiously enhanced programs. In: Yang, H. (ed.) Programming Languages and Systems - 26th European Symposium on Programming, ESOP 2017, Held as Part of the European Joint Conferences on Theory and Practice of Software, ETAPS 2017, Uppsala, Sweden, April 22-29, 2017, Proceedings. Lecture Notes in Computer Science, vol. 10201, pp. 83–110. Springer (2017). https://doi.org/10.1007/978-3-662-54434-1_4, https://doi.org/10.1007/978-3-662-54434-1_4
7. Dimitrova, R., Gazda, M., Mousavi, M.R., Biewer, S., Hermanns, H.: Conformance-based doping detection for cyber-physical systems. In: Gotsman, A., Sokolova, A. (eds.) Formal Techniques for Distributed Objects, Components, and Systems - 40th IFIP WG 6.1 International Conference, FORTE 2020, Held asPart of the

15th International Federated Conference on Distributed Computing Techniques, DisCoTec 2020, Valletta, Malta, June 15-19, 2020, Proceedings. Lecture Notes in Computer Science, vol. 12136, pp. 59–77. Springer (2020). https://doi.org/10.1007/978-3-030-50086-3_4, https://doi.org/10.1007/978-3-030-50086-3_4

8. Faymonville, P., Finkbeiner, B., Schwenger, M., Torfah, H.: Real-time stream-based monitoring. arXiv preprint arXiv:1711.03829 (2017)
9. Gou, M.S., et al.: Kaspar Explains: the effect of causal explanations on visual perspective taking skills in children with autism spectrum disorder. In: 2023 32nd IEEE International Conference on Robot and Human Interactive Communication (RO-MAN), pp. 1407–1412. IEEE (2023)
10. Joint Research Centre (European Commission), Zardini, A., Bonnel, P.: Real Driving Emissions Regulation: European methodology to fine tune the EU real driving emissions data evaluation method. Publications Office of the European Union, https://data.europa.eu/doi/10.2760/176284
11. Jonson, J.E., Borken-Kleefeld, J., Simpson, D., Nyíri, A., Posch, M., Heyes, C.: Impact of excess NOx emissions from diesel cars on air quality, public health and eutrophication in Europe. Environ. Res. Lett. **12**(9), 094017 (2017)
12. Köhl, M.A., Hermanns, H., Biewer, S.: Efficient monitoring of real driving emissions. In: Colombo, C., Leucker, M. (eds.) RV 2018. LNCS, vol. 11237, pp. 299–315. Springer, Cham (2018). https://doi.org/10.1007/978-3-030-03769-7_17
13. Kurtyka, K., Pielecha, J.: The evaluation of exhaust emission in RDE tests including dynamic driving conditions. Transp. Res. Proc. **40**, 338–345 (2019)
14. Navaratnarajah, M., Armony, M., Biewer, S., Hermanns, H., Mousavi, M.R.: Lolaprompts (2025). https://doi.org/10.6084/m9.figshare.28431935
15. Oldenkamp, R., van Zelm, R., Huijbregts, M.A.: Valuing the human health damage caused by the fraud of Volkswagen. Environ. Pollut. **212**, 121–127 (2016)
16. Union, E.: Commission regulation (EU) 2018/1832 of 5 November 2018 amending directive 2007/46/EC of the European parliament and of the council, commission regulation (EC) no 692/2008 and commission regulation (EU) 2017/1151 for the purpose of improving the emission type approval tests and procedures for light passenger and commercial vehicles, including those for in-service conformity and real-driving emissions and introducing devices for monitoring the consumption of fuel and electric energy. Official J. European Union L **301**, 1–314 (2017)

Author Index

A
Affeldt, Reynald 182
Aldini, Alessandro 75
Altisen, Karine 154
André, Étienne 114
Araujo, Hugo 17
Armony, Ma'ayan 211

B
Bernardo, Marco 75
Biewer, Sebastian 211
Bordis, Tabea 55
Bozga, Marius 154
Bugliesi, M. 202

C
Capra, Lorenzo 193
Comini, Marco 96

D
De Pierro, Massimiliano 193
Di Giusto, Cinzia 173

E
Esposito, Andrea 75

F
Foederer, Johan 37
Franceschinis, Giuliana 193

G
Garrigue, Jacques 182
Gemolotto, Luca 96
Genovese, Gabriele 173
Gerking, Christopher 55
Ghosh, Bineet 114

H
Hermanns, Holger 211

J
Jéron, Thierry 134

L
Lanese, Ivan 173
Laneve, C. 202
Laurent, Mathieu 134

M
Miculan, Marino 96
Mousavi, Mohammad Reza 17, 211

N
Navaratnarajah, Melane 211
Nejati, Shiva 17

Q
Quinson, Martin 134

R
Rensink, Arend 37
Ressi, D. 202
Rønneberg, Rasmus C. 55
Rossi, S. 202

S
Saikawa, Takafumi 182
Schaefer, Ina 55
Spanò, A. 202

T
Tabar, Asmae Heydari 55
Tuosto, Emilio 3, 173

V
van den Bos, Petra 37
Vidal, Germán 173

W
Weng, Cheng-Hui 182

Z
Zameni, Tannaz 37

The manufacturer's authorised representative in the EU is Springer Nature Customer Service Centre GmbH, Europaplatz 3, 69115 Heidelberg, Germany. If you have any concerns regarding our products, please contact ProductSafety@springernature.com

Printed and bound by CPI Group (UK) Ltd, Croydon, CR0 4YY

26/03/2026

02078952-0003